PURSUIT
of
PERFECTION

PURSUIT *of* PERFECTION

Significance of the Perfection Motif
in the Epistle to the Hebrews

―――――――

BY SETH M. SIMISI

WIPF & STOCK · Eugene, Oregon

PURSUIT OF PERFECTION
Significance of the Perfection Motif in the Epistle to the Hebrews

Copyright © 2016 Seth M. Simisi. All rights reserved. Except for brief quotations in critical publications or reviews, no part of this book may be reproduced in any manner without prior written permission from the publisher. Write: Permissions, Wipf and Stock Publishers, 199 W. 8th Ave., Suite 3, Eugene, OR 97401.

Wipf & Stock
An Imprint of Wipf and Stock Publishers
199 W. 8th Ave., Suite 3
Eugene, OR 97401

www.wipfandstock.com

PAPERBACK ISBN: 978-1-4982-9024-1
HARDCOVER ISBN: 978-1-4982-9026-5
EBOOK ISBN: 978-1-4982-9025-8

Manufactured in the U.S.A.   10/28/16

THIS BOOK IS DEDICATED to the memory of my father, the Reverend André L. Simisi, who went to be with the Lord on August 12, 1996, exactly two months after my graduation from college. He laid the foundation for my Christian faith and my walk with the Lord. Motivated not by reckless self-fulfillment and impelled instead by confidence in the faithfulness of God, he consistently encouraged me to pursue the highest goal.

Contents

Preface | ix
Acknowledgments | xi
Abbreviations | xiii

CHAPTER 1
Introduction | 1
  The Need for This Study and Its Purpose | 4
  The Thesis of This Study and Its Anticipated Contributions | 5
  The Scope of This Study and Its Design | 9

CHAPTER 2
Survey of Major Interpretative Approaches and Related Literature | 13
  Formal Meaning of Τέλειος | 13
  Technical Meaning of Τέλειος | 16
  A Case for an Eschatological Approach | 38
  Summary and Evaluation | 43

CHAPTER 3
The Notion of Perfection in the Ancient World | 44
  Lexical Meaning of Τέλειος | 44
  Classical World | 46
  Second Temple Judaism | 62
  New Testament World | 69
  Summary and Evaluation | 78

CHAPTER 4
The Literary Nature and Purpose of Hebrews | 80
  Issues of Authorship and Date | 80
  Historical Setting of Hebrews | 93
  Literary Character and Message of Hebrews | 108
  Summary Argument of Hebrews | 125

CHAPTER 5
The Notion of Τέλειος in Hebrews | 128
　Significance of the Τέλειος Notion | 129
　The Τελείωσις of Christ | 131
　Inability of the Old Covenant to Effect Τελείωσις | 155
　The Τελείωσις of the Believers | 176
　Summary and Evaluation | 210

CHAPTER 6
Summary Assessment and Conclusions | 211
　Summary Assessment | 211
　Theological and Practical Implication | 215
　Bibliography | 217

Author Index | 237
Subject Index | 241
Scripture Index | 251

Preface

THE CONCERN OF THIS book is the concept of τέλειος, or "perfection," in the Epistle to the Hebrews. This study explores the significance of the perfection motif in Hebrews, addressing the controversial interpretation of the notion of perfection in an attempt to discover its significance for the argument of Hebrews. The need for this study is evident in the lack of adequate treatment of the subject in the last four decades. This book's discussion focuses on the precise meaning to be attached to the notion of perfection and its import for the argument and interpretation of Hebrews. The thesis of this book is that the notion of perfection in Hebrews has a futurist eschatological significance and is related to the better provisions of the new covenant that guarantee believers' future salvation and eternal inheritance. Hebrews' strong emphasis on the finality of God's eschatological revelation in the Son calls for a re-examination of scholars' approaches to the notion of perfection. The writer of Hebrews sets his argument in an eschatological context, as if the end time has already begun and readers are living at the close of the age. Future eschatology occupies a place of prominence and is the determining setting for interpreting the concept of perfection.

A review of relevant literature reveals two major interpretative views related to the scholarly understanding of the notion of perfection. On the one hand, there is the fundamental formal meaning assigned to the notion of perfection, which suggests the idea of totality, completion, or accomplishment—a formal understanding that unfortunately many scholars have departed from in their interpretation of Hebrews.

On the other hand, there is the technical or material understanding of perfection most scholars have embraced. The technical understanding of perfection conveys various qualities of completion, such as the idea of fitness, adequacy, and maturation that are found in various ancient sources. Most modern commentators have interpreted Hebrews' terminology of perfection based on this latter lexical foundation. Does the notion carry a purely moral-ethical meaning, a cultic-religious meaning, or a vocational experiential meaning? Alternatively, should the concept instead be taken as carrying the notion of exaltation-glorification, a "definitive attestation," or "divine philanthropy"? As readers of this study will find, these fascinating questions concerning the meaning of τέλειος are directly related to the message and argument of Hebrews.

This book argues that the concept of perfection is best understood eschatologically in terms of the world to come. Hebrew believers have tasted the powers of the age to come (Heb 6:5) and are grateful to have received (proleptically) a kingdom that cannot be shaken (12:28). Yet their search presses on for the city that is yet to come (13:14), where God's people will experience their sabbatical rest (4:9). Believers are described as those who have already tasted the benefits of this unshakable city but who understand that its reality is yet to be fully realized until the time comes when they will be made perfect forever. Future eschatology becomes the determining element in the interpretation of the language of perfection in Hebrews.

This study proves that the notion of τέλειος—"perfection" or "completeness"—has futurist eschatological significance and is linked to the better provisions of the new covenant that guarantee believers' future salvation and their eternal inheritance. I argue in this book that this serves as an incentive for God's people to continue walking by faith with perseverance as they look forward with great anticipation to the fullness of their salvation to come, which although already guaranteed in Jesus Christ, will be fully realized upon the second coming of our Lord Jesus Christ. Thus, the call to pursue the goal of perfection becomes a call to commitment to the gospel message as Christians of all ages follow the example of Jesus, who endured suffering in order to bring many followers to their future complete, eternal glory in Christ Jesus.

Acknowledgments

THIS BOOK IS A revision of my doctoral dissertation accepted by the faculty of Dallas Theological Seminary in 2012. During the course of my academic pursuit at the Seminary, I was blessed and privileged to study under the discipline of and alongside numerous fine men who were both profoundly scholarly and truly godly. Their intellectual rigor and personal integrity will always be cherished. Completion of this study would not have been possible without the support of the faculty, friends, and family. To all these people, I would like to express my sincere gratitude—far more than I can even mention here. My thoughts go to all the friends, colleagues, and loved ones who prayed and encouraged me throughout the entire course of my PhD studies.

I am particularly indebted to the faculty whose combined scholarship, pastoral care, and servant leadership provided me with a true model of Christian servanthood that I will always covet in my future ministry. I am greatly indebted to my dissertation committee's three readers: Dr. Stephen J. Bramer, Dr. Stanley D. Toussaint, and Dr. Buist M. Fanning III. They provided the careful supervision and excellent direction I needed to complete the work. Their confidence in my ability to break new ground in Hebrews, coupled with their insightful and difficult questions, captivated my curiosity. Even when my responses were superficial or lacking, they were gracious enough to show interest and approval of my work. Their loving attitude fueled my motivation even further. My sincere thanks go to Dr. Richard A. Taylor, who helped me greatly in formatting my work. My thoughts go also to Marvin and Debbie Hunn, who recognized my dissertation proposal's contribution to current scholarly debates and who swiftly secured numerous valuable library resources for my research project, respectively. My study could not have been completed without the generous support of Mrs. Martha Johnston of LAMB Foundation, who in the early stage of my studies approved my candidacy as one of the beneficiaries of the LAMB scholars program, without which I could not have undertaken this project. Also, special thanks go to the Reverend Ted Witmer (Shalom University of Bunia) who not only demonstrated particular interest in my study project since the very start, but also mobilized additional support when needed on behalf of my family.

Finally, I am very grateful to the four greatest contributors to my life, study, and ministry: my lovely wife, Sophie, and my daughters Armelle, Angela, and Arlene. During various periods of research, writing, and revision, they have been a source of encouragement as they demonstrated their total support, unconditional love, and service throughout my research project. It is a blessing and privilege to pursue the goal of perfection alongside such faithful, special companions, friends, and teammates. May God bless and reward you mightily in ways that surpass all human wisdom and understanding.

Soli Deo Gloria!

Abbreviations

AB	Anchor Bible
AnBib	Analecta biblica
BDAG	Bauer, W., F. W. Danker, W. F. Arndt, and F. W. Gingrich. *Greek-English Lexicon of the New Testament and Other Early Christian Literature.* 3rd ed. Chicago: University of Chicago Press, 2000.
BDB	Brown, F., S. R. Driver, and C. A. Briggs. *A Hebrew and English Lexicon of the Old Testament.* Oxford: Clarendon, 1907.
BDF	Blass, F., and A. Debrunner. *Greek Grammar of the New Testament and Other Early Christian Literature.* Translated by Robert W. Funk. Chicago: University of Chicago Press, 1961.
BECNT	Baker Exegetical Commentary on the New Testament
BJRL	*Bulletin of the John Rylands Library of Manchester*
BKC	*Bible Knowledge Commentary*
BNTC	Black's New Testament Commentaries
BR	*Biblical Research*
BSac	*Bibliotheca sacra*
BSL	Biblical Studies Library
BZ	*Biblische Zeitschrift*
BZNW	Beihefte zur Zeitschrift für die neutestamentliche Wissenschaft
CaE	Cahiers évangile
CNT	Commentaire du Nouveau Testament
ConBNT	Coniectanea neotestamentica or Coniectanea biblica: New Testament Series
CTJ	*Calvin Theological Journal*

EBC	Expositor's Bible Commentary
EBib	*Études bibliques*
EvQ	*Evangelical Quarterly*
ExpTim	*Expository Times*
FRLANT	Forschungen zur Religion und Literatur des Alten und Neuen Testaments
GNC	Good News Commentary
GTJ	*Grace Theological Journal*
HALOT	Koehler, L., W. Baumgartner, and J. J. Stamm. *The Hebrew and Aramaic Lexicon of the Old Testament.* Translated and edited under the supervision of M. E. J. Richardson. 4 vols. Leiden: Brill, 2001.
HTR	*Harvard Theological Review*
ICC	International Critical Commentary
IB	Interpreter's Bible
JBL	*Journal of Biblical Literature*
JBR	*Journal of Bible and Religion*
JETS	*Journal of the Evangelical Theological Society*
JSNTSup	Journal for the Study of New Testament: Supplement Series
KEK	Kritisch-exegetischer Kommentar über das Neue Testament
KJV	King James Version
LCL	Loeb Classical Library
LEC	Library of Early Christianity
LQHR	*London Quarterly and Holborn Review*
LXX	Septuagint: Greek Version of the Old Testament
MCNT	Meyer's Commentary on the New Testament
ML	*Memorial Lagrange*
MP	*Monatschrift für Pastoraltheologie*
MT	Masoretic Text
NAB	New American Bible
NASB	New American Standard Bible
NCBC	New Century Bible Commentary
NET	New English Translation
NIBC	New International Bible Commentary
NICNT	New International Commentary on the New Testament

NIDNTT	*New International Dictionary of New Testament Theology*. Edited by C. Brown. 4 vols. Grand Rapids, 1975–1985.
NIGTC	New International Greek Testament Commentary
NIV	New International Version
NJB	New Jerusalem Bible
NJV	New Jerusalem Version
NLT	New Living Translation
NovT	*Novum Testamentum*
NRSV	New Revised Standard Version
NT	New Testament
NTC	New Testament Commentary
NTL	New Testament Library
NTS	*New Testament Studies*
OT	Old Testament
OPTT	Occasional Papers in Translation and Linguistics
PNTC	Pillar New Testament Commentary
RB	*Revue biblique*
REB	Revised English Bible
RevQ	*Revue de Qumran*
SBLDS	Society of Biblical Literature Dissertation Series
SBLMS	Society of Biblical Literature Monograph Series
SC	Sources chrétiennes. Paris: Cerf, 1943–.
SEÅ	*Svensk exegetisk årsbok*
SJT	*Southwestern Journal of Theology*
SNTSMS	Society for New Testament Studies Monograph Series
StudNeot	Studia neotestamentica
SubBi	*Subsidia biblica*
TB	*Theologische Berichte*
TDNT	*Theological Dictionary of the New Testament*. Edited by G. Kittel and G. Friedrich and translated by G. W. Bromiley. 10 vols. Grand Rapids, 1964–1976.
TEV	Today's English Version
TJ	*Trinity Journal*
TNTC	Tyndale New Testament Commentaries
TRu	*Theologische Rundschau*

TSMK	*Theologische Studien für M. Kähler*
TSK	*Theologische Studien und Kritiken*
TynBul	*Tyndale Bulletin*
TZ	*Theologische Zeitschrift*
UBSGNT	United Bible Societies' Greek New Testament
WBC	Word Biblical Commentary
WTJ	*Westminster Theological Journal*
ZNW	*Zeitschrift für die neutestamentliche Wissenschaft und die Kunde der älteren Kirche*

Chapter 1

Introduction

THE CONCEPT OF ΤΕΛΕΙΟΣ, OR "PERFECTION," is central to the Epistle to the Hebrews, but its meaning has puzzled theologians and Bible scholars throughout Judeo-Christian history.[1] The focus of this study is not historical theology but rather the τέλειος, or "perfection," motif and its significance in the argument of Hebrews, which is described as a "word of exhortation" (Heb 13:22).[2] Along with its cognates, the term appears forty-eight times in the Greek New Testament, with at least fourteen major instances in Hebrews alone. That is more than twice as often as in any other NT book.[3] This concept is of central importance

---

1. The quest for religious or spiritual perfection has been an important goal over the centuries due to Jesus' command in the Sermon on the Mount: "Be perfect therefore, as your heavenly father is perfect" (Matt 5:48). For a summary examination of how Matt 5:48 has been variously interpreted, see Shelton, "Perfection, Perfectionism," 902–906. For further details, see also Flew, *Idea of Perfection*, 73–91.

2. The description of the book as τοῦ λόγου τῆς παρακλήσεως, "a word of exhortation" (Heb 13:22) has led many students of the Bible to view it more as a written sermon than a letter. For further details, see Guthrie, *New Testament Introduction*, 668–69. See also Ellingworth, *Epistle to the Hebrews*, 732.

3. See Bachmann and Slaby, *Concordance to the Novum Testamentum*, 1777–78. Some scholars add to the fourteen major occurrences of τέλειος the τέλος word-group, and thus propose that τέλειος with its cognates appears no less than twenty-four times in Hebrews alone: "*telos* occurs five times (Heb 3:6, 14; 6:8, 11; 7:3); *teleios* twice (Heb 5:14; 9:11); *teleioo*, nine times (Heb 2:10; 5:9; 7:19, 28; 9:9; 10:1, 14; 11:40; 12:23); *teleiosis* once (Heb 7:11); *teleiotes* once (Heb 6:1) and *teleiōtēs* once (Heb 12:2); *sunteleo* once (Heb 8:8); *sunteleia* once (Heb 9:26); *epiteleo* twice (Heb 8:5; 9:6) and *teleutao* once

to the argument of Hebrews, as evidenced in the way the term is used throughout Hebrews.⁴ First, the author refers to the perfecting of Christ three times (Heb 2:10; 5:9; 7:28). Second, he points out four times that the old covenant ritual was unable to "perfect" the worshipers (7:11, 19; 9:9; 10:1). Third, the author specifies at least three times that Christ alone is the source of "perfection" for the believer (10:14; 11:40; 12:23). Fourth, he urges the readers to "perfection" (5:11– 6:1) as he points them to Christ as the "Perfecter" of their faith (12:2). Thus, the notion is clearly central to the argument of Hebrews.⁵ Two questions arise: What does the concept of perfection mean, and why is the concept so central to the author's thoughts in Hebrews? These questions continue to be central in scholarly debate today.

Scholars are divided as to how the τέλειος notion in Hebrews should be interpreted,⁶ as illustrated in the following examples. Some scholars interpret the notion following a moral or ethical perspective.⁷ Other scholars reject the moral approach in favor of a "glorification or exaltation view of perfection."⁸ An early expression of this latter position is found in the work of Julius Kögel, who argues that the τέλειος concept in the Epistle to the Hebrews is closely related to the idea of glorification or exaltation of Christ at the right hand of God the Father.⁹

Other commentators are not persuaded by either the moral or glorification views. They contend that a cultic or religious interpretation of the motif of perfection makes better sense based on the evidence in Hebrews. For instance, Theodor Häring argues that in Hebrews the τέλειος terminology functions in the cultic sense.¹⁰ This approach suggests the idea of "consecration,"¹¹ which additionally hints at priestly ordination. However,

---

(Heb 11:22)" (Welch and Allen, *Perfection or Perdition*, 35–36).

4. The focus of this study is on the fourteen major usages of the τέλειος, or "perfection," notion in Hebrews (cf. Heb 2:10; 5:8–9; 5:14; 6:1; 7:11, 19, 28; 9:9, 11; 10:1, 14; 11:40; and 12:2, 23). See also Scholer, *Proleptic Priests*, 185.

5. For further details, see Peterson, *Hebrews and Perfection*, 1. See also Vanhoye, "La Teleiosis du Christ," 321–38.

6. A detailed examination and survey of the various interpretative approaches to the τέλειος notion is given in the second chapter of this book (see pp. 13–44) [x-ref].

7. For example see Wikgren, "Patterns of Perfection in Hebrews," 160–61. See also Cullmann, *Christology of the New Testament*, 93–97.

8. For this model of interpretation, see Käsemann, *Wandering People of God*, 144.

9. Kögel, "Der Begriff," 35–68.

10. Häring, "Über einige Grundgedanken des Hebräerbriefs," 267.

11. The great influence of Häring's views is seen, for instance, in the work of Dibelius, "Der himmlische Kultus," 170. Also, DuPlessis observes in the notion of Christ's

many scholars are not convinced by the cultic approach and argue for a "vocational or experiential approach."[12] David Peterson advocates the vocational model of perfection when he argues that the author of Hebrews viewed the suffering of Christ as a vocational, experiential test or an educational process into the depth of Christ's authentic obedience to the Father.[13] The vocational approach, however, is also unconvincing, as will be shown in the second chapter of this book.

In a recent monograph, Kevin B. McCruden examines the concept of perfection in Hebrews in relation to a broader theological theme of what he terms "divine beneficence and philanthropy."[14] In his attempt to answer the question of what has been fundamentally attested, revealed, and made manifest in Christ, McCruden proposes that "it is the beneficent character of Christ that has been definitively attested to."[15] He rejects the above approaches to the notion of perfection, arguing for a technical application of "perfection" as a definitive attestation. There is no doubt that the incarnation of Christ was an expression of divine goodness and love towards mankind, but interpreting the τέλειος motif following McCruden's model is questionable and fails to appreciate the literary, grammatical, and theological content of Hebrews as a whole.

The argument that the perfection motif in Hebrews denotes any or several of the above models remains debatable, as will be argued in the second chapter of this book. For this purpose, at least three major issues present themselves: (1) What exactly does the author of Hebrews connote by his use of "perfection," (2) why is the concept of perfection such an important notion for Hebrews, and (3) what is the significance of this concept and its contribution to the argument of Hebrews?

---

perfection what he calls a "cultic sacral character"(DuPlessis, Τέλειος: *The Idea of Perfection*, 43, 217). Among modern interpreters, Ellingworth argues for the cultic model of perfection, contending that the perfect passive participle τετελειωμένον in Heb 7:28 should be taken as carrying the notion of priestly ordination (Ellingworth, *Hebrews*, 397). In his early work, Vanhoye also argues for the viability of the equation between the notion of Christ's perfection and cultic consecration (Vanhoye, *Situation du Christ*, 326).

12. An early expression of the vocational or experiential view of perfection is seen in Otto Michel's work. See Michel, *Der Brief an die Hebräer*, 139.

13. Peterson, *Hebrews and Perfection*, 67, 94. See also Attridge, *Epistle to the Hebrews*, 87.

14. See McCruden, *Solidarity Perfected*, 1–139.

15. This argument is based on what McCruden describes as "divine beneficence and divine *philanthropia*," borrowing from a representative selection of some Greek non-literary papyri's use of the notion of perfection (ibid., 44, 139).

THE NEED FOR THIS STUDY AND ITS PURPOSE

Until recently Hebrews, when compared to other New Testament books, has been neglected in scholarly studies. Many scholars would agree that Hebrews is one of those portions of Scripture that remains underrepresented.[16] This statement is also valid when it comes to the study of major themes in Hebrews. Scholars affirm not only the scarcity of studies, but also an enduring lack of scholarly consensus on the precise meaning of themes such as that of perfection in Hebrews.[17] Thus, there is a need for a comprehensive study aimed at seeking to unravel the meaning of τέλειος that appears to be so central in Hebrews. This is reflected in Otto Michel's remark that an understanding of the notion of perfection is crucial—indeed central—to a sound interpretation of Hebrews.[18] If it is true that the notion of τέλειος with its cognates appears fourteen times in Hebrews,[19] then the theme of perfection has some special significance for the book. The frequency of its occurrence is important, but the notion's central role in the author's argument is crucial.[20]

The enduring lack of scholarly consensus on the precise meaning of the notion of perfection and differing positions of various scholars who are sometimes diametrically opposed to one another calls for a comprehensive study aimed at ascertaining the meaning of the τέλειος or "perfection," motif in Hebrews. Only such a comprehensive study would help the reader understand not only the notion, but also its importance on the argument of the book of Hebrews. If the quest for religious perfection has been an important goal throughout Judeo-Christian history, then a comprehensive presentation of a biblically-based understanding of the concept of perfection in Hebrews becomes crucial.[21] There is a need to invite all students of the Bible to take Hebrews seriously. This study aims at providing such an opportunity for students of Hebrews to reconsider the terminology of τέλειος in Hebrews, its contribution to the argument of the book, and its implications for practical living. This is possible only through a comprehensive study of the above notion of perfection as we seek to develop a correct

---

16. Lane, *Hebrews: A Call to Commitment*, 9. For detailed factors that have traditionally hampered the study of Hebrews, see Ellingworth, *Hebrews*, viii–ix.

17. Kurianal's work underscores this very truth. For further details, see Kurianal, *Jesus Our High Priest*, 220–34.

18. Michel, *Der Brief an die Hebraer*, 230.

19. Silva, "Perfection and Eschatology in Hebrews," 60.

20. Rathel, "Examination of Soteriological Terminology," 125.

21. Shelton, "Perfection, Perfectionism," 909.

framework for interpretation of the perfection motif and determine its significance to the argument and message of Hebrews.

The general purpose of this study is to conduct an investigation into the perfection motif in Hebrews in order to appreciate its gravity on the argument of the book. Specifically, this study seeks to provide a comprehensive investigation that shows how the concept of perfection unlocks an understanding of Hebrews' uniqueness as a "word of exhortation" that presents a case for the superiority of the Son as the perfected High Priest and Mediator of the better provisions of the new covenant. This study will show how the author of Hebrews develops his arguments around an overriding theme of τέλειος, or "perfection," using a series of comparisons whose aim is to present Christ's priestly ministry of the new covenant as far superior to the Levitical system. Christ has been perfected and became the pioneer of believers' sanctification in order to enable worshipers to attain the same goal of true perfection.

THE THESIS OF THIS STUDY AND ITS ANTICIPATED CONTRIBUTIONS

The concern of this study is the τέλειος motif and its contribution to the argument of Hebrews. In essence, this study argues that the terminology of "perfection" has an eschatological significance and is linked to the better provisions of the new covenant such that it provides meaning and an overriding theme to the entire Letter to the Hebrews. The author of Hebrews adopts the τέλειος terminology to convey to his readers the effectiveness of the priestly ministry of the perfected Christ as the Mediator of the better promises of the new covenant. Furthermore, this guarantees the eschatological fulfilling of God's design of bringing many sons to their future glory. This concept is related to the writer's general argument about the better provisions of the new covenant. It connotes the completion of God's plan of salvation, as the author sees the historical process of God's redemptive design of salvation as moving towards the completion, fullness, and perfection of all things. Specifically, the "perfection" terminology provides meaning and significance to the better provisions of the new order as an incentive for believers to endure and press on toward the goal of completeness. The thesis of this study is that the terminology of τέλειος, or "perfection," has an eschatological significance and is related to the better provisions of the new covenant that guarantee believers' future salvation and their eternal inheritance. The concept provides an overriding theme and meaning for Hebrews.

A survey of the major literature written on Hebrews reveals that most scholars treat the τέλειος motif either too briefly or analyze only certain aspects of the concept of perfection in both the Old and New Testament.[22] A comprehensive treatment of the perfection motif in Hebrews and its contribution to the argument of the book is lacking. The following three examples illustrate this point.

First, Paul J. DuPlessis's work, which appeared in 1959 as a doctoral dissertation, is probably one of the first comprehensive studies on the concept of perfection in the broader area of biblical studies. His work provides valuable insights, including basic definitions and discussion regarding the notion of perfection in the NT. It suggests that the "perfection" terminology was widely used in the classical Greek world, especially in a purely formal sense. It is also used with the same sense in both the Masoretic Text (MT) and the Septuagint (LXX). For instance, a person who is "perfect" (τέλειος) is complete, whole, or adequate with reference to the notion of wholehearted devotion to God. DuPlessis moves away from the purely formal meaning as he observes what he calls "a cultic sacral character," which he then applies to the concept following a "cultic or priestly consecration approach."[23]

DuPlessis is not specific as to the extent the formal usage of τέλειος and τελειόω in classical Greek literature applies to the NT in general and specifically to Hebrews. Out of his dissertation's 255 pages, only twenty-six are devoted to the notion of perfection in Hebrews; of these twenty-six pages, only a few actually survey the text.[24] It is no wonder DuPlessis only provides his readers with general observations on the use of the "perfection" terminology in Hebrews. The author of the present study is compelled to present a more comprehensive approach to the τέλειος motif in Hebrews in an attempt to provide a better framework for interpreting both the concept and its contribution to the argument of Hebrews.

Second, David Peterson's monograph appeared after a modification to his doctoral dissertation at Manchester University in 1978.[25] Peterson's

---

22. The only exception appears to be Peterson's monograph published in 1982 (cf. Peterson, *Hebrews and Perfection*, 1–195). However, some Bible students would argue that Peterson's presentation of the perfection motif in terms of vocational/experiential/educational development or growth (into becoming qualified to carry on priestly prerogatives) is disputable. Furthermore details are provided in the second chapter of this book.

23. DuPlessis, Τέλειος: *The Idea of Perfection*, 75, 159–67, 217, 243. However, he is also willing to see the viability of the "vocational" or experiential model at least to some degree, as he argues for the "experiential acquisition of obedience" with respect to Christ (ibid., 220–21).

24. DuPlessis, Τέλειος: *The Idea of Perfection*, 217–30.

25. Peterson, *Hebrews and Perfection*, 1–313.

monumental work is commendable as an attempt to elucidate the meaning and purpose of the notion of perfection in Hebrews. His overview of hermeneutical approaches and proponents, together with his penetrating exegesis, is helpful. Peterson examines the theme of perfection in Hebrews and proposes a "vocational approach" to the notion of perfection. For Peterson, the idea of perfection as it is applied to Christ signifies a process of vocational development or education through the experience of suffering and temptation that culminated in the Son's qualification to become a merciful High Priest and Savior for his people.[26] Applied to believers, the notion has a similar vocational significance. According to Peterson, believers are perfected as worshipers who are now able to approach God through faith and obedient service.[27]

Many scholars would agree that Peterson provides the most thorough analysis of this subject matter in the English language—a valuable tool for any Bible student interested in the study of Hebrews. However, Peterson's monograph, with his "vocational" approach to the notion of perfection, does not help the reader appreciate how the word choice contributes to the overall message and argument of Hebrews.[28] In addition, Peterson's monograph falls short in one important aspect in Hebrews: the eschatological dimension of the notion of τέλειος and its significance in the argument of Hebrews. This study emphasizes that in Hebrews τέλειος, unlike many instances in the NT, anticipates a future completion of God's design for salvation to be fully realized at the second coming of Christ (Heb 9:28).[29] It shows how this concept carries significant eschatological overtones, the appreciation of which promises to unlock great insights into the eschatology of the New Testament, particularly Hebrews.

This book argues for an eschatological model of perfection, taking into account the Hebrews author's argument with regard to the perfecting of Christ (Heb 2:10; 5:9; 7:28), the contrast between the old and new order by which he demonstrates how the old covenant ritual was unable to "make perfect" the worshipers (7:11, 19; 9:9; 10:1), and his presentation of Christ as the source of "perfection" for believers (10:14; 11:40; 12:23) in the process (cf. 5:11–6:1) of being brought to their future glory. Through a lexical, conceptual and literary analysis, this study defines what the "perfection" terminology entails and provides a comprehensive treatment of how this

---

26. Peterson, *Hebrews and Perfection*, 67. When the notion of τέλειος is applied to believers, he argues that it has a similar "vocational" significance: "they are perfected as worshipers who are enabled to approach God" through faith, hope, and love (ibid.).

27. Ibid., 146–47, 166–67.

28. For further details, see the second chapter of this book.

29. For similar reasoning, see Barrett, "Eschatology of Hebrews," 363–93.

notion contributes to the overall message of Hebrews. This approach to the notion of perfection in this book seeks to provide a better understanding than earlier works.

Third, McCruden's work is perhaps the most recent piece dealing with the concept of perfection in Hebrews, particularly with regard to Christ.[30] He examines the notion of perfection in relation to the broader theological themes of divine beneficence and philanthropy. Rejecting all the previously stated positions, McCruden argues in favor of a material application of perfection in terms of an "official, legal or definitive attestation."[31] In response to the issue of what has been fundamentally attested, revealed, and made manifest in Christ, McCruden advocates that "it is the beneficent character of Christ."[32] He argues that "the language of Christ's perfection in Hebrews functions as a Christological grammar for reflecting upon the character of Christ."[33] Accordingly, Christ is characterized in Hebrews not by his state of being remotely transcendent but by his divine beneficence and *philanthropia*, coupled with a motivation to draw close to the community of the faithful gathered around his memory.[34]

There is no doubt that the incarnation of Christ was an expression of divine mercy and love towards mankind, but interpreting the τέλειος motif in Hebrews following the model proposed by McCruden does not help Bible students appreciate crucial theological dimensions of τέλειος in Hebrews. McCruden's work falls short of providing sound exegetical and theological conclusions. It does not help the reader appreciate the soteriological and eschatological dimensions of the text. Reading Hebrews through the lens of a few occurrences of this terminology in some non-literary papyri,[35] apart from offering sound biblical exegesis and theological study, is limited in its ability to provide a comprehensive understanding of such a crucial theme.

The present investigation strives instead to present a comprehensive study of the notion of τέλειος with the hope of providing a greater

---

30. McCruden, *Solidarity Perfected*, 1–147. This work appeared first as a dissertation entitled "The Perfection of Divine Intimacy" McCruden defended at Loyola University in 2002.

31. Ibid., 37–44. See also McCruden, "Christ's Perfection in Hebrews," 40–62.

32. This argument is based on what McCruden describes as "divine beneficence and divine *philanthropia*," borrowing from a representative selection of some Greek non-literary papyri's use of the notion of perfection (ibid., 44, 139).

33. Ibid.

34. Ibid.

35. For examples, see: P.Oxy 27.2471; P.Oxy 42.3054; P.Oxy 3.510; P.Oxy 1.68; P.Oxy 2.271; P.Oxy 2.268; P.Oxy 22.2349; P.Oxy 2.286; P.Oxy 12.1262; P.Oxy 1.63; P.Oxy 2.238; P.Mich 9.568–69; Ptebt. 2.316 (cf. McCruden, *Solidarity Perfected*, 25–44).

contribution to the wider area of Hebrews' eschatology, which is, in my view, future-oriented. Thus, this study endeavors to provide a better framework for interpretation of the τέλειος motif in Hebrews.

THE SCOPE OF THIS STUDY AND ITS DESIGN

This study faces significant limitations. First, the study of Hebrews is burdened with several problems. Not only is the letter anonymous, its destination and purpose are also obscure.[36] Over the years, various scholars have referred to Hebrews as "an enigma,"[37] "a perpetual challenge,"[38] and "the riddle of the NT."[39] As many authorities indicate, the book stands alone among the NT epistles both in style and approach. Hebrews is the only NT book whose authorship remains a mystery from the standpoint of both external and internal evidence.[40] The place and date of the book's writing, as well as its historical occasion, are almost impossible to establish except through a reasonable estimate.[41] While the focus of this study is the entire letter, this investigation is limited to one particular theme: namely, perfection and its significance to the overall message of Hebrews.

The author of Hebrews refers to the perfecting of Christ (Heb 2:10; 5:9; 7:28) and states four separate times that the old covenant ritual was unable to "perfect" the worshipers (7:11, 19; 9:9; 10:1). The author specifies three times that Christ alone is the source of "perfection" for the believer (10:14; 11:40; 12:23). Furthermore, the Hebrews author uses related terminology in his argument to convey similar truths as he urges his readers to walk toward the goal of "perfection" (5:11—6:1) and points them to Christ as the "perfecter" of their faith (12:2). Through an examination of each section of Hebrews using lexical, conceptual, and literary analysis, this author will

36. Guthrie, *New Testament Introduction*, 668. Since these problems affect both the approach to the epistle as well as the understanding of the Hebrews author's argument, this study will briefly examine these issues further in the fourth chapter. The purpose of such a discussion is not to reach a particular dogmatic conclusion but rather to create awareness of these issues among readers.

37. Manson, *Epistle to the Hebrews*, 1.

38. Barton, "Date of Hebrews," 195.

39. Scott, *Epistle to the Hebrews*, 1. Related issues to the above problems remain unanswered. See also Scott, *Literature of the New Testament*, 198.

40. For further detailed discussion of these issues, see the third chapter of this study, which provides a detailed account and discussion of the nature of the letter of Hebrews. As mentioned above, this discussion cannot be ignored in a study such as this one, since these issues affect one's approach to the epistle as a whole as well as the argument of the entire book.

41. For such estimate, see Attridge, *Hebrews*, 6–9.

define the scope of the "perfection" terminology. This book will demonstrate that perfection in Hebrews has a futurist eschatological significance and is linked to the better provisions of the new covenant, which serve as an incentive for believers to persevere and press on to maturity. This approach provides a more comprehensive understanding of "perfection" in Hebrews.

This study's methodology consists of an expositional analysis based on biblical exegesis and theological method. Exegesis serves as the heart of the task of interpretation,[42] as one seeks to analyze the text in "its historical, cultural and literary setting with concern for its lexical, grammatical and theological content."[43] For the purpose of this investigation, exegesis serves as the foundational step in determining the meaning of the terminology of "perfection" in Hebrews because it provides the building block for biblical exposition and theology. Exegesis is used as a method of Bible interpretation to develop a comprehensive understanding of "perfection" in Hebrews.

A theological method is also necessary because the author of Hebrews uses the notion of perfection throughout the epistle. By way of clarification, biblical theology can be defined as "the branch of theological inquiry concerned with tracing themes through the diverse sections of the Bible. . . and then with seeking the unifying themes that draw the Bible together."[44] Grant R. Osborne states that "while biblical theology provides a bridge to systematic theology and the contextualization of Scripture, it remains primarily within the sphere of exegetical research because its major goal is to discover the views of the biblical period."[45] Darrell L. Bock observes that "while the task of exegesis is a microscopic examination of each unit of the passage, biblical theology involves analysis and synthesis of the individual contributions of a given writer or given period to the canon's message."[46] Exegesis deals with the immediate context of particular expressions of God's revelation in order to discover the meaning of individual surface structures; biblical theology seeks overall themes and unity behind individual passages

---

42. Johnson, *Expository Hermeneutics*, 135.

43. Bock, introduction to *Biblical Theology*, 12. The concept is well defined by Charles Ryrie when he states that exegesis consists of "the actual interpretation of the Bible, the bringing out of its meaning" (Ryrie, *Basic Theology*, 125).

44. Osborne, *Hermeneutical Spiral*, 349. Interpreters believe that while "sound exegesis furnishes the raw material that is the data, biblical theology correlates the results of exegesis in relation to the progress of revelation" (ibid.). For further insights, see BDAG, 276.

45. Osborne, *Hermeneutical Spiral*, 349–50.

46. Bock, *Biblical Theology*, 13.

to reveal larger truths behind particular expressions within the context of the progression of divine revelation.[47]

To accomplish this purpose, chapter 1 of this investigation underlines the need and thesis of this study, followed by a survey of major interpretative approaches to the notion of perfection and related literature in chapter 2. Specifically, chapter 2 provides a brief working definition of the τέλειος notion, followed by a survey of five major interpretative approaches to the notion of τέλειος, including related literature and the main proponents of each approach. These interpretative approaches include: (1) a moral or ethical approach, (2) a cultic or religious approach, (3) a glorification or exaltation approach, (4) a vocational or experiential approach, and (5) a definitive attestation approach. This study proposes an alternative approach: namely, an eschatological approach.

Chapter 3 examines the notion of τέλειος in the ancient world, including the classical Greek and the Jewish tradition, Second Temple Judaism, and the NT in order to provide a general historical and conceptual background prior to a close examination of Hebrews. Chapter 4 examines the literary nature and purpose of Hebrews in light of that historical background, including issues as the authorship and date, historical setting, literary genre, occasion, purpose, and message of Hebrews. In addition, chapter 4 offers an overview of key issues with regard to the literary structure and proposes a summary argument of Hebrews in order to help the reader appreciate a broader perspective of Hebrews and broader context of the notion of τέλειος. The aim of the chapter is to serve as a bridge to the heart of the book, which readers will find in chapter 5.

The fifth chapter is a detailed analysis of the τέλειος notion in Hebrews. The major occurrences of this concept are examined both exegetically and theologically in three major sections: (1) the perfecting of Christ, (2) the inability of the old covenant ritual (versus the new) to effect perfection, and (3) the perfecting of the believers. The aim of this chapter is to foster readers' appreciation of the importance of the notion of τέλειος in the argument of Hebrews. The study concludes with a sixth chapter consisting of a summary evaluation that underlines key theological implications to clarify major points of the book.

This study makes a unique contribution in the area of eschatology of Hebrews by showing the consistent eschatological fulfillment motif in Hebrews not just as realized eschatology but, more significantly, as unrealized eschatology. According to the author of Hebrews, the better things to come serve as an incentive for the Hebrew believers and believers of all ages to

---

47. Osborne, *Hermeneutical Spiral*, 349–50.

continue their walk of faith in perseverance, pursuing the goal of τελείωσις, or "perfection," which guarantees their future uninhibited access to God and their eternal inheritance in glory. The τελείωσις of Christ is the determining factor for the perfecting of believers. It allows believers ultimate, complete, and unhindered access to God. The Son was made perfect as the source, the leader, and the forerunner of the believers' sanctification with the purpose of leading them to future completeness that guarantees their inheritance of eternal salvation.

Chapter 2

Survey of Major Interpretative Approaches and Related Literature

THIS CHAPTER SURVEYS MAJOR interpretative approaches to the notion of τέλειος, or "perfection," in Hebrews. It does not include an extensive analysis of these viewpoints or detailed exegetical discussions. Rather, its aim is to list and evaluate various alternatives in order to make a case for an eschatological approach. As a starting point, it is essential to keep in mind the fundamental formal meaning assigned to the notion of τέλειος in Hebrews.

FORMAL MEANING OF ΤΕΛΕΙΟΣ

The formal interpretation is based on the general meaning of the adjectival form τέλειος, which carries the notion of "having attained the end or purpose, complete, perfect."[1] Anything that has attained its *telos* is *teleios*, complete or perfect.[2] DuPlessis rightly observes that the approach is termed formal "in so far as it recognizes the basic properties of *teleios* as expressing totality and entirety, but then as abstract form without established material

---

1. Bauer, *Greek-English Lexicon*, 809.
2. Schippers, "τέλος," *NIDNTT* 2:59.

relationship."³ This approach is rooted in the work of Kögel,⁴ who established what could be termed a formal interpretation. Kögel's approach was a reaction to many nineteenth-century writers' assumption that any reference to τέλειος in the NT should be understood technically in terms of moral sinlessness. From his analysis of the verbal form of τέλειος in classical Greek sources, Kögel concluded that the notion is a general term to be taken as a "purely formal expression."⁵ He underscores this fact in the following words: "Es ist ein rein formaler Ausdruck, der lediglich äusserlich gilt und nichts Bestimmtes einschliesst, welcher erst sein besonderes, näheres Gepräge erhält durch das Objekt, das ihm beigefügt wird, resp. durch den Zusammenhang, dem er sich eingliedert."⁶ Kögel rightly implies that it is the circumstantial object to which the quality is attributed and its context that should determine the particular meaning used in each occurrence.⁷

For example, the expression ἡ τελεία ἀγάπη in 1 John 4:18 is translated as "perfect love" in the sense of its totality or fullness, not as an inner quality of moral development. Also, when considered as a personal attribute (1 Cor 2:6; 14:20),⁸ the notion may imply the idea of fullness of both physical and spiritual development, as in "full manhood or maturity in contrast to childhood and puerility."⁹ In classical Greek literature, an example of formal usage is found in Aristotle's suggestion that both a doctor and a thief can be said to be "perfected" in the sense of being brought to an accomplishment, a desired end, or completion.¹⁰ The passive mood of τελειόω, or "to be made perfect," is used to describe not only human adulthood, but also fully-grown plants.¹¹ Anything that has reached its τέλος is τέλειος ("complete" or "perfect").¹² Thus, Aristotle provides a classical definition when he writes, "A thing is perfect not only when it lacks nothing in respect of goodness or

---

3. DuPlessis, Τέλειος: *The Idea of Perfection*, 15. DuPlessis contrasts this approach to the "mystic interpretation" rooted in the mystery religions of the Hellenistic period and the so-called "gnostic interpretation," such as the gnostic myth of "a redeemed redeemer," which is rooted in the gnostic religious systems (ibid., 16–32).

4. Kögel, "Der Begriff, 37–68.

5. For further details, see Peterson, *Hebrews and Perfection*, 2–3.

6. Kögel, "Der Begriff," 39.

7. For further details, see Peterson, *Hebrews and Perfection*, 2.

8. See also Col 1:28, Jas 3:2, and Heb 5:14.

9. For further details, see DuPlessis, Τέλειος: *The Idea of Perfection*, 16.

10. Aristotle, *Metaphysics*, IV. 16p. 102b; LCL, 15–16. As a courtesy to the reader, select ancient works are cited with reference to the Loeb Classical Library, specific editions of which are listed in full in the bibliography.

11. Plato, *Symposium*, 192a; Aristotle, *Generation of Animals*, 776a; LCL, 31.

12. For this discussion, see Schippers, "τέλος," *NIDNTT* 2:59.

Survey of Major Interpretative Approaches and Related Literature 15

excellence, but also when it has attained its intended goal or end."[13] Accordingly, that which cannot be surpassed in goodness or excellence is perfect, mature, whole, or complete.[14]

The verbal form τελειόω is related to the noun τέλος, which originally connoted the idea of "the turning point" or "culminating point" but later came to connote the idea of "the goal" or "the end."[15] The verb carries the notion of "to bring to an end," "to complete," "to accomplish," "to fulfill," or "carry out the will of God."[16] Like other verbal forms ending in -όω, the verb is factitive,[17] that is, derived from the adjective and denoting the idea of acting upon objects or individuals to render them τέλειος, or "perfect, whole or complete."[18] The formal[19] or plain (as opposed to the technical) meaning of the verb carries the idea "to make perfect," "to fulfill," "to finish," "to bring to an end," or "to accomplish."[20] Unlike the technical understanding,[21] the formal understanding of the notion of τέλειος appears to be common not only in numerous ancient writings, but also in the writings of the NT.[22] Furthermore details will be presented in the next chapter of this book.

13. Aristotle, *Metaphysics*, V. 16; LCL, 266–67.
14. Ibid. Also see Aristotle, *Generation of Animals*, 284–85.
15. Schippers, "τέλος," NIDNTT 2:60.
16. Delling, "τέλειος," TDNT 8:73–78.
17. The basic factitive understanding of the verbal form underlies what will henceforth be referred to as the formal meaning of τέλειος, connoting the notion of consummation, accomplishment, or completion. For further details on the formal application of the concept of τέλειος, see McCruden, *Solidarity Perfected*, 5–6.
18. Ibid., 79. See also BDAG, 996.
19. McCruden rightly states, "If the formal application of τελειοῦν suggests the notion of totality, completion, and accomplishment, then the material [technical] application conveys various kinds or qualities of completion, e.g., the idea of fitness, adequacy, or maturity" (McCruden, *Solidarity Perfected*, 6).
20. For further details, see BDAG, 996. See also Delling, "τέλειος," TDNT 8:79.
21. In Gnosticism, τέλειος is considered a technical term in the myth of the "redeemed Reedemer" who is seen as "the perfect man" (Hippolytus, *Refutation of All Heresies*, 5, 7, 37), so that anyone saved by him through true knowledge is considered "the perfect gnostic" (ibid., 5, 8, 30). For further details on the technical understanding of "perfection," see Schippers, "Τέλος," NIDNTT 2:60. See also Käsemann, *Wandering People of God*, 133–44.
22. The formal understanding of τέλειος can be found in various ancient sources ranging from the Hellenic to the imperial period, including Aristotle, *Metaphysics*, V. 16; ibid., *Nichomachean Ethics*, X. 4; Thucydides, *History of the Peloponnesian War*, VI. 32 (3); Herodotus, *Persian Wars*, I. 120; Plato, *Statesman*, 272d (3); Epictetus, *Discourses*, IV. 4. 35 (2); Josephus, *Jewish Antiquities*, XV. 1 (8); Philo, *On the Creation of the World*, 89 (1); ibid., *Allegorical Interpretation*, II. 61 (1); ibid., *On Agriculture*, 158 (3); ibid., *On Flight and Finding*, 172 (5); ibid., *On the Cherubim*, 35 (2); ibid., *On the Life of Abraham*, 62–63 (6); ibid., *On the Life of Moses*, I. 283, II. 261, II. 275. Also, the

The formal understanding of τέλειος may be said to suggest the notion of totality, completion, or accomplishment, as the following discussion will demonstrate. Many scholars, however, do not follow this formal understanding of τέλειος but instead prefer a technical or material understanding that conveys various qualities of completion,[23] as described in the following discussion.

TECHNICAL MEANING OF ΤΈΛΕΙΟΣ

In addition to the formal understanding or formal application of the notion of τέλειος, scholars[24] also identify the material or technical application of the τέλειος motif in Hebrews. This understanding conveys "various kinds or qualities of completion, e.g. the idea of fitness, adequacy, or maturation"[25] and is also found in various ancient sources.[26] In fact, most modern commentators attempt to interpret the τέλειος notion in Hebrews following a discrete technical or material paradigm[27] based on this latter lexical foundation. The five approaches illustrated below are the most prevalent of the technical approaches to the τέλειος notion in Hebrews. These include:

> (1) the moral or ethical development view, (2) the cultic or religious consecration view, (3) the vocational or experiential

---

formal understanding of τέλειος seems to dominate the witness of the NT as evidenced, for example, in Luke 2:43; Acts 20:24; John 4:34, 5:36, 17:4, 23, 19:28; 1 John 2:5, 4:12, 4:17–18; Jas 2:22; Phil 3:12 (McCruden, *Solidarity Perfected*, 5). The purely formal usage is distinguished from the technical (e.g., mystical, religious, and cultic) usage. For further details on the formal interpretation of τέλειος in contrast with the technical interpretation, see Peterson, *Hebrews and Perfection*, 24–30.

23. McCruden, "Christ's Perfection in Hebrews," 6. He refers to the technical understanding in terms of the material application or material understanding.

24. For examples, see Peterson, *Hebrews and Perfection*, 25–30; McCruden, *Solidarity Perfected*, 6–26, and DuPlessis, Τέλειος: *The Idea of Perfection*, 14–32.

25. For an overview of the material/technical paradigm of perfection in Hebrews, including related literature, see Peterson, *Hebrews and Perfection*, 1–20.

26. Ancient sources include: Sophocles, *Electra*, 1508–1510; Aristotle, *Generation of Animals*, III. 2. 752a, III. 7. 757b, IV. 7. 776a; Plato, *Symposium*, 192a (5); ibid., *Republic*, VI. 487 (2), ibid., *Laws*, VIII. 834c, (10); Xenophon, *Cyropaedia*, I. 2. 4 (1); Epictetus, *Discourses*, I. 15. 8 (1); Philo, *On the Virtues*, 157 (8), ibid., *On the Special Laws*, IV. 209 (8); ibid., *On Rewards and Punishments*, 128 (8). Several references will be made to these sources in the following chapter.

27. Peterson, *Hebrews and Perfection*, 1–20. See also Scholer, *Proleptic Priests*, 185–200.

qualification view, (4) the glorification or exaltation view, and (5) the definitive attestation approach.²⁸

Moral or Ethical Approach

Some scholars follow a moral-ethical approach²⁹ in their interpretation of the "perfection" terminology in Hebrews using a straightforward moral view. This approach contends that by "perfection," the author of Hebrews suggests completion of a process of inward training and human moral development.³⁰ This approach gained prevalent acceptance in Methodism, pietist circles, and other holiness movements, especially the works of John Wesley.³¹ Following this paradigm, to be perfect is a moral achievement.³² According to this approach, there is a connection between the "perfection" terminology and the human character of Christ and believers. The notion of moral or ethical perfection presupposes the idea of a progressive moral development toward sinlessness, or moral achievement, in Jesus' humanity and believers. The implication is that just as Jesus learned obedience through his suffering and death, believers learn obedience through their trials and suffering and are thus made perfect or sinless.

Brooke Foss Westcott argues that the language of "perfection" (τελειῶσαι) applied to Jesus in Heb 2:10 (cf. 5:9; 7:28) points to the notion of bringing Christ to the full moral perfection of his humanity (cf. Luke 13:32), which carries with it the completeness of power and dignity.³³ Christ is seen as the one who progressed through and attained this state of perfection only after death (Heb 5:9; 7:28). Westcott argues that such "perfection lies in part in the triumph over death by the Resurrection and carries with it the

---

28. For an overview of these interpretative models of perfection, see McCruden, who argues for what he calls a "definitive attestation model" (McCruden, *Solidarity Perfected*, 6–24). Furthermore treatments of some of the above interpretative approaches are also found in Scholer, *Proleptic Priests*, 187–207; and Kurianal, *Jesus Our High Priest*, 220–34.

29. The moral-ethical approach was popular in the nineteenth century. Not many scholars would seriously hold this view today (see Weiss, *Handbuch über den Brief*, 13).

30. Cullmann, *Christology of the New Testament*, 92–93, 97.

31. For detailed development of John Wesley's thinking on the issue of "perfection," see Wesley, *Plain Account of Christian Perfection*, 5–100. See also Wesley, "Christian Perfection," 96–124.

32. For further details, see DuPlessis, Τέλειος: *The Idea of Perfection*, 12–14.

33. Westcott, *Epistle to the Hebrews*, 49.

completeness of power and dignity, bringing Christ to a complete moral perfection of his humanity."[34]

Allen Wikgren sees an emphasis on the moral perfection of the historical Jesus and believers. However, he also recognizes that such a reading might entail some theological difficulties. He states, "There appears throughout to be an underlying assumption of an ethical-moral content and development in the use of τέλειος and its cognates, an element that significantly and explicitly appears as ethical exhortation and moral encouragement when the Epistle deviates from its main argument, as well as in its three concluding chapters."[35] To Wikgren, just as the historical Jesus was made morally perfect (Heb 2:10; 5:9), believers are also made perfect by him (2:11) through initiation and participation in the community of faith (10:14; 11:40; 12:2, 23). Through such initiation and participation, they progressively attain the state of moral perfection. This is similar to Lala Kalyan Kumar Dey's contention that the notion of τέλειος involves proximity and access to God (6:1, 19; 7:19; 9:8–9; 10:14–24; 11:40; 12:2), implying separation from the realm of flesh and blood, mortality and weakness, or, stated differently, "sinlessness," which is procured through faith, hope, and a process of moral growth.[36] Following this approach, the notion of τέλειος is perceived as carrying the idea of moral development or moral growth through the believers' participation in the blessings of the new covenant, which are now available to all the members of the community of faith.

Similar reasoning is also found in Oscar Cullmann's work, in which he first equates the verb τελειοῦν (2:20) with ἁγιάζειν (2:11) and then argues that Christ's participation in humanity presupposes a moral development within his personality.[37] However, this does not suggest that Jesus sinned. Culmann posits, "Although he lived under the very same human conditions as we, he was the one human being without sin: 'in every respect tempted as we are, yet without sinning' (Heb 4:15)."[38] Philip Edgecumbe Hughes also affirms the notion of progressive development or moral achievement. He

---

34. Ibid. For further discussion of the concept of perfection in terms of its ethical implications, both in ancient and modern times, see Flew, *Idea of Perfection in Christian Theology*, 73–91.

35. Wikgren, "Patterns of Perfection," 160. Recognizing some viability of other approaches (e.g., cultic or religious), Wikgren argues in favor of a moral-ethical dimension. However, he rightly indicates that the perfecting of Christ does not imply a prior disobedience but ratther "that obedience reached a fuller measure" (ibid., 165).

36. Dey, *Intermediary World and Patterns of Perfection*, 228–29.

37. For this discussion, see Cullmann, *Christology of the New Testament*, 93–97. Similarly, Westcott, *Epistle to the Hebrews*, 315.

38. Culmann, *Christology of the New Testament*, 93.

argues that the Incarnate Son progressively learned obedience to the will of the Father, thus achieving perfection as he moved on toward the cross, which marked the consummation of his suffering and obedience. According to Hughes, such perfection consisted of Christ's retention and establishment of his integrity, without which his perfection would have been lost and he would have consequently been disqualified as High Priest.[39]

For believers, Christ's perfection is central to their perfection (Heb 10:14; 11:40; 12:2, 23). Through Christ's unique offering, believers are made morally perfect. For instance, Hughes asserts that the last moral reality and the last judgment took place at the cross, where Christ became the Eternal Judge and his enemies were put under his feet.[40] He observes that perfection has already been realized for all God's people (11:40) because in his view, the new covenant promise has already been fulfilled. Hughes declares, "In him [Christ] the blessings of the new covenant are a reality here and now."[41] This reasoning makes sense insofar as, apart from Christ, believers have no ground or object to their faith. However, the argument that the goal of perfection has already been realized is disputable in view of Hebrews' teaching pointing to some future aspects of God's promises that are guaranteed in Christ (12:2, 23; cf. 2:10). Hughes overlooks such future aspects. He is convinced all the promises have already been fulfilled in the work of Christ.[42] He is correct that in looking to Christ, believers are looking at the one who is the supreme exponent of faith—that is, the one who not only set out on the course of faith, but who pursued it without wavering to the end. He is thus qualified in some unique way to be the one who supplies and sustains the faith of the worshipers.[43] Yet, for the writer of Hebrews, the faith journey of believers finds its final destination in the future as believers of all ages are perfected forever.

Westcott's argument seems similar to Hughes' when he argues that the promises of the new covenant have been fulfilled in Christ, with τέλειος having been potentially obtained but progressively realized in Christ (Heb 10:14; 11:40).[44] He contends that to believers today, the fulfillment has been granted, opening their access to the kingdom of God, a kingdom which

39. Hughes, *Commentary on Hebrews*, 187–88.

40. Ibid., 402. The delay of the Day of the Lord (2 Pet 3:9–10) is perceived by Hughes as an act of grace and mercy of God, since the final judgment has already taken place.

41. Ibid., 517. For a detailed critique, see chapter 5 of this book.

42. Hughes takes this as the primary sense intended in the original Greek expression that reads, τὸν τῆς πίστεως ἀρχηγὸν καὶ τελειωτήν, or "the pioneer and perfecter of faith" (Heb 12:2). See ibid., 522.

43. Ibid.

44. Westcott, *Epistle to the Hebrews*, 315.

cannot be shaken (11:28). Westcott indicates that such perfection, perceived in terms of moral or ethical grounds, calls for believers' perseverance as members of the kingdom of Christ in progress toward their sanctification. He further indicates that such perfection must involve the perfection of Christian society. For Westcott, the perfection that Christ gained for humanity is to be appropriated by every member of the Christian community. While it is doubtful whether the notion of perfection should be perceived in terms of "moral or ethical development," Westcott insightfully argues that such perfection has been partly reached by the OT saints by virtue of Christ's exaltation (11:40), yet it awaits the final triumph of the Savior, when all the better promises of the new covenant on behalf of God's people will be fulfilled.[45] It may be argued here that Westcott rightly perceives in the notion of τέλειος not only some past and present aspects, but also future realization of God's purpose on behalf of believers.

The moral or ethical view of τέλειος appears to have been quite popular in the nineteenth century, but only a few recent scholars would seriously affirm it. For many scholars, the consideration of the notion of τέλειος in terms of moral development or growth is disputable[46] because of a few major problems that are implied by this interpretative approach.

First, critics of the moral-ethical approach would posit that the notion of moral growth or inner development contradict passages in Hebrews that testify to Christ's supreme stature. Such passages emphasize Christ's sinlessness and his holy, blameless, and undefiled character or moral purity (Heb 4:15; 7:26, and 9:14).[47] McCruden states that "such passages would appear to belie any necessity for the development of Christ's personhood."[48] Accordingly, such passages and the general tenor of Hebrews would exclude any moral development understanding of the concept of perfection. Also, James Kurianal concludes that "Hebrews' emphasis on the sinlessness of Jesus, his divine sonship, the pre-existence of the Son, and his superiority over the angels are sufficient reasons to exclude any moral-ethical meaning for τελειοῦν when it is said that Christ *has been made perfect*."[49] When applied to Jesus, τέλειος cannot be understood as implying that Christ progressed

---

45. Ibid., 382.

46. For instance, Dibelius, "Der himmlische Kultus," 165.

47. Scholer, *Proleptic Priests*, 187. This position was held not only by Dibelius, but also by J. Kögel, who consistently rejected the moral-ethical approach to the τέλειος motif in Hebrews even earlier, since according to the author of Hebrews, Christ was morally pure from the beginning. See Kögel, "Der Begriff," 41, 62, 65–66. For further details, see Dibelius, "Der himmlische Kultus," 165.

48. McCruden, "Christ's Perfection in Hebrews," 19.

49. Kurianal, *Jesus Our High Priest*, 224.

from a lower moral status to a higher status of perfection since the Letter to the Hebrews itself rules out such an interpretation.[50] In his humanity, Christ was without sin, holy, blameless, and unstained in every aspect such that any interpretative model that suggests otherwise, even by implication, is disputable.

Second, some scholars argue from a general viewpoint held in antiquity that presumes character is fixed and cannot change even with time.[51] According to this belief, an individual's character could be displayed differently given time, but it was not assumed that one's character or personality could actually undergo a developmental process or transformation.[52] Thus McCruden remarks, "The argument that Christ's perfection denotes a moral-ethical development within the context of inner personhood is in some ways a projection of modern psychological methodology into the Greco-Roman period."[53] However, some scholars would also object, instead supporting the notion that some kind of inner moral development is suggested in the language of Christ's obedience through suffering (Heb 2:10; 5:8–9). While it is true that the author of Hebrews is concerned about the conquest of sin, the concept of τέλειος does not denote the notion of the moral ideal except insofar as that is entailed in the broader theme of the completion of God's design of salvation for humankind.[54]

Third, scholars use grammatical aspects of Hebrews' language to contend that there is no evidence that would support a moral or ethical approach to the notion of τέλειος. For instance, a careful examination of the language of Heb 2:10; 5:9, and 7:28 reveals that the implied subject of the verb is God the Father, not the Son, as evidenced by the passive verbal construction. John M. Scholer suggests that such "perfection" could not have been an act of acquisition on Christ's part but was rather God the Father acting upon the Son.[55] The parallelism in Heb 10:14, where the notion is used with reference to believers, also indicates that such perfection is not an

---

50. See also Hoekema, "Perfection of Christ in Hebrews," 31. Hoekema presents a more balanced position that recognizes some aspects of the moral approach. According to this position, the language does not indicate a change from sinful to sinless character but rather a greater experience in all that obedience entails.

51. For further details, see Aune, *New Testament and Its Literary Environment*, 85.

52. For this discussion, see McCruden, "Christ's Perfection in Hebrews," 19–20.

53. Ibid., 20.

54. Lindars, *Theology of Hebrews*, 44.

55. Scholer, *Proleptic Priests*, 188. One may argue, however, that there is an implication in Heb 5:8–9 that both the Son and God the Father operated together: "he learned from suffering and was made perfect," which may be said to cohere nicely with Heb 2:10: "he was made perfect through suffering."

act of acquisition on the part of believers. The author of Hebrews writes, "He [Christ] has made perfect forever those who are purified from sin." In the former, God the Father is depicted as the implied subject acting upon Christ in making him perfect or complete; in the latter, Christ is the one depicted as the subject of the verb τετελείωκεν: Christ has made them (believers) complete.[56] If this reconstruction is correct, then in both instances Jesus is not the one achieving perfection, nor is it the believers who are achieving perfection. Rather, Christ is made perfect by God the Father as the passive form of the verb indicates (2:10; 5:9; 7:28); believers are made perfect (Heb 10:14) by means of Christ's accomplished work so they can enjoy the spiritual privilege of this accomplished work. One may argue that the moral content of the τέλειος notion is absent, particularly since its efficacy occurs independently of any action by believers themselves.[57]

The moral or ethical model of τέλειος can be said to be valuable in conveying some, if not all, the aspects of the τέλειος notion in Hebrews. One must therefore search for another model that adequately accounts for all aspects of this notion to provide a sound interpretation of the perfection motif in Hebrews. The most obvious problem is the language, but the implied moral growth and ethical progress that many scholars find contradictory to the teaching of Hebrews is also problematic, particularly in those passages where the author speaks of Christ's supreme stature and depicts Christ as holy, sinless, and blameless in every aspect.

Cultic or Religious Approach

There are scholars who interpret the τέλειος notion in Hebrews following a cultic, religious, or consecratory view.[58] This interpretative approach is based on the technical usage of the terminology as found in the Greek phrase τελειοῦν τὰς χεῖρας ("to perfect or complete the hands") that occurs

56. The Greek perfect active indicative τετελείωκεν indicates a continuing result of Christ's act as an accomplished work. See Lane, *Hebrews 9–13*, 267.

57. For this discussion, see also Scholer, *Proleptic Priests*, 188. The same may be said of τελειοῦν in Heb 11:40. For this discussion, see Kögel, "Der Begriff," 55–56.

58. The origin of this approach was thought to be in the Mysteries, where similar terminology was used to describe procedures pertaining to consecratory initiations. Bauer argues that the notion was used as a technical term for initiation into the mystic rites. See BDAG, 809; and Haring, "Über einige Grundgedanken," 386–89. Later, however, scholars thought of this origin as improbable. See, for instance, Delling, "τέλειος," *TDNT* 8:69. See also Dibelius, "Der himmlische," 166. As Scholer indicates, a cultic, consecratory interpretation of τέλειος may be said to have its origin in the Septuagint (LXX) usage (Scholer, *Proleptic Priests*, 188–89). For further details, see DuPlessis, Τέλειος: *The Idea of Perfection*, 206–33.

Survey of Major Interpretative Approaches and Related Literature 23

in the Septuagint (LXX) as a designation for the installation of the high priest.[59] Drawing from this expression, proponents of this model argue that the τέλειος notion assigned to Jesus in Hebrews denotes essentially the notion of priestly consecration or ordination (Heb 2:10; 5:9; 7:28). Scholars behind this approach see in the expression τελειοῦν τὰς χεῖρας an established *terminus technicus* in both the Septuagint and in Hellenistic Judaism.[60] Gerhard Delling maintains that the use of the verbal form is applied to priests in the LXX and indicates that one's hands are made free from stain and that the one consecrated is free to practice the *cultus* (cf. Lev 21:10).[61] He suggests that the verb τελειοῦν, which appears alone in Hebrews, follows this technical usage in the LXX and points to the idea of putting a consecrated individual in a position in which he can stand before God in priestly service (Heb 7:19; 10:1).[62]

Modern interpreters identify Häring as the leading scholar behind this influential view. According to Häring, the τέλειος notion in Hebrews functions in a religious or cultic sense. The notion of perfection assigned to Jesus in Hebrews is seen as denoting essentially the idea of priestly consecration and signifying his cultic installation as High Priest.[63] For Häring, even though Hebrews does not directly borrow the technical expression τελειοῦν τὰς χεῖρας as it occurs in the LXX, the conceptual linkage between the notion of perfection and consecration influences the author of Hebrews in his application of the notion of τέλειος to Christ. Häring states,

> Aus dieser Untersuchung des technischen τελειοῦν τὰς χεῖ ρας in LXX ergibt sich für unsre direkte Verwendung jenes technischen Gebrauchs nicht vorliegt, sofern eben τὰς χεῖρας

---

59. For example: in Exod 29:9, the Masoretic Text (MT) reads מִלֵּא יָד (piel) "to fill the hands," an expression that points to the notion of consecration or ordination with respect to the high priest Aaron and his sons. See also Exod 29:29, 33, 35; Lev 4:5; 8:33; 16:32, 21:10; Num 3:3. In most of these passages, the verbal notion τελειοῦν is used in conjunction with the accusative noun phrase τὰς χεῖρας. The expression as a whole is seen as functioning to express the idea of "ordination" or "consecration" with respect to such things as priestly sacred vestments, regulations concerning food, acts of priestly consecration, priestly anointing, etc. For further evidence of this technical or material usage of the verbal form of τέλειος in the LXX, see 2 Chr 8:16; cf. Jdt 10:8; Sir 7:25, 32, 50:19; and 4 Macc 7:15.

60. So Scholer states, "The apparent derivation of τελειοῦν in Heb from the 'terminus technicus' τελειοῦν τὰς χεῖρας in the LXX has been used to establish the absolute use of τελειοῦν as a 'terminus technicus' for 'priestly consecration'" (Scholer, *Proleptic Priests*, 189).

61. Delling, "τέλειος," *TDNT* 8:80–81.

62. Ibid., 82.

63. Häring, "Über einige Grundgedanken," 267.

fehlt. . . daß aber τελειοῦν überhaupt im Sinn von 'weihen' in LXX gebraucht wird, mithin auf den Sprachgebrauch unsres Briefes eingewirkt haben kann. Und daß dies das weitaus Wahrscheinlichste sei, ist wohl im Blick auf die strenge Parallelität (Synonymität im weitern Sinn) von τελειοῦν mit ἁγιάζειν und καθαρίζειν, die oben nachgewiesen wurde unleugbar.[64]

Häring's point is that the perfection of Christ bears the significance of his cultic installation in order to carry out the high priestly work of redemption and sanctification in relation to the faithful. Similarly, DuPlessis perceives what he calls a "cultic sacral character" in the notion of Christ's perfection, pointing to the notion of τέλειος in Hebrews in terms of priestly consecration.[65] Paul Ellingworth adheres to the cultic or religious model when he argues, "By virtue of his sacrificial death, Jesus the ordained high priest and eternal Son allows others to partake of the divine presence mediated through his own death"[66] by associating the verbal form of τέλειος with the notion of priestly ordination. Following the cultic approach, Ceslas Spicq refers to the perfected Christ as "'le consacré par excellence, ὁ ἱερεὺς ὁ Χριστὸς ὁ τετελειωμένος (Lév. 4: 5; Héb 7:28),'"[67] that is, the one truly consecrated as the high priest.

For believers, these scholars see in the notion of τέλειος a cultic or religious participation or membership into the new, perfect cult of the new covenant against the old, imperfect cult of Judaism. Thus, Spicq alludes to the notion of the perfect religion, which consists of participation in the blessings of the new covenant as a reality that believers can experience now.[68] According to Spicq, through faith believers participate in the fruits of

64. Ibid.

65. DuPlessis, Τέλειος: *Idea of Perfection*, 43, 217. Such a material or technical application of the τέλειος notion is found especially in the Torah and deals primarily with prescriptions for the priests. See, for example, Exod 29:9, 29, 33, 35; Lev 4:5, 8:33, 16:32, 21:10; Num 3:3. The LXX does offer evidence for a material application of the verbal form in a more technical sense of priestly service, but this always agrees with the context. For an overview of these LXX passages, see McCruden, *Solidarity Perfected*, 12–18.

66. Ellingworth, *Epistle to the Hebrews*, 397.

67. Spicq, *L'Épître aux Hébreux*, 222. Spicq concedes the applicability of the religious-cultic view of τέλειος in Hebrews, but he is willing to affirm that the notion may be susceptible to other interpretations, such as a moral-ethical and even an eschatological interpretation, depending on the context (ibid., 221–24). Spicq's argument is supported by Vanhoye, who also sees a relationship between the perfection of Christ and cultic consecration. For further details, see Vanhoye, *Situation du Christ*, 326.

68. Spicq states, "Alors que le Judaïsme n'était qu'une religion imparfaite, puisqu'il n'a jamais pu atteindre le but (τέλος), celle du Christ est parfaite" (Spicq, *L'Épître aux Hébreux*, 310). Τελείωσις is thus regarded as the character of the perfect religion which was introduced by Christ.

Christ's sacrifice and have access to God because of their union with Christ. Perfection is perceived as a present reality that has been made possible by the perfected Christ and acquired through faith (10:14; 11:40; 12:2, 23). Faith in Christ is perceived as essential to allowing access and participation in the blessings of the new covenant. Spicq words his position well when he states, "La foi, en effet, permet de s'approcher de Dieu, d'avoir accès près de lui (3), elle est la base de la religion. . . de tous les rapports avec Dieu, et sans elle il est impossible de lui plaire (11:6)."[69] Accordingly, everything humankind needs for salvation has been acquired in Christ (cf. 10:14). All that humankind needs is the faith element, which allows access and participation in the new covenant and the blessings already acquired for members of the perfect religion, the church.

Correspondingly, DuPlessis submits that the notion of τέλειος connotes the idea of reintegration into covenant community through consecration achieved by "the unblemished beast," that is Christ. The unblemished physical character of Christ is transferred to the believer with the effect that he or she is reintegrated into fellowship and atoned for. As such, τέλειος becomes a present reality experienced by the people of God, or those who are saved or drawing near to salvation.[70] Believers' participation now as members of the church-believing community is vital, since believers are perceived as having permanent access to the Father as a result of Christ's suffering and death, and they enjoy communion with Christ (10:14; 11:40; 12:2). Ellingworth contends that consecrated believers, or members of the faith community, have access to the inner sanctuary and are now living in the age of fulfillment. He emphasizes the present—not future—aspect of salvation (5:9).[71]

Despite voluminous literature in support of this reading and its significant influence on the interpretation of Hebrews, many scholars would argue that this technical interpretation is disputable and problematic. Considering the witness of the LXX, it is true that the expression "to perfect the hand" (τελειοῦν τὰς χεῖρας) is certainly a technical phrase used in various contexts to suggest the notion of priestly consecration. However, it is illegitimate to suggest that the verbal form in itself (τελειοῦν), even when isolated from the entire phrase, connotes the same technical notion of priestly ordination or consecration.[72] Kurianal rightly argues that the verb τελειοῦν alone, without the addition of τὰς χεῖρας cannot be given the technical meaning of

---

69. Ibid., 376.
70. DuPlessis, Τέλειος: *Idea of Perfection*, 229–32.
71. Ellingworth, *Hebrews*, 636.
72. Attridge, *Epistle to the Hebrews*, 85.

priestly consecration.⁷³ DuPlessis agrees with this position to some extent, but he contends that the strong evidence in Lev 21:10 (LXX), where the verb alone is used with a connotation of priestly inauguration, should not be ignored.⁷⁴ Consequently, the context becomes the only important clue in determining the meaning of the notion.

In Lev 21:10 (LXX), the verbal form τελειοῦν is used without its object in a cultic context to give a general meaning of "to sanctify" or "to consecrate." In Hebrews, "the verbal form τελειοῦν occurs invariably in the more experiential context of Jesus' suffering as described in Heb 2:10 and Heb 5:9."⁷⁵ Clearly, the emphasis in Hebrews appears to be on the surpassing nature of Christ's priesthood in contrast to the Levitical priesthood rather than an establishment of his qualifications to act as priest. McCruden rightly observes,

> For the author of Hebrews, Christ's priesthood is superior not on any legal ground of valid qualification, but because it is inherently superior by nature. This nature of qualitative difference between the two priesthoods is seen especially in Heb 7:24 where the eternal permanence of Jesus' priesthood, not its legal validity or cultic qualification, marks it as superior to the earlier priesthood of Aaron" ὁ δὲ διὰ τὸ μένειν αὐτὸν εἰς τὸν αἰῶνα ἀπαράβατον ἔχει τὴν ἱερωσύνην⁷⁶

As Scholer indicates, it is the context that should determine the meaning of conferring "priestly consecration" for τελειοῦν, but this is not because it is a *terminus technicus* for priestly consecration.⁷⁷ Since the verbal form τελειοῦν is used in the LXX with different meanings than its connotation in the Greek language, it cannot be assumed that the verb in itself connotes the cultic meaning "to confer priestly ordination" or "to consecrate."⁷⁸ David Peterson's argument that only the expression as a whole (τελειοῦν τὰς χεῖρας) connotes a technical, cultic meaning but not the verbal form (τελείουν) per se is correct.⁷⁹ While the technical sense is in keeping with the cultic context of the LXX passages, the hypothesis that Christ needed to be consecrated is unclear with respect to the theological emphasis of Hebrews.⁸⁰ Harold W.

73. For this discussion, see Kurianal, *Jesus Our High Priest*, 221.
74. DuPlessis, Τέλειος: *Idea of Perfection*, 212–16.
75. McCruden, *Solidarity Perfected*, 17.
76. Ibid.
77. Scholer, *Proleptic Priests*, 190.
78. For this discussion, see also Kurianal, *Jesus Our High Priest*, 221.
79. Peterson, *Hebrews and Perfection*, 28–30.
80. See also Riggenbach, "Der Begriff," 193.

Attridge accurately states that whether or not Hebrews uses the τέλειος notion in a technical sense of "to consecrate," this meaning cannot be inferred from its use in the LXX, nor from later Christian usages.[81]

For some scholars,[82] it makes sense that the perfection assigned to Christ signifies his cultic installation to carry out his priestly work of redemption and sanctification on behalf of the believers. However, one may argue that it is hard to establish that the meaning of τέλειος is primarily concerned with Jesus' consecration as High Priest. It is safer to argue that the Hebrews' author is more concerned with the surpassing nature of the character of Christ's priesthood. As some would argue, Christ's priesthood is superior because it is inherently superior by nature, not because it is primarily based on any legal ground of valid qualifications.[83] While the LXX expression τελειοῦν τὰς χεῖρας clearly points to the notion of consecration or priestly ordination, this does not automatically apply to the verbal form alone as used in Hebrews. For this reason, many scholars are not totally convinced by the cultic or religious approach to the τέλειος notion but prefer to argue instead for the "glorification" or "exaltation" approach.

Glorification or Exaltation Approach

Some scholars find no satisfaction with either the moral or ethical approach *or* the cultic or religious interpretative approach but argue instead for the glorification or exaltation model of perfection in Hebrews. According to this view, the τέλειος terminology in Hebrews is closely related to the idea of the glorification or exaltation of Christ to the right hand of God the Father.[84] For proponents of this view, it is by virtue of his sacrifice for the redemption of humankind and as a direct consequence of his passion that Christ has been crowned with glory and honor (2:9) and is sitting at the right hand of God the Father (10:12). The perfecting of Christ here carries the notion of Christ's triumphant entry into heaven, where he intercedes on behalf of the believers in order to fulfill the eschatological goal of bringing many believers to glory (2:10; 9:28).

---

81. Attridge, *Hebrews*, 85. For a critical evaluation and further details, see Peterson, *Hebrews and Perfection*, 26–30.

82. For example: Windisch, *Der Hebräerbrief*, 44–46; Dibelius, "Der himmlische Kultus," 170–71. Dibelius seems to combine some elements of both the cultic and exaltation model, as discussed below. See also Vanhoye, *Situation du Christ*, 326.

83. McCruden, *Solidarity Perfected*, 17.

84. For proponents of this view, the language of perfection functions essentially to express the theological notion of Christ's exaltation or glorification.

This majority-view approach has its root in the works of Kögel,[85] who associates the perfecting of Christ with his exaltation. By his exaltation, Christ opens the way for those drawing near to God's glory in the process of being perfected by Christ. For Kögel, Christ was perfected as the ἀρχηγός in order to bring about the perfecting of many sons, whom he calls "brothers," and is in the process of bringing them to glory and honor.[86] Similarly, James Moffat alludes to the idea that Jesus was the ἀρχηγὸν τῆς σωτηρίας αὐτῶν in the sense that he led the way for those who followed him: "He did not die simply to show mortals how to die; he experienced death ὑπέρ παντός and by this unique suffering made it possible for many sons of God to enter the bliss which he had first won for them."[87] This approach has greatly influenced many scholars in the twentieth century. A few examples will be sufficient to illustrate this point.

Building on Kögel's work, Ernst Käsemann links the notion of perfection to the concept of glorification when he concludes that "perfection" in Hebrews is synonymous with "glorification" or "entrance" into the heavenly sphere.[88] Contrary to Kögel, Käsemann connects the notion of τέλειος to the gnostic notion of a descending and ascending redeemer myth. Referring to the Mandaean literature, he suggests that "the gnostic myth offers precisely the same train of thought in bewildering variety."[89] Käsemann states,

> Among the Valentinians, the gathering of the parts of Urmensch as the divine seed is called τελειωθῆναι. . . . If according to Heb. 2:7 the completed Christ is crowned with *doxa* as the attribute of the heavenly sphere, then, according to the *Odes of Solomon* 36:2, perfection and heavenly *doxa* unite when the Holy Spirit sets the redeemed "on my feet in the Lord's high place, before His perfection and glory." It is instructive that according to 36:2 the Redeemer has anointed the redeemed "with His perfection;

---

85. For this discussion, see Kögel, "Der Begriff," 35–68. For a summary of Kögel's contribution to this discussion, see Peterson, *Hebrews and Perfection*, 2–3.

86. Kögel, "Der Begriff," 61.

87. Moffatt, *Critical and Exegetical Commentary*, 31. The point is that by perfecting Jesus through his suffering, God carries out his purpose of bringing many believers to glory.

88. Käsemann, *Wandering People of God*, 137, 44. For Käsemann, however, the notion is connected to the mythological tapestry of a comprehensive gnostic notion of a redeemer myth wherein Christ appears as a descending redeemer from heaven to earth and back again. As Peterson indicates, however, there is a metaphysical emphasis in Käsemann's presentation that is not found in Kögel's presentation. See Peterson, *Hebrews and Perfection*, 6, 298.

89. Käsemann, *Wandering People of God*, 138.

and I became one of those who are near him." The τελειοτής thus enables access to the heavenly Man.⁹⁰

Because of his dependence on the gnostic myth of the heavenly redeemer, Käsemann concludes that obedience and the process of perfection are two contrasting stages in the journey of Christ from heaven to earth and back to heaven again. Accordingly, only Christ is the "perfecter" (12:1), and the believers are perfected by their attachment to him (10:14; cf. 11:40; 12:2, 23), and thus they are called τέλειοι, "the perfect ones" (5:14). Such perfection for the believers is associated with their transfer to a higher position in the heavenly assembly as a new covenant people (11:40; 12:23; cf. 7:11, 19), but is also connected with the concept of sthe anctification and purification Christ accomplished through his sacrifice (9:9; 10:1, 14).⁹¹ For Käsemann, believers are members of the heavenly sphere while they are still on earth.⁹² Whether the notion of τέλειος is seen as compatible with the gnostic myth of a descending and ascending redeemer is disputable. It is clear, however, that for Käsemann, there is a link between the notion of perfection and the concept of glorification.

Moffatt builds on this argument and suggests that the notion of τέλειος should be seen as corresponding to the larger divine intention that encompasses the eschatological glory of humanity—an intention he contends has been fulfilled by Christ.⁹³ Accordingly, the better promises of the new covenant and its benefits are already in effect for believers. Similarly, Moisés Silva interprets the notion of perfection within the larger structure of an eschatological fulfillment motif with an emphasis on the present realization of God's promise. According to this paradigm and as a result of Christ's exaltation, the promise of the new covenant, including its benefits, has finally arrived and is therefore in effect.⁹⁴ Building on both arguments by Moffatt and Silva, William L. Lane attests that "the eschatological exaltation of Christ in fulfillment of the divine promises constitutes the concrete designation of perfection."⁹⁵ Lane sees the whole process leading to Christ's

---

90. For further details and parallels in the *Odes of Solomon* and the Epistle to the Hebrews, see ibid., 138–39.

91. For this discussion, see also Peterson, *Hebrews and Perfection*, 6.

92. For a contrast with the moral-ethical approach, especially Michel's work, see ibid., 4–6.

93. Moffatt, *Hebrews*, 28–32.

94. Silva, "Perfection and Eschatology in Hebrews," 68.

95. Lane, *Hebrews 1–8*, 195. For Lane, the exaltation motif in Hebrews' teaching corresponds to the notion of Christ as "perfect." The idea is that "while the final goal of Christ's perfection is to fulfill the divine intention for the eschatological glory of the faithful, this intention itself is contingent upon Christ's exaltation to glory" (ibid.). See

exaltation as also important. Hence, he assigns to the verbal form τελειοῦν a dynamic sense that refers to the whole process by which Christ was personally and vocationally prepared to qualify for his continuing ministry at the right hand of God the Father.[96] Christ's exaltation is seen as qualifying him for ministry as High Priest, enabling him to serve as priestly intercessor on behalf of his faithful followers.[97] This is similar to the position of Craig R. Koester, who assigns multiple dimensions of Christ's death and exaltation to the verbal notion of τελειοῦν. He believes that to be made complete has to do first with Christ's exaltation to eternal glory, and second, to overcoming death through exaltation to everlasting life in God's presence, which enables him to be a source of eternal salvation for his followers and to serve as a High Priest forever (Heb 2:10, 17–18; 4:9–10; 5:9–10; 7:26; 11:39–40; 12:2, 22).[98]

Significantly, most of these scholars recognize a present-day eschatological dimension of the τέλειος notion in Hebrews. They connect it with an expansive belief of the completion of God's redemptive plan in the sense that humanity's eschatological destiny has already been made possible in the Christ event.[99] Realized eschatology becomes these scholars' focus in their interpretation of Hebrews. There is much to appreciate in terms of the relevance of an exaltation-glorification model within the context of Hebrews' Christology. The problem, however, is that the model does not exhaust all the aspects of the τέλειος motif as applied to Christ and to believers.[100] More importantly, because of its emphasis on the death and exaltation of Christ, the model does not help describe how the exaltation of Christ relates to the perfecting of believers. Proponents of this interpretative approach are unclear as to how the past is related to the future eschatological dimension of perfection in Hebrews. The suggestion that all the better provisions of the new covenant are now in effect, coupled with a failure to realize some future dimensions at the second advent of Christ, appears to be misleading. This issue, which is essential to this study, will be dealt with in the fifth chapter. At this point, however, it is important to consider an alternative approach held by other scholars.

---

also McCruden, *Solidarity Perfected*, 8.

96. Lane, *Hebrews 1–8*, 196. For further details, see DuPlessis, Τέλειος: *Idea of Perfection*, 221.

97. Saucy, "Exaltation Christology in Hebrews," 43–58.

98. For further details, see Koester, *Hebrews*, 123–25.

99. Lindars, *Theology of Hebrews*, 45. See also Silva, "Perfection and Eschatology in Hebrews," 68.

100. For this criticism, see McCruden, "Christ's Perfection in Hebrews," 11.

Vocational or Experiential Approach

Some scholars argue for a vocational or experiential view of perfection in Hebrews. According to this view, the concept of τέλειος connects with the concept of the "testing and proving of Christ."[101] This is linked to the notion of an educational experience.[102] David Peterson, using Michel's phrase, submits that Christ's perfection—his *berufliche vollendung*—signifies an entire developmental process forged through the experience of suffering and temptation that culminates in the Son's qualification to become a merciful High Priest and Savior for his people.[103] Hence, Christ's endurance of suffering is seen as an experiential, existential test, or an educational experience-learning process delving into the depths of authentic obedience to the Father.[104] Accordingly, Christ has become acquainted with the depth of true obedience by virtue of his temptations and sufferings, with the result that the Son became preeminently qualified to carry out his priestly activity.[105] This interpretative approach has influenced many scholars.

George B. Caird presents his case from this interpretative model when he observes that Christ was made perfect because he fully experienced all conditions of human life, including a learning or educational process through suffering. For Caird, it was through his dependence on God that Christ won the right to enter God's presence.[106] The implication is that worshipers can be called "just men made perfect" for no other reason than the fact that they have been admitted to the presence of God by virtue of their faith in the resurrected Savior.[107] From the same perspective, John R. Walters observes that the perfection notion involves "an educative process

---

101. Scholars believe that the earliest expression of this approach is found in the work of Michel. For further details, see Michel, "Die Lehre von der Christlichen," 139.

102. Walters, *Perfection in New Testament Theology*, 88.

103. Peterson, *Hebrews and Perfection*, 93.

104. F. F. Bruce highlights this experiential acquisition of obedience in his observation that it was only through suffering that Jesus learned the nature of human obedience. See Bruce, *Epistle to the Hebrews*, 131.

105. Peterson, *Hebrews and Perfection*, 94. Foundational to Peterson's model of vocational fitness or qualification is what Attridge describes as an existential or experiential model of perfection (Attridge, *Hebrews*, 87). One of the earliest and most skillfully articulated argument for this interpretative approach is found in Caird, "Just Men Made Perfect," 89–98.

106. Caird, "Just Men Made Perfect," 93.

107. Ibid. Hoekema makes a similar observation, maintaining that Jesus' perfection entails some kind of development or growth in the sense that through his sufferings and temptations, Christ learned "experientially" the true meaning of obedience made perfect on the cross. See Hoekema, "Perfection of Christ," 36–37.

in suffering, and of course a willingness to embrace death itself for a greater purpose."[108] Christ's endurance of temptation and suffering is regarded as an educational or experiential test into the depth of authentic obedience to the Father that opens up the way for his qualification to carry out his High Priestly activity. Similarly, F. F. Bruce observes that it was through experience that Christ learned the true nature of obedience.[109] DuPlessis, who argues for a cultic model, is willing to recognize the viability of the experiential model to some degree. The same can be said of Albert Vanhoye, who reinvigorates the experiential model of perfection in Hebrews.[110] Lane proposes that Christ's experience of suffering allowed him to be acquainted with a new dimension of obedience.[111]

Christ's experience becomes a model for the readers' experience of suffering as the author of Hebrews recalls times in the past when believers were publicly subjected to insult and outrage, stripped of their goods, accepted hardship, sympathized with prisoners, and knew that there was a great and enduring reward reserved for them (Heb 10:32–34).[112] Thus, the experience of suffering and death is regarded as the fitting way for Jesus to be made perfect.[113] Thomas G. Long wholeheartedly proposes that Christ was made perfect in two distinct ways. In terms of vertical participation in the life of God, suffering made Christ perfect by testing his obedience and faithfulness. In terms of horizontal participation in human life, Jesus is made perfect in the sense that he is joined completely and emphatically to the human condition.[114] Because he was tested by what he suffered, he is qualified to help believers who are being tested and made perfect. Believers, therefore, are called to the same kind of suffering and obedience. Contrary to his previously-held position, Vanhoye reasons similarly. Reinvigorating the vocational or experiential approach, he suggests that the sacrificial

108. Walters, *Perfection in New Testament Theology*, 88.
109. Bruce, *Hebrews*, 131.
110. Vanhoye, "La 'teleiosis' du Christ," 332.
111. Lane, *Hebrews: A Call to Commitment*, 81–82.
112. Manson, *Epistle to the Hebrews*, 41.
113. Long, *Epistle to the Hebrews*, 41.
114. Ibid., 42. Similarly Vanhoye observes,

La teleiosis du Christ est vraiment sacerdotale, par ce qu'elle est doublement relationnelle: elle a rendu le Christ 'parfait' dans sa relation avec Dieu, grâce à une obéissance poussée à l'extrême, et 'parfait' en même temps dans sa relation avec ses frères (Heb 2 :11–12, 17 [Cf. Heb 5:8–9; 8:1, 9 :15, and 10:19–21]) grâce à une solidarité poussée également à l'extrême dans les souffrances et dans la mort. (Vanhoye, "La 'teleiosis' du Christ," 337).

Survey of Major Interpretative Approaches and Related Literature 33

character of Hebrews has a lot to do with an existential interpretation.[115] Hence, with an emphasis on the theme of suffering and obedience following the example of Christ, the call to be willing to suffer loss and obedience is compellingly made in view of the reward to come (Heb 10:32–39).[116] The application derived from this concept is that the way of faith is obedience to the will of God; the sacrifice of obedience is the essence of a life lived in relationship with God.[117]

In the last twenty years, Hebrews scholars have associated the vocational or experiential approach with David Peterson.[118] Scholars have identified value and insight in this approach not because of its applicability to Christ's suffering and death but rather to the recipients of the letter. Under this model, the sufferings of believers serve as discipline that trains them to become fit for participation in divine holiness (Heb 12:10–11).[119] Christ's educative process in suffering and death becomes a model for the believer's experience of suffering in view of the great, enduring reward to come. This interpretative paradigm is an attempt to move beyond the notion of perfection in Hebrews conceived strictly on a moral or ethical ground as found in scholars such as Westcott[120] and Cullmann,[121] although many would agree that the two interpretative paradigms are closely related. The vocational model puts more emphasis on the Christ event as a whole. In this case, the notion of τέλειος is perceived as implying the fulfillment of a comprehensive redemptive process, which includes not only the experience of suffering and death, but also Christ's exaltation to glory,[122] without which his present intercessory ministry as High Priest would not be possible.

Although David Peterson argues that Christ's perfection includes the necessity for his experiences of suffering and death as the training ground for the Son's full appreciation of what obedience to the Father entails, he also admits that a vocational approach to the perfection motif in Hebrews

---

115. Speaking of the language of Hebrews, Vanhoye observes, "lorsqu'il s'agit du Christ, ce n'est plus à des cérémonies rituelles qu'il [le language] s'applique. . . . [Les termes utilisés] expriment les plus dures réalités de l'existence: la mort en Heb 9:15, [et] la souffrance en Heb 9: 26." (ibid., 332).

116. Konkel, "Sacrifice of Obedience," 2–3.

117. Ibid., 9. The experience of the worshipers becomes crucial in this interpretative approach to the τέλειος notion.

118. This interpretative model is founded on what some scholars describe as an existential or experiential model of perfection. See Attridge, *Hebrews*, 87.

119. Peterson, *Hebrews and Perfection*, 194.

120. Westcott, *Hebrews*, 49–50.

121. Cullmann, *Christology of the New Testament*, 93–97.

122. Peterson, *Hebrews and Perfection*, 67.

assumes to some degree the concept of the necessity for Christ's developmental process, if only in the sense of Christ having to prove himself to be vocationally fit.[123] If this is true, then McCruden may be said to be correct that David Peterson's model opens itself to the same criticism brought to bear against the moral or ethical approach to the notion of perfection in Hebrews.[124] Therefore, it becomes difficult to reconcile the notion of perfection conceived along vocational-experiential development or growth with passages in Hebrews that emphasize such qualities as Christ's supreme stature (Heb 4:15; 7:26).[125] This highlights the need to consider a better alternative approach. Before this author proposes a better approach, there is a relatively new approach that deserves some attention.

Definitive Attestation Approach

The most recent interpretative proposal is what may be termed the "definitive attestation" view proposed by K. McCruden.[126] In his fine work, McCruden examines the τέλειος notion in relation to the broader theological theme of "divine beneficence or *philanthropia*."[127] McCruden's definitive attestation approach argues in favor of a new material or technical application of the concept of τέλειος that attempts to answer the question of what has been fundamentally attested or made perfect, complete, fulfilled, or manifest in Christ. He argues that it is "the beneficent character of Christ that has been definitely attested to"[128]—a strange approach that is based on selected non-literary papyri. Whereas the purpose of this discussion is not to offer a detailed analysis of McCruden's findings, it is important to examine a few examples from a representative selection of the non-literary papyri McCruden uses to make his case—in particular, the papyrological evidence

---

123. Ibid., 103. Similarly, A. B. Bruce sees perfection as the process through which Christ became skillful in his vocation as the Savior—that is, in learning the art of saving (Bruce, *Epistle to the Hebrews*, 101–103). Bruce, however, proposes that a moral-ethical dimension should be understood to be implied in the notion of perfection in Hebrews.

124. McCruden, *Solidarity Perfected*, 21.

125. For further details, see Scholer, *Proleptic Priests*, 188.

126. McCruden, *Solidarity Perfected*, 44–69.

127. Ibid., 66–7. His primary focus, like that of many other scholars, is not primarily on the notion of perfection as it relates to the believers, but rather to Christ.

128. Ibid., 25, 44–69, 139. This argument is based on what McCruden describes as "divine beneficence and philathropia," which he borrows from his reading of a representative selection of some Greek non-literary papyri wherein the verbal form τελειοῦν is used in a technical sense. For an overview of these non-literary papyri, see McCruden, *Solidarity Perfected*, 26–44.

from Oxyrhynchus that, according to McCruden, has some relevance to Hebrews' Christology.[129]

McCruden posits that there is enough papyrological evidence to demonstrate consistent usage of the verbal form of τέλειος in a material, technical sense of legal execution in the form of public notarization or execution (or implementation) of a legal document.[130] One example used to validate this notion is found in P.Oxy XXVII.2471, a papyrus dated approximately AD 49 that deals with the repayment of a loan made to a man named Chaeremon by two brothers, Demetrius and Isodorus, and paid back in installments through the bank of Narcissus. The document serves as a contract or agreement of cancellation of a loan.

A portion of the contract reads,

> We agree between ourselves as follows, . . . by the present draft made by Chaeremon and τετελειωμένην executed through the aforesaid exchange-bank of Narcissus—the thirteen talents which they lent to Chaeremon himself. . . together with the interests, that the loan σψνχηορεσισ be null and void. . .[131]

Whether the verb τελειόω translated "executed" may be said to carry the notion of "notarization" by the action of the exchanged bank or the notion of "executed" (cf. "accomplished" or "fulfilled") through the bank action of repaying the loan, given the terms or conditions as stipulated in the written drafts, contract, or agreement, is unclear.[132] It is also true that there is an idea of accomplishment or fulfillment of an agreement, promise, or condition as found in the act of formal payment of the loan. This makes sense, since any acceptance of such a loan or debt presupposes a formal acceptance of some terms and conditions that must be honored or fulfilled. Whatever the case, whether such a notion of τέλειος as "official notarization" can be read into Hebrews' language is highly debatable.

Another example is found in P.Oxy III.483, dating from around AD 108. McCruden points to the verbal form of τέλειος as carrying the notion of "legal execution" in reference to a memorandum by a public official

---

129. McCruden is, however, not certain that his approach constitutes the key to the interpretation of the τέλειος notion in Hebrews. See McCruden, "Christ's Perfection in Hebrews," 27.

130. For further details, see Moulton and Milligan, *Vocabulary of the Greek Testament*, 629.

131. Turner et al., "P.Oxy 27.2471," 147–48. See also P.Oxy 27.2473; P.Oxy 42.3030, 3054; P.Oxy 3.510.

132. The idea that this technical notion of notarization or execution of a legal document has any relevance to Hebrews' Christology is highly disputable.

giving an order to public recorders "to execute" or "complete" some deeds as underlined in a public document, following proper procedures. A portion of the papyrus reads,

> I present this application in order that you may instruct the αγορανομοι of Oxyrhynchus, who are also recorders, to execute (τελειῶσαι) the deed in the proper way.[133]

From the document, one may deduce that public recorders are instructed "to execute," "to complete," "fulfill," or "to accomplish" some deeds following proper procedures in the contract or legal document. Again, whether one should take this reading as having some relevance to Hebrews or its Christological language remains disputable.[134]

The same idea is also found in P.Oxy XII.1462, a document dated from about AD 90 in which a woman named Taeuemeros promises to fulfill her obligations by repaying a soldier a certain amount of money owed to his mother in order to fulfill the terms and conditions found in a loan contract. A portion of the document reads:

> Taeuemeros, daughter of Marcus, . . . acknowledges to Marcus Anthestius Gemellus, soldier of the third Ituraenan cohort of the century of Titius. . . that she will perforce repay to Marcus Anthestius Gemellus within the. . . days, which she has asked him for (?) as indulgence on the loan. . . the silver drachmas owed to the mother. . . in accordance with a contract of. . . drawn up [τελειωθεῖσαν] through the *grapheion* of the village of Karanis. . . in the sixth year of Domitian in the month of Pharmouthi.[135]

In the verbal form, there is a notion of "completion" or "fulfillment" of the woman's obligations to repay the loan as stipulated in the contract's terms and conditions. It is debatable whether the technical sense of "legal notarization" or "definitive attestation" constitutes a better reading of the τέλειος notion in this document. Even when such reconstruction could be said to be valid in terms of the notion's broader context in these documents, its applicability to the Christology of Hebrews remains questionable. Nevertheless, the proposal deserves some serious thought and more investigation.

---

133. Grenfell and Hunt, "P.Oxy III.483," 173.

134. For further details, see P.Oxy I.68; P.Oxy II.237. The same formal notion of completion of some deeds is seen in these documents, such that McCruden's proposal of the notion of "definitive attestation" in the sense of an "official notarization" is a distortion of the facts found in Hebrews. See especially Lobel and Roberts, "P.Oxy 27.2349," 145.

135. Husselman, "P.Mich 9.568–569," 116–18.

Survey of Major Interpretative Approaches and Related Literature 37

The question as to what, exactly, McCruden proposes and its relevance to Hebrews is significant.

In most of the selected excerpts from the papyri, McCruden argues the terminology of "perfection" functions essentially as a confirmation of the business or legal matter at hand. For instance, when the notion is applied directly to a person, it is used as formal registration of a slave.[136] McCruden recognizes, however, that many Hebrews scholars would doubt that the author would apply a technical term typically reserved for legal or business transactions to the person of Christ, his work, and the believers.[137] Perhaps the issue does not reside in the technical term reserved for legal matters and business transactions per se, but rather in whether the language in the papyri can be transferred to the language of Hebrews. The context becomes the defining factor in determining what the "perfection" terminology implies. Before pointing specifically to what McCrudem perceives in Hebrews' Christology as a "technical or material meaning of perfection," it suffices to indicate that while the meaning assigned to the notion of τέλειος in the papyri is somewhat unclear, there seem to be instances where the verbal form can be seen as carrying its formal connotation of completion, accomplishment, or fulfillment, as evidenced in many other ancient writings referred to previously.[138]

Considering the language the authors use in both the selected excerpts in the papyri and in Hebrews, scholars who support this approach would point to the central function of the concept of τέλειος as intending to make something clear and demonstrative in a definitive sense. For example, the opening verses of Hebrews would be seen as an assertion that God has now spoken in a definitive way in the person of the Son (Heb 1:1–2). McCruden proposes that the same connotation is found in the verb βεβαιόω which means "to confirm" or "to establish" (Heb 2:3; 3:14; 6:16, 19; 9:17; 13:9). This also points to the idea of an "official or definitive attestation." Furthermore, the contrast between the old Levitical system as provisional and the new as complete is seen here as a definitive attestation of divine beneficence or *philanthropia*. McCruden concludes that it is Christ's personal sacrifice that accounts for both the more perfect priesthood of Christ and the specific failure of the old institution of the Levitical priesthood. A definitive, complete sacrifice was made by Christ, the perfect High Priest; the personal quality of

---

136. Grenfell and Hunt, "P.Oxy I.63," 136.

137. For this discussion, see McCruden, "Christ's Perfection in Hebrews," 37.

138. For this reading, see for example, Lobel and Roberts, "P.Oxy 22.2349," esp. lines 3–4. See also Grenfell et al., "P.tebt 2.316," esp. lines 10–12.

his salvific activity has been displayed clearly with the unique and personal qualities the Levitical priesthood lacked.[139]

The definitive attestation approach sees some parallels between selected excerpts in the papyri and the language of Hebrews. This approach claims that in Hebrews, God spoke in a definitive way in the person of the Son. If one assumes that such a clear attestation is unmistakably evidenced in the work of the perfected Son as the authentic new priest, then some aspects of this approach could be said to be similar to the vocational-existential approach. For instance, it is Christ's own experience of offering up of his own life (rather than animals') to God that makes him perfect. There is no doubt that the incarnation of Christ is an expression of divine goodness and mercy toward mankind. However, interpreting the τέλειος motif in Hebrews following the definitive attestation model leaves readers with some unanswered questions because the model does not help readers appreciate the content and message of Hebrews. As will be shown in subsequent chapters, the text and context remains the key for proper interpretation of τέλειος in Hebrews. The strong emphasis on the finality of God's eschatological revelation in the Son in Hebrews calls for a better approach.

A CASE FOR AN ESCHATOLOGICAL APPROACH

This author contends that the eschatological approach accounts for all the evidence found in Hebrews and presents a better alternative as an interpretative approach to the τέλειος notion. This approach is based on the premise that the author of Hebrews places his message in an eschatological context, as if the end time has already begun. The readers are living at the close of the age, as evidenced in the phrase ἐπ' ἐσχάτου τῶν ἡμερῶν τούτων (Heb 1:2).[140] To the author of Hebrews, the messianic mission of Jesus falls at the close of the age, which points to the completion of God's redemptive plan of salvation and God's definitive and final provision in Christ. The goal of direct access to God has been attained by the Son, who opened the way toward the same goal for believers through him (Heb 6:19–20).[141] The goal of the τέλος and final access to God in glory (*parousia*), becomes the deciding

---

139. For this discussion, see McCruden, "Christ's Perfection in Hebrews," 37–40.

140. In the first chapter of Hebrews, the author begins his exhortation with a solemn statement that clearly sets the context of the message when he states, "In these last days, God has spoken through the Son. . ." (1:2). The phrase ἐπ' ἐσχάτου τῶν ἡμερῶν τούτων establishes clearly from the very outset of the exhortation an atmosphere of impending eschatological dimension that can be seen through the rest of the book. For further details, see Mackie, *Eschatology and Exhortation in Hebrews*, 40–41.

141. See also Lindars, *Theology of Hebrews*, 47.

feature in the interpretation of the τέλειος motif in Hebrews. The complete or final access to God is conceived here as an eschatological future event.[142] As will be shown in subsequent chapters, future eschatology occupies a central place in Hebrews; it is the determining element in the interpretation of the τέλειος notion in Hebrews.[143]

"Eschatology" Defined

The concept of "eschatology" needs to be understood properly to avoid any misconception of the use of the word when applied to Hebrews. Ellingworth is correct that the word "eschatology" can be used in its strict sense to refer to the last things, more generally in reference to the future.[144] However, sometimes scholars use the word in a broad sense to point to the temporal rather than special categories, or even more broadly to indicate a concern with soteriology rather than cosmology.[145] It is pivotal to assume that the author of Hebrews is not primarily concerned with cosmological, Hellenistic, or special categories, but rather with soteriological, temporal, and future goal-oriented categories. Soteriologically, Hebrews seems to be concerned with the attainment of fullness of salvation for many worshipers in the process of drawing near to the goal of "completeness," which coincides with the full realization of all the better provisions of the new covenant. While the present facts are critical as the foundation for what is yet to come, the future reward or promise becomes the key incentive, driving force, and motivating factor for the believer's perseverance. Some aspects of Hebrews' language become very important to appreciating this eschatological dimension of Hebrews.

---

142. For a similar argument, see Preisker, *Das Ethos des Urchristentums*, 130–34. Preisker argues,

> Τέλειος gibt sich also als eindeutig eschatologischer Begriff, der den Frommen von der Endhoffnung, vom Reich Gottes her bestimmt sein lässt, aber um den Abstand von Gott und vom τέλος weiss. (Preisker, *Das Ethos des Urchristentums*, 131)

According to Preisker, the eschatological kingdom of God gives direction to every action.

143. For further details, see Barrett, "Eschatology of Hebrews," 363–93.

144. Ellingworth, *Hebrews*, 76.

145. Ibid.

Eschatological Aspects of Hebrews

Hebrews, like other writings in the NT, can be understood within an eschatological orbit. Eschatology occupies a vital dimension in the author's mind as evidenced in the letter as a whole, beginning with its opening verses. This does not suggest that eschatology is the burden of the book, nor that eschatology functions in the letter as an end in and of itself. The point is that eschatology can be considered as the context of the book. While Hebrews is not intended to provide detailed teaching or explanations on the subject of eschatology, this context provides the framework within which the word of exhortation is functioning. The following facts illustrate this point.

Assuming that Hebrews was written primarily to a Hellenistic Jewish audience living outside Palestine, perhaps in Rome or near Rome,[146] as will be discussed in the next chapter, it naturally follows that Hebrews' audience would embody some eschatological hopes of the Jewish people in the final or definite reconstitution of the Hebrew people as a nation. It is for this reason that the author's eschatological convictions cohere in many ways with other NT writings.

From the start of the letter, the author lays out the setting of his message when he states: ἐπ' ἐσχάτου τῶν ἡμερῶν τούτων ἐλάλησεν ἡμῖν ἐν υἱῷ, , "in these last days God has spoken to us through the Son" (Heb 1:2). From the majestic opening statement of Hebrews, Christ's future possession of all things is given a degree of prominence even before his role in creation. In fact, the same theme reappears in Heb 1:14, where it is applied to the people of God but with an emphasis on the eschatological future.[147] The phrase ἐσχάτου τῶν ἡμερῶν τούτων. . ., "in these last days. . .," establishes an atmosphere of the impending eschatological fulfillment.[148] While the author takes the theme of "the world to come" (cf. Heb 2:5) as a starting point, there is a tension between Christ's present exaltation and the future fulfillment of God's purpose. From the outset, however, the Son's messianic mission can be understood as falling at the close of the age, when God completes his redemptive plan to bring many believers to their eternal glory. For

---

146. For this position and alternative views, see Guthrie, *New Testament Introduction*, 682–87. See also, Bruce, *Epistle to the Hebrews*, 3–4. A complete treatment is given in the fourth chapter of this study.

147. This naturally leads to the author's first expression of his warning for the worshipers' future in Heb 2:1–4. The other warning passages in Hebrews are Heb 3:7–4:13; 5:11–6:8; 10:26–39; and 12:25–29. For further details on the eschatological aspects of the warning passages, see Toussaint, "Eschatology of the Warning Passages, 67–80.

148. Mackie, *Eschatology and Exhortation*, 40.

this reason, the author's emphasis on both the present and future come out strongly as illustrated in the following examples.

The first example is seen in the word "salvation" and related concepts. To the author of Hebrews, "salvation" is something already present and available through the Christian message first announced by Jesus (Heb 2:3), and it comes as a result of Christ's self-sacrifice.[149] Jesus is already the pioneer of salvation for his many believers (2:10) and is the source of their salvation (5:9). Yet the context suggests that the full realization of such a salvation is still in the future.[150] The author of Hebrews is confident that readers will come to fully share in this salvation.[151] In Heb 6:9, the future aspect clearly reveals that such a salvation is yet to happen, especially in view of the promise to come.

The second example is the use of the description of the Hebrew believers as God's people. They are already identified as God's "house" or "household" (3:6), yet their hope (cf. 6:18–20) is not yet fully realized. They are already sharing in Christ (3:14), yet they are still, like OT saints, seeking full participation in what is variously described as God's κατάπαυσίς "resting-place" (3:11),[152] as a "homeland" (11:14), or as a "city" (11:16). Although they are already sharing in the promise of Christ, they have yet to inherit or take permanent possession of what God has promised (6:12; cf. 9:11; 10:36; 11:39). Furthermore evidence of the future element is that only at the last judgment will the temporary be destroyed so that what is permanent may be seen to survive (12:25–29).[153] Thus, the author of Hebrews vividly depicts the idea that the OT heroes of faith walked in obedience, enduring by faith with anticipation of Christ (11:26), but are still waiting until later believers in Christ are joined together with them as God's restored people so that they may all be made perfect together (11:40).[154]

Third, the recurrent language of "hope" (Heb 3:6; 6:11, 18; 7:19; 10:23; cf. 11:1) conveys to the readers a future dimension of the promises or

---

149. Thus, Ellingworth recognizes the tension between the present exaltation and future fulfillment, but correctly observes that the starting point of this opening section is the theme of "the world to come" (cf. Heb 1:2, 14; 2:5). See Ellingworth, *Hebrews*, 77.

150. Bruce states, "The salvation here spoken of lies in the future; it is yet to be inherited, even if its blessings can already be enjoyed in anticipation" (Bruce, *Hebrews*, 25–26).

151. The work of Christ, his suffering and death, and the future salvation are inextricably bound together (Heb 2:5–10). See also Ellingworth, *Hebrews*, 77.

152. For a detailed but concise treatment of the concept of "rest," see Toussaint, "Eschatology of the Warning Passages," 70–74.

153. For this discussion, see Ellingworth, *Hebrews*, 73–74.

154. Ibid., 74. For further details, see chapter 5 of this book.

benefits that flows from the self-sacrifice of Christ. The κατάπαυσίς remains a promise of entering God's future resting place (Heb 4:1; cf. σαββατισμός in v. 9). The nature of such an assurance constitutes the object of the Christian hope—that is, "what is hoped for," rather than the subjective hopefulness.[155] Interpreters believe that this theme of hope is closely related to the prominent theme of God's promise as found in Hebrews (4:13), which refers to what God promises rather than the act of promising. In fact, given the pastoral purpose of Hebrews, the exhortation "to the readers to hold fast to their confession of faith" become almost by definition, future-oriented,[156] but clearly without the minimization of its present aspect. The author's exhortation to hold fast in 10:23 is undeniably related to the past event of Christ's sacrifice (10:19–21), the consequent cleansing of worshipers (10:22), and their present life as a believing community that sees "the Day drawing near" (10:24–25).[157] At the end of chapter 12, the author refers to the final cataclysm, which points to the expectation that the final judgment is near as a characteristic of early Christian teaching. The future-oriented hope becomes an incentive for the believers, in view of the coming future judgment, to persevere and hold fast to the confession of their faith.

Finally, the author's eschatological convictions cohere in many ways with other NT writings. For example, to the author of Hebrews, not only have Jesus' death and exaltation occurred at "the end of the age" (Heb 9:26; 1 Cor 10:11; 1 Pet 1:19–21),[158] but also in a little while Jesus will return to earth in order to bring judgment and salvation (Heb 9:28; 1 Thess 4:13–18; 1 Pet 1:3–9). It is obvious that in the interim, the believers live in a time of eschatological ambiguity as they experience "the powers of the age to come" (Heb 6:5; 1 Cor 12–14). Yet they are eagerly waiting for the full unveiling of God's eschatological kingdom, which is envisioned in Hebrews as the "unshakable kingdom" (Heb 12:28) and as the "heavenly city" (13:14). Indeed, the key stages in the Hebrews' past, present, and future seem to converge in the vocabulary of what may be termed the "traditional Jewish apocalyptic

---

155. Ellingworth, *Hebrews*, 77.

156. Some characteristic terms in this connection include μακροθυμία (Heb 6:12), ὑπομονή (10:32, 36), πίστις (4:2–3), and verbs of exhortation such as κατανοήσατε (3:1; cf. 10:24) and ἀναλογίσασθε (12:3) with similar connotations, φοβηθῶμεν (4:1); and κατέχωμεν (10:23). Yet even in such passages as these, past, present, and future are closely related. For further details on this discussion, see Ellingworth, *Hebrews*, 77.

157. Ibid., 77–79.

158. The phrase "end of the ages" (Heb 9:26) is seen by many students of the Bible not only as the climax of the Old Testament eras, but also as the climax of all things. This is perhaps the reason why the author points readers to Christ's second coming in the following passage. For further details, see Hodges, "Hebrews," 803.

two-age eschatology," although clearly with the distinctive Christological focus that is characteristic of early Christianity (13:8, 13).[159]

SUMMARY AND EVALUATION

Hebrews is framed within an eschatological setting. The eschatological dimension of the letter sets up the motivation for the way the Hebrew worshipers are to lead their lives in perseverance. Such motivation comes from both the present and future eschatological perspective of the letter. As the eschatological age has already begun, the readers are to lead their lives not only in accordance with their present status of new rebirth, but also in view of what is yet to come. Since they are living in "these last days," the author reminds the believers of what they should pursue if they are to stand before the coming judgment seat of God. The future judgment, while acting as a warning to the Hebrew believers, also serves to encourage their perseverance. The result of such perseverance is the inheritance of the future provisions of the new covenant. It is within this context that the author employs the language of τέλειος in Hebrews. As will be argued in subsequent chapters, the Hebrews author's concern does not primarily consist of the moral-ethical ideal, nor does it meet the cultic or vocational qualifications. His concern does not consist solely of Christ's exaltation, despite a number of scholarly insights from this approach. The author is more concerned with the completion of God's plan of salvation and the attainment of complete access or fellowship with God (cf. Jer 31:31–34) when all the promises made to Abraham will be finally brought to completion.

The notion of perfection is best understood eschatologically in terms of "the world to come." Hebrews believers have tasted the powers of the age to come (Heb 6:5); they are grateful for receiving (proleptically) a kingdom that cannot be shaken (12:28). Yet their search is for the city that is yet to come (13:14). There, the people of God will experience their sabbatical rest (4:9). The city has fixed foundations, its maker and designer being God himself (11:10). While the believers are described as those who have already spiritually tasted the benefits of this unshakable city, its reality has yet to be fully realized. Future eschatology becomes the determining element in the interpretation of the τέλειος terminology in Hebrews. In order to fully appreciate this insight, this study now turns to an examination of how the notion of τέλειος would have been used in the ancient world. This will serve as a broader historical background to the notion of perfection in Hebrews that will be examined later in this study.

159. For this discussion, see Mackie, *Eschatology and Exhortation*, 3.

Chapter 3

The Notion of Perfection in the Ancient World

THIS CHAPTER EXAMINES HOW THE τέλειος terminology of "perfection" was used in the ancient world. The basic assumption is that the biblical text is illuminated when it is examined against its historical, conceptual, and theological background. To this end, the lexical meaning is examined first, followed by an examination of the usage of the concept of perfection in the classical Greek world, Jewish tradition, Second Temple Judaism, and the rest of the New Testament.

LEXICAL MEANING OF ΤΕΛΕΙΟΣ

The meaning of the root word must be determined in order to shed light on the notion of τέλειος as used in various contexts. As lexicographers indicate, the adjectival form τέλειος is derived from the word τέλος,[1] which carries primarily the sense of "an end" but also other nuances such as "termination," "the limit at which something ceases to be," "the last part of a process," "close," or "conclusion," "that to which a thing is finished, its close," and "the end to which all things relate, the goal, purpose."[2] The idea of achievement,

---

1. The word τέλος is seen by older interpreters as the deciding feature in the interpretation of the τέλειος notion in Hebrews. For further details, see Preisker, *Das Ethos des Urchristentums*, 131.

2. Bauer, *Greek-English Lexicon*, 998–99. As a *nomen actionis*, τέλος carries the

fulfillment, and completion are implied in the word τέλος, and are closely related to the concept of τέλειος and cognates as found in both the adjectival and verbal forms.

The adjectival form carries the notion of "bringing to an end." Joseph Henry Thayer observes that the adjective connotes the idea of "brought to its end, finished, wanting nothing necessary to completeness, perfect."[3] The verbal form τελειόω carries the notion of "to fulfill," "to carry out," or to complete the will of God.[4] Like other verbal forms ending in -όω, this verb is factitive,[5] denoting the notion of acting upon objects or individuals to render them τέλειος perfect, whole, or complete.[6] The verb carries the notion of "to complete," "to bring to an end," "to fulfill," "to finish," or "to accomplish."[7] This is related to the idea of "totality," "completion," or "fullness." This idea is also present in the Septuagint (LXX) rendering of the corresponding Hebrew terminology in the Masoretic Text (MT), תָּמִים and שָׁלֵם. This terminology connotes the idea of complete, wholehearted devotion to God. Thus, an individual who does the "whole" will of God is תָּמִים and the heart that is undivided in obedience to Yahweh is שָׁלֵם.[8]

The concept is used once to translate three other Hebrew words: כָּלָה, כָּלַל, and עָשָׂה. When the verbal form of τέλειος is used to translate כָּלָה, the emphasis is on the notion of completion or accomplishment of a task.[9] For instance, it is used in reference to the completion of Solomon's temple in 2 Chr 8:16. In Ezek 27:11, it is used to translate כָּלַל with reference to completion of beauty, such that it is rendered in the NJB as "they completed your beauty." The general idea is "to make perfect," such that other translations

---

notion of "achievement" (Aeschylus, *Suppliant Women*, 624), "fulfillment" (Aristotle, *Politics*, VI. 8. 1322b. 13), and "carrying out of an Old Testament prophecy" (Josephus, *Jewish War*, IV. 387). Also, the notion carries the idea of "completion" as a state of "perfection," such as in Plato, *Laws*, VI. 772c; and Josephus, *Jewish Antiquities*, X. 58. For further details, see Delling, "τέλος, τέλειος," *TDNT* 8:49.

3. Thayer, *Greek-English Lexicon*, 618–19.

4. Delling, "τέλειος," *TDNT* 8:81. See also BDAG, 996.

5. Spicq emphasizes the factitive notion of "consummation" to the verbal form τελειοῦν in Hebrews when he explains the notion: ". . . il s'agit toujours de porter quelque chose ou quelqu' un au but qui lui est assigné" (Spicq, *L'Épître aux Hébreux*, 224).

6. Attridge, *Epistle to the Hebrews*, 83.

7. See Blass and Debrunner, *Greek Grammar of the New Testament*, 996.

8. For further details, see Delling, "τέλειος," *TDNT* 8:73. For further treatment of the LXX usage, see the discussion below.

9. See *HALOT*, s.v. "כָּלָה," Qal 2, 477, where the word is listed to signify "completed" or "to be finished." For further details, see BDB, s.v. "כָּלָה," Qal 1b, 478.

render it as "they perfected your beauty."[10] The general thought of completing a task is also seen in the passive stem of נַעֲשָׂה ("to be done"), where the concept refers to Nehemiah's building project in order to highlight the divine agency aspect in the completion of the task.[11]

As to the semantic field of τέλειος, lexicographers attribute the sense of "having attained the end, purpose, or completeness," in the sense of persons who are fully up to the standard in some respect or virtue.[12] It is this notion of virtue that most readers generally assign to the English word "perfect," with the connotation of "flawlessness" or "sinlessness."[13] It is partially true that τέλειος may carry this connotation, but it should not be confined to this definition. Transition from one language to another may render the expression difficult if one is tempted to transfer meaning from one cultural setting to another. The notion carries the general idea of "goal" or bringing something (or someone) to its intended end, fulfillment, or completeness. Before drawing such a conclusion, it is important to examine various usages of the τέλειος terminology in order to appreciate its full-orbed meaning as evidenced in its usage in the classical Greek world, Jewish tradition, Second Temple Judaism, and the NT world.

CLASSICAL WORLD

This section demonstrates how the τέλειος notion in Hebrews is indebted to its larger context and can be understood against this background. The concept of τέλειος appears to be widely used in a formal sense in ancient writings.[14]

General Usage of τέλειος

In the ancient Greek world, the τέλειος terminology was widely used in a formal sense, with a few technical usages of the notion depending on the context.[15] A careful examination of both the adjectival and verbal forms shows how the notion is commonly used in various ways in reference to

---

10. For details see *HALOT*, s.v. "כָּלַל," 480.
11. For further details, see Oyediran, "Lexical and Exegetical Analysis," 65–67.
12. BDAG, 995.
13. Anderson, "Root *Teleios*," 4.
14. Liddell and Scott offer an extensive treatment of the notion of τέλειος and show how the notion was used in the classical Greek world with a variety of nuances, as alluded to in the following lines (Liddell and Scott, *Greek-English Lexicon*, 1769–70).
15. Ibid. For further details, see Attridge, *Hebrews*, 84–87.

animals, sacrifices, persons, arithmetic, prayers, and vows in a general sense to convey the notion of completeness. Ancient writers like Homer used the notion in a technical sense, referring to an animal that was fit for sacrifice. In such cases, the sacrificial victim is described as "being without spot" or "without blemish."[16] Similarly, the notion is used in reference to one who is made suitable for office.[17] In Thucydides, τέλειος is used in reference to sacrifices "performed with total rites" and said to be perfect. Full-grown men and even animals are referred to as τέλειος.[18] Also, a number is said to be full, complete, or perfect when it is equal to the sum total of its divisors, for example: 28=14+7+4+2+1.[19] Such numbers were said to be τέλειοι, or "complete." Furthermore, the adjectival form is also used in referring to the gods. For example, Zeus is described as Ζεῦ Ζεῦ τέλειε, "O perfect Zeus."[20] This description connects with the nouns "end" or "goal" (τέλος) to indicate that the gods have the powers to fully accomplish what they set out to do or to fulfill (τελεῖν).[21] All these examples demonstrate a general sense of totality, fullness, maturation, or completion that indicates the notion carries a formal rather than a technical connotation.

The verbal form has the same variations in nuances as those found in the adjectival form, but these may be identified as stressing the general sense of fulfillment, consummation, or completion. Thucydides, for example, uses the term "perfection" in reference to the execution of a treaty or completion of a deed like that of libation.[22] Similarly, Herodotus uses the verbal form

16. Boisé, *First Six Books of Homer's Iliad*, 3. For further details, see Homer, *Iliad*, I. 66. 6.

17. See Sophocles, *Electra*, lines 1508–10, where the passive voice is used in reference to one who has come to the end of his labor, thus obtaining his freedom. Here, the formal connotation of "completion" is emphasized by the same author when he used the verb in reference to an ambush carried out or completed successfully (Sophocles, *Electra*, LCL, 250–51).

18. See Thucydides, *History of the Peloponnesian War*, V. 47; LCL, 240. In Xenophon, *Cyropaedia*, I. 2. 4 (cf. Heb 5:14), full-grown men are referred to as τέλειοι, while full-grown animals are referred to as perfect in Aeschylus, *Agamemnon*, 1504. In Isocrates, *Panathenaicus*, XII. 32. 242, the notion of τέλειος is used in reference to men who are said to be accomplished or perfect in their kind, especially in relation to quality. See also ibid., XII. 9.

19. For further examples see Aristophanes, *Lysistrata,* 104; and Aristotle, *Nicomachean Ethics*, I. 16.

20. Aeschylus, *Agamemnon*, 973; LCL, 82–83. The notion is also used in the same reference of the gods (i.e., Zeus) as having the power to fulfill prayers of his worshipers.

21. This was a further way to point to the power of Zeus and other gods as having powers to accomplish the worshipers' prayers. See DuPlessis, Τέλειος: *The Idea of Perfection*, 77.

22. Thucydides, *History of the Peloponnesian War*, VI. 32; LCL, 240–41.

in reference to the notion of "bringing to completion" or "consummation" of one's wish, desire, or deed, such as a claim to a monarchy's throne.[23] The passive voice is used in Sophocles in reference to one who has been made suitable for office. The concept of "completion" is emphasized by the same author when he refers to an ambush "carried out" completely or successfully.[24] It is only at a later stage that the image of the ideal sage is developed in Stoicism and the notion of τέλειος is perceived in terms of possession of all virtues.[25] For example, speaking of the lives of eminent philosophers in their perpetual exercise of virtue, Diogenes remarks, "For virtue can never be lost, and the good man is always exercising his mind which is perfect τέλεια."[26]

While the dominant or fundamental sense of the adjective τέλειος is "fullness," "totality," "maturation," or "completion," the verb carries the notion of "to carry out fully," "to fulfill," or "to complete."[27] David Peterson concludes there is no evidence of the use of the notion of τέλειος in classical Greek in a technical or material sense. In any case, only very limited technical usages of this term can be justified. In most instances, the notion carries a formal rather than a technical connotation.[28]

Based on this, τέλειος can be said to carry the ordinary or general notion of "consummation," "completion," or bringing to the fullness for which something was intended. In this case, the term carries more of a formal, rather than a technical or material connotation. This formal connotation is also found in Greek philosophy, which reveals a sense of "ideal," "fullness," or "completeness" sometimes seen as future-oriented and one that is very difficult to acquire, as evidenced especially in Plato and Aristotle.[29] Since these two figures are the most influential, they are examined in order to appreciate any influence they may have had on the writing of Hebrews.

---

23. Herodotus, *Persian Wars*, V. 11–12; I. 120; III. 86; LCL, 10–11.

24. Sophocles, *Electra*, 1508–10; LCL, 251. The perfect voice is used here to refer to one who has been perfected or made suitable for office through some kind of test, as implied in a chorus performed to the House of Atreus.

25. Attridge, *Hebrews*, 84.

26. Diogenes Laertius, *Lives of Eminent Philosophers*, VII. 128; LCL, 233.

27. Peterson, *Hebrews and Perfection*, 23.

28. See ibid., 21–23.

29. Hartin, *Spirituality of Perfection*, 18.

The Notion of Perfection in the Ancient World

Platonic Usage of Τέλειος

Platonism is the most popular conceptual background posited for Hebrews thought. The basic assumption alleges a link or similarities between the Hebrews concept of reality and the Platonic theory of ideas.[30] The uses of antitheses like the contrasts between the earthly and the heavenly (cf. Heb 8:1–13; 9:23–24), between the created and the uncreated (9:11), and the passing and the abiding (7:3, 24; 10:34; 12:27; 13:14) have raised the issue of whether the author of Hebrews, like Philo, was influenced by Platonic dualism.[31] For some scholars, Platonic dualism so dominates Hebrews that the author must be regarded as an Alexandrian Jew who learned this approach from contact with Philo's teaching. An examination of the Platonic usage of τέλειος, however, raises some doubts as to whether or not the author of Hebrews was directly influenced by the Platonic theory of ideas.

In Plato's writings, the concept of τέλειος reveals a meaning of "perfection" that has a future orientation, a state that is very difficult to acquire. As one of the world's most significant thinkers, Plato believed that a man is τέλειος only when he attains what he calls Φρόνησις, "insight," "wisdom," "a firm and true view," or a philosophical insight or total knowledge including all the benefits carried by these things.[32] Accordingly, the notion of perfection lies in the ideal order of things. In his work *Phaedo*, Plato refers to the notion of perfection as that which is withdrawn from the present order of existence in one's pursuit of truth and wisdom.[33] The notion of perfection conceived in terms of the ideal becomes future-oriented, and is perceived as something very difficult, if not impossible, to acquire.[34]

Plato answers the question of how such perfection is attained by suggesting that the philosopher's responsibility consists of striving to remember what had once been seen in the world of ideas. Through the process of liberating oneself from the shadows of this world and ultimately attaining

---

30. The alleged similarities and link between Hebrews and Plato were first posited by Eusebius, who commented on Heb 8:5 by citing Plato's *Republic* (Eusebius, *Preparation for the Gospel,* 12). For a summary examination of terminological similarities between Hebrews and Plato, see Oyediran, "Lexical and Exegetical Analysis," 7–8.

31 This dualism is seen in Plato's theory of ideas, as eloquently presented in his distinction between the eternal idea and temporal (or corporeal) things (Plato, *Republic*, VII. 1–2). The Platonic theory of ideas regards what is seen as unreal—a mere shadow of what is not seen or the reality behind the shadow (cf. Oyediran, "Lexical and Exegetical Analysis," 7). For further details, see also Guthrie, *Letter to the Hebrews*, 43.

32. Plato, *Laws*, II. 653a.

33. Ibid., *Phaedo*, 65–66; LCL, 229.

34. For this discussion, see Hartin, *Spirituality of Perfection*, 18–19.

the world of ideas, one can reach the world of true being or "perfection."[35] Plato's premise is that before the soul was united with the body, it was in a state of "perfection." One must rekindle such memories in order to attain the world of ideas, which may lead to the state of "perfection."[36] The path to "perfection" is followed through "contemplation of the world of ideas through the eyes of the soul"[37] as one contemplates what is good and morally conforms to the nature of good.

This is similar to the religious and philosophical notion of perfection in Plato's mentor, Socrates. He suggests that the perfection of felicity to be strived for is the ὁμοίωσις Θεοῦ, "the being made like God, a God who is rational, wise and good."[38] Perfection of the soul can only be reached beyond this life when the soul is completely freed from all the hindrances of the mortal physical body.[39] However, while the pursuit of self-knowledge, insight, and virtue remains the way to "perfection," the notion of virtue is primarily synonymous with "philosophical knowledge" or "intellectual insight."[40] For Plato, man's greatest problem is ignorance because the one who knows what is good is by nature capable of doing good, but such a person must also be willing to do so through the imitation of God. Culbert G. Rutenber observes,

> The true imitator of God is the philosopher, for the inmost nature of philosophy is the struggle to imitate God. . . By participating in wisdom the philosopher assimilates himself to God, growing in divinity and likeness to God. . . the culmination of the educative and reasoning process: the vision of the idea of the Good. . . This insight in the structure of reality is the point of imitation at which man is most godlike, for he sees God as he really is and is transformed into the likeness of his image.[41]

Furthermore, Plato often uses the language of perfection in the sense of initiation into mystery religions. There are disagreements among scholars regarding the significance of the τέλειος notion in regard to the mystery religions. According to Walter Bauer, the notion was used as a technical

---

35. For details, see DeVogel, *Greek Philosophy*, 135.
36. Plato, *Phaedrus*, 249 c, d; LCL, 480–83.
37. Ibid., *Republic*, VII. 533 d; LCL, 202–203. For further details, see ibid., *Statesman*, 272 d (8).
38. For this discussion, see LaRondelle, *Perfection and Perfectionism*, 11.
39. Plato, *Phaedo,* 118 d, e.
40. LaRondelle, *Perfection and Perfectionism*, 11.
41. Rutenber, *Doctrine of the Imitation of God*, 58, 62. See also Plato, *Phaedrus*, 278d; ibid., *Republic*, 533 b, c, 490 a, b; 505a–509c.

term for initiation into the mystic rites.⁴² Delling finds the technical usage for such initiations disputable.⁴³ According to DuPlessis, the concept of τέλειος cannot be proven to mean "initiation" into the mystery religions, but "rather more the perfection of being, attained by such cultic act."⁴⁴ This notion appears to have been an important concept in gnostic thought, where it was used as a technical term with reference to the redeemer and those he has enlightened.⁴⁵ It is perhaps in this sense that τέλειος is seen as an attribute of Zeus in the sense of "actualizing," "mighty," and "efficacious,"⁴⁶ so that to both Plato and Socrates, the notion of perfection is conceived in terms of being like the gods with all their fullness of power and thus as being complete.⁴⁷

Platonic perfection consists in the contemplation of the world of ideas through "the eyes of the soul."⁴⁸ Philosophical virtue—seen as full insight or total knowledge or fullness of wisdom—becomes the goal and also the basis for one's every act of goodness in pursuit of perfection.⁴⁹ This necessitates concentration on the activity of one's soul, or "thinking."⁵⁰ Under the Platonic theory of ideas, only through philosophical reason is the soul capable of disengaging itself from the body to attain a vision of its own divine being, which Plato⁵¹ describes as the ανάμνησις, or the remembrance of the soul's pre-existent divinity. Such language is different from Hebrews concept of reality. In Platonic dualism, "perfection" is far removed from the philosopher and difficult to acquire; in Hebrews, it is attainable by the faithful and is both a present and also a future reality. There may be some element of vertical dualism in Hebrews, but there is no strong evidence that such an element is a direct result of Platonic influence.

---

42. Cf. BDAG, 995.

43. Delling, "τέλειος," *TDNT* 8:69.

44. DuPlessis, Τέλειος: *Idea of Perfection*, 85.

45. Rathel, "Soteriological Terminology in Hebrews," 60. This does not suggest, however, that the author of Hebrews uses the terminology of τέλειος in a manner similar to that found in the mystery religions, as some scholars have indicated.

46. Delling, "τέλειος," *TDNT* 8:68.

47. See also LaRondelle, *Perfection and Perfectionism*, 11, 13.

48. Plato, *Republic*, 203. For further details, see also Plato, *Statesman*, 272 d (8).

49. For this discussion, see Drake, *Plato's Complete Works*, 46, 87. See also Edman, *Works of Plato*, xx–xxii.

50. LaRondelle, *Perfection and Perfectionism*, 12.

51. Plato, *Phaedo*, 73 e ff.; ibid., *Phaedrus*, 247 c ff.

Aristotle and Stoicism

Aristotle, originally a student of Plato's, was greatly influenced by his master's metaphysical and religious teaching. In spite of this great influence, however, scholars believe Aristotle developed his own scientific interests.[52] According to Aristotle, τέλειος implies that no further change or development is needed in the quality of something; it is the idea of "lacking in nothing, but excellent in all aspects."[53] For Aristotle, there is a link between τέλος ("end" or "goal") and τέλειος ("perfect"): something is "perfect" or "complete" when it achieves its intended goal or arrives at its end.[54] The term τέλειος, when taken in the strict sense of the word, is an ideal condition that may never be realized in this present, imperfect world. Aristotle observes that something is "perfect" only when it lacks nothing in respect to goodness or excellence and cannot be surpassed in its kind.[55]

The notion of τέλειος is viewed in terms of ethical philosophy founded on the observation of nature. Aristotle proposes that there is in all things, including man, "a dynamic idea or form principle,"[56] which is "a teleological principle which by nature propels man to his goal of perfection, the fulfillment of the natural destination of man."[57] Moral virtue is acquired and perfected through the habit of doing what is morally good.[58] Man is seen as carrying perfection in himself, derived from human nature as well as from specific human characteristics such as freedom of choice and reason. According to Aristotle, the highest value or claim of τέλειος, "completeness," is to live in accordance with reason or common sense, which is a mere formal principle as far as moral ethics is concerned.[59] This assumes that a philosopher or rational man can make good choices upon which virtue and happiness depends; nature does not prevent him. On the contrary, nature commends him to strive for the orderly conduct of life[60] in pursuit of the ideal, or that which is "complete" or "wisdom."

---

52. See Hartin, *Spirituality of Perfection*, 20.

53. See Aristotle, *Metaphysics*, V. xvi. 1021b, 12–25; LCL, 266–67.

54. For this discussion, see Hartin, *Spirituality of Perfection*, 21. See also DuPlessis, Τέλειος: *Idea of Perfection*, 73.

55. For this discussion, see Campbell, "Perfection," 730.

56. LaRondelle, *Perfection and Perfectionism*, 14.

57. Ibid.

58. See Aristotle, *Nicomachean Ethics*, II. 1. 1103, 32–33, b 1–2; cf. II. 5. 1105b, 9–10; LCL, 71–116.

59. Ibid., X. 7. 1178a 6.

60. LaRondelle, *Perfection and Perfectionism*, 15.

Aristotle's highest wisdom (as derived from nature) is a pragmatic ideal for a rational person: to make oneself immortal as by striving to live in accordance with the best thing imbedded in one's being, reason.[61] Like Plato, Aristotle suggests that perfection is something one strives for, something one may fully attain in the future: one is on the way to "perfection." This is closely related to the idea of attaining completeness as one attains the goal (τέλος) for which one strives. The concept of τέλειος is not taken as carrying a technical connotation, but as bearing the understanding of maturity and the formal idea of bringing the process of formation to completion or consummation.[62]

The notion of living according to subjective reason or nature is further developed in Stoicism, especially by the Stoic philosopher Zeno. Zeno follows Plato and Aristotle in principle as he narrows down his findings and develops the notion of man's virtuous living in pursuit of τέλειος. The τελείωσις of an individual is identical with the perfection of his individual nature.[63] In this case, virtue is not qualified as a habit, as Aristotle suggests, but as a diathesis, or "a certain state of the mind."[64] Virtue becomes a matter of human intellect. It is no longer the way to perfection but is instead perfection itself, bringing "salvation," perfect happiness, and freedom, which is a state of blessedness here and now.[65]

This same notion is developed by Seneca (AD 3–65), whose cult of virtue is said to be his true religion.[66] The pursuit of τέλειος is perceived as a ladder of moral progress on which mankind dominates moral wickedness or sin. For this to be true, an individual must have a certain natural disposition or the effectiveness of the natural human will or the ability to make good choices.[67] Accordingly, since humans are naturally good, sin is to be blamed for bringing the perversion of nature. The problem of sin is viewed here as originating from without,[68] which is contrary to the biblical claim regarding the fall of man and the need for God's revelation in the Son. According to Stoicism, there is perfect harmony between human reason and nature, so perfection of reason becomes similar to perfection of human nature.

---

61. Aristotle, *Nichomaean Ethics*, X. 7. 1177b, 32–35.
62. Ibid., *Generation of Animals*, III. 2. 252a; LCL, 284–85.
63. Diogenes Laertius, *Lives of Eminent Philosophers*, VII. 94.
64. For this discussion, see LaRondelle, *Perfection and Perfectionism*, 16.
65. Ibid., 17.
66. Ibid., 18.
67. Seneca, *Moral Epistles*, 71.
68. Ibid., 94, 53; 115, 11–12.

Contrary to Hebrews' teaching, Stoicism implies that man can rely not solely on God's provision in the Son, but rather on his own strength by striving to live in accordance with his own nature, which is perceived to be good [69] in order to attain "perfection" or "completeness." For Seneca, when one's whole being is founded on reason, then one's perfect and complete state of mind allows one to follow the perfect duties that lead to becoming full of divine virtue.[70] This reasoning assumes that sin is just a deviation from the path of reason because of ignorance, not a conscious transgression of a positive divine command.[71]

There is very little evidence to suggest that Hebrews was influenced by Aristotle or Stoicism. One general observation is that the formal nature of the τέλειος terminology prominent in classical Greek[72] is carried through the language and argument of Hebrews. However, the nuance philosophers attach to the notion of perfection is strange to the language of Hebrews. The Aristotelian understanding of "perfection," perceived in terms of ethical philosophy based on reason, is contrary to Hebrews understanding of "perfection," which is based on faith in Christ. Furthermore, the notion of living according to subjective reason or nature as found in Stoicism is also strange to the teaching of Hebrews, which calls for faith-endurance based on God's redemptive work of salvation already accomplished through the perfected Christ. Hebrews' thought assumes that man is sinful and in need of the Savior. Only through Christ is God's promise of salvation guaranteed. Such salvation is on the basis of faith in Christ, not on philosophical virtue or human intellect. One must look elsewhere for the conceptual and theological influence behind Hebrews' thought.

Hebrew Scripture and the Septuagint

The Hebrew Scripture (OT) and the Septuagint (LXX) constitute the most immediate context for Hebrews. Several features in Hebrews align particularly well with a Jewish background. The author's general tenor and subject matter indicate that the OT cultic system is pivotal for a proper understanding of his message. This is evidenced in his extensive appeal to details of the OT sacrificial system.[73] Interpreters are unanimous in their opinion that the

---

69. Cf. ibid., 92, 2.

70. Ibid., 71, 4; 75, 9.

71. For this discussion and further details, see LaRondelle, *Perfection and Perfectionism*, 18.

72. See Peterson, *Hebrews and Perfection*, 23.

73. Interpreters do not agree on the number of citations or allusions from the OT

The Notion of Perfection in the Ancient World

Scripture the author cites comes from the Greek translation of the Hebrew text.[74] The Hebrew Scripture and LXX are significant as the main Jewish influence on Hebrews. The following comments examine how they may have illuminated the author of Hebrews in the use of the concept of τέλειος.

In the LXX, τέλειος is used mainly to translate the two key Hebrew adjectives תָּמִים and שָׁלֵם that connote the idea of "unblemished, undivided, complete, and whole."[75] The Hebrew תָּמִים is used with reference to animals in the context of sacrificial worship of Israel, where is carryies the sense of "unblemished" with reference to an animal that is without defect and therefore fit for sacrifice.[76] Furthermore, the Hebrew word תָּמִים is also used with reference to human action or conduct and carryies the idea of one who walks wholeheartedly before Yahweh, meaning "belonging to Him" as opposed to those who practice idolatry, sorcery, and other abominations.[77] For example, in Deut 18:13, Moses tells the Israelites, "You shall be blameless [τέλειος] before the Lord your God." The meaning is one who is "perfect" or "complete" in one's relationship with God, in the sense of being fully devoted to Yahweh.[78]

---

text in Hebrews. Yet the extensive use of the OT is an essential element in the author's design and intention. For further details, see Lane, *Hebrews 1–8*, cxv–cxvi.

74. For a survey, see Thomas, "Old Testament Citations in Hebrews," 303–25. Occasionally, the wording of these citations does not conform in every detail to the extant witnesses to the LXX. Attridge observes:

> (1) it is hardly surprising that first-century texts should show some variations from the fourth-century witnesses to the LXX; (2) it's also clear that the author felt the freedom to change the wording of scripture (cf. Jer 31:31–34 at Heb 8:8–12; and the partial quotation at 10:16–17); and (3) some variations between the citations in Hebrews and witnesses to the LXX may be due to tendentious handling of the text.

For this discussion and various ways Hebrews makes use of Scripture, see Attridge, *Hebrews*, 23–27.

75. See Delling, "τέλειος," *TDNT* 8:72. Cf. Gen 6:9; Exod 12:5; Deut 18:13; 2 Kgs 22:26 (LXX). The adjective τέλειος translates the two Hebrew forms תָּמִים and שָׁלֵם at least seven times. As Rathel indicates, the verb τελειοῦν often translates the piel of תָּמִים and שָׁלֵם (Rathel, "Soteriological Terminology," 60). For further details, see Koehler and Baumgartner, *Hebrew and Aramaic Lexicon*, 1748–50.

76. For example, in Lev 1:3, 10; 3:1, 6; 4:3 the word used in the LXX to translate the Hebrew תָּמִים is ἄμωμος ("unblemished"), but in Exod 12:5 the word τέλειος is used: "Your lamb shall be without blemish [πρόβατον τέλειον], a one year-old male." For further details, see *HALOT*, 2:1749.

77. For further details, see Schnackenburg, "Christian Perfection According to Matthew," 160–61.

78. For example, Gen 6:9; 17:1; 1 Kgs 8:61; 11:4; 15:3, 4; 2 Kgs 20:3; 22:26; 1 Chr 28:9; 2 Chr 15:17. For instance, תם is an attribute of Job as a righteous man or one fully devoted to Yahweh (Job 1:1; 8:20; 9:21–22). There is also the sense of upright conduct

The most frequent occurrences of the adjective are found in the Psalms and the Writings, where they are used at times in close relationship with concepts such as "purity" and "righteousness." H. K. LaRondelle observes, "A perfect heart is not an attributive of human nature or product of law and morality, but the gracious gift of redemption."[79] For this reason, some scholars suggest the notion of τέλειος should not be perceived in terms of moral, cultic, or religious development, or even Platonic or Philonic categories. One should consider its conceptual relationship with other related terminologies in the Hebrew Scriptures and the LXX.[80] Such terminologies that are seen as related to the concept of perfection in the LXX include: "righteousness," "integrity," and "wholeness"—considered to be closely related by one fundamental supposition, which is not cultic, mystical, or ethical, but is instead purely the relationship of humankind to God as the only criterion for these qualities.[81] DuPlessis observes that "perfection is God's goodwill and bounty toward man, and man's obedient response,"[82] which encompasses the fullness of what God has intended for humankind—a perfect relationship with the Creator.

The Hebrew word שׁלם is linked in a few instances with the Hebrew word לב to convey the idea of a heart that is whole or perfect, and it is rendered also as τέλειος in the LXX (1 Chr 28:9; 2 Kgs 20:3).[83] The concept encompasses wholehearted devotion or complete allegiance to Yahweh.[84] It carries the general meaning of what is truly "perfect" or "complete" or "finished" as evidenced in the use of the adjective. On the other hand, the Hebrew verbs also convey the general meaning of "to complete, fulfill or

---

in this terminology as found, for instance, in Noah, who is declared to be "perfect in his generation" (Gen 6:9). The idea is that he was found to be blameless or righteous in his time. For this discussion, see Rathel, "Soteriological Terminology," 61.

79. LaRondelle, *Perfection and Perfectionism*, 116.

80. Michel, *Der Brief an die Hebräer*, 139.

81. To Michel, these concepts are closely related by one mutual and fundamental supposition, which is not cultic, mystical, or ethical. Rather, the relationship of man to God is the only criterion to these qualities (ibid.). For further details on other terms used in the LXX to translate the Hebrew תמים, see also DuPlessis, Τέλειος: *Idea of Perfection*, 33.

82. Ibid., 33–34.

83. See also Judg 20:26; 21:4; 3 Kgs 8:61; 11:4; 15:3, 14; Jer 13:19. The general meaning behind the Hebrew adjective is to be "whole, perfect," and "complete," while the general meaning of the root שׁלם is "completion or fulfillment of entering into a state of wholeness and restored relationship." For details, see Tregelles, *Gesenius' Hebrew and Chaldee Lexicon*, 830. See especially *HALOT*, 2:1996.

84. For this discussion and other related words, see DuPlessis, Τέλειος: *Idea of Perfection*, 94–102. For further details, see also Waanders, *History of Telos and Teleo*, 237.

finish."[85] While תָּמִים is used with reference to animals and individual persons, the word שָׁלֵם is used specifically to refer to individual persons.

Although the two words carry similar connotations and are almost synonymous,[86] the former comes from the root תמם which means "to complete, to finish," while the latter comes from the root word שלם which means "to be whole, sound, safe."[87] The former conveys the idea of upright conduct, blamelessness, or completeness as far as man's relationship to Yahweh is concerned. However, for animals, there is also the sense of "being without blemish" referring to an animal that is fit for sacrifice. For example, in Exod 12:5, the unblemished character of the sacrificial animal is emphasized, denoting that only what is whole, complete, and without defects could be offered to God as sacrifice. In this context, one can clearly see the notion of perfection. If an animal remains true to its original constitution, then it is considered to be perfect. Unlike Greek philosophy, where perfection is seen as an ideal toward which one strives, in Jewish thought perfection is conceived in terms of an "intimate relationship to the original state of being, to its wholeness as originally constituted."[88] An individual is "perfect" and "complete" when the individual is firmly rooted in this relationship with Yahweh.

The latter word שָׁלֵם carries the connotation of "being devoted to God and at peace with him."[89] For example, this nuance is present in King Solomon's charge to the Israelites: "Let your heart therefore be perfect with Jehovah our God, wholly devoted to keep his statutes and to keep his commandments as at this day" (1 Kgs 8:61). In a similar fashion, the heart of Asa is said to have been שָׁלֵם, "perfect," with the Lord (1 Kgs 15:14). The word is also used in David's address concerning the temple, in which he urges all his officials including his son Solomon to serve the Lord with a שָׁלֵם, or "perfect," heart (1 Chr 28:9). This emphasizes the idea of "fullness" or "consummation" in a formal sense.[90] The conviction of loving God and proper conduct are clearly implied as man's obedient response to God's goodwill and bounty toward men, but this does not mean that τέλειος should be primarily interpreted in terms of moral or ethical development in the sense of sinlessness or moral achievement on the part of the worshipers. Yet if one perceives the

---

85. Tregelles, *Gesenius*, 867. Cf. *HALOT*, 2:1749.

86. Both terms are taken to mean fundamentally, undivided disposition and complete devotion to Yahweh. See DuPlessis, Τέλειος: *Idea of Perfection*, 33.

87. Tregelles, *Gesenius*, 884. Cf. *HALOT*, 2:1996.

88. DuPlessis, Τέλειος: *Idea of Perfection*, 101.

89. Tregelles, *Gesenius*, 830. Also see *HALOT*, 2:1996.

90. For this discussion, see also Anderson, "Root Teleios," 10.

notion as a "gift" of God's goodwill and his bounty toward humankind, then an obedient response from the worshiper is anticipated in one's daily walk with the Lord.

In Wisdom of Solomon (4:13), Enoch is not allowed to experience death because he has been perfected or made complete. The aorist passive participle τελειωθείς is taken as functioning like a circumlocution for God's activity as the one who perfects Enoch. In 4 Macc 7:15,[91] Eleazar is praised as the leader of the Maccabean movement. Mark A. Rathel indicates that the ultimate result (ἐτελείωσεν) of Eleazar's commitment to the law was his perfection in death.[92] It is best understood that Eleazar is not perfected in death, but rather in his zeal for the law. David Peterson argues that Eleazar's faithfulness to the law found its ultimate or complete expression in his torture and death. The verb is used in a purely formal sense to describe the consummation of one's life of faith, as evidenced in his martyrdom with no special cultic, moral, or mystical implications.[93]

The verbal form τελειόω carries a seemingly different nuance, but it still holds the formal idea of bringing something to a desired or accomplished end. Almost uniformly, the verbal form is used in the expression τελειῶσαι τὰς χεῖρας to convey the notion of consecration or priestly ordination in the LXX. This does not imply that the verb should be taken by itself to imply cultic consecration apart from the whole expression as a syntactical unit.[94] Some scholars argue that the use of the verbal form is applied to priests in the LXX and indicates that someone's hands are made free from stains and that the one consecrated is free to practice the *cultus* (cf. Exod 29:6; Lev 21:10).[95] Based on this observation, Delling suggests that the verb in Hebrews follows this special usage in the LXX to indicate that someone is in a position to stand before God (Heb 7:19; 10:1).[96] The phrase τελειῶσαι τὰς χεῖρας is translated from the pi'el of the verb מלא (מִלֵּא יָד) which carries the notion of "to fill one's hand."[97] Scholars disagree on the significance of this expression.

---

91. Dey argues that 4 Macc 7:15 speaks about "religious perfection" as "unmediated access to God" in a way that parallels Philo's use of "perfection" (Dey, *Intermediary World*, 78).

92. Rathel, "Soteriological Terminology," 62.

93. Peterson, *Hebrews and Perfection*, 25.

94. Ibid., 28.

95. Delling, "τέλειος," *TDNT* 8:80–81.

96. Ibid., 82.

97. Tregelles, *Gesenius*, 474. There are at least nine usages of the verb in this sense as in Exod 29:9 dealing with the consecration of Aaron and his sons. See also 2 Chr 8:16 and Neh 6:16. For details, see Anderson, "Root *Teleios*," 10. The phrase is used with

The Notion of Perfection in the Ancient World

Roland de Vaux proposes that the meaning of this expression suggests the act of "appointing or investing a priest," although the original meaning has been forgotten and is debatable.[98] Some differing positions have been put forth. First, some scholars believe the original meaning of the phrase "filling of the hand" may be payment of the priest with the first installment of his salary at the beginning of his ministry. Support for this hypothesis is found in Judg 17:10; 18:4 in the account of a Levite Micah engaged for service. The Levite's hand is filled with payment, and he is engaged for ten silver shekels per annum, plus food and clothing. Second, other scholars suggest the expression may be connected with an Akkadian expression "to fill someone's hand," meaning "to put a man in charge of something." Third, some scholars interpret the act of distributing booty assigned by right to certain officers (as found in some archives from Mari, including some texts from the time of Hammurabi), as "the filling of the hand."[99]

De Vaux indicates that the latter meaning is perhaps the closest parallel to the expression in the Hebrew phrase. He suggests that "the priest was given the right to a part of the revenues accruing to the sanctuary and to a share of the offerings made there."[100] The expression has nothing to do with priestly ordination since priests in ancient Israel were not "ordained." Instead, they began their priestly service without any religious rite conferring power upon them. Priests were made holy and sacred by virtue of their priestly work.[101] Evidence from Hebrew Scripture points to a rite involved, as for example in Exod 29 and Lev 8, where there are references to the "filling of the hand." De Vaux refers to the same passages and appropriately describes the significance of this expression as follows: "by so performing for the first time the ritual gesture of minister of the altar, the man was invested with priestly power."[102] David Peterson observes that the translators of the LXX had in mind a literal "filling of the hands" with sacrifices "to convey

---

a technical meaning of priestly investiture or priestly ordination. Cf. Exod 29, where more than half instances are found in the context of God's instructions for priestly installation (vv. 9, 29, 33, and 35). The phrase is further elucidated by its association with the χρίω root (Exod 29:29; Lev 16:32; 21:10) and ἁγιάζω (Exod 29:33) to indicate that there is a connection between the priest's ordination, installation, and consecration. For further details, see Oyediran, "Lexical and Exegetical Analysis," 66.

98. DeVaux, *Ancient Israel*, 346.
99. For this discussion, see ibid., 346–47.
100. Ibid., 347.
101. Ibid.
102. Ibid.

the sense that the high point of the consecration was the action to 'perfect' or 'qualify' the man himself to act as a priest in offering a sacrifice to God."[103]

Some scholars, including Martin Dibelius, argue that the verb in this context should not be interpreted in a purely formal sense, but solely in terms of a technical linguistic usage, which is familiar to the LXX and its intended readers. The verbal form τελειοῦν should be rendered "to consecrate" to indicate that the person consecrated has the necessary qualifications for priestly service.[104] Others see the passages as pointing to the usual formal sense of the verb.[105] Delling pursues a cultic interpretation of the verbal form τέλειουν, suggesting the LXX expression τελειοῦν τὰς χεῖρας should be interpreted in terms of "someone's hand made free from stain" or "one who is made free from stain."[106] Similarly, Silva takes Lev 21:10 as clear evidence that the technical sense of this idiom is in fact transferred to the "head word,"[107] but rightly acknowledges that one may not assume that a "head word" would take the sense of the whole expression. David Peterson notes, "It is too far-fetched to suppose that Lev 21:10 alone influenced the writer of Hebrews or that his readers would have made the necessary connection."[108] One may posit that the ceremony the verb in the Leviticus passage alludes to is not about ritual cleansing but is rather about the subsequent rite of filling the hands with offerings—that is, the act of being invested with priestly power. The assumption that the verbal form τελειοῦν in the LXX could acquire a cultic significance, apart from the expression as a whole, is debatable. The assumption that the author of Hebrews would have expected his readers to understand he was using the word that way is also debatable. David Peterson concludes,

> Τελειοῦν, used in the combination τελειοῦν τὰς χεῖρας in the Pentateuch, retains its formal sense 'to accomplish, make full, perfect' and, although not as literal a rendering of Hebrew as ἐμπιπλάναι/πληροῦν τὰς χεῖρας, it is nevertheless to be understood in context as taking full account of the literal meaning of the Hebrew expression, as indicated by the narratives of Exod 29 and Lev 8. The formula as a whole has a technical, cultic

---

103. Peterson, *Hebrews and Perfection*, 28.

104. Dibelius, "Der himmlische Kultus," 166, 170. Accordingly, the consecration of Christ is effected through his sacrifice, the action that preceded his entrance into the heavenly sanctuary.

105. For further details, see Peterson, *Hebrews and Perfection*, 29.

106. Delling, "τέλειος," *TDNT* 8:81.

107. Silva, "Perfection and Eschatology in Hebrews," 61.

108. Peterson, *Hebrews and Perfection*, 29.

meaning but not the verb per se. If the verb in Hebrews is to be given any cultic sense, it cannot be argued from this source.[109]

The technical application of the notion of τέλειος in the MT and the LXX is limited.[110] Significantly, the purely formal connotation of τέλειος observed in classical Greek is also present in both the MT and the LXX.[111] Furthermore, as mentioned in the previous discussion, the verbal form τελειόω used in the expression τελειοῦν τὰς χεῖρας in the Pentateuch is not to be taken as carrying a technical application that naturally assigns a cultic or religious meaning to the concept. Instead, it retains its formal meaning, "to accomplish, complete, fulfill or perfect." As many scholars indicate, it is the whole expression (τελειοῦν τὰς χεῖρας) as a unit that has a technical, cultic, or religious meaning, not the verb per se.[112] If one is compelled to assign a cultic meaning to the verb in Hebrews, that meaning cannot be argued from the use of the expression as a whole as found in the LXX, but must rather be argued from the context of the verbal form as used in Hebrews.

The contribution of the Hebrew Scripture and the LXX to the Hebrews' concept of reality is commendable. The author's extensive appeal to details of the OT sacrificial system helps readers appreciate the message about the finality of the work of Christ as the perfected High Priest. It has been shown that the conceptual meaning of τέλειος emerges from a wide range of contexts that embrace the notions of completeness, wholeness, and wholehearted dedication or relationship to the Lord. The OT and LXX notion of perfection (as completeness, the giving of oneself to God wholeheartedly or unconditionally, and the wholehearted dedication to the Lord) is amplified in Hebrews' calling to faith and endurance, as exemplified in the perfected Christ. The goal of such complete devotion to the Lord as anticipated in the OT is actualized and fulfilled in the person and work of the perfected

---

109. Ibid., 30.

110. This is contrary to DuPlessis' notion that the Masoretic Text (MT) uses *Tamim* predominantly in a cultic and qualitative sense, suggesting "wholeness, entirety and intactness" (DuPlessis, Τέλειος: *Idea of Perfection*, 94). Peterson indicates, however, that apart from Exod 12:5, it is not τέλειος but rather αμωμος that is the usual LXX rendering in the technical contexts. Translators choose to use the former when *tamim* is used in a personal qualitative sense (Gen 6:9; Deut 18:13; 2 Kgs 22:26 [LXX: 2 Sam 22:26]). See also Peterson, *Hebrews and Perfection*, 26.

111. Exceptions are found in 2 Sam 22:26 (LXX: 2 Kgs 22:26 and Sir 31:10) that are free from both textual and exegetical problems in this regard, as opposed to the purely formal usage of the notion in at least eleven references. Peterson (*contra* DuPlessis, Τέλειος: *Idea of Perfection*, 94) indicates, "the two or even four 'religious' applications can hardly be described as setting precedent for NT usage" (Peterson, *Hebrews and Perfection*, 26).

112. Ibid., 30.

Christ. Only in him are believers also made perfect, even as they anticipate their glorification at the second coming of Christ.

SECOND TEMPLE JUDAISM

The concept of τέλειος as conveyed by the Hebrew word תָּמִים continued to have some importance in the lives of Jewish people. This was evidenced in the way the LXX gave attention to the notion of τέλειος. In addition, its importance can be observed in two different contexts of Second Temple Judaism: the Qumran community and Philo of Alexandria.

Qumran Community

This discussion of the Hebrew Scripture and the Septuagint pointed out that the two relevant words that are rendered τέλειος in the LXX are תָּמִים and שָׁלֵם. At Qumran, the word תָּמִים was more prominent in denoting the perfection of the members of the Qumran community. Some scholars have identified distinct parallels between the language of Hebrews and several Qumran documents.[113] The context in which the word is used at Qumran points to the concept of fulfillment of God's will as far as the law is concerned, but also to the keeping of the rules of the community.[114] The use of "perfection" in the Dead Sea Scrolls reveals that the sectarian community used the concept as a means of self-designation. The members referred to themselves as "the perfect ones" (1QS 3:3), "the men of holy integrity" (1QS 8:20), and the "council of holiness" (1QS 8:21). Those outside the community are considered people who do not belong—"the imperfect ones."[115] Those who belong to the secluded house of the community are seen as those to whom "perfection" belongs as people who walk in the path of "perfection."[116] Their daily

---

113. For details on these suggested parallels, see Rigaux, "Révelation des Mystères," 237–62; Spicq, "L'Épître aux Hébreux," 365–90; Yadin, "Dead Sea Scrolls and Hebrews," 36–55; Coppens, *Affinités qumraniènnes d'Hébreux*, 128–41; Batdorf, "Hebrews and Qumran," 16–35; and Fitzmyer, "Further Light on Melchizedek," 25–41.

114. Delling, "τέλειος," *TDNT* 8:73. For example: 1QS 1:8; 1QS 2:2; 1QS 8:18, 21; 1QS 9:6, 8; 1QS 9:9.

115. For instance, 1QS 3:3 reads, "In the source of the perfect, he shall not be counted." In 1QS 8:1, the writer states, "In the community council [there shall be] twelve men and three priests in everything." See also 1QS 5:20; 1QS 8:20, 21; 1QS 5:13, 20; 1QS 8:17, 23; and 1QS 9:8. Unless stated otherwise, the English translation used is taken from García Martinéz, *Dead Sea Scrolls Translated*, 3–463.

116. For example, 1QS 1:8; 2:2; 3:9; 8:18, 21; 9:6, 8; 9:9; 9:19. See also Delling, "τέλειος," *TDNT* 8:73. For further details, see Rigaux, "Revelation des Mystères,"

preoccupation consisted of scrutinizing, studying, and meditating on Scriptures in order to discover the secret divine revelation that they believed was intended exclusively for the community that held a deep passion to walk in the way of "perfection."[117] At the core of this belief is the idea that the community was living in the last days of the cosmic conflict between truth and falsehood, light and darkness—a radical dualism that regards perfection and wickedness as polarized into two contrasting communities.

Members of the Qumran community engaged in careful study in order to exact Scripture's hidden meaning and apply it to their own situation as its eschatological consummation. This is especially apparent in their expositional commentaries on Ps 37, Isaiah, Micah, Nahum, and notably Habakkuk.[118] Their consciousness of being the "elect" for the end of times springs from the comment in Hab 2:3 that reads, "Though it tarry, yet await it; for it will surely come, it will not delay."[119] Such knowledge and mysteries are seen as eschatological and soteriological revelation in history derived from the OT teaching. Building on the OT notion of complete devotion to God, the community adds to this notion a sense of exclusion, such that the one who is *tamim*, or "perfect," is the one who follows the ascetic path of the desert. This entails giving up the world in order to retreat to a sanctuary of holiness into which one is accepted only after strict censure and rites of purification. DuPlessis notes,

> Perfect is he who pledges absolute alliance to the New Covenant and obeys unflinchingly the Law of God, to the extent or maintaining every single item, turning neither left nor right or deviating one single step on his way (1QS i. 15). In this pursuit of diligence and zeal for the Law, there are grades of accomplishment, from the highest superior in perfection to the lowest. Yet everyone as such is *tamim*. Perfect is finally, he who has insight into the decrees of God as revealed to His prophets—some more, some less—and illumined to the minds of men occupied

---

237–62.

117. Ibid.

118. A patent example is seen in the *Pesher* on Hab 2:1–3 (1QP Hab 7:1–15; cf. 1QP Hab 2:1–10). The writer is concerned with the vision of Habakkuk without insight into the fact and timing of its realization. Yet he further contends that he knows the significance of the events for God has revealed it to the "teacher of righteousness" what was concealed to the prophets. For this discussion, see DuPlessis, Τέλειος: *Idea of Perfection*, 109.

119. Ibid.

with its search day and night, by the Holy Spirit (1QS iii.13-iv. 26).[120]

The members of the Qumran community used the τέλειος terminology exclusively in reference to themselves as "the perfect ones,"[121], but they also recognized human inability to walk in absolute perfection by ourselves and our need for divine help to achieve perfection.[122] For the secluded community, תָּמִים was not in fact attainable by humankind, but rather through the work of God on behalf of the secluded covenantal community gathered at Qumran.[123] However, the goal of the community as well as individual members remained that of a "perfect walk" defined in terms of a "complete obedience to the path as outlined in Torah as well as fidelity to the rules of the community as a necessary ingredient for the preservation of the bonds of their society."[124] This path is seen as the way of the new covenant that necessitates a retreat to secluded desert community life as a sign of wholehearted devotion to God.[125] At the same time, the word has a connotation of "knowledge" or "revelation" from God, imparted by the Holy Spirit (1QS 3:13–4:26), that is essentially described as a divine gift reserved for the end times—but exclusively for the sectarian Qumran community.[126]

Though the Qumran community borrowed the concept of perfection from the OT, the community used "perfection" to mean obedience to divine precepts as exclusively practiced at Qumran. This included the acceptance of a total monastic life conceived as an outward expression of God's will.[127] The use of "perfection" at Qumran not only carries the connotation of obedience to the path outlined in the Torah, but also obedience to the rules of the community. Such rules are perceived as necessary to the preservation of the bonds of the community. The path of obedience is perceived as the way of the new covenant that, according to Qumran, necessitates withdrawal from the corrupt world into secluded community life as the mark of a wholehearted devotion to God resulting from knowledge of God's revela-

---

120. Ibid., 111.

121. For further details, see ibid., 104–15.

122. For example, see 1QS 11:2, 11; 1QS 5:23–24; 1QS 1:1–8. For this discussion, see also Hartin, *Spirituality of Perfection*, 28–29. See also 1QH 1:36.

123. 1QS 11:2, 3; 1QH 4:31, 32.

124. Hartin, *Spirituality of Perfection*, 26.

125. Rigaux states, "Cette voie parfaite est une désignation de la voie de l'alliance nouvelle de la forme de vie que procure la retraite au désert" (Rigaux, "Révelation des Mystères," 238).

126. Ibid., 239.

127. Ibid., 238.

tion to worshipers (1QS 2:2; 1:12).¹²⁸ Such revelation is described as a divine gift reserved for the end times that is exclusively for the sectarian members of the community at Qumran.¹²⁹ The realized eschatological aspect of the notion of perfection at Qumran is significant for Hebrews. However, the understanding of "perfection," perceived in terms of exclusion and particularization, is obviously strange to the concept of τέλειος in Hebrews. The message of Hebrews indicates that the privilege of access to God is not limited to a secluded community but is instead available to all the worshipers who are willing to draw near.

Philo of Alexandria

Some scholars posit that both Philo and the author of Hebrews are to be understood in terms of some kind of "Platonized Hellenistic Jewish thought."¹³⁰ This is similar to the general perception among some scholars that the author of Hebrews is directly dependent on Philo.¹³¹ Alleged evidence includes the two authors' shared understanding of the concept of τέλειος and its cognates.¹³² One must seek to examine Philo's understanding of the concept of perfection in order to appreciate any similarities and see how the Philonic concept of perfection might have illuminated the author of Hebrews.

Philo's writings show widespread usage of the concept of τέλειος and its cognates. It is no wonder that some scholars view the τέλειος terminology in Hebrews as directly related to the world of thought characteristic of Hellenistic Judaism and especially of Philo.¹³³ The adjectival form τέλειος alone is used more than 400 times in Philo, and the verbal form τελειόω

---

128. DuPlessis sees a positive relationship between knowledge (understood as truth or insight into the mysteries) and the notion of perfection at Qumran. For details, see DuPlessis, Τέλειος: *Idea of Perfection*, 107.

129. For further details, see Rigaux, "Révélation des Mystères," 239.

130. Carlston, "Vocabulary of Perfection in Philo," 33.

131. This is the central argument Spicq posits when he suggests there are profound similarities between the two authors: "les caractéristiques de la mentalité intellectuelle, littéraire, morale, religieuse de Hébreux sont celles même de l'alexandrin." Thus, Spicq concludes that the author of Hebrews "est un philonien converti au Christianisme" (Spicq, *L'Épître aux Hébreux*, 91).

132. This study is limited to some general observations, since a detailed examination of the comparisons between Philo and the author of Hebrews is beyond the scope of this book. For further details on similarities between Philo and the Hebrews author, see Carlston, "Vocabulary of Perfection," 133–60.

133. Dey, *Intermediary World*, 7.

appears fifty-three times.¹³⁴ Rathel points out that most of Philo's usage of τέλειος is similar to other Greek writers' works, but Philo's distinctive usage is in the context of his religious and philosophical speculations,¹³⁵ which distinguishes his approach from other ancient writers'. In the following, some examples are enlisted to illustrate the significance of this concept in Philo and briefly examine whether Hellenistic Judaism (especially Philo) might have influenced Hebrews' thought.

In his account of the world's creation, Philo uses the verbal form τελειόω in reference to the bringing forth of creation to its completion.¹³⁶ Furthermore, Philo alludes to the idea that a thought cannot be perceived as perfect or complete until it has resulted in some actions.¹³⁷ In his work *On the Special Laws*, Philo uses the verb to refer to the maturation of plants and the physical maturation of humans.¹³⁸ Interestingly, Philo also uses the verbal forms (τελειωθέσεται and τελειοῦσθαι) when he refers to fulfillment of God's Word.¹³⁹ Philo's system of values is controlled by his religious thought, which he links to the idea of wisdom or virtue—God being the source of both.¹⁴⁰ Implicitly, to be controlled by wisdom and virtue becomes for Philo the path to perfection.¹⁴¹ This is perhaps based on his premise that God alone is perfect and thus no one is really perfect in any endeavor except God.¹⁴² Accordingly, it is only through the working of God in his grace that perfection can be found in any created thing, such that perfection becomes

---

134. For further details, see Peterson, *Hebrews and Perfection*, 30. See especially Mayer, *Index Philoneus*, 275–76.

135. Rathel, "Soteriological Terminology," 63.

136. See Philo, *On the Creation of the World*, 89; LCL, 72–73. Furthermore, Philo uses the same notion when he alludes to the "completion" of the city and tower of Gen 11 (ibid., *On the Confusion of Tongues*, 89.155; LCL, 94–95). For similar reasoning, see also ibid., *Allegorical Interpretation*, I. 6; I. 10.

137. Ibid., *Allegorical Interpretation*, II. 61; LCL, 262–63.

138. Ibid., *On the Special Laws*, IV. 209; LCL, 138–41. For Philo, crops might develop differently, but they would ultimately reach their perfection, completion, or maturation at the same time. See also ibid., *On the Virtues*, 157; and ibid., *On Rewards and Punishments*, 127–28, 131.

139. Ibid., *Life of Moses*, I. 283; LCL, 260–63. A similar reasoning is found in Josephus, *Jewish Antiquities*, XV. 4; LCL, 5. See also Maier, *New Complete Works of Josephus*, 62. The notion of τέλειος has the connotation of completion, fulfillment, or carrying out a divine direction. Cf. Peterson, *Hebrews and Perfection*, 30–32.

140. Philo, *On the Migration of Abraham*, 36–37; LCL, 152–55. See also ibid., 36–42.

141. Delling, "τέλειος," TDNT 8:70–71.

142. See Philo, *On Giants*, 45; ibid., *Who Is the Heir?* 121; ibid., *On the Special Laws*, I. 277.

only a gift of God to humankind.¹⁴³ As many scholars would posit, human perfection is of great significance for Philo,¹⁴⁴ but such perfection does not mean sinlessness,¹⁴⁵ although it is related to the leaving behind of bodily passions¹⁴⁶ and the attainment of the wisdom of God, which he refers to as "a vision of God."¹⁴⁷

Philo is both Jewish and Hellenistic in his thought; he combines both worlds. DuPlessis comments, "Philo was not Greek enough to relinquish his adherence to the Jewish idea of God's love."¹⁴⁸ Similarly, Patrick J. Hartin also remarks, "With him the world of Judaism and Hellenism intersect, for his thought owes much to both traditions."¹⁴⁹ As the greatest Jewish philosopher of Second Temple Judaism who also lived outside Palestine in Egyptian Alexandria, Philo owes much both to Platonic and Stoic understandings of the world of ideas and the contrasts these schools of thought draw between heavenly patterns and worldly copies.¹⁵⁰ Most theologians agree that Philo's system of values is controlled by his religious thought, which he ties to the notion of wisdom and virtue, with God as the source of both and thus constituting the path to perfection.¹⁵¹ As a Jew, Philo believes that humanity could not attain the state of τέλειος by its own effort, but rather through the divine gift of grace that originates from the great cause of all things. Wisdom (σοφία), which emanates from God, is the perfect path (τέλεια ὁδός) to God, since he alone can be truly perfect. Philo observes, "perfection is found in no created thing, but. . . it does appear in them at times owing to the grace of the great cause of all things."¹⁵² God alone is the one who creates virtue in the soul to lead it to perfected happiness, and he alone is the climax of

143. Ibid., *That God Is Unchangeable*, 92; ibid., *On Planting*, 93. See also ibid., *On Agriculture*, 169.

144. Carlston, "Vocabulary of Perfection," 141.

145. Philo, *On Special Laws*, 252.

146. Ibid., *On Drunkenness*, 103; ibid., *Migration of Abraham*, 214.

147. See Philo, *On the Sacrifices of Cain and Abel*, 7; ibid., *Allegorical Interpretation*, III. 44, 74. For further details, see also Rathel, "Soteriological Terminology," 64. For a complete analysis of alleged similarities (including linguistic, terminologies, themes, and use of Scripture) between Philo and the author of Hebrews, see Williamson, *Philo and Hebrews*, 277–308, 434–48, 519–38.

148. DuPlessis, Τέλειος: *Idea of Perfection*, 116.

149. Hartin, *Spirituality of Perfection*, 29.

150. For details, see Carlston, "Vocabulary of Perfection," 145, 59, n. 492.

151. Philo, *Migration of Abraham*, 36, 38–42. For further details, see Delling, "τέλειος," *TDNT* 8:70–71.

152. Philo, *On Planting*, 93; LCL, 260. Since none but God is τέλειος, Philo includes himself among those who are ἀτελεῖς ("not perfect").

true and perfect happiness.[153] The implication is that a person who strives to live in accordance with the ordinances of the Torah is "a perfect person."[154] Such a person must be pure in word and deed, and his whole conduct; and as such he has already received through the body a share in eternal life.[155]

Philo's emphasis on God shows that despite the importance he assigns to the human ability to strive toward philosophical virtue or perfection, ultimately the state of perfection remains something that is granted only by God. It is the divine power (by his own gift) that leads the soul to God. Some scholars may suggest this language is similar to the language of Hebrews, but a careful examination reveals Philo is different.[156] Philo's interest in philosophy, his view of progress towards philosophical virtue, his stress on ethics, and the notion of training or pedagogy all differ from the language of Hebrews.

While both Philo and the author of Hebrews were perhaps influenced by the same general Platonic worldview, they were clearly citizens of two different countries.[157] For instance, the privilege of τελείωσις is limited to a philosophical minority who are committed to the way of virtue for Philo. However, for the author of Hebrews, the privilege of access to God is available to all believers who are drawing near to God. In addition, while it is true that both writers use the Hebrew Scripture, it is used to accomplish different goals. Philo used the OT with the goal of extracting philosophical truths; the author of Hebrews used the Hebrew Scripture as "a sustained endeavor to demonstrate that the OT in its entirety pointed forward prophetically to Christ."[158] This approach is not based on Hellenistic philosophy's model, but is in accord with the teaching of the NT as a whole. Yet examining how the NT writers in general would have perceived the notion of τέλειος remains significant. Are they similar to Qumran or Philo, as scholars such as Dey[159] suggest, or perhaps different?

---

153. See also ibid., *Allegorical Interpretation*, III. 207.

154. Ibid., *On the Special Laws*, IV. 140; LCL, 95. See also ibid., *On Planting*, 231–33.

155. For further details, see ibid., *On the Special Laws*, IV. 140; LCL, 95. See also ibid., *On the Life of Moses*, II. 150; cf. Exod 20:12.

156. Williamson thus concludes that "there is no proof that the choice of words displayed in the Epistle to the Hebrews has been influenced by Philo's lexicographical thesaurus" (Williamson, *Philo and Hebrews*, 576).

157. Carlston, "Vocabulary of Perfection," 148.

158. See Williamson, *Philo and Hebrews*, 576.

159. See Dey, *Intermediary World*, 7–8.

NEW TESTAMENT WORLD

Having examined the notion of τέλειος in its wider Greco-Roman context as well as in the Hebrew Scriptures, the Septuagint, and Second Temple Judaism, one final noteworthy area remains to make this overview examination complete—namely, the distinctive traditions that form the rest of the NT. This sub-section is a brief overview of the concept of τέλειος in the rest of the NT, which serves as the more immediate context of Hebrews. Its appreciation illuminates the understanding of Hebrews' thought, which emerges more clearly when examined against this more immediate context of Hebrews.

Synoptic Gospels, John, and Acts

The substantive use of τέλειος is rare in the Synoptic Gospels, where it occurs only three times, all of which are found in the Gospel of Matthew. It is found twice in the Sermon on the Mount (Matt 5:48) and once in Jesus' encounter with the rich young man (19:16–30).[160] In Matt 5:48, Jesus states, "You therefore must be perfect [ἔσεσθε οὖν ὑμεῖς τέλειοι], as your heavenly father is perfect [ὡς ὁ πατὴρ ὑμῶν ὁ οὐράνιος τέλειός ἐστιν]." If isolated from the context of the Sermon on the Mount[161] and treated as an independent moral or religious logion, the passage becomes susceptible to serious misinterpretations. The particle οὖν points to the preceding verses (vv. 43–47). Clearly, the phrase ἔσεσθε οὖν ὑμεῖς τέλειοι recapitulates what these verses convey in terms of a message that is given as a positive command.[162] The imperative tone is clear, as the grammatical construction indicates. The sentence forms part of the impressive series of commendations on good works, beginning in 5:13, that immediately follow the Beatitudes

---

160. The adjective τέλειος appears twice in Matt 5:48 and once in 19:21. In both passages it is used in a personal attributive way, reflecting closely the world of Judaism. See Hartin, *Spirituality of Perfection*, 32.

161. For various interpretative approaches, see Martin, "Dispensational Approaches to the Sermon," 34–48.

162. The future ἔσεσθε (indicative middle, second plural of εἰμί) is imperatival and may be taken as an ethical one to suggest a moral sense (sinlessness) as taught by Wesley, *Plain Account of Christian Perfection*, 5–100. DuPlessis takes the imperative of Matt 5:48 as an absolute positive command based on the redemptive indicative that precedes it and gives it a religious dimension by tracing its origin to the Hebrew *tamim* or *shalem*. See DuPlessis, Τέλειος: *Idea of Perfection*, 169. It is perhaps best to take the command as eschatological, considering the context of the passage. See Preisker, *Das Ethos des Urchristentums*, 135.

in the Sermon on the Mount.[163] These commendations are put forward as descriptions of heirs of the kingdom of God, the focus of the Sermon on the Mount.

Jesus calls his disciples to be "complete" (τέλειος) in accordance with the kingdom's standards of righteousness, as evidenced in love for even their enemies. He does not lower the standards to accommodate humans but rather sets forth his absolute "completeness" as the kingdom standard, specifically in the circle of love. This notion of "completeness" in the circle of love is similar to the OT notion of wholehearted or complete devotion to the Lord, as expressed in a life of total obedience to the will of God as a kingdom prerogative.[164] According to Jesus' teaching, there is no place for relative or limited devotion in the kingdom. Not only does Jesus denounce limited love or limited devotion to God (Matt 5:43-47), he makes his point conclusively, calling upon the disciples to be τέλειος in this respect. As kingdom people, the disciples are not to be satisfied with half measures in their loving devotion, they should strive to attain God's original intention or will. Significantly, the Evangelist uses the correlative ὡς ("as") in order to point to the Father as the supreme example of completeness for imitation (cf. Matt 5:45)[165] by those who are as children to him.

The same notion of τέλειος is also found in Matt 19:21, where Jesus, speaking to the rich young man states, "If you wish to be perfect [εἰ θέλεις τέλειος εἶναι], go [ὕπαγε] sell your possessions and give the money to the poor."[166] This command is a challenge to the rich young man to choose poverty as a means to attain τέλειος, "completeness," or "perfection." Roman Catholic exegetes consider the understanding of "perfection" here as something limited to a few individuals who have a special calling to a higher

---

163. BDAG, 996.

164. France observes that the use of *teleios* ("perfect") instead of "holy" derives from the OT requirement of total loyalty to God (cf. Deut 18:13), where the Hebrew *tamim* ("complete," "unblemished," "blameless," or "perfect") is rendered by *teleios* in the LXX (France, *Gospel of Matthew*, 228).

165. For this discussion, see also Hartin, *Spirituality of Perfection*, 33.

166. Roman Catholic exegetes use the text as a vindication for the higher standard of morality called forth by one of the three *consilia evangelica*—namely, poverty, chastity, and obedience. To these scholars, the command has only a limited application and should not be interpreted universally. The reason advanced is that not all followers of Christ can renounce their possessions and serve God in this exceptional way of "poverty." So the absolute renunciation of wealth is looked at as a higher form of life governed by precepts that supersede the Decalogue as one only embarked upon by those who are ambitious of τέλειος. For this discussion, see DuPlessis, Τέλειος: *Idea of Perfection*, 13, 172.

standard of religious perfection in a monastery or convent.[167] Some compare the issue with a similar passage in *Didache* (1:4; 6:2) and translate the τέλειος motif in a perfectionistic sense, giving it a predominantly moral or ethical meaning. The context makes this interpretation questionable. Jesus' call to renunciation should be seen as a means to convey the real import of the Law, which is love for God and for others (Matt 22:37–40; Mark 12:30; Luke 10:27; cf. Deut 6:5) from an undivided heart. This is evidenced in complete obedience to God's will and in carrying God's command to the fullest possible extent.[168] It is in the promotion of this greater standard of perfection that Jesus Christ himself fulfills the OT expectations for God's people.

For Matthew, true faith, as evidenced in a renunciation of all other allegiances, is a precondition for everyone who wishes to find the way into God's kingdom. Such faith involves a willingness to surrender all at Christ's bidding (Matt 16:24), which the rich young man failed to do (Matt 19:22). Matthew's message of the kingdom of God calls for a greater righteousness (unlike that of the scribes and Pharisees [Matt 5:20]) for those who belong to the new order that has been fulfilled in the person and work of Christ.[169] One might argue that Matthew uses the τέλειος language in order to procure compliance from those wishing to enter the kingdom of heaven.[170] In Matt 19:14, Jesus indicates the kingdom of God belongs to those of faith, like little children. In verse 26, he shows that it is impossible for a rich person to enter God's kingdom unless God himself intervenes. It is clear from the context that τέλειος does not come as a result of any moral, religious, or vocational effort on the part of the individual, but rather God's gracious intervention in bringing about "completeness," which is a prerequisite for kingdom participation. In both Matt 5:48 and 19:21, the adjectival nominatives τέλειος ("perfection") should be perceived as carrying the general idea of "wholeness," "completeness," or "totality."

---

167. Ibid.

168. For a similar notion of perfection, see *Did.* 6:2: "For if thou canst bear the whole yoke of the Lord, thou wilt be perfect [τέλειος ἔσῃ], but if thou canst not, do what thou canst" (Goold, *Didache*, 319).

169. This is in accord with all the fulfillment passages in Matthew that show the early church believed Jesus fulfilled not only OT direct prophecies, but also the eschatological expectations of God's people. For further details, see Osborne, *Matthew: Exegetical Commentary*, 184.

170. The image of entering into τὴν βασιλείαν τῶν οὐρανῶν ("the kingdom of heaven") is understood in terms of both conversion and eternal life, as found also in Matt 7:21; 18:3, 8–9; 19:17, 23, 24; 23:14 (Osborne, *Matthew: Exegetical Commentary*, 184).

The verbal form τελειοῦν appears more frequently in the Gospels of Luke and John and bears some similarities to τελεῖν (Luke 1:45; 2:43;[171] 13:32; Acts 20:24), which also carries the meaning of "bringing something or someone to a state of entirety," that is, "to make complete and perfect."[172] For Luke, the notion of τέλειος carries the dominant theme of "fulfillment" of God's purposes as recorded in Scripture and prophecy. For example, in Luke 1:45, the word τελείωσις is used to express Mary's belief in the fulfillment of God's prediction to her. Bock comments that God's promise of coming to completion is part of Luke's "fulfillment" motif, the key term being τελείωσις, "fulfillment" or "completion."[173] This is related to the final execution or completion of God's promises. The fulfillment of the promise to Mary becomes an assurance to readers that the final completion of the rest of God's promise will come to pass. The context indicates not only the present aspect of the fulfillment, but also future eschatological fulfillment that is yet to come. François Bovon notes that verse 45 speaks of the eschatological fulfillment (τελείωσις) Mary awaited.[174] Validating his point about the eschatological context of the passage, Bovon states that for the evangelist, "les vv. 51–55 celèbrent l'accomplissement eschatologique encore attendu dans la foi."[175]

Another example is found in Luke 13:32, where Jesus replies to the Pharisees who come to tell him to flee because Herod wants to kill him. In response, Jesus predicts the approaching completion of his work in death and resurrection as τελειοῦμαι: "Behold, I am casting out demons and performing healings today and tomorrow, but on the third day I will complete [τελειοῦμαι] my work."[176] That his mission will be brought to completion or consummated is indicated in this passage. The verb carries the notion of "completion" or "fulfillment" of God's plan[177] in his death and resurrection. If the verb is taken as passive, the emphasis is on Christ's messianic work

---

171. The phrase τελειωσάντων τὰς ἡμέρας when "they have completed the days" (of festivities in Jerusalem) compares with the use of τελεῖν in Matt 7:28; 11:1; 13:53; 19:1 and 26:1. For details, see DuPlessis, Τέλειος: Idea of Perfection, 173.

172. For an examination of similarities, see ibid., 120.

173. Bock, Luke 1:1—9:50, 139.

174. Bovon, L'évangile selon Saint Luc (1:1–9:50), 93.

175. Ibid. See also Wallace, Exegetical Syntax, 563. Not only the present, but especially the future aspect of fulfillment, becomes key.

176. Luke 13:32 is the only place in the NT (apart from Hebrews) where the verbal form τελειοῦν is used in connection with the person of Christ. The perfecting of Christ is linked with the perfecting of his work in the passage (Peterson, Hebrews and Perfection, 33).

177. See also Luke 12:50; 22:37; John 19:30.

being brought to completion by God and on the perfecting of Jesus as the Messiah.[178] This is similar to the saying attributed to Paul in Acts 20:24 and translated as "But I do not consider my life worth anything to myself, so that I may complete the course and the ministry. . ." (ὡς τελειῶσαι τὸν δρόμον μου καὶ τὴν διακονίαν). For Jesus, not only is his work or ministry in view, his redemptive mission in death and resurrection is also apparent (Luke 13:32; cf. 12:50; 22:37; John 19:30).[179] Some scholars, such as Joseph A. Fitzmyer, take the notion of τέλειος here as carrying the sense of attaining his goal,[180] to support the idea that Jesus will be fulfilling the purpose for which he was sent here on earth.[181] From the Gospel of Luke account, it is clear that one of Jesus' goals is to go to Jerusalem (13:33). But more importantly, his goal is to complete the mission he was sent for, including his death and resurrection as the means of salvation for the world.[182] These facts cannot be ignored in the context.

The Apostle John's account does not differ much from Luke's. In John 4:34, Jesus' messianic mission is presented as τελειώσω αὐτοῦ τὸ ἔργον ("to complete or accomplish his work"), an idiom that correlate with ἵνα ποιήσω τὸ θέλημα τοῦ πέμψαντός με ("to do the will of the one who sent me"). Having spoken figuratively in verse 32, "I have food to eat that you know nothing about," Jesus explains to the disciples what he means: that his food is to do the will of the one who sent him, the Father, and to complete or accomplish his work (John 4:34; cf. 5:36; 17:4; 19:28). This leads naturally to Jesus' metaphor of the harvest.[183] The fruit of his mission is palpable in the fact that the Samaritans are coming to him. The dominant theme is similar to Luke: the fulfillment of God's purpose or mission in the person of Jesus Christ and in fulfillment of Scripture.[184] As DuPlessis states, the dormant *telos* notion that lies behind the pronouncements of Jesus agrees with the overall NT impression that Jesus Christ not only carries redemptive history to its eschatological end, he is also its *Telos*.[185]

178. Delling, "τέλειος," *TDNT* 8:84.

179. For this discussion, see also Peterson, *Hebrews and Perfection*, 33–34.

180. Fitzmyer, *Gospel According to Luke*, 1031.

181. For the same fulfillment motif as seen in the τέλειος notion, see Luke 18:31; 22:37; and Acts 13:29; cf. Acts 20:24.

182. Some scholars posit that the verb carries a technical meaning with reference to Jesus' consecration or enthronement into his messianic office. See Ellis, *Gospel of Luke*, 189.

183. John 4:35: οὐχ ὑμεῖς λέγετε ὅτι ἔτι τετράμηνός ἐστιν καὶ ὁ θερισμὸς ἔρχεται;, "do you not say, 'there are four months, and then comes the harvest'?"

184. Cf. John 19:28, 30.

185. For this discussion, see also DuPlessis, Τέλειος: *Idea of Perfection*, 172–74.

John uses this concept with reference to the notion of "completeness or totality." In John 17:23, Jesus prays for perfect unity of his disciples ἵνα ὦσιν τετελειωμένοι εἰς ἕν, "that they may be perfected into one." While the dominant theme seems to be the idea of totality as far as unity of Christ's followers is concerned, the ultimate achievement of unity is really a matter of the end times. Despite interpreters who dismiss these future aspects, there is an indication that perfect unity can only be achieved when the number of the elect is accomplished at the second coming of Christ. This does not imply that the present aspect is ignored,[186] since there is an implication that believers would strive to be complete in unity at every stage of their growth.[187]

One of the most fundamental uses of τέλειος, especially in reference to God's love, is found in John. The theme of "love" that dominates the Fourth Gospel is also seen as forming the core of his First Epistle (1 John 2:5; 4:12, 17, 18). For instance, John describes God's love as ἡ τελεία ἀγάπη, or "perfect love" (1 John 4:18). He writes, "There is no fear in love, but perfect love casts out fear; for fear has to do with punishment and whoever fears has not reached perfection in love." In verse 16, he says, ". . . God is love. . ." The context indicates God's supreme love is consummated and conditioned by true fellowship with him. John uses τέλειος in his description of the sum total of all humankind's affection in reference to an undivided love and loyalty to God. As Hartin contends, "Such love enables one to remain in communion with God."[188] Clearly, the concept of τέλειος conveys the notion of complete fellowship with and sharing in the very nature of God, who is love. It consists of striving through every action to abide in this fellowship of love with God. However, one may argue that while believers have tested this fellowship, the full realization of "perfect love and perfect communion" may only be perceived as a future reality when believers are glorified.

Pauline Tradition

The Apostle Paul uses the adjectival form τέλειος widely (Rom 12:2; 1 Cor 2:6; 13:10; 14:20; Eph 4:13; Phil 3:12, 15; Col 1:28; 3:14, and 4:12).[189] The term is used with reference to the idea of "maturity" or "completeness."

---

186. Peterson, *Hebrews and Perfection*, 36. In the strict sense of the word, perfect unity can only be achieved at the end times when the Lord intervenes to make everything new.

187. See Barrett, *Gospel According to St. John*, 428.

188. See Hartin, *Spirituality of Perfection*, 35.

189. Delling, "τέλειος," *TDNT* 8:76. The verbal form τελειοῦν is used only once by Paul in Phil 3:15. For an insightful summary of Pauline usage of the τέλειος notion, see DuPlessis, Τέλειος: *Idea of Perfection*, 204.

For example, in Col 1:28, Paul writes, "It is he whom we proclaim, warning everyone and teaching everyone in all wisdom so that we may present everyone τέλειον ἐν Χριστῷ complete [or perfect] in Christ."[190] What Christ has accomplished is complete or perfect as far as God's redemptive plan is concerned.[191] However, there is also an implicit acknowledgement that believers would grow in their allegiance to Christ to attain the fullness of life in Christ. This is seen in 1 Cor 14:20, where the apostle presents a contrast between "children" (παιδία) on one hand and the "mature" (τέλειοι) on the other. Only the adults are considered spiritually mature (τέλειοι) or fully human. Similarly, in Eph 4:12–13, Paul envisions that the church as the body of Christ would grow to full maturity or completeness to become "the perfect person" (εἰς ἄνδρα τέλειον) to the measure of the full stature of Christ. There is a future goal to be attained. Paul's concern is that all the members of the body labor toward this final goal of being presented as mature believers before the Lord.[192] In essence, there is a difference between the present reality and future world yet to come. Thus, in 1 Cor 13:10, Paul alludes to the present condition of the believers as humans who are fragile and fragmentary by their very nature, in contrast to the future world in which everything will be made anew. It is in this sense that DuPlessis refers to the present inter-advent period of tension, which he interprets in verse 12 as "the progression from the now till then."[193] DuPlessis is correct that there is, by necessity, a future dimension to the present state of affairs. It is best to look at this not necessarily as a progression from "the non-perfect" now to "the perfect" future, but rather as the necessary abrogation of the former by the latter, which will be complete and perfect.[194] Such complete victory can only be perceived as a future reality (1 Cor 15:54–55) even though believers have tasted some of its benefits (cf. 1 Cor 2:6).

The verbal form τελειοῦν is used only once in Phil 3:12, but the apostle often uses τελεῖν and its compounds. Speaking about the hope of the resurrection of the dead, the apostle states, ". . . I have not already been

190. NASB, NAB. Cf. NKJV and NIV.

191. See also 1 Cor 13:10, where Paul alludes to the notion of perfection as characteristic of the eschatological end times. It is fitting to suggest that the most distinct aspect of the notion of τέλειος in Paul and other NT writers is the eschatological fullness of the redemptive state, or the supreme soteriological bounty of belief in Jesus Christ. The context points to the redemptive significance of Jesus Christ as the one who has ushered in the eschatological salvation for those who believe in him. For further details, see DuPlessis, Τέλειος: *Idea of Perfection*, 205.

192. See Delling, "τέλειος," *TDNT* 8:76. For further details, see DuPlessis, Τέλειος: *Idea of Perfection*, 177–204.

193. Ibid., 185.

194. For this discussion, see also Hartin, *Spirituality of Perfection*, 36.

perfected [τετελείωμαι], but I strive to lay hold of that for which Christ also laid hold of me." Most commentators suggest Paul uses the notion of τέλειος (3:12; cf. v. 15) because his opponents used the terminology. In order to understand what the apostle meant, one needs to have a clue not only of the identification of the opponents, but also what they taught. Some scholars believe Paul's opponents were gnostic Christian missionaries.[195] Other scholars, like A. F. J. Klijn, argue the opponents were Jewish missionaries who preached that "a better way to perfection can be shown than according to Paul's preaching."[196] Similarly, F. W. Beare argues that Paul's opponents are "Christians of the Judaizing faction of the early Palestinian church, who appear to have carried on a kind of counter-apostolate against Paul among his Gentile churches in Syria, in Galatia, and Achaea."[197] But Beare's conclusion that the verbal form τετελείωμαι ("I have attained perfection") belongs to the language of the mysteries,[198] is difficult to substantiate from the context. Robert Jewett acknowledges that the opponents were truly Judaizers but, at the same time, also libertine heretics claim to have attained the goal of perfection.[199] According to David Peterson, Jewett's argument makes a lot of sense given the context. Based on his conversion, Paul possesses a knowledge of Christ (Phil 3:8), a righteousness from God by faith (v. 9), and a realization of the power of Christ's resurrection (v. 10). But he is also waiting in anticipation of the consummation of all these at the resurrection from the dead (v. 11).[200]

The context of Phil 3:12 seems to indicate that Paul's opponents were Jewish Christian missionaries (Judaizers) who advocated that Gentiles should become Jews in their practices.[201] As many interpreters suggest, the context also conveys an eschatological implication of what being in Christ involves (vv. 10, 11, 14, 20, 21).[202] Paul is talking about the hope of the future

---

195. For further details, see Schmithals, "False Teachers of the Philippians," 65–122.

196. See Klijn, "Paul's Opponents in Philippians 3," 279.

197. Beare, *Commentary on Philippians*, 109. For an alternative to Beare's approach, see Koester, "Purpose of the Polemic of a Pauline Fragment," 317–32.

198. Beare, *Commentary on Philippians*, 229. In the mysteries, the person initiated into the cult is said to be admitted to the highest grade, and is therefore called τέλειος— perfect. Beare uses this language to refute the notion of moral perfection in favor of the notion of "transition to a higher order of being through the operation of sacramental rites," and thus having attained the highest level of Christian life with no further progress to make (cf. ibid., 130).

199. Jewett, "Conflicting Movements in Philippians," 362–90.

200. For this discussion, see Peterson, *Hebrews and Perfection*, 39.

201. Hawthorne, *Philippians*, 142–48.

202. For this discussion, see Peterson, *Hebrews and Perfection*, 38–39.

resurrection of the dead. His opponents argue they have achieved perfection by means of complete righteousness by the Law, but also that they now possess the eschatological promise, including the spiritual experience of such heavenly gifts as resurrection and freedom from suffering and death.[203] In his reply, Paul is concerned with what has not yet been received in Christ; it follows naturally that he must still await the goal of consummation at the resurrection of the dead, when he will lay hold of the hope set before him. The verbal form τελειοῦν in Phil 3:12 should be taken as pointing to the eschatological consummation at the second coming of Christ.[204] In this context, "perfection" cannot be perceived in terms of moral, religious, or vocational concepts; rather, its significance lies in and depends on the work of God, in his redemptive history, to bring to completion what he has already started in Christ by leading many followers to a full or complete realization of their salvation. Taken in this sense, the notion of τέλειος cannot be perceived as far removed from the same notion as used by the author of Hebrews.

From Pauline context, a few observations may be highlighted. First, the τέλειος notion carries the concept of "completeness" as far as the redemptive state is concerned (1 Cor 2:6; Phil 3:15; Col 1:28 and 4:12). Second, Paul uses the metaphor of adulthood to imply the idea of maturity (versus "babes") or full development of the believer's spiritual growth. Within the state of this salvation, the believer is seen as being in the process of moving toward full realization or completeness (1 Cor 14:20). Third, Paul uses the concept of τέλειος to refer to the idea of total agreement with the perfect will of God (cf. Col 4:12). Also, the apostle alludes to the perfecting of the body of Christ in corporate unity (Eph 4:13; Col 3:14). In each of these passages, one can see either directly or indirectly some constitutive perfection motif as characteristic of the future eschatological end times. This is especially clearer in 1 Cor 13:10 and Phil 3:15, 21. One may discern that for Paul, the most distinct aspect of τέλειος as he (and perhaps many other NT writers, including the Hebrews author) envisages it is the future eschatological fullness of the redemptive state, or the supreme soteriological bounty of belief in the person of Jesus Christ.[205] This undoubtedly demonstrates the redemptive significance of Jesus' person and his work of salvation revealed in the end times, the full benefits of which—though already tasted—remain in the future for those who believe in him.

203. See also Koester, "Purpose of the Polemic," 321–23. For an evaluation of Koester's viewpoint, see Peterson, *Hebrews and Perfection*, 39.

204. For further details, see Peterson, *Hebrews and Perfection*, 39.

205. DuPlessis, Τέλειος: *Idea of Perfection*, 205.

The Epistle of James

A New Testament survey of the notion of τέλειος would be incomplete without a consideration of the Epistle of James. One could argue that the concept of perfection is more central to James than to Paul.²⁰⁶ As Walters observes, James uses the adjectival form τέλειος five times in his first chapter alone compared to an almost equal number in the entire Pauline corpus, and both texts use the verbal form once.²⁰⁷ Scholars believe that "perfection" is one of James' favorite words. He uses it twice in the fourth verse of his opening chapter and a total of four times in the entire chapter (Jas 1:4, 17, 25). In addition, the concept occurs in two other instances in James (2:22; 3:2).²⁰⁸ According to DuPlessis, James' usage of τέλειος can be traced back to the OT notion of תָּמִים, but James applies the notion in his own distinct way to the basic theme of his letter, which is the profound unity of faith and works.²⁰⁹ For example, the mutual relationship between faith and works is clearly expressed in the use of the verbal form in Jas 2:22 (ἡ πίστις συνήργει τοῖς ἔργοις αὐτοῦ καὶ ἐκ τῶν ἔργων ἡ πίστις ἐτελειώθη). The faith of Abraham was "made complete" by his works. The idea is that his faith "was made fully effective according to the properties expected of true faith."²¹⁰ The verb carries the meaning of bringing something to its end, its completeness or fullness. It is like a fruit tree that does not reach the fullness of its purpose until it bears fruit. Similarly, James seems to indicate that true faith does not reach its end until it demonstrates itself in a righteous life.

SUMMARY AND EVALUATION

This chapter surveyed the usage of the τέλειος notion in the ancient world, including the classical Greek world, Jewish tradition, Second Temple Judaism, and the New Testament world. As one seeks to understand the conceptual and theological background behind Hebrews' thought, the following observations emerge from this discussion.

First, there is adequate evidence that the notion of τέλειος carries its ordinary formal connotation of totality, completion, consummation, or the bringing to the fullness for which something was intended, its ultimate goal,

---

206. For a full treatment of the notion of perfection in James, see Hartin, *Spirituality of Perfection*, 57–161. See also DuPlessis, Τέλειος: *Idea of Perfection*, 233–40.

207. Walters, *Perfection in New Testament Theology*, 183.

208. See Bachmann and Slaby, *Concordance to the Novum Testamentum*, 1777–78.

209. DuPlessis, Τέλειος: *Idea of Perfection*, 240.

210. Peterson, *Hebrews and Perfection*, 41.

or a desired end as far as the will of God is concerned. In Greek philosophy, this notion sometimes connotes a future ideal, but such a goal is not guaranteed even for the one who pursues such a philosophical virtue. Unlike Greek philosophy, Hebrews and the rest of the NT assumes that complete access to God has been made possible through Christ. The goal of τέλειος is attainable by everyone who approaches God by faith in Christ. Like the rest of the NT, the Jewish Scripture and the LXX constitute the more immediate conceptual and theological influence behind Hebrews' thought. For the author of Hebrews, the undivided and wholehearted devotion to God anticipated in the OT has been illustrated, exemplified, and fulfilled in the perfected Christ. The goal of complete access to God is possible, not exclusively for philosophical elites or small, secluded groups like that at Qumran, but is instead available to all believers who draw near during the process of their sanctification.

Second, since the rest of the NT constitutes the immediate context for Hebrews, a soteriological terminology in Hebrews is not isolated from similar notions in the rest of the NT. In Matthew, for instance, Jesus calls his disciples to be τέλειος in accordance with God's kingdom's standards of righteousness. This message of the kingdom has eschatological implications. Whereas believers may have tasted some benefits of salvation, its full and complete realization remains a future reality and will not come as a result of any moral, religious, or vocational effort. Rather, it will come as a result of God's intervention in the world as he makes everything new. For this reason, Jesus' pronouncements in the Synoptic Gospels agree with the overall NT impression, especially in Hebrews, that Jesus Christ not only carries God's redemptive history to its eschatological end, but also that he is its end.

Since the notion of τέλειος carries the idea of sharing in the very nature of God, it is clear that while believers have tasted fellowship with God in Christ, the full realization of such fellowship of perfect love and perfect communion can only be perceived as a future reality. For instance, the most distinct aspect of τέλειος as envisaged by the Apostle Paul is the eschatological bounty of belief in Christ. Like Hebrews, this points to the redemptive significance of Jesus' person and work of salvation already revealed in these last days. Believers have already tasted some of its benefits, yet the full realization of their salvation remains a future reality.

Chapter 4

The Literary Nature and Purpose of Hebrews

THIS CHAPTER EXAMINES THE literary nature and purpose of Hebrews. The previous chapter has shown that the concept of τέλειος is not isolated from the larger context of the Biblical world that influenced Hebrews' thought of reality. Before endeavoring to make a detailed analysis of this notion in Hebrews, one must understand the immediate literary context of Hebrews. This section therefore examines issues related to authorship and date, historical setting, conceptual background, and the literary character of Hebrews in order to allow a clear understanding of the notion of τέλειος. Thus, this chapter serves as a bridge to the heart of the study in the fifth chapter, which will provide a detailed analysis of τέλειος, perfection, in the Epistle to the Hebrews.

ISSUES OF AUTHORSHIP AND DATE

There have been more scholarly suggestions related to the issue of authorship[1] than can be handled in the present study. This section consists of an overview rather than a detailed discussion of these matters. Suggested can-

---

1. Major suggestions for authorship include Paul, Luke, Clement of Rome, Barnabas, Apollos, Silas (Silvanus), Philip, Priscilla and Aquila, and others. For a survey of contemporary issues related to authorship of Hebrews, see Guthrie, *New Testament Introduction*, 197–219. See also Ellingworth, *Epistle to the Hebrews*, 3–21.

didates for authorship include Paul, a companion of Paul,[2] or an unknown author. Some scholars believe that the author of Hebrews is Paul[3] or someone associated with him. Other scholars reject Pauline authorship in favor of Luke as a possible candidate based on alleged similarities in the polished Greek style of Luke-Acts and Hebrews.[4] Some scholars are not satisfied by either of the above positions and suggest other possibilities, such as Barnabas or Apollos, that maintain Pauline connections. To some, Barnabas is a possible candidate for authorship of Hebrews.[5] Among those who advocate an author with Pauline connections is the Reformer Martin Luther, who first supported Pauline authorship in his commentary on Hebrews (1517), a position that he also defended in his Magnificat in 1521. However, in his latter work (1522), Luther attributed Hebrews' authorship to Apollos,[6] a position that is held by many modern commentators.[7] Other suggestions for authorship include Priscilla and Aquila[8] or Clement of Rome because of his quotations from sections of Hebrews.[9] Silas is also suggested as a candidate

2. Such companions include Barnabas, Apollos, Silas, or Priscilla and Aquila. For a detailed discussion of these possible candidates, see Spicq, *Hébreux: Introduction*, 197–219.

3. Pauline authorship is suggested by Leonard, *Author of Hebrews*, 1–43. Following his critical analysis of parallelisms between Hebrews and Pauline literature, Leonard concludes, "There is solid external historical evidence and strong positive internal evidence for the Pauline origin of the Epistle" (ibid., 43). Some modern scholars, especially among Roman Catholics, do not support Leonard's position but instead contend for an associate of Paul's. See Grässer, "Der Hebräerbrief 1938–1963," 128–36.

4. Calvin, *Commentaries on Hebrews*, xxviii, 353. For a recent argument for Lukan authorship of Hebrews, see Allen, *Lukan Authorship of Hebrews*, 376–79. Allen contends that the most significant argument for Lukan authorship is the linguistic argument (lexical, stylistic, and text-linguistic evidence) (ibid., 78–174). He posits that "both the vocabulary and style of Hebrews are more like Luke-Acts than any other New Testament book" (ibid., 377). Allen concludes: "based on all the evidence, I conclude that Luke himself [independently] wrote the Letter to the Hebrews from Rome c. AD 67" (ibid., 376, 379).

5. Barnabas was first suggested in Tertullian, *Modesty*, xx. See also Bartlet, "Barnabas and His Genuine Epistle," 381–96; and ibid., "Hebrews as the Work of Barnabas," 381–96. Bartlet later abandoned this view in favor of Apollos' authorship. For further support of Barnabas' authorship, see Hughes, *Commentary on Hebrews*, 24–29.

6. Luther's shift is based on his observation that the confrontation of Gal 1:1, 12, and Heb 11:3 clearly excludes Paul as a possible candidate for authorship and instead supports a disciple of Paul, namely Apollos. Spicq follows Luther in support of Apollos as the most probable candidate for authorship, on the basis of his hypothesis on alleged Philonism of Hebrews. For further details, see Spicq, *Hébreux: Introduction*, 39–91, 210.

7. For example, Manson, "Problem of the Epistle," 1–17. See also Lenski, *Interpretation of Hebrews and James*, 23–24.

8. Harnack, "Probabilia," 16–41.

9. Scholars have alluded to some remarkable parallels between Hebrews and the

for authorship, since he was also an associate of Paul's and functioned also as an amanuensis of the First Epistle of Peter, which is believed to bear some literary affinities with Hebrews.[10] Whether there is historical and internal evidence to support a particular candidate for authorship,[11] the issue remains debatable.

Historical or External Evidence

The influence of the early church authorities on the study of Hebrews, including both interpretative approaches by the Eastern and Western church fathers, is important for this discussion. From earliest days, the Eastern Church at Alexandria considered Hebrews to be Pauline, although some made only an indirect connection.[12] According to Eusebius (ca. AD 339), Clement of Alexandria (ca. AD 200) claimed that Hebrews was written in the Hebrew language by Paul and that it was later translated by Luke into Greek. It is believed that Clement himself derived this opinion from "the blessed presbyter," who is generally taken as his predecessor, Pantaenus (ca. AD 190), at Alexandria.[13] In his *Ecclesiastical History*, Eusebius provides a record of the views of Clement of Alexandria as follows:

> As for the Epistle to the Hebrews, he [Clement of Alexandria] says that indeed it is Paul's, but that it was written for Hebrews in the Hebrew tongue and that Luke, having carefully translated it, published it for the Greeks. Hence it [Hebrews] is as a result of this translation, the same complexion of style is found in the Epistle and in Acts; but that the words "Paul and apostle" were naturally not prefixed. For he says, "In writing to Hebrews who

---

epistle sent by Clement of Rome to the Corinthians. Examples of such parallels are: Heb 11:7 and 1 Clem 9:4; 12:1; Heb 1:3-4; and 1 Clem 36:1-2. Such parallels may suggest that Clement of Rome was in possession of a copy of Hebrews that he freely cited. For this discussion, see Ellingworth, "Hebrews and 1 Clement," 262–69. In spite of these parallels, there is no evidence to support the claim that Clement of Rome was the author of Hebrews. See Bruce, *Epistle to the Hebrews*, 14.

10. For further details, see Spicq, *Hébreux: Introduction*, 202–203.

11. To many scholars, Hebrews' vocabulary, style, and various literary characteristics do not clearly support any particular author.

12. As early as the second century, there was a common belief that Paul wrote Hebrews. Actually, the oldest extant manuscript of Hebrews (P46), which is an Egyptian text (ca. AD 200), placed the text of Hebrews immediately after Paul's letter to the Romans, perhaps because of the length of the epistle and the mention of Italy in Heb 13:24. For this discussion, see Koester, *Hebrews: New Translation with Introduction and Commentary*, 21.

13. For this discussion, see Guthrie, *New Testament Introduction*, 669.

had conceived a prejudice against him and were suspicious of
him, he very wisely did not repel them at the beginning by putting his name."[14]

Clement explains the non-Pauline character of the Greek style by
claiming that Luke translated the original Hebrew letter by Paul—a statement that might explain why Hebrews is seen as presenting some affinities in vocabulary and style with Lukan writings.[15] This historical evidence by Clement[16] accounts for the absence of a salutation in the letter as Paul's attempt to conceal his identity in the face of Jewish prejudices against him and some suspicions about his ministry. Furthermore, Eusebius quotes a statement by Clement regarding Pantaenus' view on Hebrews' authorship:

> But now as the blessed elder [Pantaenus] used to say, since the Lord, being the apostle of the Almighty was sent to the Hebrews, Paul through modesty, since he had been sent to the Gentiles does not inscribe himself as an apostle to the Hebrews, both to give deference to the Lord and because he wrote to the Hebrews also out of abundance, being a preacher and apostle to the Gentiles.[17]

If this reconstruction is correct, then Paul does not identify himself as the author for reasons related to modesty. Apparently, he does not see himself as one who was sent (as an apostle)[18] to the Hebrews but rather as an apostle to the Gentiles.

In addition to Clement, Origen (ca. AD 254) proposes that the composition as well as style of Hebrews should be seen as belonging to one who

---

14. Clement of Alexandria, *Hypotyposes*, qtd. in Eusebius, *Ecclesiastical History*, IV. 14. 2–3; LCL, 47.

15. For an examination of these affinities, see Koester, *Hebrews*, 43. As many scholars indicate, there seems to be nothing in Hebrews that would suggest Luke as the author. Thus, Koester concludes the alleged similarities in vocabulary and style point only to the fact that they were both influenced by the same Hellenistic environment. For further details, see Spicq, *Hébreux: Introduction*, 198–99.

16. Furthermore, Clement quoted from Hebrews in his own writings and, in many instances, he attributed the text to Paul (Clement of Alexandria, *Miscellanies*, V. 10. 62; VI. 7. 62). See, for example, Clement d'Alexandre, *Les Stromates: Introduction, texte critique et index*, 127–29.

17. Eusebius, *Ecclesiastical History*, IV. 14. 4; cf. ibid., IV. 14. 3.

18. The word ἀπόστολος is used of Jesus in Heb 3:1. Presumably, Paul would not identify himself as an apostle in Hebrews, since he was never an apostle to the Hebrews. For this discussion, see Koester, *Hebrews*, 20–21.

calls to mind the Apostle Paul, but one who made short notes of what his master said.[19] Origen, in his Homilies, has this to say:

> If I may state my own opinion, I should say that the thoughts are of the apostle [Paul], but that the style and composition are the work of someone who called to mind the apostle's teaching and wrote short notes, as it were, on what his master said. If any church, then, regards this epistle as Paul's, let it be commended on this score; for it was not for nothing that the men of old have handed it down to us as Paul's. But as to who actually wrote the epistle, God knows the truth of the matter. According to the account which has reached us, some say that the epistle was written by Clement, who became bishop of the Romans; others, that it was written by Luke, the writer of the Gospel and Acts.[20]

While it is evident that Origen's remark suggests that only God truly knows the author of Hebrews, Origen commonly refers to Paul as Hebrews' author.[21] Particularly, he suggests that someone who was influenced by Paul must have written Hebrews. Furthermore, he is aware of the other opinions that Clement of Rome or Luke wrote the epistle. He is evidently also aware that many in the Eastern Church accepted Pauline authorship of Hebrews while at the same time recognizing that the Western Church, particularly those in Rome, disputed Pauline authorship. Eusebius states, "the fourteen letters of Paul are obvious and plain."[22] He recognizes that such a position is not universally held, particularly by the church in Rome. He states, "Yet it is not right to ignore that some dispute the letter to the Hebrews saying that it was rejected by the church at Rome as not being by Paul."[23] It is clear that while some thought Paul did not write Hebrews, Origen and many in the Eastern Church believed that there was nothing in Hebrews that would disqualify Paul as the author, at least partly or indirectly.

The Latin or Western Church differed sharply from the Eastern Church. Eusebius records that in the Western Church, Hebrews was not universally accepted as Pauline.[24] Early evidence for rejection of Pauline authorship comes from the Presbyter Gaius (ca. AD 200). In his defense of the Catholic position against Montanism, Eusebius refutes the idea that

---

19. Ibid.

20. Origen, qtd. in Eusebius, *Ecclesiastical History*, IV. 25. 11–14.

21. For further examples of ascriptions of authorship to Paul, see Origen, *On First Principles*, I. 1; ibid., *Commentary on John*, II. 72 (FC 80.113).

22. Eusebius, *Ecclesiastical History*, III. 3. 4; LCL, 193.

23. Ibid.

24. Ibid.

Hebrews could be counted among the epistles composed by Paul. He refers to the work called *Dialog of Gaius* in which the author mentions only thirteen epistles written by Paul, excluding Hebrews, and concludes, "even to this day among the Romans there are some who do not consider it to be the apostle's."[25] Irenaeus (ca. AD 130), Hyppolytus (ca. AD 235), and Tertullian rejected Pauline authorship of Hebrews. For instance, Tertullian held that Hebrews was not written in a Pauline style, even though it preserved his apostolic teaching. Tertullian believed Hebrews was written by Barnabas, who followed Paul by practicing self-denial (1 Cor 9:6–12). He considered the letter to be authoritative because it preserved its apostolic status.[26]

Clearly, the Eastern Church differed from the Western Church in its assessment of Hebrews. Interpreters believe that such differences were due to the fact that they worked within different interpretative frameworks. Koester observes, "rather than dealing with the soul's pilgrimage to God, western writers tended to focus on the patterns of church order which affected their views of authorship and authority of the Book."[27] Although the church in the West rejected Pauline authorship of Hebrews, its authority and canonicity were never rejected. This explains Hebrews' influence on the work of Clement, who became Bishop of Rome and wrote his two letters as early as the first century. Most interpreters see some early usages of Hebrews in the West in 1 Clement (ca. AD 96), written in Rome and addressed to the church at Corinth.[28] As some scholars would indicate, the author of 1 Clement does not explicitly refer to Hebrews, but there are striking similarities between the two documents.[29] In spite of specific early usages, Hebrews is absent from both the Marcion and Muratorian canons. Toward the end of the first century, specific references are made in relation to Hebrews.[30] The letter is present in the early manuscript of the *Corpus Paulinum* (ca. AD 200), but modern scholars do not consider this as enough evidence in favor

---

25. Ibid., IV. 20. 3. Irenaeus apparently knew about Hebrews, but he did not cite it in his extant theological writings. His attitude regarding Hebrews is unclear.

26. This is mentioned only once in his writings (Tertullian, *Modesty,* 20). Cf. Tertullian, *La Pudicité,* 432–33.

27. Koester, *Hebrews,* 21.

28. If this reconstruction is correct, then it also provides some clues to the dating of Hebrews, at least by conjecture.

29. As referred to above, such similarities can be seen at Heb 1:1–4 and 1 Clem 36:2–5; Heb 2:17–18; 6:1 and 1 Clem 36:1; Heb 12:1–2 and 1 Clem 19:2; and Heb 4:12 and 1 Clem 21:2. For a detailed discussion, see Koester, *Hebrews,* 22–3. See also Ellingworth, "Hebrews and 1 Clement," 262–69.

30. Eusebius, *Ecclesiastical History,* IV. 14. 2–3.

of Pauline authorship. That calls for some contextual considerations in the text itself as basis for authorship of Hebrews.

Internal Evidence

There is no name given for the author of Hebrews. Unlike all NT epistles (except 1 John), Hebrews has no salutation in which the author identifies himself. This may suggest that it was the author's intention to remain anonymous. From contextual evidence, one may conjecture that the author was not an immediate disciple of Jesus Christ (Heb 2:3). The author appears to have been well versed in the OT, which he cites from the LXX. Most scholars would also agree that he probably had some acquaintance with Timothy (Heb 13:23). Furthermore, the author assumes that his audience knows him (Heb 13:19, 22, 23).[31] Although a number of suggestions for authorship have been proffered (Paul,[32] Barnabas,[33] Luke or Clement,[34] Apollos,[35] Priscilla,[36] and others such as Philip, Peter, Silvanus or Silas, Aristion, and Jude),[37] Origen's agnosticism that when it comes to Hebrews' authorship, only God knows, is still valid.[38] However, internally, it is safe to posit that the author may have been associated with Paul.

---

31. See Tenney, *New Testament Survey*, 357–58.

32. Leonard, *Author of Hebrews*, 385–87. See also Manson, "Problem of the Epistle," 1–17.

33. Tertullian first proposed the argument for Barnabas. For further details, see Tertullian, *La Pudicité*, 263. See also Spicq, *Hébreux: Introduction*, 199. For further details on Tertullian and other insights, see Milligan, *Epistle to the Hebrews*, 10–18.

34. See Calvin, *Epistle to the Hebrews*, xxviii, 353. Rejecting Pauline authorship of Hebrews, Calvin advances an argument for Luke or Clement.

35. Luther also suggests Barnabas, given Barnabas' connection with Paul, but he later suggests a disciple of Paul—namely, Apollos—as the author based on the conflict of Gal 1:2, 12, and Heb 2:3. As Spicq remarks,

> Dans son commentaire sur Hébr. de 1517, Luther accepte l'épître comme étant de Paul, et il garde la même opinion dans son explication du *Magnificat* en 1521 (edit. Weimar, vii, p. 600). Mais dans la préface à Hébr de 1522 il l'attribue à Apollos (x, 1, p. 143), car il a observé que la confrontation de Gal. I, 1, 12 et Hébr. II, 3, exclut l'authenticité paulinienne de celle-ci, il l'attribue donc à un disciple de l'Apôtre. (Spicq, *Hébreux: Introduction*, 210)

36. Harnack, "Probabilia," 16–41.

37. For further details, see Spicq, *Hébreux: Introduction*, 202–203. See also Guthrie, *New Testament Introduction*, 669.

38. Origen, qtd. in Eusebius, *Ecclesiastical History*, VI. 25. For further studies, perhaps Wallace is correct that Hebrews may be considered as the work of dual authorship, based on the argument that the first-person pronoun plural "we" is used throughout

The Literary Nature and Purpose of Hebrews

There are similarities that are worth noting—both in terms of circumstances and doctrine—between Hebrews and other Pauline writings. For example, the mention of Timothy (Heb 13:23; cf. Col 1:1; Phil 1:1; 2:19, 22) suggests some similarities in circumstances with other epistles, especially Ephesians, Philippians and Colossians.[39] In addition, the author displays a high regard for OT Scriptures, especially with reference to the Law. Direct citations from the OT are found in every chapter of Hebrews.[40] This may be said to be similar to Paul's argument in Phil 3:4–7, where the Apostle Paul argues that he has abandoned what is good for what is superior while holding the Law to a higher esteem. Furthermore, the blessings of the new covenant made available through Christ are presented as being of greater benefit than any found under the old order. The author presents a case for the superiority of the new order over the former—an aspect that is almost similar to Paul's attitude toward the Law when he emphasizes the faith of the believer over any fleshly attempt to keep Jewish rules, practices, and regulations.[41]

In spite of such language similarities, there are some factors that would argue against Pauline authorship.[42] Regardless of such arguments, one must keep in mind that Pauline authorship was never disputed in the Eastern Church centered at Alexandria from the close of the second cen-

---

the epistle (cf. 2:5; 5:11; 6:9, 11; 8:1; 9:5; 13:18). For a discussion of the editorial "we" and relevance for the Epistle to the Hebrews, see Wallace, *Exegetical Syntax*, 393–99.

39. The mention of Timothy may be said to be similar to Paul's reference to his young companion in his epistles. If this assumption is correct, Hebrews could have been written by an associate of Paul either at the same time or immediately after Paul's writing of Ephesians, Philippians, and Colossians. For details, see Pentecost, *Faith That Endures*, 4–10. Lexicographers assume that the Timothy mentioned in Heb 13:23 is the same as the one mentioned in Pauline letters. For further details, see BDAG, 1006.

40. For the listing of these citations, see ibid., 6–7.

41. Examples of similarities in wording and allusions between Hebrews and Paul are found in Heb 1:2 and Eph 3:9; Heb 1:3 and Col 1:15, 17; 2 Cor 4:4; Phil 2:6; Heb 1:4 and Eph 1:21; Phil 2:9; Heb 1:5 and Acts 13:33; Heb 1:6 and Rom 8:29; Col 1:15; Heb 2:2 and Gal 3:19; Heb 2:4 and 1 Cor 12:4, 11; and many other references (Pentecost, *Faith That Endures*, 8–9).

42. For arguments against direct Pauline authorship, see Spicq, *Hébreux: Introduction*, 155–68. The most striking evidence against Pauline authorship is the author's explicit statement that he received the message of the gospel indirectly (Heb 2:3). This is in contrast with Paul's claim that he received his commission directly from the risen Lord (Gal 1:1). Second, Paul's name does not appear in the prologue or anywhere else, contrary to his custom with his thirteen epistles. Third, Hebrews lacks the characteristic salutation found in each of the Pauline letters. Fourth, there is in Hebrews a marked absence of characteristics of Pauline thought, themes, motifs, and theology. For further details on differences between Paul and Hebrews, see also Ellingworth, *Hebrews*, 7–12; and Allen, *Hebrews*, 38–43.

tury onward. Through Jerome and Augustine, the general belief in Pauline authorship was also accepted in the Western Church centered in Rome. Similarities in both doctrine and circumstances point with some merit to the suggestion that just as the Gospel of Mark was written under Peter's apostolic oversight, so Hebrews was perhaps written under Paul's apostolic oversight. Thus, the truth contained in Hebrews and its doctrine would be Pauline.[43] Due to similarities in theological affinities, and assuming that the Timothy mentioned (13:23) is Paul's young companion, one may posit that the author was perhaps connected to the Pauline circle. However, as most commentators would conclude, the best reading of all the evidence would suggest that Paul is not the author of Hebrews. The question of dating Hebrews is also relevant to this discussion.

Date of Composition

Scholars are divided over the dating of Hebrews. According to Westcott, the date of Hebrews should be placed just before the outbreak of the Jewish War between AD 64 and AD 67.[44] The majority of modern critics, including Adolph von Harnack and Oskar Holtzmann, contend that Hebrews was written after the destruction of the temple between AD 81 and AD 96 under the rule of Domitian.[45] A few critics propose a latter date toward the end of Trajan's rule (AD 117), when the Jews attempted to rebuild their temple. However, as Spicq indicates, such an extreme date cannot be legitimate.[46]

There is both historical and internal evidence that provides some clues for the dating of Hebrews.[47] The *terminus ad quem* is certainly fixed by Clement's epistle to the Corinthians, which contains several parallels with Hebrews.[48] If Clement of Rome (ca. AD 96) used segments of Hebrews, then Hebrews would have been penned before AD 96. If this reconstruction is correct, then the next issue becomes whether Hebrews was written before the destruction of the temple (AD 70) or after this historical event. The *terminus a quo* must be determined by one's answer to the issue of Hebrews'

---

43. For further details, see Pentecost, *Faith That Endures*, 10.

44. Westcott, *Epistle to the Hebrews*, xlii.

45. Robertson, *John and Hebrews*, 330. This is the majority view held by modern critics. Other proponents include: H. von Soden, J. Réville, Wrede, G. Hollman, Th. Häring, J. Goodspeed, V. Taylor, H. Strathmann, Th. H. Robinson, A. M. Hunter, and O. Michel.

46. Spicq, *Hébreux: Introduction*, 253.

47. For a detailed discussion, see Carson and Moo, *Introduction to the New Testament*, 605–608.

48. Ellingworth, "Hebrews and 1 Clement," 29–33.

relationship to the destruction of Jerusalem.[49] The two major views can be grouped under two subtitles: (1) a date before AD 70, or (2) a date after AD 70. In either case, however, a precise date may not be possible to determine.[50]

Date of Composition before AD 70

As stated before, there is evidence that Clement of Rome was familiar with Hebrews. This places the date of its composition firmly within the first century of the Christian era, specifically before AD 96.[51] Interpreters refer to parallels between Hebrews and the Shepherd of Hermas as having some role in the dating of Hebrews before AD 70.[52] These parallels are perhaps due to Hermas' borrowing from Hebrews and would have some significance if the Shepherd were dated early (that is, before AD 70).[53] More important, however, is the internal evidence.

First, the language of Hebrews indicates that the temple in Jerusalem was still standing at the time of composition, since the author does not give any clues that indicate the temple was destroyed. This argument is supported by the author's consistent use of the present tense in his description of the entire Levitical system.[54] Although, for some scholars, the use of the present tense by itself can hardly be decisive for establishing that the Levitical priesthood was still functioning at the time of composition—especially since other writers after the event of AD 70[55] also used the present tense in their description of the same practice, even though they knew the temple

---

49. For significance of the event of Jerusalem's fall, see Robinson, *Redating the New Testament*, 200. See also Guthrie, *New Testament Introduction*, 701.

50. Ibid., 703.

51. Hughes, *Epistle to the Hebrews*, 30.

52. Robinson, *Redating the New Testament*, 208.

53. Guthrie, *New Testament Introduction*, 703.

54. Examples of the present tense usages are found in Heb 5:1–4; 7:21; 7:23, 27, 28; 8:3–4; 8:13; 9:6, 9, 13, 25; 10:1, 3, 8, 11; and 13:10, 11. Some scholars have questioned the use of the present tense by itself as an indicative that the Levitical priesthood was still functioning at the time of Hebrews' composition. Robinson argues that many of these present tenses are used to indicate a timeless manner in the author's description of Jewish rituals (e.g., Heb 5:1–4; 8:3–5; 9:6, and 10:1). For this discussion, see Robinson, *Redating the New Testament*, 200.

55. The Jewish historian Josephus, writing two decades after the destruction of the temple, regularly uses the present tense with reference to the tabernacle and its furnishings (Josephus, *Jewish Antiquities*, IV. 6. 1–8; LCL, 102–150). In his description of the vestments of the priests, Josephus alternates between the present and the past tenses (ibid., IV. 7. 1–7; LCL, 151–87), but he regularly uses the present tense in his reports on the Levitical sacrifices (ibid., IV. 9. 1–7; LCL, 224–57).

was already destroyed.[56] One may thus conclude that the use of the present tense is not by itself enough proof that the temple was still standing. Attridge posits that "the cultic language could, in some secondary fashion, allude to contemporary practice, but it need not."[57] It is the OT ritual, not contemporary practice, that is in view. In fact, the author always refers to the Tabernacle and not to the temple.

Second, the lack of any reference to the destruction of the temple indicates Hebrews was written prior to AD 70. Most scholars argue that the absence of any indication of the catastrophe of the temple is of greater weight.[58] John A. T. Robinson posits Heb 10:2-3 would make very little sense if sacrifices had in fact ceased.[59] Although for scholars such as K. W. Clark, Jewish sacrifices did not necessarily cease with the fall of Jerusalem.[60] Donald Guthrie argues that this view is certainly not correct.[61]

Following Guthrie, some scholars vie for the dating of Hebrews prior to AD 70, either in the early part of the decade or when the threat of the siege had become imminent.[62] The tone of the letter and the exhortation to "come out" (Heb 13:13) would naturally point to the doom of the city as an imminent reality, especially in light of Jesus' warning in Mark 13:14-15. In addition, the reference to Timothy, Paul's companion, would make more sense to scholars who argue that Hebrews was perhaps written by a member of the Pauline circle. This would be a strong reason to place the letter chronologically as near as possible to the time of Paul.[63] For these reasons, one may hypothesize that "the use of the present tense" together with "the lack of any reference to the destruction of the Temple in Jerusalem," plus the tone of the epistle itself, together argue for a date prior to the destruction of the temple in AD 70.

---

56. For this discussion, see Attridge, *Epistle to the Hebrews*, 6-9.

57. Ibid., 8. For further details, see Guthrie, *New Testament Introduction*, 701-702.

58. For this discussion, see Manson, "Problem of the Epistle," 1-17. Manson maintains an early date when the temple was still standing, appealing to the use of the Melchizedek high priesthood argument instead of a direct appeal to the destruction of the temple.

59. Robinson, *Redating the New Testament*, 202.

60. Clark, "Worship in the Jerusalem Temple," 268-80. According to Clark, although the temple was destroyed in AD 70 and its sacred objects carried away, the Roman conqueror pronounced no edict against the continuation of religious worship until late in AD 135 (see especially ibid., 271-72).

61. Guthrie, *New Testament Introduction*, 701.

62. Ibid., 702.

63. For further details, see ibid.

Date of Composition after AD 70

The second major view is that Hebrews was written after the fall of Jerusalem (after AD 70). This allows for a broader range of it being written between AD 70 and 96.[64] Proponents of this view base their argument on the apparent imminence of persecution under the rule of Domitian.[65] Also, the high Christology evidenced especially in the exordium, in the parallels with the Lukan corpus, in the Pastorals, and in 1 Peter are taken by many scholars as warranting a post-70 date.[66] For instance, the use of some of Pauline epistles (especially the prison epistles), is taken as evidence to support a later date for Hebrews, since time would be required for the circulation of these letters. Accordingly, any date prior to the fall of Jerusalem (AD 70) would be considered premature.

On the other hand, there is a reason most students of Hebrews agree with the general consensus that the epistle could not have been penned after AD 96, a date that coincides with the epistle of Clement of Rome to the Corinthians that refers to several portions of Hebrews.[67] Because of this general consensus, some scholars feel safe to set the *terminus ad quem* for Hebrews at AD 96, allowing for a broader range of dating around AD 60–96. However, as many scholars indicate, this broader range can be significantly narrowed to a date not later than AD 70 and not earlier than AD 64, which is the date associated with Paul's death. This would allow one to confidently

---

64. This view is held by the majority of the critics. For early opinions on this view, see Spicq, *Hébreux: Introduction*, 253. For recent opinions, see Fiorenza, "Der Anführer," 264; Stadelmann, "Zur Christologies Hebräerbriefes," 138. See also Kistemaker, *Exposition of Hebrews*, 16.

65. Guthrie, *New Testament Introduction*, 704.

66. For this discussion, see Attridge, *Hebrews*, 9. Commenting on Hebrews' high Christology, Spicq shows how the Christology of Hebrews reaches such a completeness that would require a long period of reflection. He states,

> Elle [Hebrews' Christology] traduit en particulier une connaissance approfondie des épîtres de la captivité; si bien que quelques année sont necessaries depuis la publication et la diffusion de celles-ci pour donner à l'auteur de l'Hébreux le temps de les assimiler et de les incorporer à sa synthèse doctrinale. (Spicq, *Hébreux: Introduction*, 253–54).

67. For further details, see Ellingworth, "Hebrews and 1 Clement," 262–69. See also Hagner, *Use of the Old and New*, 179–95. Interestingly, Robinson has argued for a date as early as AD 70 for 1 Clement (Robinson, *Redating the New Testament*, 327–34). On the other hand, some scholars have argued for a later date ranging from AD 80 to 140 (For details, see Attridge, *Hebrews*, 7–8; see also Lane, *Hebrews 1–8*, lxii–lxiii). However, the general consensus is that 1 Clement was composed about AD 95–96. For this discussion, see also deSilva, *Perseverance in Gratitude*, 20. See also Salevao, *Legitimation in Hebrews*, 104.

set an upper limit for the dating of Hebrews at AD 70, the year during which the temple of Jerusalem was destroyed by the Romans under Titus.[68] Most scholars think the mention of Timothy (Heb 13:23) is a clear indication that "the *terminus ad quem* might be earlier than the uppermost limit allowed by the date range of 1 Clement,"[69] especially when one presumes that the Timothy mentioned is Paul's young companion.[70] In addition, proponents of the later date use Heb 2:3, where the author implies second-generation Christianity by placing himself outside the immediate circle of the apostles.[71] Such an argument is favors the view that Hebrews was written at a later date, perhaps after AD 70.

There is reason to believe that Hebrews must have been penned prior to AD 70 and before the Jewish wars of AD 67, which culminated in the fall of Jerusalem (cf. Heb 8:13). The tone of Heb 3:7 (cf. 11:34) clearly suggests an immediate urgency to the readers' enduring faith. Furthermore, they must be ready to face the likelihood of some intense persecution (12:4) and to imitate the heroism of their leaders (13:7). They must be prepared to hold fast to the confession of their faith in the Lord Jesus Christ and to persevere in the midst of trials (3:14; 10:39) in view of the danger of infidelity, disobedience, and apostasy (Heb 3:12, 18; cf. 4:11; 10:27; 12:25). Based on the text, it is clear that some approaching desolation or calamity (cf. 10:25) is in mind of the author,[72] which is similar to Jesus' prophetic prediction of the ruins of Jerusalem as described in the Synoptic Gospels. Spicq sees the second coming of Christ (cf. Heb 10:37) as coming into perspective with the desolation of the Temple, Jesus being the center of the new order of the new covenant and crown of the presence of the glory of God.[73] In the immediate context of Hebrews, the threat of an approaching desolation over Jerusalem leads naturally to not only the author's tone of urgency, but also to his exhortation to the readers to hold fast to the confession of their faith in the process of their journey to their intended goal of completeness and

68. For further details, see Thomas, "Case for a Mixed-Audience," 134.

69. Attridge, *Hebrews*, 9.

70. Some scholars are skeptical about the reference to Timothy on the grounds that nothing is known about the date of his birth or death. For further details, see Morris, "Hebrews," 8.

71. For further details, see Harrison, *Introduction to the New Testament*, 377.

72. Spicq compares this to Jesus' predictions of the ruination of Jerusalem as found in the Synoptic Gospels (Mark 13, Matt 24 and Luke 21) but also points further to its eschatological significance, looking forward to the second coming of Christ: "La ruine de Jerusalem va preparer un avenement nouveau du règne de Dieu . . . qui sera pour les élus une période de delivrance ἀπολύτρωσις (cf. Heb 11: 35; Luke 21:28)" (Spicq, *Hébreux: Introduction*, 258).

73. Ibid., 259.

glory. Philip E. Hughes rightly observes that "the author foresaw that the judgment which Christ predicted would come upon Judaism and its temple, was close at hand (cf. Mk 13:14ff.; Matt 24:15ff.; Luke 21:5ff.)."[74]

From the foregoing discussion on the dating of Hebrews one may deduce the following: first, that the temple was still standing at the time of writing of Hebrews; second, that the arrest of Paul's young companion, Timothy, was connected to his association with the apostle; third, that he was imprisoned immediately after the death of Paul (AD 64) to which fact Heb 13:21 seems to bear witness. If this reconstruction is correct, then one can confidently posit that Hebrews was penned not after AD 70, but shortly after the death of the Apostle Paul, at around AD 65–66.[75]

HISTORICAL SETTING OF HEBREWS

Understanding the historical setting of Hebrews will yield a greater appreciation of the notion of τέλειος ("perfection") and its contribution to the message of Hebrews. For this purpose, three aspects of the historical background will be delineated: the geographical location, the socio-political milieu, and the religious or spiritual context of the original readers.

Geographical Location and Recipients

Some clues about the geographical location of the recipients are needed before attempting to address particular issues pertaining to their identity. The major options for their locale range from Palestine in the east to Spain in the west.[76] However, the general consensus among modern scholars today favors Rome as the destination of Hebrews. The question becomes: Why Rome and not some other places in Palestine or Egypt?

Palestinian Destination

Traditionally, commentators have defended the view that Hebrews was written to the Jewish Christian community in Jerusalem or a sister church

---

74. For further details, see Hughes, *Hebrews*, 30.

75. See also, Thomas, "Case for a Mixed-Audience," 134–35.

76. For this discussion, see Bruce, *Hebrews*, 10. For further details, see also Spicq, *Hébreux: Introduction*, 234.

within the Palestinian region.⁷⁷ William M. Ramsey,⁷⁸ for instance, argues that Hebrews was written to the Jerusalem church from Caesarea during Paul's imprisonment in that city (AD 57–59) by one of his companions, possibly Philip the Evangelist. Some proponents of this view believe Hebrews was sent to the Jerusalem church shortly prior to the outbreak of the war against the Romans in AD 66.⁷⁹ Arnold Ehrhardt believes Hebrews was sent to the believers as "a message of consolation that originated from the church in Rome to the believers in the Holy Land after the fall of the city of Jerusalem."⁸⁰ The arguments⁸¹ in support of this view are compelling. First, Hebrews "gives an impression that its readers must have lived in the neighborhood of the temple, the antithesis throughout not being that of συναγωγή and church, but of temple and ἐπισυναγωγή of Christians."⁸² Second, there is patristic evidence indicating the Jerusalem church was made up entirely of "Hebrews" and was called "the church of the Hebrews."⁸³ Third, the imminent crisis in view (Heb 1:2; 3:13; 10:25; 12:27) is generally understood as the approaching siege of Jerusalem.⁸⁴ Fourth, the absence of any controversy between Jews and Gentiles can only be justified by an assumption that the original readers were Jewish Christians who lived in a Jewish congregation in Palestine.⁸⁵

A number of objections⁸⁶ have been leveled against this traditional view. First, some scholars argue that the members of the Jerusalem church could not have been addressed in the terms of Heb 2:3 since many among them would have heard Jesus personally. However, to some interpreters, this objection can be removed if the destination of Hebrews is moved from the Jerusalem assembly to some other sister church nearby or around Pales-

77. For a defense of the traditional view, see Delitzsch, *Epistle to the Hebrews*, 21–22. See also Westcott, *Hebrews*, xl-xli; Bruce, *Epistle to the Hebrews*, 6–7; Spicq, *Hébreux: Introduction*, 220–52; Hughes, *Epistle to the Hebrews*, 11, 19; and Thiessen, *Introduction to the New Testament*, 301–303.

78. For further details, see Ramsey, *Luke the Physician*, 301–28.

79. For this discussion, see Bruce, *Epistle to the Hebrews*, 10.

80. Ehrhardt, *Framework of the New Testament Stories*, 109. This view counters the argument that Hebrews does not make any reference to the destruction that befell the city of Jerusalem, including the destruction of the temple.

81. For further details on these arguments from the traditional viewpoint, see MacLeod, "Theology of Hebrews, 76–78.

82. Delitzsch, *Hebrews*, I. 21; Westcott, *Hebrews*, xxxix-xli.

83. See especially Eusebius, *Ecclesiastical History*, IV. 5. 1–2.

84. For further details, see Westcott, *Hebrews*, xli.

85. Salmon, *Books of the New Testament*, 427–28.

86. Moffatt, *Epistle to the Hebrews*, 446. For further details, see Guthrie, *New Testament Introduction*, 712.

tine.[87] Second, some argue that it would have been more appropriate for the author of Hebrews to write in Aramaic if he was addressing an audience in Palestine—an objection that was removed in ancient times by the suggestion that Hebrews was first written in Hebrew and translated later into Greek.[88] Third, some scholars reason that the terms of Heb 5:12 would not be considered as appropriate for the Hebrew believers in Jerusalem—an objection that may also be removed if Hebrews is considered to have been written to one of the sister assemblies in the Palestinian region.[89] Fourth, the context seems to indicate that the group to which Hebrews was addressed had never suffered any martyrdom (Heb 12:4), yet from the Lukan account, it appears clearly that Christian martyrdom started with the church in Jerusalem (Act 7:54–8:3).[90] Fifth, a number of references in Hebrews (6:10; 10:34; 13:2, 5, 16) indicate that the recipients were materially generous, yet as many interpreters point out, the church in Jerusalem was known for its poverty and its need for support from other churches in the region. For some scholars, the issue of poverty does not exclude the possibility of some generous acts of kindness toward fellow believers.[91] Sixth, some scholars assert that the extensive usage of the LXX would not favor an audience of

---

87. MacLeod, "Theology of Hebrews," 78. Other places in Palestine are suggested for Hebrews' destination, including Samaria, specifically Sychar (Bowman, *Hebrews, James, I and II Peter*, 13–16). Spicq suggests Caesarea as the place of Hebrews' destination but regards Syrian Antioch as more probable (Spicq, *Hébreux: Introduction*, 247–52; Cf. Burch, *Epistle to the Hebrews*, 137). For these scholars, the incidents noted in Heb 10:32–34 could be placed in the context of the tension between the Jewish and Gentile populations of Caesarea in the decade that preceded AD 66 (see Josephus, *Jewish War*, II. 266–70; ibid., *Jewish Antiquities*, XX. 173–84). Manson, on the other hand, detects in Hebrews an early form of the "Colossian heresy," and thus points to Colossae or a neighboring town in the Lycus Valley as its geographical destination (Manson, *Studies in the Gospels and Epistles*, 242–58; cf. Manson's previous article, ibid., "Problem of the Epistle," 1–17). For a summary of how Hebrews is associated with the Lycus Valley, see Bruce, *Hebrews*, 11. Another suggested place for Hebrews' destination is Ephesus (Howard, "Epistle to the Hebrews," 80–91), because of the assumption that the original recipients constituted a group of wealthy and learned Jews who had been converted during Paul's Ephesian ministry, but whose faith waned following the apostle's imprisonment and subsequent execution in Rome; see also, Bartlet, "Riddle of Hebrews," 448–51. In addition, Corinth (Montefiore, *Hebrews*, 11–16), Cyprus, which was associated with Barnabas' authorship of Hebrews (Riggenbach, *Der Brief an die Hebräer*, xlvi), and also Antioch (Brown, "Authorship and Circumstances of Hebrews," 505–38; Burch, *Epistle to the Hebrews*, 137) have been suggested as Hebrews' destination.

88. Ibid.

89. Ibid., 79.

90. For this discussion, see Lightfoot, *Jesus Christ Today*, 34.

91. See Peake, *Hebrews*, 23.

Jewish believers in Jerusalem or Palestine.⁹² This objection is not decisive since other educated Jewish people⁹³ frequently used the LXX, which is an indication that the Greek OT was held in much better standing in Palestine than some current scholars believe.

Alexandrian Destination in Egypt

Egypt's Alexandria is the second major place suggested by a good number of scholars for the destination of Hebrews.⁹⁴ According to this view, the Jews of Alexandria, the largest population of all the Jewish communities of the diaspora, were in fact very receptive to the message of the gospel. The testimony by Eusebius is especially compelling in this regard when he states that "Mark was the first to be sent to Egypt where he preached the message of the Gospel that he had written and started churches first at Alexandria. Since the very beginning, the number of believers among men and women increased tremendously, and their way of living was in accord with the way of wisdom. . ."⁹⁵ There is some evidence that the author of Hebrews was associated with Alexandria, Egypt, as many scholars note.⁹⁶ F. F. Bruce states that "the author is evidently acquainted with the literature of Alexandria Judaism, like Wisdom and 4 Maccabees, and especially the writings of Philo."⁹⁷ However, as many indicate, this may have to do more with his association with the city of Alexandria than those who lived there. There is no reference to Hebrews in the Muratorian Canon, which refers to another letter "to the Alexandrines." This does not mean Hebrews should be identified with the so-called letter to "the Alexandrines."⁹⁸

Many scholars claim that the Alexandrian destination has much that could be argued in its favor. However, there is one major obstacle

---

92. Moffatt, *Hebrews*, 446.

93. MacLeod, "Theology of Hebrews," 80.

94. For various opinions in support of this view, see Spicq, *Hébreux: Introduction*, 237–38.

95. Eusebius, *Ecclesiastical History*, II. 16. 1–2. Some scholars attribute Hebrews' authorship to Mark and argue that several Scriptural citations in Hebrews follow the *Codex Alexandrinus* (Heb 1:3 and Wis 3:25; Heb 1:5 and Psa 2:7; Heb 10:5 and Psa 40; Heb 11:21 and Gen 46:21). For this discussion, see Spicq, *Hébreux: Introduction*, 238.

96. For this discussion, see Anderson, "Hebrews and Pauline Letter Collection," 429–38.

97. Bruce, *Hebrews*, 12.

98. Spicq observes, "Vouloir identifier *Hébr* avec la lettre *ad Alexandrinos* mentionnée par le canon de Muratori (Hug) est une erreur manifeste"(Spicq, *Hébreux: Introduction*, 238).

The Literary Nature and Purpose of Hebrews 97

that presents a strong objection to this view. While it is true the belief in Pauline authorship of Hebrews arose first in Alexandria, it is also true that the church at Alexandria did not lay any claim to Hebrews; the early Alexandrian Fathers did, in fact, assume that the epistle was addressed to the Hebrew people who lived in Palestine.[99] If this had not been the case, the church fathers at Alexandria would have included the subscription πρός Ἀλεξανδρίνους[100] instead of πρός Ἑβραίους. The author of Hebrews shared a mutual background with Alexandrian authors of such literature as Wisdom, Fourth Maccabees, and especially Philo, but the likelihood of Alexandria as the destination for Hebrews is disputable.

Roman Destination

Many interpreters today argue for a Roman destination for Hebrews.[101] There is compelling evidence in support of this view. The salutation οἱ ἀπὸ τῆς Ἰταλίας, "those from Italy" (Heb 13:24),[102] is taken by interpreters as a strong evidence that Hebrews was destined for Rome. Those referred to had left their place of origin (Italy) and were then living outside of Italy.[103] Most commentators today favor this understanding of the salutation, which linguistically provides the more natural sense of the preposition ἀπό. It is also found in a phrase like "those from Cicilia and Asia" who lived in Jerusalem (Acts 6:9; cf. 21:27; 24:18).[104] If this reconstruction is correct, somewhere in Italy (e.g., Rome) is the most likely destination. The allusions to the gen-

---

99. Guthrie, *New Testament Introduction*, 700.

100. Speaking about the unlikelihood of an Alexandrian destination, Spicq is emphatic: "En tout cas, ses scribes si nombreux, auxquels on doit tant des copies de l'Epître, n'auraient point manqué d'ajouter la suscription πρὸς Ἀλεξανδρίνους" (Spicq, *Hébreux: Introduction*, 238).

101. Lane is one of the strongest modern supporters of the Roman destination. He presents a number of pieces of evidence as indicting a Rome as the location for the recipients of Hebrews. For further details, see Lane, *Hebrews 1–8*, lviii–lx.

102. The salutation, οἱ ἀπὸ τῆς Ἰταλίας, may be understood as referring to "those in Italy," "the Italians," or "those who come from Italy," to imply that they had left their native home and are now living outside of Italy (cf. BDAG, 106). While linguistically the first option may not be excluded, commentators believe that the second option provides a more natural sense of the preposition ἀπό (cf. Matt 21:11; Mark 15:43; John 1:44; 21:2; Acts 6:9, and 18:2). For interpreters who prefer the first reading ("those in Italy"), see Spicq, *Hébreux: Introduction*, 261–65. For some detailed illustrations that the preposition ἀπό could refer also to one's place of residence (cf. Acts 10:23; 17:13), see Koester, *Hebrews*, 581–82.

103. For further details, see Ellingworth, *Hebrews*, 29.

104. For further details, see Koester, *Hebrews*, 581.

erosity of the community (Heb 6:10-11 and 10:33-34) are consistent with the history of Roman Christianity as described by other ancient writers like Ignatius of Antioch and Dionysius of Corinth, both of whom are cited by Eusebius.[105] In addition, the reference to the community's endurance of early sufferings (Heb 10:32-34) seems to reflect the circumstances the Roman church was subjected to, the edict by Claudius expelling Jews and Jewish Christians from Rome around AD 49.[106] The terminology used for the "leaders" of the community, ἡγούμενοι (Heb 13:7, 17, 24), is said to also be found in other Christian literature associated with the setting of Rome.[107] Lane indicates that Hebrews was first known and used in Rome. Clement of Rome is the first author to have cited Hebrews in his pastoral letter to the Corinthians (cf. *1 Clem* 35:1-6),[108] an indisputable indication that Hebrews was already circulating among the churches in or around Rome.[109] Lane observes, "Not only are there striking parallels to the form and statement of Hebrews throughout First Clement, but also Clement is literally dependent upon Hebrews in First Clement 36:1-6."[110] This observation provides some clues regarding the identity of the original recipients of the letter.

Original Recipients of Hebrews

Having discussed the major opinions related to the geographical location of the recipients of Hebrews, one is now compelled to answer the question pertaining to the identity of the first readers. The title πρός Εβραίους, "to the Hebrews"[111] is often dismissed on the grounds that it was never part

---

105. Eusebius, *Ecclesiastical History*, IV. 23. 10.

106. For a discussion on "The Edict of Claudius" and its connection with Hebrews, see Lane, *Hebrews 1-8*, lxiii-lxvi.

107. Examples are found in *1 Clem* 36:1-6; Herm. *Vis.* 2.2.6; 3.9.7. For further details, see ibid., lviii-lix. See especially Lane's comment on Heb 13:7 (Lane, *Hebrews 9-13*, 526-27).

108. See also Ellingworth, "Hebrews and 1 Clement," 262-69. For further details and parallel passages between Hebrews and Clement, see also Lightfoot, *Jesus Christ Today*, 28-30.

109. For this discussion, see also Lane, "Social Perspectives on Roman Christianity," 196-244.

110. Lane, *Hebrews 1-8*, lviii. For this discussion, see also Mitchell, *Hebrews*, 6-7.

111. For a detailed examination of the usage of the title in both early and late Greek manuscripts, see Westcott, *Hebrews*, xxvii-xxx: this title is alluded to in the earliest extant manuscripts (P46 ℵ A B C). Most scholars would argue that there are no manuscripts of Hebrews that do not bear this title. For further details, see also Guthrie, *Letter to the Hebrews*, 22. The epistle has been known by this title since as early as Clement of Alexandria and Tertullian. Therefore, there is no patristic evidence that would suggest

of the original text. While it is true that the title may have not been part of the original document, interpreters agree that it must have been added at a very early date due to the relation the book occupies vis-à-vis the message of the gospel. Thus, Westcott posits that "the arguments and reflections in their whole form and spirit, even more than in special details, are addressed to 'Hebrews' men, that is, whose hearts were filled with the thoughts, the hopes, the consolations of the Old Covenant, such perhaps as, under another aspect, are described as οἱ ἐκ περιτομῆς (Acts 10:45; 11:2; Gal 2:12; Col 4:11; Titus 1:10)."[112] Similarly, Theodor B. Zahn comments, "there is not the slightest trace of evidence that Hebrews was ever known by another title in any part of the church."[113] Therefore, many see no reason to disqualify the title's genuineness.

The title πρός Εβραίους appears also in P46, which is the oldest extant codex containing Hebrews (ca. AD 200). As pointed out in chapter 3, Clement of Alexandria, writing at about AD 130, spoke of the epistle as written "to the Hebrews."[114] Also, Tertullian, writing at about AD 220, refers to the letter as an epistle "to the Hebrews" (*ad Hebraeos*).[115] There is compelling evidence that this traditional title ("to the Hebrews") was widespread at a very early date. If Hebrews was never known by another title, then the above historical evidence should be taken as arguing strongly for the traditional view that Hebrews was written primarily to a Jewish Christian audience.[116] Some scholars reject the traditional view in favor of the view that Hebrews was directed primarily to a Gentile audience.[117] Moffat, among others, suggests that the use of the LXX (and not the MT), the lack of any reference to either the temple or circumcision, point more to a Gentile readership rather

---

any reason to doubt this tradition. For further details, see Guthrie, *Letter to the Hebrews*, 22.

112. Westcott, *Hebrews*, xxviii. The Greek phrase οἱ ἐκ περιτομῆς, "those from the circumcision," simply refers to "the Jewish Christians."

113. Zahn, *Introduction to the New Testament*, 294.

114. Clement of Alexandria, qtd. in Eusebius, *Ecclesiastical History*, VI. 14. 3–4.

115. See also Tertullian, *Modesty*, 20.

116. For a detailed argumentation in favor of the traditional view (Jewish audience), see Delitzsch, *Hebrews*, 1:20–21; Westcott, *Hebrews*, xxxv; Bruce, *Hebrews,* 2–4; Burch, *Hebrews*, 1–31; Manson, *Epistle to the Hebrews*, 18–23; Spicq, *Hébreux: Introduction*, 220–52; Hughes, *Hebrews,*18–19; and Guthrie, *Introduction*, 699–703. See also Filson, "Epistle to the Hebrews," 22–3; Dahms, "First Readers of Hebrews," 365–75; and Zahn, *Introduction to the New Testament*, 2:296–97.

117. For arguments in support of the Gentile audience hypothesis, see Manson, *Epistle to the Hebrews*, 16; Moffatt, *Hebrews*, xvi–xvii; and Vos, *Teaching of Hebrews*, 14–23. An earlier defense of this hypothesis is found in Scott, *Hebrews: Its Doctrine and Significance*, 14–19. See also Strachan, *Historic Jesus in the New Testament*, 90–91.

than Jewish. He specifically observes, "The LXX is for him and his readers the codex of their religion, the appeal to which was cogent for Gentile Christians in the early church."[118] This argument is put forth to establish some aspect of Gentile character for Hebrews. However, there is sufficient evidence to establish the Jewish character of the original recipients. The title πρός Εβραίους should be regarded as genuine and primarily intended for a group of Christians who were predominantly Jewish.

Many scholars agree that the content of Hebrews is entirely drawn from themes of direct and vital interest primarily to first-century Jews.[119] Not only is the argument Jewish in character, the theological antitheses between Christ and Moses, Christ and Melchizedek, Christ's high priesthood and Levitical priesthood, as well as between the old and new covenant are designed to primarily address Jewish eschatological hopes to come. This does not imply that Hebrews is lacking in applications to Gentile believers. The point is that the whole spectrum of Hebrews is so impregnated with Judaism that the content can only be explained on the premise that it was written primarily to a Jewish Christian audience, in or around the city of Rome.[120]

The title "the Epistle to the Hebrews" is used in reference to both Jews and Jewish Christians in distinction from the Gentile audience.[121] The traditional view suggests Hebrews was written primarily to a Jewish audience based on the assumption that the readers were familiar with the OT and the old Levitical cultic system. Perhaps it is best to argue that the audience was predominantly Jewish Christians, or Hellenistic Jewish Christians based on the high level of Greek and the citations from the LXX. These Hellenistic Jewish believers lived outside Palestine, perhaps around the city of Rome. This does not exclude the presence of some Gentile believers.[122] However, this position is not meant to overlook scholars who genuinely prefer to take a safer position that although Rome's destination is more likely, it is not conclusive. For such scholars, the destination of Hebrews remains uncertain.[123]

---

118. Moffatt, *Hebrews*, xvi.

119. Filson, "Epistle to the Hebrews," 22.

120. For detailed analysis of this hypothesis, see Sanford, "Addressees of Hebrews," 24–35. The original recipients would have been predominantly Jewish believers meeting in a house church in or around Rome.

121. Purdy and Cotton, "Epistle to the Hebrews," 592.

122. For this discussion, see Ellingworth, *Hebrews*, 682–87.

123. See Carson and Moo, *Introduction to the New Testament*, 608–609. See also Bruce, *Hebrews*, 9–14. For further details, see also Ellingworth, *Hebrews*, 28–29.

Socio-Political Setting of Hebrews

Assuming that Hebrews is a document that goes back to the mid-sixties of the first century, one may argue that its contents should be regarded as related to the circumstances immediately prior to the Jewish War (AD 66–70),[124] which is considered as a key to understanding Hebrews.[125] Historically, the recipients would be converts who lived in Rome at that time period, which implies that they would have lived through the reign of Claudius (AD 41–54) and into the reign of Nero (AD 59–68). One can assume that they had experienced not only past sufferings under Claudius[126] but also anticipated even more suffering under Nero[127] because of their Christian faith. The emergence of Christianity on the scene of the first-century Greco-Roman world meant hardship, persecution, social and economical isolation for Christians in general. As Everett Ferguson notes, idolatrous practices permeated all sectors of society and aspects of life, causing Jews and Christians to be at a severe social and political disadvantage. Syncretism was encouraged and polytheism was acceptable to the extent that monotheistic movements like Judaism and Christianity were hardly welcomed.[128] As far as the Jewish Christians were concerned, it was a period of troubles characterized by looting, imprisonments, ostracism, and even violence.[129]

While Roman authorities showed an attitude of tolerance for Christianity, they also demonstrated some general distaste for Christians. This is especially seen in a report by the Roman historian Tacitus, who refers to first-century Christianity as "a deadly superstition" and "mischief." He asserts that the "Christians were notoriously depraved," such that their guilt

---

124. Moule, reflecting on Nairne's commentary, observes that the outbreak of the Jewish War presented a crisis for the Hebrews' faith. It is against this background that Hebrews should be understood. He writes, "The outbreak of the Jewish war in AD 66 must have led to a great upsurge of Jewish nationalism. . . with the result that Jewish Christians would have been sorely tempted to rejoin the ranks of Orthodox Judaism from which they had come from" (Moule, "Commentaries on Hebrews," 228).

125. Also, Spicq observes, "Les données de l'Epître correspondent exactement aux circonstances qui caractérisèrent les prodromes de la guerre juive" (Spicq, *Hébreux: Introduction*, 259). See also Westcott, *Hebrews*, xxxviii.

126. For a detailed discussion of the state of Christianity in relation to Judaism under Claudius and the expulsion of the Jews from Rome, see Benko, "Edict of Claudius," 403–18. For further details, see Bruce, "Christianity under Claudius," 303–26. See also, Schürer, *History of Jewish People*, 3:76–78, 122.

127. For a discussion of the state of affairs under Nero, see Ferguson, "Religion, Greco-Roman," 1006–11.

128. Ibid., 1007. For this discussion, see also Thomas, "Case for a Mixed-Audience," 136.

129. For further details, see Spicq, *Hébreux: Introduction*, 259.

as Christians deserved "ruthless punishment" and their presence in Rome proved that all degraded and shameful practices flourished in the capital city of Rome.[130] Also, Pliny expressed some concern that Christianity was stealing people away from the state religion, referring to the Roman temples as having been deserted for a long time on account of Christianity.[131] However, from a general point of view, scholars believe that "the Romans usually left Christians alone,"[132] perhaps because they sensed no major threat to public order from first-century Christianity. This explains why the Apostle Paul was frequently able to escape accusations from his Jewish opponents even when the Roman authorities were aware of his religious activities. Also, Paul's status as a Roman citizen was more important than his religion. This does not imply that the Christians were always exempted from Roman persecution. From a socio-political point of view, the state of affairs during the reign of two Roman emperors—Claudius and Nero—is relevant to the timing of Hebrews.[133]

In AD 49, Claudius issued an edict expelling the Jews from the city of Rome.[134] Some conflicts had arisen in Alexandria opposing Jewish from non-Jewish communities. In Alexandria and other cities, Claudius admonished tolerance toward the Jews and their practices; in Rome, he took serious measures against them, apparently because conflicts had arisen among them.[135] Reporting on the Jews' expulsion from Rome, Suetonius says, "Since the Jews constantly made disturbances at the instigation of Chrestus, he [Claudius] expelled them from Rome."[136] Interpreters are not certain whether Suetonius is referring here to Jesus Christ or another figure in Rome. In his report, Suetonius refers to Chrestus as "a rabble rouser in Rome," and

---

130. Tacitus, *Annals*, XV. 44. For further details, see Jeffers, *Greco-Roman World*, 106.

131. Pliny, *Letters*, X. 96.

132. Jeffers, *Greco-Roman World*, 107.

133. The author of Hebrews points to early sufferings endured by the recipients and anticipated future sufferings (cf. Heb 10:32–35). Bible scholars believe that this description of early suffering is congruent with circumstances of those who suffered under the decree of expulsion by Claudius. Insults, public abuse, and even loss of property are all believed to have been normal circumstances under the conditions of an edict of expulsion. For further details, see Lane, "Social Perspectives on Roman Christianity," 217–18. Under Nero, the edict of Claudius was lifted, allowing the Jews to return to Rome. However, further persecution of Jewish believers arose at Nero's instigation, especially following a dreadful fire in which many Roman structures were consumed (AD 64). For further details, see Lohse, *New Testament Environment*, 205.

134. Benko, "Edict of Claudius," 403–18.

135. For further details, see Lohse, *New Testament Environment*, 204.

136. Suetonius, *Deified Claudius*, V. 25. 4; LCL, 53.

spells the name with an "e" instead of an "i" as *Chrestus* and not *Christus*.[137] It is generally acknowledged that the mention of "Chrestus" here is a reference to Jesus Christ.[138] This may justify the theory that one of the major reasons for the edict of Claudius was "the prevalence of a theological dispute among Jews of Rome which sometimes took on violent proportions."[139] Floyd V. Filson thinks it "possible and even probable that what happened in Rome was a series of riots or excited disputes between Jews who believed in Jesus as the Christ and Jews who rejected that claim."[140] The disruption may have been caused by Jewish believers in the Lord Jesus Christ who preached about their resurrected Messiah, causing some violent debates among Jewish communities,[141] which ended up attracting the unfavorable attention of the Roman imperial authorities.[142] C. Adrian Thomas reasons that one may infer from Suetonius' statement that the "earliest Roman Christianity was an inner-Jewish phenomenon and that the disorders he mentions were caused by controversy within the Jewish community about the truth or falsehood of the Christian message."[143]

If the contents in Hebrews can be seen as corresponding in one way or another with the circumstances of the Jewish War (AD 66–68), then an elucidation of the situation during this time becomes of a particular significance for understanding the message of Hebrews. As mentioned, this was a period of increasing trouble for the Jews and Jewish Christians. Historians

---

137. According to Lane, it was a popular practice in antiquity, especially among those who were not Christians, to interchange the two forms. In the manuscript tradition of the NT, the same confusion is reflected in the spelling of the name "Christian" in Acts 11:26; 26:28; and in 1 Peter 4:16. The uncial codex Sinaiticus (א) reads Χρηστιανός (i.e., *Chrestianos*). Early apologists anonymously agree that "pagans often confuse the two spellings, much to the dismay of the Christians" (see Justin, *Apology*, I. 4; Tertullian, *Apology*, 3; Lactantius, *Divine Institutes*, IV. 7). For further details, see also Lane, *Hebrews 1–8*, lxv; and Bruce, "Christianity under Claudius," 316.

138. For this discussion, see Thomas, "Case for a Mixed-Audience," 136.

139. For further details, see Benko, "Edict of Claudius," 409.

140. Accordingly, "Suetonius mistakenly thought that the riots were stirred up by a Roman Jew named Chrestus" (Filson, *New Testament History*, 66).

141. For the Roman authorities, there would not have been a distinction between Jews and Christians. Bruce explains this well: "Christianity under Claudius would not have been isolated from the fortunes of the Jewish people throughout the Empire during his reign" (Bruce, "Christianity under Claudius," 310). In other words, the lot of the Christians at this time was almost invariably cast with that of the Jews. This explains the case of Priscilla and Aquila (Acts 18:2) who were, ironically, evicted from Rome not for being Christians, but for being Jews. For this discussion, see also Thomas, "Case for a Mixed-Audience," 138.

142. Lane, "Hebrews," 448.

143. Thomas, "Case for a Mixed-Audience," 138.

connect these increasing troubles and persecution with the martyrdom of James,[144] also referred to as James the Just, who later became a leader in the Jerusalem church according to Jewish Christian tradition.[145] There is historical evidence that connects the Roman invasion of the Holy Land to Jewish persecution against the leaders of the church in Jerusalem.[146] According to Eusebius, all men considered James, the brother of the Lord, to be a man of great righteousness because of his Christian devotion and constant prayers for the forgiveness of people, so that "he became a true witness both to Jews and Greeks that Jesus is the Christ, right at the time when Vespasian began to besiege them."[147] Some scholars see the death of James and others, even before the siege, as leading to an increase in Jewish nationalism in Palestine and surrounding regions, resulting in provocative riots and inciting people to violence. This atmosphere of terrorism would lead to Roman intervention.

As part of the Roman intervention, Gessius Florus, the Roman procurator, confiscated seventeen talents from the temple's treasury and ordered a massacre of approximately 3,000 Jews around AD 66–67. This led to a revolt by the Jerusalem population, the killing of Roman guards, and an insurrection in all Judea and neighboring countries.[148] The Romans, under Gestius Gallus, attempted to reconquer Jerusalem but were scattered by the Jews

---

144. This James is said to be one of the sons of Mary, one of the women present at the crucifixion (Matt 27:56; Mark 16:1; Luke 24:10; see especially Mark 15:40, KJV). Some scholars think that he may have been called James the "less" or James the "young" because of his small stature. For this discussion, see Beardslee, "James," 791. Eusebius refers to him as James the Just and James, the brother of the Lord (Eusebius, *Ecclesiastical History*, II. 23. 3–18).

145. Jewish Christian tradition distinguishes "James the Less" from James, the brother of John, who was referred to as "James the Great," and a son of Zebedee.

146. Eusebius reports: "James was indeed a remarkable man and famous among all for righteousness, so that the wise even of the Jews thought that this [his martyrdom] was the cause of the siege of Jerusalem immediately after his martyrdom, and that it happened for no other reason than the crime which they had committed against him" (Eusebius, *Ecclesiastical History*, II. 23. 19–23; LCL, 177). Furthermore, he reports that the suffering endured by the Jews during the war against the Romans was ascribed by Josephus to God's vengeance for the death of James. However, there seems to be no such reference in Josephus' work, unless James the Less is to be identified as James, the brother of Jesus, in Josephus' account. See Josephus, *Jewish Antiquities*, LCL, 109.

147. Eusebius, *Ecclesiastical History*, II. 23. 14–18. Around AD 68, Vespasian followed Nero's order. He invaded the region of Galilee and became emperor following Nero's death. Later, his son Titus took the command of military operations that led to the control and destruction of Jerusalem on August 10, AD 70, after a seven-month siege. See also Spicq, *Hébreux: Introduction,* 260; and Eusebius, *Ecclesiastical History*, II. 23. 3–9.

148. Cf. Tacitus, *History,* V. 10.

under the leadership of Ananias, the high priest.[149] The troubles did not end there; more serious ones were anticipated not only in Jerusalem but also in Antioch, Ceasarea, and surrounding countries. The threat of calamity was very serious not only for the Jews but also for Jewish Christians in the whole Greco-Roman world. One example is the devastating fire in Rome and the blame Nero directed against the Christians as instigators, in spite of rumors that he himself had ordered the fire. Tacitus thus reports, "to scotch the rumors, Nero substituted as culprits and punished with the utmost refinement of cruelty, a class of men loathed for their vices, whom the crowd styled Christians."[150] This opened the door to intensified persecution around AD 68 and perhaps the beginning of some intense struggles that ultimately led to the destruction of Jerusalem under the military command of Titus on August 10, AD 70, after a seven-month siege.[151]

During the reign of Nero, the socio-political situation of the empire severely deteriorated. As Salevao notes, "More than anything else, Nero is remembered primarily for his cruelty and madness which, as Eusebius (cf. *Eccl. Hist.* 11. 25) described it, 'led him to the senseless destruction of innumerable lives,' including Peter and Paul in Rome."[152] Eventually, Nero took his own life by committing suicide, but prior to this, he had already murdered countless of others, especially Christians, Jews included.[153] Most scholars would agree that Hebrews is to be placed at the later end of this period of turbulence for the Christians in general and Hebrew believers in particular.[154]

This socio-political setting fits well with what one can understand from Hebrews about the experience of the readers. The author knew how great the threat was for those readers caught up in the midst of these

---

149. The high priest Ananias is said to be the one who executed James the Just (see Josephus, *Jewish Antiquities*, XX. 200. 223). For an account of Jewish troubles in Palestine and surrounding countries, see also ibid., *Jewish War*, IV. 288; IV. 289–315. Josephus reports there were already signs (or "divine warnings") announcing the threat of desolation. For further details, see ibid., IV. 289–315.

150. Tacitus, *Annals*, XV. 44; LCL, 283.

151. For further details, see Spicq, *Hébreux: Introduction*, 260.

152. Salevao, *Legitimation in Hebrews*, 125.

153. Most scholars agree that blame for the fire that swept through fourteen districts of Rome (July of AD 64) and caused accusations against Christians had no legal foundation except for greed and the senseless will of one man: Nero. Thus, Tacitus reports, "In spite of a guilt which had earned the most exemplary punishment, there arose a sentiment of pity due to the impression that they were being sacrificed not for the welfare of the state, but to the ferocity of a single man" (Tacitus, *Annals*, XV. 44).

154. For further details, see also Lane, "Social Perspectives on Roman Christianity," 215.

socio-political circumstances, especially in light of the growing troubles of AD 66–67. They had endured some trials and sufferings and could expect even more (Heb 10:32–34; 11:26; 13:13).[155] From the general tenor of Hebrews, one can argue that not only socio-political hostility but also alienation was a continuous circumstance for the Hebrew believers (cf. 3:6, 12–14; 4:14; 10:19–24; 12:1–29; 13:12–16). Prolonged suffering had weakened them to some extent,[156] causing a few serious effects on both their religious and spiritual lives.

Spiritual and Religious Setting

The overall impression from the text is that the community it addresses had experienced a socio-political threat that led to a crisis of faith. The text indicates the recipients had heard and made a commitment to the gospel (Heb 2:1–4; 3:1, 14; 10:23). They had demonstrated "the fruits that accompany salvation" (6:9), referred to in the text as their work and love for God, through their service on behalf of the saints (6:11; 10:39). For the most part, the recipients appear to have been true believers. This does not exclude the possibility that some among them were rebellious at heart and on the verge of the threat of "falling away."[157] It is possible, even probable, that some among the recipients may have been professing but not genuine believers. They had made a profession of faith in Jesus Christ "but were seriously considering returning to Judaism."[158]

From the text, it appears that the recipients endured suffering, including being "publicly exposed to abuse and affliction" (10:32, 33); they shared in the suffering of those in prison and joyfully accepted the loss of their

---

155. Lane notes that "the social history of the audience can be read in terms of its response to humiliation and public abuse" (Lane, *Hebrews 1–8*, lvii). The significance of the above passage is also alluded to in DeSilva's description as "a passage that sketched an intense experience of dishonor and rejection at the hands of society" (DeSilva, *Despising Shame*, 145).

156. Salevao, *Legitimation in Hebrews*, 132.

157. Arminian scholars would take "apostasy" here as a deliberate repudiation and abandonment of the Christian faith resulting in one's loss of salvation. Perhaps a better position is that some in the readership had made a profession of faith in Jesus Christ but had considered returning to Jewish rituals and legalism. Toussaint rightly posits that "they were about to abandon Christianity to slip back to the works system of Judaism" (see Toussaint, "Eschatology of the Warning Passages," 68). See also MacLeod, "Theology of Hebrews," 135, *contra* the Arminian view that a genuine believer could lose salvation.

158. Toussaint, "Eschatology of the Warning Passages," 68.

property (v. 34), which was an indication of their religious devotion.[159] As a result of continued suffering, they showed signs of spiritual lethargy or retrogression from their initial faith commitment to the gospel, which could then lead to final defection or apostasy.[160] The result of this spiritual lassitude was that some had forsaken their past commitment of faith and participation in regular community gatherings due to spiritual negligence (cf. Heb 10:25).[161] Those receiving the Epistle include the leaders of the community whose faith commitment is obvious and are represented as those who must be obeyed and submitted to (13:17) as well as those who have abandoned the regular gatherings of the assembly (cf. 10:25). Between these two extremes are others who showed a lack of interest. The recipients were not necessarily all at the same level of spiritual regression. Lane observes that within the house church addressed, some individuals were stronger than others, which is one reason why the author exhorts them to encourage one another (cf. 3:13; 10:25; 12:12–15).[162]

Generally, it appears the recipients exhibited signs of discouragement and weariness in their Christian walk of faith (12:1–4). It seems they forgot that their suffering was part of the Lord's discipline (12:5–12). They needed to refocus their attention on the Lord Jesus Christ (12:2) and to remember that discipline is a sign of divine Sonship (12:5–8). The context indicates that some had become lazy in their spiritual race of faith (5:11–14) and neglected to move on to "perfection" (6:1). For the author of Hebrews, the antidote for such spiritual lethargy was clear: pursue their τελειότης, "perfection, completeness," build themselves up in the basics of their faith, and persevere in Christian love and service (cf. 6:1–2, 10–12). The context supports the notion that the readers struggled with the general problem of ongoing trials and personal sins in their lives,[163] resulting in their need for

159. For further details, see Lane, *Hebrews 1–8*, 144.

160. Koester delineates three phases in the spiritual journey of the readers: first, they converted to Christianity through the proclamation of the gospel; second, they experienced some trials and persecution from non-believers who instigated hostilities against them; and third, they witnessed a time of friction and spiritual malaise that led to tendencies to neglect the faith and regular community gatherings (Koester, *Hebrews*, 64–72). According to Koester, it was perhaps during this third phase that the Epistle to the Hebrews was written.

161. For further details, see ibid., 72. Fanning describes their negligence as follows: "They were spiritually exhausted, weakened, and lame" and were in need of spiritual renewal in order "to run their race of endurance" (10:36; 12:1–2) (Fanning, "Theology of Hebrews," 408).

162. Lane, *Hebrews 1–8*, lvi. See also Thomas, "Case for a Mixed-Audience," 162.

163. Their struggle with personal sins is evidenced in Heb 13:1–5, which suggests a general waning of their Christian love (v. 1), lack of hospitality (v. 2), disregard for

forgiveness and the cleansing of their troubled consciences.[164] This problem exposed them to a temptation to return to the Jewish ritual system in the hope it would provide them with material cleansing to ease their consciences (9:9, 14; 10:2). In this case, the readers' temptation to return to the old sacrificial system looms behind the central argument of Hebrews (4:14–5:10; 7:1–10:31), in which the author presents a compelling case for the perfect or complete work of Christ as abiding and efficacious in perfecting the believers in order to bring them to their final eschatological glory.

The readers are called upon to pay close attention to what they have heard (2:1) and not to refuse the one (God) who is speaking (12:25), since this would amount to becoming like those of the unbelieving wilderness generation who rebelled against God and forfeited their promised rest (3:7–4:13). Such a refusal after having tasted the blessings of the gospel would indicate that one has forsaken the living God (3:12; 6:4–6). For the author of Hebrews, the spiritual condition of the recipients is critical. Their confidence in God's promise has been shaken, with the result that they are on the verge of hard-hearted unbelief and rebellion against God (cf. 3:6–14; 4:1, 11; 10:35–36; 12:25).[165] Thus, the author of Hebrews sends his "word of exhortation" (ὁ λόγος τῆς παρακλήσεως, 13:22) to the Hebrew believers in or around Rome in order to build their hope in the better things that are yet to come. The literary nature and conceptual background of Hebrews thought should be understood in the light of this setting.

LITERARY CHARACTER AND MESSAGE OF HEBREWS

The author speaks of Hebrews as a "word of exhortation"[166] (Heb 13:22), leading many students of the Bible to view it more as a written sermon than a letter.[167] It becomes crucial to examine the literary genre of this piece of writing in an attempt to understand how well this concept fits with the message of Hebrews.

---

prisoners (v. 3), lack of sexual purity (v. 4), and the growing love of money (v. 5). For further details, see also Thomas, "Case for a Mixed-Audience," 163.

164. Fanning, "Theology of Hebrews," 406.

165. For further details, see ibid.

166. If τοῦ λόγου τῆς παρακλήσεως means a homily as in Acts 13:15, then there is a possibility that the structure of Hebrews owes its origin to an earlier sermon that was adapted into a letter form with some addition of personal comments at the end. For this discussion, see Guthrie, *Letter to the Hebrews*, 31.

167. For a discussion of Greek style, rhetoric, and literary structure, see Witherington, *Letters and Homilies for Jewish Christians*, 138–346.

Literary Genre of Hebrews

The message of Hebrews must be regarded as fitting with the literary genre of the book.[168] The question of genre presents some problems. Hebrews does not appear to be a letter or an epistle,[169] because it lacks the epistolary salutation and thanksgiving formula found in NT letters or epistles. While the author includes an epistolary postscript common to other NT letters, some commentators question its originality by claiming it was added at a later date.[170] Traditionally, if Hebrews is to be placed among the Pauline letters, then the issue becomes even more complicated. For this reason, the following classifications are examined: (1) Hebrews as a midrash, (2) Hebrews as a written homily or sermon, and (3) Hebrews as a letter or epistle.

Hebrews as a Midrash

Some commentators contend the author of Hebrews uses the midrashic method of exegesis that was basic to Jewish Christian understanding of the role of Scripture in their religious life.[171] By "midrash" commentators mean "a method of Jewish scriptural exegesis that was common in rabbinical Judaism,"[172] and consisted of "an actualization of the biblical text, applied to a particular situation that occasioned it."[173] A common feature of the

---

168. According to some scholars, the literary genre and its relationship to the contents and purpose of Hebrews is not clear at all. For further details, see Koester, *Introduction to the New Testament*, 277. For an examination of problems faced with the classification into genres of NT writings, especially Hebrews, see Ellingworth, *Hebrews*, 59–62.

169. Attridge notes there are discrepancies between the opening of Hebrews and its conclusion, which presents a "literary riddle" to many commentators (Attridge, *Hebrews*, 13).

170. Mitchell states that "not every commentator has been confident that it was part of the original document" (Mitchell, *Hebrews*, 13). As some scholars would indicate, the integrity of chapter 13 has been substantially demonstrated and is generally assumed. Attridge states, "The conclusion is not an afterthought or a secondary addition by an interpolator's hand, but is part of the literary plan of the whole work, a device that makes the elaborate rhetorical exercise of Hebrews suitable for delivery at a distance" (Attridge, *Hebrews*, 405).

For further details, see also Spicq, "L'Authenticité du chapître XIII d'Hébreux," 226–36. See also, Filson, *"Yesterday": A Study of Hebrews*, 226–36; and Tasker, "Integrity of Hebrews," 136–38.

171. For example, see Buchanan, *To the Hebrews*, ix-xxi.

172. Mitchell, *Hebrews*, 16.

173. Ibid. The practice of midrash was a central feature of rabbinic interpretation aimed at uncovering the deeper meanings the rabbis assumed were inherent in the

midrashic method of exegesis would be citing one or several OT Scriptures and applying them to a given situation such as those found in Hebrews. It is for this reason that George Wesley Buchanan refers to Hebrews as a "homiletical midrash,"[174] which is based on Ps 110.[175] Elke Tönges is not convinced by this categorization of Hebrews, but rather sees in Hebrews what she calls a "Jesus midrash," meaning that though the author uses a Jewish method of Scriptural interpretation, his midrashic exposition is different; it is Christological.[176]

Classifying Hebrews as "midrash" has not been popular among modern commentators.[177] The problem with this hypothesis is the lack of documentary evidence in support of reading Hebrews either as a "homiletical midrash" or "Jesus midrash." The suggestions by Buchanan and Tönges should be considered with some degree of caution. There is no clear evidence that would support one's reading of Hebrews as midrash in the context of a synagogue worship service. Also, there is no evidence that would point to Hebrews conforming to the later midrashic form of a homily.[178]

Hebrews as a Written Homily or Sermon

There is a growing consensus among scholars that Hebrews should be read as a written homily or sermon.[179] A major argument for this view is that the author of Hebrews refers to the literary character of Hebrews as τοῦ λόγου

---

actual wording of Scriptures. Ultimately, the rabbis' motive was pastoral—to provide some logical biblical principles for situations not directly covered in Scriptures. For this discussion, see also Klein, Blomberg, and Hubbard, *Introduction to Biblical Interpretation*, 24.

174. For further details, see Buchanan, *To the Hebrews*, xxi. According to Buchanan, similar examples are found in Philo, namely: *On the Creation of the World, Allegorical Interpretation, On the Cherubim, The Tower of Babel, Moses,* and *The Ten Commandments*.

175. "Homiletic midrashim" are defined as "sermons or essays which expound important subjects or texts in the Old Testament" (Buchanan, *To the Hebrews*, xxi); cf. Heb 1–12.

176. For details, see Tonges, "Hebrews as a 'Jesus Midrash,'" 90.

177. Ellingworth, *Hebrews*, 61.

178. Mitchell, *Hebrews*, 16–17.

179. For instance, Lane remarks, "Hebrews is a sermon prepared in response to a crisis of faith" (Lane, *Hebrews: Call to Commitment*, 27). Attridge defines this category more technically as a "paraclesis," a subgenre of the more "generic classification of paraenesis," in which "exhortation is grounded in exposition and application of traditional materials" (Attridge, "Paraenesis in a Homily," 223).

τῆς παρακλήσεως a "word of exhortation" (Heb 13:22).[180] The phrase "word of exhortation" is descriptive for a sermon or homily following the reading from the Law and the Prophets in the synagogue service.[181] For instance, when the Apostle Paul is asked to provide a word of exhortation (τοῦ λόγου τῆς παρακλήσεως) in the synagogue at Pisidian Antioch (Acts 13:15), he stands and delivers a sermon or homily.[182] Some scholars believe there is nothing in Hebrews that would not have been spoken by a preacher to an audience,[183] except perhaps for the postscript, which is typical of any other epistolary writing of the NT. As far as the literary characteristics of Hebrews are concerned, Hartwig Thyen refers to the book as "the only example of a completely preserved homily."[184] Such characteristics include "homiletic language marked by a communal tone, the use of the LXX as a source, the introduction of Scriptural citations with rhetorical questions, and the use of paraenesis and exhortation."[185]

If ὁ λόγος τῆς παρακλήσεως means a "homily" or "sermon" as found in Acts 13:15, then the structure of Hebrews may owe its origin to an earlier sermon that was perhaps adapted into a letter form with some additional personal comments at the end.[186] Lawrence Wills uses Acts 13:14–41 plus other illustrations from Hellenistic Jewish and other early Christian sources as models to show that there is a discernible pattern establishing the form of this "word of exhortation." Wills shows how this developed into the form of a sermon in Hellenistic synagogues.[187] His conclusion is that in the case

180. For further details, see Guthrie, *New Testament Introduction*, 722; and Bruce, *Hebrews*, xlviii.

181. For further details, see Lane, *Hebrews: Call to Commitment*, 18.

182. The descriptive (τοῦ λόγου τῆς παρακλήσεως) "word of exhortation" in Heb 13:22 is seen by many scholars as one way to describe a "synagogue homily." For further details, see Koester, *Hebrews*, 80–81. In her recent work, Gelardini also refers to Hebrews as a "synagogue homily" with its *sitz im leben* being the Sabbath gathering (Gelardini, "Hebrews, an Ancient Synagogue Homily," 108). Wills critically examines Acts 13 and suggests that it contains features consistent to a sermon labeled a "word of exhortation." For further details, see Wills, "Form of Sermon in Hellenistic Judaism," 277–99.

183. Lane observes, "When we read Hebrews we are exposing ourselves to early Christian preaching" (Lane, *Hebrews: Call to Commitment*, 17). For further support of this view, see Bruce, *Commentary*, xlviii; Moffatt, *Introduction*, 428; Jewett, *Hebrews*, 241; Filson, *Hebrews*, 20; Swetnam, *Hebrews*, 261–69; and Lane, "Hebrews: Sermon in Search of a Setting," 13–18.

184. Thyen, *Der Stil des judisch-hellenistischen Homilie*, 106.

185. Ibid. For further details, see also Vanhoye, *Homilie für haltbedurftige Christen*, 11.

186. For this discussion, see Guthrie, *Letter to the Hebrews*, 31.

187. Wills, "Form of the Sermon," 293.

of repeated cycles (like in Hebrews), the assumption that the form of a sermon lies behind the texts is compelling.[188] Similarly, in the body of the text referred to in its conclusion as a "word of exhortation" [ὁ λόγος τῆς παρακλήσεως (Heb 13:22; cf. Acts 15:32)], Attridge sees what he terms "an epideictic oration" similar to Aristotle's style,[189] but he specifically refers to Hebrews as a sermon or homily.[190]

In spite of the growing consensus that Hebrews should be read as a homily or a sermon, many other scholars think this classification is too vague to be applied with certainty to Hebrews. For Helmut Koester, the classification of Hebrews as a written homily or a sermon "is too vague in terms of literary genre, although it certainly contains a good deal of homiletical material in the style of Jewish diaspora preaching."[191] Perhaps Ben Witherington III is correct when he concludes that Hebrews should be seen as "a situation-specific homily" addressed as a letter to Jewish Christians in or around Rome, who had endured the trauma of persecution in that city since AD 49.[192] There seems to be some agreement among scholars that Hebrews was delivered first as a sermon and perhaps put in a written form (as a letter) at a later date.

Hebrews as a Letter or Epistle

Hebrews does not begin as most NT letters or epistles normally do. The book lacks the identification of the author and the recipients.[193] However, its final chapter contains epistolary characteristics like other NT epistles. The issue becomes whether one can confidently call Hebrews a letter or an epistle in the same way one will normally refer to NT letters such as Romans or Ephesians. Most early commentators including Henry Alford,[194] Alexander Nairne,[195] J. Dickie[196] had no doubts about the identification of Hebrews as a letter or epistle, because of their shared understanding that Hebrews was sent as a letter to a specific group, but also because of its clos-

---

188. Ibid., 299. For further details, see also Lane, *Hebrews 1–8*, lxxiii.

189. Aristotle, *Rhetoric*, I. 3. 1358b.

190. Attridge, *Hebrews*, 14. For further details, see ibid., "Paraenesis in a Homily," 211–26.

191. Koester, *Introduction to the New Testament*, 277.

192. Witherington, *Letters and Homilies*, 32.

193. For this discussion, see Hagner, *Encountering the Book of Hebrews*, 29–30.

194. Alford, *Greek New Testament*, 62.

195. Nairne, *Epistle of Priesthood*, 10–11.

196. Dickie, "Literary Riddle of Hebrews," 374.

ing chapter (Heb 13) which has some epistolary features, including personal information, greetings, a doxology, and a benediction.[197] Adolf Deissmann, attempting to distinguish between a letter and an epistle, classifies Hebrews as an epistle (a tract or treatise) addressed to the church in general.[198] For many scholars, there are specific references in Hebrews that point to a local group,[199] rather than a general audience, a position that argues against Deissmann's view of Hebrews as a universal tract for a general audience. Franz Delitzsch observes, "We seem to have a treatise before us, but the specific hortatory references interwoven with the most discursive and dogmatic portions of the work soon show us that it is really a kind of a sermon addressed to some particular and well-known auditory; while the close of the homiletic form (the *Paraclesis*) changes into that of an epistle. . ."[200]

There are other substantial arguments supporting the view of Hebrews as a letter or an epistle. Spicq emphasizes the inclusion of hortatory sections of Hebrews and shows how they are typical of a letter or epistle.[201] If it is true that Hebrews is addressed to a specific group or community, then this would imply the text is meant to be read as an epistle or letter.[202] This would shed light on the reason why Hebrews was included in collections of the Pauline Epistles or letters from an early date. While it is true that Hebrews appears more as a homily or a sermon than a typical letter (or epistle), many expositors also believe that Hebrews should also be read as a letter (or epistle).[203] This phenomenon is not strange to the NT epistolary writings. For instance, the First Epistle of John does not begin like a typical letter nor end like one. On the other hand, the Epistle of James begins like a typical NT letter but does not conclude like one.[204] Lastly, the final chapter of Hebrews indicates that the book is meant to be read as a letter (or epistle).[205] Assuming the

---

197. For further details, see Doty, *Letters in Primitive Christianity*, 1–81.

198. Deissmann, *Bible Studies*, 49–55 (cf. Deissmann, *New Testament in the Light of Modern Research*, 51–2). His view is adopted by Jon M. Isaak, who argues that Hebrews was composed as a normal literary product aimed at a general audience (Isaak, *Situating Hebrews in Early Christian History*, 54–55).

199. Filson, "Epistle to the Hebrews," 20.

200. Delitzsch, *Hebrews*, 1:3–4.

201. Spicq, *Hébreux: Introduction*, 21–22.

202. Mitchell, *Epistle to the Hebrews*, 13–14.

203. For further details, see Hagner, *Encountering Hebrews*, 29.

204. Mitchell, *Epistle to the Hebrews*, 14.

205. Some have gone further by referring to Hebrews as an "encyclical letter" arguing that it contains characteristics that are typical of NT encyclical. See, for example, Dunnill, *Covenant and Sacrifice in Hebrews*, 22.

integrity of Heb 13,²⁰⁶ the implication is that several exhortations point to a specific community to which Hebrews was addressed. Such specific exhortations include the commands to remember their former leaders (13:7), imitate their life of faith (13:7), and obey and submit to their current leaders (13:17). This implies a vested concern of the author. From 13:18–19, there is an indication that he belongs to the community, perhaps one of its leaders. While he may be absent from among them, he hopes to "be restored to them soon." This can be substantiated from both the benediction (13:20–21) and the postscript (vv. 22–25) as an indication of some personal knowledge and close ties between the author and recipients. As Ellingworth suggests, the mention of Timothy (13:23) also speaks volumes to the readers; yet, until he is joined to them, his λόγος τῆς παρακλήσεως is sufficient enough as a substitute for his presence.²⁰⁷

While Hebrews lacks the formal characteristics of a letter (or epistle), the epistolary elements replicated in its final chapter (Heb 13) should be regarded as contributing to its functioning as an epistle.²⁰⁸ The book, which includes an appropriate epistolary ending, can be regarded as a "carefully constructed treatise like sermon"²⁰⁹ written by the author; like other NT epistles it was written to a specific community of believers who were facing a serious crisis of faith.

Conceptual Background of Hebrews

Understanding the issue of Hebrews' conceptual background or the origin of Hebrews' thought is significant in order to appreciate the full-orbed meaning of the τέλειος concept in Hebrews.²¹⁰ The major issue over the years is whether the conceptual influence behind Hebrews' thought and theology is mainly philosophical (Platonic, Philonic, or Hellenistic Philosophy)²¹¹ or Jewish apocalyptic-eschatological.²¹² Platonic influence, as stated earlier,

---

206. As Attridge comments, there are "no good reasons for attributing the conclusion [of Hebrews] to a second hand" (Attridge, *Epistle to the Hebrews*, 13).

207. Ellingworth, *Hebrews*, 60. See also Thomas, "Case for a Mixed-Audience," 158.

208. For this discussion, see Ellingworth, *Hebrews*, 62. See also Lindars, *Theology of Hebrews*, 6–7.

209. Hagner, *Encountering Hebrews*, 30.

210. For a standard work providing a good analysis and survey of various posited backgrounds, see Hurst, *Hebrews: Its Background of Thought*, 7–133.

211. See Thompson, *Beginnings of Christian Philosophy*, 15–16.

212. Barrett, "Eschatology of Hebrews," 363–93; Hurst, "Eschatology and 'Platonism' in Hebrews," 41–74; and Hurst, *Epistle to the Hebrews*, 131–33.

has been the most popular conceptual background posited for Hebrews' thought. This assumption is based on the alleged link and similarities between Hebrews and the Platonic theory of ideas. A. H. McNeile argues, "Hebrews conceptual basis is the Platonic theory of ideas."[213] The same approach is embraced by Moffat who asserts, "The philosophical element in the author's view of the world and God is fundamentally Platonic."[214] Thus, Aelred Cody warns interpreters against "forcing Hebrews to speak in terminology and categories quite foreign to its own brand of Platonism."[215] Most scholars in this camp argue for a Platonic influence either directly or as mediated by the Philonic approach.[216]

The first half of the twentieth century saw the emergence of the Philonic conceptual approach to the study of Hebrews. This view reached its apex in 1952 with Spicq's massive commentary that was considered to be a *tour de force* probing vocabulary, hermeneutical techniques, psychology, and special parallels between Hebrews and Philo of Alexandria. The author's use of the argument from silence about Melchizedek was of particular significance for Spicq to whom the lack of genealogy is theologically important, since Philo uses the same argument in other connections.[217] Spicq's conclusion was that the author of Hebrews was a Philonian, converted to Christianity, and even suggested that the author knew Philo personally, and was trained by him.[218] For many scholars, although Spicq's work represents a climax of over fifty years' case for Platonic, Philonic, or philosophical influence behind Hebrews' thought, his plea for a direct dependence has failed.[219] Thus, Lincoln D. Hurst suggests the linguistic similarities between Plato/Philo and Hebrews have been exaggerated.[220] This conclusion is corroborated by

---

213. McNeile, *New Testament Teaching*, 222.

214. Moffatt, *Epistle to the Hebrews*, xxxi.

215. Cody, *Heavenly Sanctuary and Liturgy*, 3.

216. Other scholars, however, refer to this more broadly in terms of Hellenistic philosophy. For this approach, see Thompson, *Beginnings of Christian Philosophy*, 15–16.

217. Cf. Philo, *Allegorical Interpretation*, I. 60, 79–82. For a complete analysis of Melchizedek in Philo and Hebrews, see Williamson, *Philo and Hebrews*, 434–49.

218. Spicq, *Hébreux: Introduction*, 91. Also, see Thompson, who argues that the author's dualistic reading of the OT, the use of Hellenistic terminology, such as in Heb 7:3 and the focus on the abiding, have their closest analogies in Philo (Thompson, *Beginnings of Christian Philosophy*, 127).

219. Hurst argues, "The work of Hanson, Barrett and Williamson ended any thoroughgoing form of the Platonic/Philonic approach to Hebrews" (Hurst, *Epistle to the Hebrews*, 41). Some modified approaches have continued to flourish.

220. Ibid., 42.

Ronald Williamson's detailed study of the linguistic similarities, themes, and ideas and the use of Scripture in Philo and Hebrews.[221]

The work of C. K. Barrett was a turning point in Hebrews conceptual scholarship. *Contra* the alleged influence of Platonic dualism on Hebrews, Barrett stressed the central role of eschatology in Hebrews. Although the author of Hebrews used a language that could have been understood by Plato and Philo, many of the features in Hebrews were derived from currents within Jewish apocalyptic-eschatology.[222] This is in accord with an observation in the second chapter of this study that several features in Hebrews particularly align with a Jewish background. For instance, if it is true that the recipients were almost certainly Jewish Christians, then this fits well with such features in the text that particularly align with a Jewish background.

Among the literary influences on Hebrews' thought, the OT was primary. However, the author not only adopts Jewish traditions, he presents them in an elaborate masterpiece using the Greek translation of the Hebrew Scripture. Since the eschatological perspective is the underlying motive, the author uses extensive details of OT features, especially its cultic system, in order to present a comprehensive adaptation of the OT prophetic-eschatological image and motif of the Hebrew Scripture. For this reason, the author of Hebrews does not refer to non-Jewish traditions, nor quote Greek or Roman literature, but rather he extensively uses the Hebrew Scripture as the word of God.[223] The author sees himself and the recipients as living in the last days as described in the exordium of Heb 1:2: ἐπ' ἐσχάτου τῶν ἡμερῶν,[224] "at the end of these days," a common conviction for authors of the NT and Jewish apocalyptic texts.[225]

For the author of Hebrews, history is divided into two ages: the present and the age to come (Heb 6:5, μέλλοντος αἰῶνος).[226] The message is connection with Ps 95 (94 LXX), cited in Heb 3–4 pronouncing the nearness of the *eschaton*: "Today, if you hear his voice, do not harden your heart as in rebellion. . . ," less you forfeit to enter God's rest. The enthronement psalm, which the author cites, carries an eschatological theme of the anticipated

---

221. Williamson concludes, "In the realm of vocabulary, there is no proof that the choice of words displayed in the Epistle to the Hebrews has been influenced by Philo's thesaurus" (Williamson, *Philo and Hebrews*, 576).

222. Barrett, "Eschatology of Hebrews," 363–93. For further details, see Hurst, *Epistle to the Hebrews*, 13–42.

223. Tönges, "Hebrews as a 'Jesus-Midrash,'" 100.

224. For text-critical remarks, see Attridge, *Epistle to the Hebrews*, 35.

225. Tönges, "Epistle to the Hebrews," 100.

226. Ibid.

rest which is yet to come.²²⁷ Furthermore, the author's treatment of the OT *cultus* as found in the Pentateuch serves as background for his argument about the finality of the perfected Christ both as High Priest and sacrifice. Also, Psalms 2, 45, and 110 play a key role in the author's development of his thought,²²⁸ with a focus on the eternal nature of Christ's ministry and his eschatological rule.²²⁹ This is also supported by the author's use of the new covenant text of Jer 31:31–34 which he cites extensively in the eighth chapter. Clearly, the author is influenced primarily by his Jewish background and uses Jewish scriptures, which he interprets as the word of God, giving them a messianic-eschatological significance.

Occasion and Purpose of Hebrews

Many interpreters believe that the recipients of Hebrews consisted of members of a household and their close associates or friends. This group may have been one of a number of specific groups scattered throughout the districts of the city of Rome.²³⁰ The group had experienced some crisis of faith characterized by defections from regular Christian gatherings (Heb 10:25), loss of confidence in the viability of their convictions, and lack of interest in the message of salvation, which they had previously embraced (2:1–4) and had formerly given them a sense of identity as the new covenant people of God. Yet, the author indicates some of the readers are no longer listening to God's message in the Scripture (2:1; 3:7–4:13; 5:11; 12:25). He describes them as lethargic and disheartened (5:11; 6:12; 12:3, 12–13), and weary (12:3–14). They are interested in traditional ritualism that conflicts with the message of the gospel (13:7–9); this has led to tension within the community (13:1, 17–18). The recipients are faced with additional problems including social ostracism, impending persecutions (12:4; 13:13–14), a general waning of enthusiasm, and erosion of confidence (3:14; 10:35).

Furthermore, the community has experienced a crisis of faith evidenced in faltering hope (3:6; 6:18–20; 10:23–25; 11:1). The author indicates

227. Toussaint, "Eschatology of the Warning Passages," 73.

228. For further details, see Kistemaker, *Psalm Citations in Hebrews*, 13–151.

229. These are combined with Nathan's oracle regarding the Davidic dynasty (2 Sam 7:14; cf. 1 Chr 17:13) pointing to the major thrust of the author's argument: the superiority of the perfected Christ and his role as the author of salvation. For further details, see Oyediran, "Lexical and Exegetical Analysis," 103–104.

230. As Lane states, the recipients "are undoubtedly a small group, consisting of members of a household and some of their associates and close friends, and whose theological vocabulary and conception were informed by the rich legacy of Hellenistic Judaism" (Lane, *Hebrews 1–8*, liv).

that some members are in great danger of turning away from God (3:12). Doing so would subject the Lord Jesus Christ to public contempt (10:26–31) because of doubt regarding the efficacy of his sacrifice on the cross. According to Hebrews, such behaviors are in complete violation of their covenant fidelity and would entail exclusion from covenant fellowship. The author is deeply concerned that members of the household church would reject the grace of God and forfeit their participation in the new covenant community because of personal carelessness (3:12–15; 4:1, 11; 6:4–8, 11; 10:26–31; 12:15–17, 25–29).[231]

In the midst of such a crisis of faith, the author sends his ὁ λόγος τῆς παρακλήσεως to the Hebrew believers to help them appreciate the hope of their eschatological salvation in Christ. In order to accomplish this goal, the author exhorts the readers to "hold fast to their confession" and not give up their hope in the better promises of the new covenant that have been made possible through Jesus' perfect sacrifice in bringing to completion the Abrahamic promises to them.[232] In view of the threat they face, the author seeks to remove all danger of apostasy while bringing hope and comfort to his readers in the midst of their trials.[233] Through his exposition of Scripture, the author presents the τελείωσις of Christ (Heb 2:10; 7:22, 25, 28 and 9:28) as a pledge for the abiding efficacy of his sacrificial work. It also points to his perfect ability to intercede on behalf of the believers in the process toward the goal of their τελείωσις, complete access to God. The author presents Christ as the pioneer and cause of eternal salvation. As the perfected High Priest, Christ has been made the new definitive agent of God's eschatological revelation and the source of eternal salvation based on the better promises of the new covenant that he mediates.

Therefore, to the Hebrew believers or those tempted to return to Jewish traditions and ritualism, the author seeks to denounce the impotence and inability of the old economy for securing their perfection or complete access to God. The author shows that such τελείωσις ("perfection") for the worshipers cannot be attained through the sacrifices of the Levitical priesthood (7:11), since "the Law made nothing perfect" (7:19). The Levitical sacrifices under the old economy can never "make perfect those who draw near" (10:1). By contrast, the one sacrifice of Jesus is permanently effective

---

231. For this discussion, see ibid., 61–73. See also Verbrugge, "Towards New Interpretation of Hebrews 6:4–6," 61–73.

232. Buchanan notes that the author exhorts the recipients to come to the promised land just as Abraham did, and if they do not lose hope, they will receive their promised rewards. See Buchanan, *To the Hebrews*, 267.

233. Spicq, *Hébreux: Introduction*, 260. For further details, see also Weiss, *Der Brief an die Hebräer*, 33.

"to perfect for all time those who are being sanctified" (10:14).[234] For this reason, the high priestly ministry of the Son as the perfected High Priest revealed in the new economy is far more superior than the old economy not only because the sphere of its service is in the heavenly sanctuary and true tabernacle,[235] but also because he is the Mediator of the new covenant enacted on better promises that guarantee complete access to God.

The author of Hebrews shows that the Son as the perfected High Priest, the supreme and definitive example of perfection, enables believers to walk in faith and hope as those who have attained the same perfection even as they share now in similar trials. The perfecting of Christ becomes of deciding importance for the perfecting of the believers. Such τελείωσις for the believers, while conceived as a present reality, it remains a future reality to be fully realized at the second coming of Christ when all the better promises of the new covenant will be realized. In his extensive exposition of numerous OT passages, the author sets out his message to prove that the Mosaic system of worship with all its limitations or failures has been superseded by the new covenant of which the perfected Christ is the Mediator bringing many sons to their eschatological glory—full, complete, and uninhibited access to God in eternal glory.

Literary Structure of Hebrews

The literary structure of a text is significant because "it affects one's understanding of how the book is to be divided and of the author's development of his argument."[236] One's appreciation of the literary framework of Hebrews is a key element for proper interpretation of its message. Vanhoye summarizes this well when he states "One must figure out the structural composition of the work as a whole in order to correctly understand the message of Hebrews."[237] Validating his statement, he further notes that "each part receives its precise meaning only when it is situated in its place in the whole."[238] While most scholars see in Hebrews a high level of literary

---

234. For this discussion, see also Lindars, *Theology of Hebrews*, 45.

235. The tabernacle is described here as τῆς τελειοτέρας (Heb 9:11). The comparative degree of the adjectival form of τέλειος denotes the completeness of the true Tabernacle in contrast to the imperfection (inefficacy) and failures of the former to effect eternal salvation for the Hebrew believers.

236. MacLeod, "Literary Structure of Hebrews," 185–97. He provides a concise discussion of the traditional approach to the structure of Hebrews and summarizes contemporary contributions to the discussion.

237. Vanhoye, *Structure and Message of Hebrews*, 18.

238. Ibid. Vanhoye's work is a one-volume publication of two of his previous

artistry,[239] they disagree on its major divisions, subdivisions, and the literary development of its argument. Many of the scholarly proposals tend to overlook the coherence of Hebrews' argument, suggesting a relatively low level of cohesion in the discourse.[240] If it is true that Hebrews is a literary masterpiece, then it is also true that a literary masterpiece must present an identifiable argument or a clear line of thought. As David Alan Black discerns, there must be relative cohesiveness and coherence in the literary development of Hebrews argument.[241]

The major approaches to the literary structure of Hebrews have included the following:

> (1) the conceptual approach (i.e. content analysis), (2) the literary approach, sometimes distinguished from the rhetorical analysis, (3) the "patchwork" approach, (4) the tripartite structure, and (5) the text-linguistic approach.[242]

Traditionally, scholars have followed the "conceptual"/"thematical" (content analysis) approach in their inquiry into the structure of Hebrews. Commentators who follow this approach structure the book into two major sections. One section is mainly doctrinal (Heb 1:5–10:18) and the other section is mainly paraenetic or practical exhortation (10:19–13:19).[243] Generally, scholars[244] who follow the traditional approach believe that these two major divisions are held together by a brief but polished introductory prologue (1:1–4) and a brief concluding epilogue (13:20–25). While the focus seems to be on the two major sections, it is significant to realize the major sections can be subdivided into two or more subdivisions as indicated in the follow-

---

booklets: (1) Vanhoye, *Structured Translation of Hebrews*, and (2) ibid., *Message de l'Épître aux Hébreux*, translated here in a slightly reedited format by James Swetnam.

239. Westfall, *Discourse Analysis Hebrews*, xi.

240. Ibid.

241. Black, "Problem of the Literary Structure," 163–77.

242. For a complete survey of the literature on the structure of Hebrews, see Westfall, *Discourse Analysis of Hebrews*, 1–21. See also, Guthrie, *Structure of Hebrews*, 3–147.

243. Some modifications may be observed among these scholars. For example, (1) doctrinal section (1:5–10:39) and (2) the practical section (11:1–13:19), or (1) doctrinal section (1:5–10:18), and (2) practical exhortation (10:19–13:7 or 13:19 or 13:25).

244. For examples: Westcott, *Epistle to the Hebrews*, xlviii–l; Nairne, *Epistle to the Hebrews*, xi–xii; Robinson, *Epistle to the Hebrews*, 52–54; Héring, *Epistle to the Hebrews*, xvi; Hiebert, *Introduction to the New Testament*, 92–100; and Guthrie, *Letter to the Hebrews*, 58–59. See also, Robert and Feuillet, *Introduction to the New Testament*, 537. This approach dominated much of conservative Protestant scholarship about fifty years ago. For further details on the traditional approach and major developments, see MacLeod, "The Literary Structure," 185–97.

ing lines. Most proponents of the traditional view do not reject the presence of paraenetic passages within the doctrinal sections and the presence of doctrinal contributions within the paraenetic sections.[245]

Scholars who do not agree with the traditional approach suggest the scheme stretches the outline too far in order to maintain the overall theme of Christ's superiority. Cynthia Long Westfall proposes that the traditional approach "fails to account adequately for the semantic content and formal significance of the commands in the first six chapters."[246] However, for many students of Hebrews, there seems to be some validity in the traditional approach in that, when contrasted to other non-thematic theories in nature, it is the only approach that highlights major thematic features of Hebrews. Therefore, the traditional approach is in a better position to help the readers appreciate not only the overall interrelationship between the major sections and subsections, but also a unified theme and overall message of the book as a whole.[247]

The purported presence of Hellenistic literary and rhetorical devices[248] in Hebrews has led some scholars to argue for a literary or rhetorical approach to the structure of Hebrews emphasizing Greek literary form and traditions. Such scholars as Attridge,[249] David E. Aune,[250] and C. Clifton Black[251] refer to Hebrews as epideictic rhetoric, since the contrasting patterns it draws between Christ and other entities or persons form one of the distinctive characters of the book. Accordingly, not only the rhetorical impact on the readers, but also "the oral nature of the discourse and its possible sermonic nature" are of great significance in determining a structural

---

245. For further details, see MacLeod, "Literary Structure," 186.

246. Westfall, *Discourse Analysis of Hebrews*, 3.

247. The outline followed in this study is based on the traditional approach, seeing two major divisions with a recognition of some contributions by other scholarly approaches, especially the "literary" or "rhetorical" approach by Vanhoye and the text-linguistic approach of G. H. Guthrie, based on the relatively new discipline of discourse analysis (Vanhoye, *Structure and Message of Hebrews*, 1–109; Guthrie, *Structure of Hebrews*, 1–147).

248. For a catalogue of literary or rhetorical devices in Hebrews, see Spicq, *L'Épître aux Hébreux*, 351–78.

249. Attridge, *Epistle to the Hebrews*, 14.

250. Aune, *New Testament and Its Literary Environment*, 212.

251. Black, "Rhetorical Form," 5.

paradigm for Hebrews.[252] Barnabas Lindars,[253] on the other hand, refers to Hebrews as deliberative rhetoric, but he sees the discourse entirely from the point of view of its intended effect on the readers.

The most elaborate approach to the structure of Hebrews is perhaps the literary analysis by Vanhoye,[254] who sees a carefully crafted chiastic structure that is "repeatedly interwoven by key words which appear at the beginning of a section and then reappear at or very near to the close of the section,"[255] thus producing a detailed synthetic structure that is considered unique by many scholars. For instance, Lane states: "I am eager to acknowledge my reliance upon the work of Vanhoye even when the analysis of the literary structure that I propose differs from his own."[256] In his approach, Vanhoye presents a chiastic structure of five concentric sections[257] with several subsections to show how the author of Hebrews wrote his masterpiece using some "structuralizing techniques" as a result of his Jewish-Hellenistic education. For Vanhoye, these techniques or literary devices include: (1) announcement of the subject, (2) inclusions indicating boundaries of units, (3) variations of literary genre such as exposition or paraenesis, (4) words

---

252. For this discussion, see Westfall, *Discourse Analysis of Hebrews*, 4–5. For further suggestions on the oral nature of Hebrews, see Lane, *Hebrews 1–8*, lxxv. For a detailed discussion of the author's usage of rhetorical figures such as alliteration, anaphora, antithesis, assonance, asyndeton, chiasm, ellipsis, isocolon, and others, see Attridge, *Epistle to the Hebrews*, 20–21.

253. Lindars, "Rhetorical Structure of Hebrews," 382–406.

254. Vanhoye, *Structure and Message of Hebrews*, 1–109, esp. 23–24; ibid., *Message de l'Epître aux Hébreux*; and ibid., *Structured Translation of Hebrews*. Vanhoye builds his work from previous works by Descamp, "Structure de l'Epître aux Hébreux," 251–58; Gyllenberg, "Die Komposition des Hebräerbriefs," 137–47; Thien, "Analyse de l'Épître aux Hébreux," 74–86; and Vaganey, "Plan de l'Épître aux Hébreux," 269–77.

255. For this observation, see also Black, "Problem of the Literary Structure of Hebrews," 168. He concludes that Vanhoye's thesis must be the starting point for any discussion of Hebrews (ibid., 176).

256. Lane, *Hebrews 1–8*, lxxxvii. For further details on the significance and influence of Vanhoye's approach, see Attridge, *Hebrews*, 16–27.

257. Vanhoye's general outline is as follows:

    a. Exordium (1:1–4); I. A name so different. . . (1:5–2:18); II. A. Jesus, high priest worthy of faith (3:1–4:14), B. Jesus, compassionate highpriest (4:15–5:10). [A preliminary exhortation (5:11–6:20)]; III. A. High priest according to the order of Melchizedek (7:1–28), B. Come to fulfill (8:1–9:28), C. Cause of eternal salvation (10:1–18) [Final exhortation (10:19–39)]; IV. A. The Faith of the men of God (11:1–40), B. The endurance required (12:1–13); V. Straight courses (12:14–13:18), and Z. Peroration (13:20–21).

For a detailed presentation, see Vanhoye, *Structure and Message*, 79–109.

that characterize a development, (5) transition by immediate repetition of an expression or a word that is labeled a "hook word," and (6) symmetric arrangements.[258] Vanhoye's methodology presents valuable insights. However, it does not help one appreciate a clear and definite structural pattern with an understandable line of thought. The issue of how the parts contribute to a unified theme is uncertain.

Some scholars, including Wolfgang Nauck[259] and Werner Georg Kümmel,[260] are not persuaded by Vanhoye's elaborate methodology on Hebrews' structure, but rather posit a so-called "Tripartite approach."[261] In this system, Hebrews is structured into three major sections, each identified by the presence of a parallel passage at the beginning and close of the section.[262] Proponents of this approach believe that Hebrews should be regarded first as paraenetic or exhortation with the expositional blocks used only as a basis for exhortations. Kümmel argues that the paraenetic passages should be seen as pointing to the real goal of the entire exposition rather than interruptions.[263] While this system enjoys some support among scholars who are unsympathetic to Vanhoye, others believe that the tripartite approach has proved to be weak in showing the internal logic of Hebrews' discourse.[264] Attridge, for instance, acknowledges that such an approach cannot be overlooked but argues in favor of Vanhoye, even enlisting five major movements

---

258. Ibid., 19–20. In his own estimation, Vanhoye indicates that the most important of these "structuralizing techniques of composition" is the announcement of subject (e.g. Heb 1:1–4). He observes, "One arrives at five announcements in all, situated first at 1: 4, then 2:17–18, then 5: 9–10, then 10: 36–39, and finally at 12: 13" (ibid., 20).

For an evaluation of Vanhoye's presentation, see Stanley, "Structure of Hebrews from Three Perspectives," 245–71. For strengths and weaknesses, see Westfall, *Discourse Analysis of Hebrews*, 8–9.

259. Nauck, "Zum Aufbau des Hebräerbriefes," 199–206.

260. Kümmel, *Introduction to the New Testament*, 390.

261. This approach was first proposed by Otto Michel. For further details, see Michel, *Der Brief an die Hebräer*, 29–35.

262. Nauck, "Zum Aufbau des Hebräerbriefes," 200–203. The three units or sections suggested by Nauck are as follows:

> (1) Heb 1:1–4:13 [with 1:2b-3 seen as parallel with 4:12–13]; (2) 4:14–10:31 [with 4:14–16 seen as parallel with 10:19–23], and (3) 10:32–13:17 [this final unit is also seen as beginning and ending with a similar type of exhortation].

Nauck's emphasis on such parallels has made his approach especially popular among scholars less convinced by Vanhoye. For further details on this discussion, see Guthrie, *Structure of Hebrews*, 17–19.

263. Kümmel, *Introduction*, 390.

264. For further details, see Koester, *Hebrews*, 84.

or sections in Hebrews in a scheme similar to that proposed by Vanhoye.[265] Attridge's proposal is also considered problematic by some scholars.[266]

For scholars who are opposed to an elaborate literary approach and not willing to support the traditional approach, the "agnostic approach," also referred to as "patchwork approach,"[267] similar to Origen's agnostic opinion on the authorship of Hebrews, makes sense. For example, F. F. Bruce[268] and Leon Morris[269] do not consider the question of literary form or structure but rather propose a content-centered outline based on chapters or changing themes with no consideration for an overriding theory of structure. Many expositors indicate how difficult it is to imagine that an author with an important message would have no structural design in a composition of such a masterpiece as Hebrews. Thus, David Alan Black states, "whatever the merits of a 'patchwork' outline, its considerable demerit is that it is achieved at the expense of a procedure which cannot commend itself as being in accordance with the principles of scientific criticism."[270] Attridge similarly observes that such a method clearly fails to illuminate the function of major sections of the book.[271] For many scholars, this criticism can be leveled as well against the five-part structure that Attridge proposes as an alternative.

The "Discourse Analysis"[272] as an alternative system has led to the "text-linguistic approach" to the structure of Hebrews. One of the leading proponents of this approach is George H. Guthrie, who has taken up the issue of

265. Attridge's structural presentation is as follows:

a. Exordium (1:1-4); I. Name superior to the angel—Eschatology (1:5-2:18); II. Faithful and compassionate high priest—Ecclesiology (3:1-5:10); III. Central exposition—Sacrifice (5:11-10:39); IV. Faith and endurance—Ecclesiological paraenesis (11:1-12:13); V. Peaceful fruit of justice—Eschatology (12:14-13:19), and Z. Conclusion—postscript (13:20-21). (Attridge, *Hebrews*, 16).

266. For further details, see Westfall, *Discourse Analysis of Hebrews*, 19.

267. Black, "Problem of Literary Structure," 175.

268. Bruce subdivides Hebrews into eight sections, each with a title reflecting the contents of the section. For further details, see Bruce, *Hebrews*, vii-x.

269. Morris, "Hebrews," 10-11. Following the same approach, Morris subdivides Hebrews into eleven sections with no attention to any major division.

270. Black, "Problem of Literary Structure," 176.

271. Attridge, *Hebrews*, 14.

272. According to Westfall, "Discourse analysis is a relatively new discipline that analyzes discourse above the sentence level by utilizing contemporary principles of linguistic study" (Westfall, *Discourse Analysis of Hebrews*, 16). For example, Neeley follows the linguistic approach set out by Longacre, which she applies to the text of Hebrews (Neeley, "Discourse Analysis of Hebrews," 1; Longacre, *Grammar of Discourse*, 7-336). On the other hand, Guthrie bases his structure on an analysis of cohesion shifts in Hebrews (Guthrie, *Structure of Hebrews*, 112-47).

Hebrews' structure from a fresh perspective in his work.[273] Many scholars think that "the application of linguistics and its research methodology to the Greek text is an exciting frontier for biblical research."[274] However, while it may be true that the method has "the potential to synthesize various areas of biblical as well as linguistic investigation into one model," the approach is perceived by some scholars as limited in providing an analysis of cohesion in the discourse or the author's choices to create continuity in the text.[275] For example, George H. Guthrie's approach focuses more on "inclusios" and "hook words" while neglecting the function of conjunctions, which leads to a problem of coherence and cohesion as well as difficulties in locating a discourse pattern. As Westfall puts it, George H. Guthrie's overview of a number of discourse issues as well as basic linguistic terminology is problematic when coupled with his adaptation of much of Vanhoye's method and vocabulary.[276] Most students of Hebrews would stand to gain significant insights from these outlined approaches. However, they are simply an enriching and insightful addition to the traditional approach adapted for this study.

SUMMARY ARGUMENT OF HEBREWS

The Epistle to the Hebrews may be subdivided into five major divisions: a prologue (1:1–4); a part one-section detailing the perfecting of Christ as God's King-Son (1:5–4:16); a part two-section detailing the perfecting of Christ as God's Priest Son (5:1–10:18); a part three-section detailing the faith response and practical effects of Christ's finality (10:19–13:19); and an epilogue that includes an epistolary benediction, farewell, and final exhortation (13:20–25).

In the opening brief but polished prologue (1:1–4), the author introduces his exhortation with a solemn statement showing how God has revealed himself to his people in these last days through the Son, Jesus Christ. This statement is followed by a part one-section that deals with the perfecting of God's King-Son (1:5–4:16). First, the author describes how the perfected God's King-Son in his nature is superior to the angels (1:5–2:18) and to Moses (3:1–4:16). Secondly, the author describes how the perfected God's King-Priest [Christ] is superior to the Levitical priesthood (5:1–10:39). The perfected Christ as God's King-Priest (5:10; 6:20; 7:1–28; cf. Gen 14; Ps 110)

---

273. Guthrie, *Structure of Hebrews*, 1–161.
274. Westfall, *Discourse Analysis of Hebrews*, 20.
275. Ibid., 19.
276. For further details, see ibid., 18–20.

is presented as the pioneer of the believer's sanctification. Having made provision for the redemption of mankind from sin, he enables worshipers to attain the same goal of true perfection (7:11, 19), which the author links with the cleansing of their consciences and complete forgiveness of sin (9:9, 22, 28; 10:1). Thus relating "perfection" to the better provisions of the new covenant (8:8–11; 9:15; 10:15–18; cf. Jer 31:31–34), the author describes the priestly ministry of the perfected Christ (unlike the former Levitical order) as efficacious (9:11, 15) in guaranteeing the eschatological completion of God's design of bringing many brethren to their future glory and eternal inheritance (2:10; 5:8, 9; 9:28; 10:1, 13, 35–37; 11:39, 40; 12:18–29). The perfected Christ is superior in all aspects.

The presentation of Christ as superior to the angels serves as a basis for an exhortation that the Hebrew believers should not drift away from the gospel (2:1–4). Since the perfected Christ is also superior to Moses, the believers should not harden their hearts like the Israelites did in the wilderness. Rather, they should make every effort to draw near in order to enter God's eschatological rest (3:1–4:13).[277] Also, since the eternal priesthood Christ mediates is superior to the Levitical priesthood, Hebrew believers should hold fast to their faith and endure until their final salvation is perfected in eternal glory (5:1–10:39).[278]

Following a presentation of the superiority of Christ as the perfected High Priest in contrast to the angels, Moses, and the Levitical priesthood, the author exhorts the Hebrew believers to endure suffering and live for others (11:1–13:19). First, he points to their faith as foundational for endurance even in suffering with hope for the reality of completion of the promise (11:1–40). Therefore, they must run with enduring hope the race set before them, following the patterns of the perfected Christ who endured the cross and was exalted to the right hand of God the Father. In a similar manner, the Hebrew believers should persevere as they pursue their inheritance of the heavenly city (12:1–29), since they have come to the perfected Christ who is the Mediator of the new covenant. Furthermore, in view of the completed work of their salvation, they should love the brethren, enjoy the freedom that they have in Christ, and honor their spiritual leaders (13:1–19).

The author of Hebrews concludes his exhortation with an epilogue in which he gives a final benediction, exhortation, and farewell to his readers (13:20–25). The author's purpose here is to urge the Hebrew believers to persevere and not return to Judaism. For the author of the Epistle to the

---

277. The τέλειος concept does not appear in chapters 3–4, but the author's argument builds on what he has already introduced in chapter 2.

278. A detailed analysis of major occurrences of the τέλειος motif is provided in the following chapter to illustrate how the notion is central to the argument of Hebrews.

Hebrews, the eschatological revelation of the perfected Christ means the final and complete access to God for the believers, because Christ, as the leader of their sanctification, has been perfected in order to lead them to their true and eschatological τελείωσις, "perfection," or complete access to God. This message permeates the author's use of the τέλειος motif as delineated in the following chapter of this book.

Chapter 5

The Notion of Τέλειος in Hebrews

THIS CHAPTER FORMS THE heart of the study and aims to illustrate the importance of the notion of τέλειος by examining how it is used by the author and its import to the argument of Hebrews. It delineates how the author presents Christ as the supreme exemplar of τελείωσις, "perfection," or "completeness," and as the one who enables believers to walk in faith and hope as people who have already attained the same goal of τελείωσις, even as they share in earthly trials and temptations. Such "perfection" or "completeness," while presented as in progress now, remains a future reality that is to be fully realized at the second advent of the glorified Christ. More specifically, this chapter shows that there is a consistent eschatological fulfillment motif not only as realized eschatology, but also, more significantly, as unrealized eschatology. The future eschatological fulfillment motif serves as an incentive for the readers to continue in faith, looking forward to their future uninhibited access to God and the full enjoyment of their eternal inheritance.

SIGNIFICANCE OF THE ΤΈΛΕΙΟΣ NOTION

That the notion of τέλειος is significant for the argument of Hebrews is evidenced in the way the notion and its cognates are used by the author.[1] Michel argues that an understanding of the concept of τέλειος is central to a proper interpretation of Hebrews.[2] First, the Hebrews author refers to the τελείωσις ("perfection") of Christ (Heb 2:10; 5:9; 7:28), linking the notion of τέλειος to the eschatological salvific import of Christ's ministry and exaltation as the perfected High Priest in the order of Melchizedek and the Mediator of the new covenant (cf. 7:22, 25 and 9:28).[3] A look at these passages shows how the author presents the τελείωσις of Christ as a guarantee of his ability to intercede on behalf of his brethren and his priestly ministry of leading them to their eternal salvation. The perfected Christ is presented as the author, the cause, and the one who will fulfill the eschatological salvation of worshipers who are being drawn closer to God.

Second, the author of Hebrews mentions four times that the Levitical system was unable to perfect the worshipers (Heb 7:11, 19; 9:9, 11; 10:1).[4] An examination of these passages shows that it is in accordance with God's promise (Ps 110:4) that a new priest has been revealed, belonging to an order other than the Levitical priesthood. This is very significant, since a change of priesthood implies that the whole legal institution on which the Levitical system was predicated has changed. F. F. Bruce observes, "If God had intended the Aaronic priesthood to inaugurate the age of perfection, the time when men and women would enjoy unimpeded access to him, why should he have conferred on the Messiah a priestly dignity of his own—different. . ., and by implication superior to Aaron's?"[5] For the author of Hebrews, the Levitical priesthood—with its inability to lead to perfection—has been replaced by a new and different priesthood that is able to accomplish

---

1. For a statistical summary data and the semantic field of τέλειος, see Ngoupa, "La perfection dans l'épître aux Hébreux," 5–15.

2. Michel, "Die Lehre von der christlichen," 333. Cf. Peterson, *Hebrews and Perfection*, 1.

3. Lehne, *New Covenant in Hebrews*, 96.

4. This affirmation is similar to the Pauline truth revealed when the apostle affirms, "You are not under the Law but under grace" (Rom 6:14). For the worshipers under the new order, the Levitical ritual system has been nullified, at least as far as acceptance and access to God are concerned.

5. The priesthood of Christ is designated not merely as another (ἄλλον), but as a different priesthood (ἕτερον. . . ἱερέα). For further details, see Bruce, *Epistle to the Hebrews*, 165. For a detailed delineation of the difference between the priesthood of Christ and the Levitical priesthood, see Vanhoye's work (Vanhoye, *Prêtres anciens, prêtre nouveaux*, 150–221).

the goal of leading many sons to their future glory. One reason why the new order is greater is because it has been instituted with an oath (Ps 2:7; 110:4). This points to the superiority of Christ as the only one who is the guarantee[6] of the better promises of the new covenant and its surety of definitive access to God (Heb 9:11; 10:1). In this context, the perfected Christ is presented in the argument as the new, definitive, and final agent of God's eschatological salvation for the believers. Accordingly, Christ is the source of eternal salvation based on the better provisions of the new covenant.

Third, the author of Hebrews states at least four times (Heb 10:14; 11:40; 12:2, 23) that Christ alone is the source of τέλειος for believers, who are presented as in a process of being perfected. Furthermore, the author exhorts readers to pursue the goal of τελείωσις (5:11—6:1) as he points them to the perfected Christ as the "Perfecter" of their faith (12:2). This is significant because it shows that the perfected Christ is the one who enables believers to continue running the race of faith to its triumphant finish.[7] The author advances his argument around an overriding theme of τέλειος through a series of contrasts aimed at presenting Christ as the one who has been made perfect in order that he might also lead believers to the goal of true perfection as the "pioneer," "champion," or "chief leader" of their sanctification. Christ is presented not only as the initiator of faith, but also as the one who leads believers to their future goal: the inheritance of the divine promise that the ancient heroes of faith saw only from afar, yet never obtained (11:13, 39).[8] The perfected Christ "provides, therefore, a perfectly adequate model of what life under the covenant involves."[9]

In order to appreciate the significance of the τέλειος notion as it develops throughout the argument of Hebrews, it is important that these major occurrences be examined to determine its magnitude on the message of Hebrews referred to as τοῦ λόγου τῆς παρακλήσεως a "word of exhortation" (Heb 13:13). The following discussion analyzes the notion of τέλειος as used in Hebrews in order to delineate how the author presents the perfection motif as an overriding theme of Hebrews.

---

6. The Greek word ἔγγυος is used only in Heb 7:22 and means "a guarantee." Some translations use the word "surety" (KJV, ASV, and RSV). The notion points to the better hopes to come based on the better promises of the new covenant. For further details, see also Attridge, *Epistle to the Hebrews*, 208.

7. Bruce, *Hebrews*, 337.

8. Attridge, *Hebrews*, 356.

9. Ibid.

THE ΤΕΛΕΊΩΣΙΣ OF CHRIST

The author of Hebrews seeks to establish the superiority of Christ over all that came before, particularly the Levitical order of worship. The primary evidence of this superiority is that the perfected Christ means the final and definitive access to God. Hebrews opens with a majestic statement pointing the readers to the surpassing greatness of the Son as the vehicle *par excellence* for the eschatological divine revelation (Heb 1:1–4). In this majestic assertion, the author contrasts Christ by implication with the prophets[10] of old and explicitly contrasts him with the angels.[11] For the author, Christ became superior to the degree that he has inherited a more excellent name (1:5–14). The author develops his argument with a description of Christ's superiority over the angels, followed by a practical exhortation that warns believers they should not drift away from the gospel (2:1–4).[12] This is followed by a doctrinal paragraph (2:5–18) resuming the theme of Christ's superiority as evidenced in his eschatological rule.[13] The angels are described as "ministering spirits" (1:14) in contrast with the Son, who is portrayed with majesty[14] not only because of his eternal Sonship, but also because of his suffering and death, which led to his resurrection and exaltation to glory. Presenting Christ's superiority as the one who fulfills the eschatological divine destiny for humanity, the author points first to the τελείωσις of Christ (2:10) as the "pioneer" or "chief leader"[15] of the believers' eternal salvation.

---

10. Christ is superior to the prophets because he is the final revelation and the image of God. In fact, whereas God's past revelation to his people was through the prophets (Heb 1:1), God's eschatological revelation is through his Son, Jesus Christ (1:2–4), who is introduced as the radiance of God's glory upholding everything, purifying sin, and exalted to the right hand of God the Father (1:3; cf. Ps 110:1).

11. Westcott, *Epistle to the Hebrews*, xlix.

12. The author shows that if the angels were the mediators of the covenant at Sinai and the penalty for disregarding that revelation was severe, then the penalty for neglecting the word of salvation proclaimed by the Son would be much more severe (Peterson, *Hebrews and Perfection*, 50).

13. The designation τὴν οἰκουμένην τὴν μέλλουσαν, "the world to come," taken as an equivalent to the expressions μέλλοντος αἰῶνος, "the age to come" (Heb 6:5), and πόλιν... τὴν μέλλουσαν, "the city to come" (13:14), reflects a class of expressions the author uses to point to the establishment of the eschatological kingdom of God. Lane takes this expression as "a designation of the eschatological realm of salvation" (Lane, *Hebrews 1–8*, 46).

14. Attridge observes, "While the Son is seated in majesty, the angels are but ministering spirits." The ministry of the angels is not envisioned in the heavenly sanctuary but rather as the "service" (διακονίαν) they perform on earth for the "heirs of salvation" (Attridge, *Hebrews*, 62).

15. For details on the Greek word ἀρχηγός (cf. Heb 12:2; Acts 3:15 and 5:31), see this author's discussion later in this chapter.

Hebrews 2:10

The author of Hebrews states, "For it was fitting for Him for whom and through whom all things exists in bringing many sons to glory, to make perfect (τελειῶσαι) the pioneer of their salvation through suffering." The author has already shown that the Son's superiority is well attested in the Scripture (1:5–13).[16] Whereas the angels are appointed to worship and serve the Son (1:5–7), the Son as the perfected priest is the eternal, righteous ruler and creator from the beginning to the end (1:8–12). The angels are ministering spirits appointed to serve even believers (1:14). At this juncture, the author introduces his first warning passage that the Hebrew readers should not drift away from the gospel of the superior Lord (2:1–4).

The validity of the author's exhortation is seen in the verses that follow detailing that Christ's superiority will be seen in his future glory (2:5–9; cf. Ps 8:4–6),[17] after defeating Satan (Heb 2:8, 14–15). For Christ, this glory has already begun, in spite of his humiliation for a short time in order to save his people. There is an idea here that Christ's superiority can now be seen in his redemptive death on the cross and exaltation to glory for the purpose of delivering his brethren from the fear of death and from the devil (2:10–18). Because he has tasted suffering and death and has been exalted to glory, believers have found deliverance from their slavery to sin and to their fear of death. The result is that he has become a merciful and faithful High Priest on behalf of his brethren. Because Christ has identified with humankind in his incarnation and suffering, he is able to help those who are tempted (2:17–18).

In Heb 2:9–10, the author provides marvelous insights into the man Jesus Christ regarding his work on the cross when the Hebrews author speaks of him as the ἀρχηγός[18] of man's salvation, bringing many sons to glory. The

---

16. By way of validation, the author includes seven citations from Scripture: Heb 1:5 is from Ps 2:7 and 2 Sam 7:4 (cf. 1 Chr 17:13); verse 6 is a combination of Deut 32:43 and Ps 97:7; verse 7 is from Ps 104:4, verses 8–9 are from Ps 45:6–7, verses 10–12 are from Ps 102:25–27, and verse 13 is from Ps 110:1. While the use of the OT is not the primary focus of this study, the author uses these OT Scriptures to stress the superiority of the Son as the perfected High Priest and final Mediator of the better promises of the new covenant. For this discussion, see Morris, "Hebrews," 18.

17. The future eschatological world is in view in the author's use of the OT as he gives messianic significance to Ps 8 and other Scriptures he uses. Pointing to this future significance in the use of the OT by the author, Padva states, "S'il est dit que toutes choses lui sont assujetties, il ne s'agit pas des choses de ce monde, mais du monde à venir." For further details on OT citations in Hebrews, see Padva, *Les citations de l'Ancien Testament*, 47.

18. The word ἀρχηγός is also used in Acts 3:15; 5:31 in contexts that speak of Christ's death, resurrection, and exaltation as pointing to his mission. Some scholars

description of Jesus as the "leader" points to Christ as the one who takes the lead as the "champion"[19] of man's future eschatological salvation.[20] F. F. Bruce remarks, "He is the Pathfinder, the Pioneer of our salvation," being "the Savior who blazed the trail of salvation along which alone God's 'many sons' could be brought to glory."[21] If DuPlessis is correct that "the appellation ἀρχηγός (cf. also 12:2) contains an undeniable reference to his mission,"[22]

connect the noun with the Hellenistic notion of the divine hero (e.g., the legendary hero Hercules, designated as "champion" or "savior") who "earns his exaltation by the service rendered to mankind" (cf. Lane, *Hebrews 1–8*, 56). This is similar to the gnostic redeemer myth's notion of a "savior" (Käsemann, *Wandering People of God*, 182–93). *Contra* Käsemann, Vanhoye observes that the alleged associations of the word ἀρχηγός to the "gnostic redeemer myth" are remote (Vanhoye, *Situation du Christ*, 325). In the LXX, the word is often a translation of the Hebrew (MT) word ראשׁ (e.g., Exod 6:14), which is also rendered in the LXX as ἄρχων (such as in Num 1:4) in the general sense of "ruler" or "leader." Some commentators indicate this may be all that the word ἀρχηγός means in Hebrews. For further details, see Ellingworth, *Epistle to the Hebrews*, 161. Further insights are found in secular literature, where ἀρχηγός is used in reference to "the founder of a kingdom" (Bauer, ἀρχηγός, 3). According to Ellingworth, the author's use of πρόδρομος (Heb 6:20) in reference to Christ suggests that the word ἀρχηγός kept alive the Hellenistic metaphor of a "pioneer" or a "leader" opening a path that others could follow (Ellingworth, *Hebrews*, 161). This seems to fit well with the immediate context—the participle ἀγαγόντα, seen as corresponding with the accusative noun ἀρχηγόν (see Delitzsch, *Commentary on Hebrews*, 117)—and also the larger context or development of the argument about Christ's superiority in 3:7–4:11.

The word is a vehicle for a broad range of nuances, both in Jewish and secular sources (Cf. Delling, "ἀρχηγός," *TDNT* 1:487–88). It may be translated as "pioneer" or "leader" (Louw and Nida, *Greek English Lexicon*, 36:6). It may be taken in the sense of an "initiator," "founder," or "originator" (BDAG, 138) and used in reference to a "prince" or "leader," the representative head of a community or family, or a "trailblazer" in the sense of one who breaks through new ground and opens the way for others to do the same. Ideas such as "author, source, originator, and initiator, are all suitable" (DuPlessis, Τέλειος: *Idea of Perfection*, 219). Thus, the phrase τὸν ἀρχηγὸν τῆς σωτηρίας αὐτῶν can be translated: "him who leads them to salvation." The connotation is that the perfected Christ leads many sons to their future eschatological salvation. Christ is portrayed as the originator, but also as the leader who opens the way for believers, helping them to follow him until the attainment of the goal of their future inheritance. For this discussion, see Miller, *Epistle to the Hebrews*, 51–52; Hughes, *Commentary on Hebrews*, 100; Alford, *Epistle to the Hebrews*, 44; and Lünemann, *Critical and Exegetical Handbook*, 121.

19. Given the literary context, some scholars prefer this rendering on the grounds that it does not restrict the interpretation of ἀρχηγός to the perspectives of verse 10 alone but instead takes into account the distinctive color of the paragraph. For this discussion, see Lane, *Hebrews 1–8*, 57. Other scholars see the stress of the vocable on the first or second syllable, respectively, and suggest that it "hovers between the senses of 'chieftain and founder'" (see, for example, Simpson, "Vocabulary of Hebrews," 35).

20. See also Thayer, *Greek-English Lexicon*, 77.

21. Bruce, *Hebrews*, 80.

22. DuPlessis, Τέλειος: *Idea of Perfection*, 218.

then to the author, Christ is the "champion" who secures the coming salvation of God's people through the suffering and death he endured in his identification with them. It is significant that the goal of Christ's leadership consists of leading many sons to their future glory (δόξαν)[23] as envisioned in the statement from Ps 8:6 (LXX) cited in verse 7:"crowned with glory and splendor."[24] The redemptive associations with the term "glory" are apparent in the subsequent phrase τῆς σωτηρίας αὐτῶν,"their salvation," the reference being made to the future heritage reserved for believers in the world to come.[25]

The author of Hebrews pursues his argument by stating that "it was fitting for him [God], for whom and through whom all things exist to make perfect through sufferings [διὰ παθημάτων τελειῶσαι], the pioneer of their salvation in bringing many sons to glory" (Heb 2:10). The verse starts a new paragraph (vv. 10-18) continuing the argument about the superiority of Christ. Not only is Christ presented as the one who shares in the believers' situation—their trials and sufferings—but as the one who leads them to their eschatological salvation. The verse is connected through the conjunction γάρ in the previous paragraph,[26] specifically in verse 9, where the author shows that Christ's superiority will be seen in his future glory (2:5-9, Ps 8:4-6). The conjunction indicates the author intends to explain fully what he just pointed out regarding the purpose of the incarnation—namely, that Jesus might taste death on behalf of everyone. For the author of Hebrews, Jesus' humiliation, death, and exaltation have their right and proper place in God's salvific design for humanity. The purpose of verse 10 and the following verses is "to show how fitting this method of salvation is and by implication how totally inappropriate any other notion must be."[27]

23. Many scholars see the motif of "Christ's leading of many sons" as being similar to some of the OT imageries, particularly in connection with the exodus of the Israelites from Egypt, where the divine initiative is often stressed (Exod 3:8, 17; 6:6-7; 7:4-5). For this discussion, see Schreiner, "Fuhrung-Thema der Heilsgeschichte," 2-8. See also Muller, *Cristos Archgos*, 114-48.

24. The crowning with glory, in the context, starts with Christ (v. 9) and extends to believers (v. 10) who are in the process of being drawn near.

25. Lane, *Hebrews 1-8*, 56.

26. Some scholars such as Alford, Hughes, and Milligan take the conjunction γάρ as indicating the reason for Jesus' suffering and death. Accordingly, Jesus endured death because it was fitting for God to perfect Jesus through suffering. More likely, the conjunction γάρ is explanatory of what is involved in the previous statement about Jesus' incarnation and his tasting of death on behalf of everyone (Ellingworth, *Hebrews*, 158; and Lane, *Hebrews 1-8*, 55). Thus, instead of connecting the conjunction to what follows (Montefiore, *Commentary on Hebrews*, 33-254), it should be connected to the preceding paragraph (Ellingworth, *Hebrews*, 158).

27. Hughes, "Epistle to the Hebrews," 98. Similarly, Ellingworth states that the

The author states, "it was fitting (ἔπρεπεν, cf. also 7:26)[28] that it should be by suffering." The appropriateness of God's action in Christ is indicated by the imperfect active indicative of πρέπω, "to be fitting."[29] This conveys the idea that it was appropriate for God and his character,[30] as opposed to any matter of chance. Significantly, the author indicates it was appropriate and in accordance with God's gracious purpose (Heb 2: 9) that Christ should suffer in order to bring many believers to glory. The fittingness of divine action as revealed in Christ is suggested by the manner in which God is designated here as Δι' ὃν τὰ πάντα καὶ δι' οὗ τὰ πάντα, "he for whom and by whom all things exist."[31] Most interpreters would indicate such circumlocution for God is completely appropriate to the context, which concerns the fulfillment of the divine intention in leading many believers to glory. DuPlessis observes that it is not a question of "rhetorical embellishment but a complement to the divine appointment of the Son to his redemptive mission"[32] in bringing many sons to glory. God, who creates and preserves all things, is precisely the one who is able to act in such a way that his intention for humankind will be achieved.[33]

God's position, as far as all creation is concerned, appears important, yet the author also uses the point to emphasize the importance of future eschatology by highlighting the results of Christ's death and exaltation within the context of God's purpose of restoring all things for and to himself. The context indicates that this will be realized in the future glorification of the "many sons" presented as already secured by the Son's suffering, death, and his present state of exaltation as the perfected High Priest. Thus, the Hebrews

---

humiliation of Jesus, his death, and his exaltation all "have their right and proper place in God's purpose" to bring many sons to their future glory. For further details, see Ellingworth, *Hebrews*, 158.

28. Some scholars believe that the formula is strange to the language of the LXX and rest of the NT but is found in ancient writings, especially Philo (Philo, *Allegorical Interpretation*, 1.48; ibid., *On the Eternity of the World*, 41; ibid., *On the Confusion of Tongues*, 175), and Josephus (Josephus, *Against Apion*, 168). For further details, see Spicq, *Hébreux: Introduction*, 53. As Lane posits, the formula "affirms that what has taken place in the experience of Jesus is consistent with God's known character and purpose" (Lane, *Hebrews 1–8*, 55). See also Bruce, *Hebrews*, 79.

29. BDAG, 861. See also Milligan, *Epistle to the Hebrews*, 47–396; Lane, "Hebrews," 443–58.

30. As Morris posits, the way of salvation is not arbitrary; rather, it is appropriate to or befitting the character of God (Morris, "Hebrews," 26).

31. This circumlocution for God as the one δι' ὃν τὰ πάντα καὶ δι' οὗ τὰ πάντα is similar to Paul in Rom 11:36. The tone of the language is doxological, suggesting a liturgical setting. For further details, see Ellingworth, *Hebrews*, 159.

32. DuPlessis, Τέλειος: *Idea of Perfection*, 217–18.

33. For further details, see Lane, *Hebrews 1–8*, 55.

author indicates, "It was fitting... πολλοὺς υἱοὺς εἰς δόξαν ἀγαγόντα to lead many sons to glory."[34] As part of God's eternal purpose, the incarnation of Christ is fitting as the effective means of achieving God's great design, namely the ultimate "restoration of all things."[35] This phrase indicates the path to future eschatological fulfillment, along which Christ leads[36] those who have entrusted their lives to him through faith to the ultimate goal. The perfected Christ, placed at the forefront of humanity, is portrayed as the one "leading" (ἀγαγόντα)[37] his many followers to their future participation in Christ's glory, which is their appointed goal for eternal salvation (cf. 2:3), including ruling with Christ,[38] who is described as the "leader," "champion," or "pioneer" of their salvation.

The author of Hebrews portrays Christ as the "pioneer" or "leader" who has secured the salvation of his people through the sufferings he endured due to his identification with them and, more specifically, his death.

---

34. The Greek word δόξα (cf. 1:3) points to the future glory. According to Alford, it has to do with "God's bliss and majesty, which believers partake of in part in this life, and fully in the future life to come" (Alford, *Hebrews*, 44). Most interpreters indicate that it implies full participation in Christ's glory and in the messianic blessedness or the splendor of eternal salvation, including ruling with Christ in the future. For this discussion, see Lenski, *Hebrews and James*, 78–82; Milligan, *Hebrews*, 108–109; Morris, "Hebrews," 26–27; Montefiore, *Hebrews*, 60; BDAG, 257–58; and Delling, "δόξα," *TDNT* 2:249–51.

35. Hughes, "Epistle to the Hebrews," 98.

36. The Greek aorist tense ἀγαγόντα, "leading," is taken by some expositors as timeless (Montefiore, *Hebrews*, 60) or the act as a completed action (Alford, *Hebrews*, 43). Others take the aorist tense as a simultaneous action (Bruce, *Hebrews*, 77; and Guthrie, *Letter to the Hebrews*, 88) occurring at the same time as the action of the verb τελειῶσαι. Ellingworth believes the aorist tense should be understood as indicating not an event prior to τελειῶσαι, but rather coincident action (Ellingworth, *Hebrews*, 160). For further details, see the following note.

37. The participle ἀγαγόντα, translated as "leading," may be taken as indicating time or temporal circumstances. For example, the NAB takes the participle as referring to the time when God acted: "it was fitting to perfect Jesus through suffering when he brought many sons into glory." Bloomfield, on the other hand, takes the participle as referring to the time of God's decree to act: "it was fitting for God to perfect Jesus through suffering after God had decreed to bring many sons to glory" (Bloomfield, *Greek New Testament*, s.v. "Hebrews," 394–480). However, it is perhaps best to take the participle as indicating the purpose of divine action of the perfecting Jesus: "it was fitting for God... in order to bring many sons to glory" (see Lane, *Hebrews 1–8*, 55; and Morris, "Hebrews," 26). DuPlessis sees no sense of time attached to this aorist; rather, he puts forth the notion of vocation as the main stress of the aorist ἀγαγόντα (DuPlessis, Τέλειος: *Idea of Perfection*, 219). The aorist suggests an ingressive force, since God will still bring many sons to glory (Vanhoye, *Situation du Christ*, 309–10).

38. Milligan, *Hebrews*, 91–92. The Greek word for "glory" is seen as related to the objective genitive noun σωτηρίας, or "salvation," which results or springs from the substance or the source. For this discussion, see also Delitzsch, *Hebrews*, 1:117.

He states, "it was fitting for him. . . to make perfect through sufferings (διὰ παθημάτων τελειῶσαι) the pioneer of their salvation, in order to bring many sons to glory." The rendering of the Greek verb τέλειοω is debatable in light of the various possibilities,[39] as suggested by a number of scholars. Some scholars take the notion of τέλειος in Heb 2:10 and the rest of Hebrews in a moral or ethical sense, arguing that Jesus' participation in humanity through the incarnation presupposes a moral or ethical development in his character.[40] P. E. Hughes writes, "As the incarnate Son who fully shared our humanity, it was absolutely necessary for him to learn obedience, since his obedience was essential for the offsetting of our disobedience."[41] Accordingly, "through his curriculum of suffering, Christ was made perfect in character by learning certain moral virtues, e.g., sympathy, patience, obedience, faith."[42] However, as many scholars rightly posit, the τέλειος concept applied to Jesus cannot be taken as implying a moral progressive development in the sense of moral growth from a lower moral status to a higher status of perfection, since evidence in Hebrews rules out such an interpretation.[43]

Other scholars take the notion of τέλειος in a cultic or religious sense,[44] arguing that the terminology found in Hebrews should be seen as functioning in a cultic or religious sense, which suggests the notion of "consecration" or "priestly ordination."[45] Using scriptural support for this approach, Delling argues that the notion of τέλειος in Hebrews is related to the notion of priestly consecration as found in the LXX expression τέλειος τὰς χεῖρας (cf. Exod 29:9, 33, 35; Lev 4:5; 8:33; 16:32; Num 3:3),[46] indicating that someone's hands are made free from stains, which frees the individual to practice priestly functions. It is true that according to some witness of the LXX, the expression τέλειος τὰς χεῖρας, "to perfect the hand," is a technical phrase that suggests the notion of "priestly consecration," but it is doubtful

---

39. For a detailed discussion, see this author's discussion in chapter 2.

40. Examples include: Wikgren, "Patterns of Perdition in Hebrews," 160–61; Cullmann, *Christology of the New Testament*, 93–97; and Dey, *Intermediary World*, 31–126), among others.

41. Hughes, *Hebrews*, 187.

42. Bruce, *Epistle to the Hebrews*, 99.

43. While the notion of some kind of development may be present in the language of Hebrews, this should not be taken as suggesting a move from sinful to sinless status (Hoekema, "Perfection of Christ in Hebrews," 31–37).

44. Examples include Häring, "Über einige Grundgedanken des Hebräerbriefs," 267; and Dibelius, "Der himmlische Kultus," 166.

45. DuPlessis argues the notion of τέλειος in Heb 2:10 carries a "cultic sacral character" (Τέλειος: *Idea of Perfection*, 43, 217). Similarly, Ellingworth argues that the notion carries the idea of "priestly ordination" (Ellingworth, *Hebrews*, 326).

46. Delling, "τέλειος," *TDNT* 8:96.

that the verbal form by itself (τελειοῦν), without the addition of τὰς χεῖρας as found in Hebrews, could be taken as having the same technical meaning as priestly consecration.[47]

Some scholars interpret the τέλειος notion in Heb 2:10 following a "glorification" or "exaltation" model,[48] maintaining that the notion is closely related to the idea of glorification or exaltation of Christ to the right hand of God the Father. Accordingly, by his suffering and death, Jesus was exalted and opened up the new way for the many believers to draw near to God. Käsemann believes that perfection in Hebrews is synonymous with "glorification" or "entrance into the heavenly sphere."[49] Although significant insights can be deduced from this approach, many scholars do not consider it the best approach and thus prefer to take the notion of τέλειος in a "vocational" or "experiential" sense.[50]

Proponents of the vocational view connect the notion of τέλειος with the idea of "testing and proving of Christ,"[51] also referred to as an "educational experience" Jesus presumably acquired through his sufferings and temptation, which culminated into his qualifications as a merciful High Priest and Savior for his people.[52] Caird, commenting on Heb 2:10, argues that Christ was made perfect because he "experienced to the full all conditions of human life, including a learning or educational process through his sufferings and temptations."[53] Such a vocational approach can be seen as assuming the premise of Christ's need for development in the sense of Christ having to prove himself. If this reconstruction is correct, then this approach opens itself to the same criticism leveled against the moral/ethical approach,[54] so that the same question remains as to how such a notion of moral development could rest harmoniously alongside passages in Hebrews that emphasize qualities such as Christ's sinlessness (Heb 4:15) and his un-

---

47. Kurianal, *Jesus Our High Priest*, 28–30.

48. For example: Kogel, "Der Begriff 'τελειοῦν' im Hebräerbrief," 35–68; Saucy, "Exaltation Christology in Hebrews," 43–58; and Koester, *Hebrews: New Translation with Introduction and Commentary*, 122–25.

49. Käsemann, *Wandering People of God*, 44, 137. He goes further, applying the notion of τέλειος to the mythological gnostic notion of a descending/ascending redeemer, a metaphysical reading that has been rejected by many scholars (Peterson, *Hebrews and Perfection*, 6, 298).

50. Attridge refers to this approach as an existential model of perfection (Attridge, *Hebrews*, 87).

51. Michel, "Die Lehre," 135.

52. Peterson, *Hebrews and Perfection*, 93.

53. Caird, "Just Men Made Perfect," 93.

54. McCruden, *Solidarity Perfected*, 18–20.

defiled character (7:28). The context becomes the only testing ground for the various possibilities in the search for a better interpretative framework for the τέλειος notion in Hebrews. With this background in mind, one is now in a position to elucidate the meaning of διὰ παθημάτων τελειῶσαι, "made perfect through suffering" (Heb 2:10).

The author of Hebrews has already presented Jesus, the perfected High Priest, as the one who fulfills the divine destiny for humanity in bringing many believers to glory. The context indicates this "glory" is the eschatological destiny of God's children, who are being sanctified.[55] It is in Christ's role as the one who fulfills the eschatological destiny of humankind that the author describes him as the one God fittingly made perfect through suffering (διὰ παθημάτων τελειῶσαι).[56] Lane notes that the phrase is clearly a repetition (in another form) of the phrases διὰ τὸ πάθημα τοῦ θανάτου, "through the suffering of death," and γεύσηται θανάτου, "he might taste death," in verse 9.[57] The linguistic or conceptual correspondences alert the reader to the fact that the author intends to build his argument or explain further (in the following paragraph) the comments he made based on Ps 8.[58] The cited words of the psalmist look at the past and future, which are inextricably tied together with the person and work of Christ.[59] It is only in the perfected Christ that believers find the pledge of their own inheritance of future salvation, which consists of the full realization of their intended glory. For Christ, this glorification is already obtained (Heb 2:9), whereas

---

55. Attridge argues that this is the same glory the Son has always had from all eternity (cf. Heb 1:3) and with which he was crowned at his exaltation (2:7–9). Accordingly, the believers live as those having this glory, i.e., their eschatological salvation as their destiny. Similar notions on the eschatological glory are found in both Jewish and early Christian traditions (Dan 12:3; 1 Enoch 39:4–6; 45:3; 2 Enoch 22:8–18; 4 Ezra 7:91, 98; 2 Bar 30:1; 32:4; 1QS 4:23; CD 3:23; 4:1–3; 1QH 17:5; see also Philo, *On the Special Laws*, 1:45). For further details, see Attridge, *Hebrews*, 83; and Kittel, "δόξα," *TDNT* 2:233–55.

56. The Greek words "to make perfect" are literally "to carry to the goal or consummation," or "fulfill." The aorist tense τελειῶσαι suggests ingressive action connoting entrance into a state with continuing effect or result since God will still bring many to glory. For this discussion, see Wuest, *Hebrews in the Greek New Testament*, 60. See also Vanhoye, *Situation du Christ*, 369.

57. Lane, *Hebrews 1–8*, 52.

58. Ibid. For further details on this reasoning, see Vanhoye, *La structure littéraire d'Hébreux*, 79.

59. Lane is correct that Christ's condescension to be made "lower than the angels" for a little while set in motion a sequence of events in which humiliation is the necessary prelude to exaltation (Lane, *Hebrews 1–8*, 50).

for believers, it is still in the future to be realized at the second coming of the glorified Christ (Heb 2:10; cf. 12:23).[60]

An interpretative key to τέλειος in 2:10 is found in the eschatological character of the discourse as a whole. Silva comments, "The eschatological exaltation of Jesus as the one who fulfills God's redemptive promises constitutes its specific designation."[61] The eternal God fulfilled his divine intention through Christ by allowing him to come in suffering and death in order to accomplish God's redemptive plan of salvation for mankind. The language of τέλειος in 2:10 does not imply that this developed from imperfection to moral, vocational, or cultic perfection in the person of Christ. In addition, there is no clear evidence that the terminology should necessarily be limited to Christ's exaltation or glorification. Rather, the context seems to indicate the terminology could be best explained in terms of a broader context of eschatological fulfillment of the divine purpose. To the author of Hebrews, the eternal divine purpose to bring many sons to their future glory has been accomplished by means of the incarnation.[62] The Son, Jesus Christ, in his genuine humanity, has been revealed in these last days. Made perfect through suffering and death, he has fulfilled divine purposes for the redemption of humankind.

Hebrews 5:8–9

The author of Hebrews continues his argument by expanding on his previous thought regarding the τελείωσις of Christ (Heb 2:10), which he describes in Heb 5:8–9: "Though he was a Son, he learned obedience through what he suffered, and having been perfected, he became the source of eternal salvation for all who obey Him." The author has already embarked on his doctrine of the superiority of Christ over the angels using OT Scriptures (1:5–14),[63] which serve as a basis for his exhortation to the readers not to

60. Vanhoye, *La structure littéraire*, 76. An examination of the author's use of the OT in Hebrews (Heb 1:5; cf. 2 Sam 7:14; 1 Chr 17:13; Ps 2:7; Heb 1:13, cf. Ps 110; Heb 1:10–12, cf. Ps 102:26–28) shows that he intends to present Jesus as the one in whom all the eschatological hopes are realized in all their fullness (Vanhoye, *Structure and Message of Hebrews*, 47).

61. Silva, "Perfection and Eschatology in Hebrews," 62–68.

62. Pentecost, *Faith That Endures*, 62.

63. Vanhoye states that the OT Scriptures cited are, for the most part, related to royal messianism in conformity with early Christian tradition: the glorified Christ is the Son of David in whom the prophetic oracle of Nathan is realized (2 Sam 7:14; cf. Ps 2). In addition, he is the Lord of Ps 110 who sits at the right hand of God the Father (Ps 110; Acts 2:34; 1 Cor 15:25). In him, all the eschatological hopes are to be realized (cf. Ps 102:26, 27–28). For further details, see Vanhoye, *Structure and Message*, 47.

neglect the message of the gospel from the superior Lord (2:1–4). Next, the author shows how Christ's superiority, seen in what has been accomplished (his redemptive death on the cross and exaltation), will also be seen in his future glory (2:5–9). Then he explains how suffering and death does not constitute an end in itself by pointing to its purpose of leading his brethren to eternal salvation (2:10–18). This theme is readdressed in 5:8–9.

Following Heb 2:10–18, the author includes a new theme describing the superiority of Christ with regard to Moses (3:1–6), showing Moses was faithful as a servant in God's house (cf. v. 5), and proving the perfected Christ was faithful as a Son over God's entire household (v. 6). Unlike Moses' servanthood, Jesus, as the Son of God (cf. Ps 2:7; 110), announced and inaugurated the eternal order.[64] For the readers of Hebrews, the eschatological moment has been inaugurated by Jesus. It is up to the worshipers to grasp its significance and application to the journey they have begun in Christ. This is the reasoning for the second exhortation to the Hebrew believers not to follow Israel's unbelieving heart, which had cost generations beforehand entrance into the promised land (3:7–4:13). Significantly, the author sets up the goal of the future rest (4:1–13; cf. 2:5) that still remains ahead for believers. Not only is the perfected Christ superior to Moses, he is also superior to Aaron. Next, the author describes Christ's superiority as the perfected High Priest in the order of Melchizedek (4:14–5:10). This is the rationale for his third exhortation to believers to press on to the goal of τέλειος, "completeness or maturity" (5:11–6:20).

Elaborating on his notion of τέλειος already introduced at 2:10, the author states in Heb 5:8, "Though he was the Son,[65] he learned obedience through what he suffered." This passage is connected to the previous verse (v. 7) through a concessive phrase, καίπερ ὢν υἱός, or "even though he was the Son," setting up a contrast between two situations. One is the Son, and the other is learning obedience through what he suffered.[66] The emphasis

---

64. Manson, *Epistle to the Hebrews*, 55. Following this line of thought, Manson notes that according to Hebrews "the believers live in the ultimate period, the last 'now' of time" (ibid.).

65. The Greek word υἱός is used without an article, but it is nevertheless definite, just like a proper name. Most interpreters would suggest that the article is absent because "Son" is a predicate. It means he was the Son. Naturally, a son would learn obedience by suffering, but as the context indicates, Jesus is not just an ordinary son—he is the Son of God, yet in God's eternal design, Jesus was not granted exemption from death. For this discussion, see Lenski, *Hebrews*, 164–65; see also Lane, *Hebrews 1–8*, 121.

66. The contrast is to be understood in terms of what the author has already said about the Son. Particular attention should be given to what he has already stated about his exalted status (Heb 1:2, 3, 8; 3:6; 4:14; 5:5). Johnson observes that the readers—who

appears to be on the main verb ἔμαθεν, or "he learned," pointing to Christ's life experience and, in the process, how it affected him. For the author of Hebrews, it is through ὧν ἔπαθεν, or "the things he suffered,"[67] that the eternal Son of God learned what obedience entails. Jesus, as the eternal Son of God, could not be tempted because God is not tempted by evil—yet in his true humanity, the Son could be tested.[68] For this reason, the author indicates that Jesus, as the appointed High Priest, learned obedience by the things he suffered (Heb 5: 8).[69] The context does not suggest that "he learned to obey"[70] but that he learned the cost of τὴν ὑπακοήν, or "the obedience."[71] This notion is similar to that of Phil 2:8,[72] as a willingness to surrender for a while his prerogatives even unto death on the cross in order to accomplish

---

have heard about the eternal Son of God as one who was involved even in creation of the universe—can now hear of the Son as one who learned obedience through what he suffered. For this discussion, see Johnson, *Hebrews: A Commentary*, 147.

67. Some scholars take ὧν ἔπαθεν, "the things he suffered," as referring to his death on the cross (Lane, *Hebrews 1–8*, 121). It is best to take this as referring to his sufferings in general, including his entire life on earth, which culminated in his crucifixion, death, and exaltation. For further details, see Ellingworth, *Hebrews*, 292; see also, Alford, *Hebrews*, 622.

68. Pentecost, *Faith That Endures*, 99.

69. The phrase ἔμαθεν ἀφ' ὧν ἔπαθεν, "he learned from what he suffered," has a rhetorical construction based on a Greek wordplay (μαθειν παθειν, or "to learn is to suffer") common in ancient Greek moral discourses. Johnson states, "the link between suffering and learning is made as early as the Greek tragedians (Aeschylus, *Agamemnon* 177; Sophocles, *Trachiniae* 143) and is widely attested in classical Greek literature (Herodotus 1.207; Aesop, *Fabulae* 134.1–3; 223.2–3; Philo, *Flight and Finding* 138; *Dreams* 2.107; *Special Laws* 4.29; *Life of Moses* 2.55, etc)" (Johnson, *Hebrews*, 147). The idiom sometimes meant that while sufferings may be unwelcome, they can become a lesson (Herodotus, *Persian Wars*, I. 207). For Philo, "people learned by their mistake" (Philo, *On Flight and Finding*, 138; ibid., *On the Special Laws*, IV. 29) "and through experience just as a foolish child would learn" (see ibid., *Who Is the Heir?* 73; *On the Life of Moses*, II. 55; II. 280). Yet Jesus did not need to learn obedience, since he was already without fault. For further details, see Koester, *Hebrews*, 290.

70. Pentecost indicates, "Jesus did not learn to obey, rather he learned all that obedience entails" (Pentecost, *Faith That Endures*, 99).

71. The obedience (τὴν ὑπακοήν) does not imply that Jesus was previously disobedient, since such a notion would be incompatible with the Son. For further details, see Hewitt, *Epistle to the Hebrews*, 98. The notion of "obedience" does not necessarily imply specific moral virtues Jesus had to learn (*contra* Lünemann). The definite article suggests the particular obedience required by the incarnation, which culminated in his passion and death on the cross. For this reasoning, see Dods, "Epistle to the Hebrews," 289.

72. Kistemaker states, "Jesus did not have to learn anything concerning obedience, because his will was the same as God's will. However, in his humanity, Jesus had to show complete obedience; he had to become "obedient to death—even death on a cross!" (Phil 2:8) (Kistemaker, *Exposition of Hebrews*, 139).

the divine intention of leading those who obey to their eschatological salvation (5:9). For Hebrews, it is the goal of eternal salvation that has been completed in Christ, as the perfected High Priest opens up an avenue of direct access to God. Jesus, the appointed High Priest in the order of Melchizedek, has become the source of eternal salvation for those who obey.

In Heb 5:9, the author writes, "And having been made perfect, he became the source of eternal salvation for all who obey him." As with the first instance of τέλειος (cf. Heb 2:10), the question in Heb 5:9 is "in what sense was Jesus made perfect?" What does the author imply, especially in view of 5:8? In the first segment of his sermon, the author established the place of the perfected Christ as the Son through an elaborate comparison with the angels (1:5–14; 2:5–9) and with Moses (3:1–6). Next, the author provides a link between the perfected Son and his priesthood[73] through a comparison with the Levitical priesthood as he advances an argument for his superiority. Just like Aaron, Jesus was appointed and offered a sacrifice as a mediator between God and the people (5:1–4). As the perfected High Priest, Jesus differs from Aaron and other earthly priests because he has higher qualifications that mark him as the High Priest (5:5–10).

Christ did not need to offer sacrifices for his own sins because his priesthood was from a different order (Heb 5:6). He was appointed High Priest as the begotten Son in order to offer himself as sacrifice to God (5:5–7). His appointment as High Priest is paralleled with his appointment as King-Son (Ps 2:7; 110:4). Thus, Alan C. Mitchell posits, "Sonship and priesthood are brought together through a common appointment."[74] The use of Ps 2, quoted earlier (Heb 1:5), proclaims Christ as the Davidic Heir destined to rule all the nations (Ps 2:8). The use of Ps 110 also quoted earlier (Heb 1:13) indicates that the future ruler is also a priest forever. Both psalms thus unites in the person of Christ and his dual office of Priest and King. Because he was appointed by God as King-Son and Priest forever, he was qualified to offers himself as a sacrifice to God on behalf of God's people (5:7–8). More than that, Christ became the source of eternal salvation to all who are willing to follow him (5:9–10). It is in this context that the author uses the notion of τέλειος for the second time (v. 9) to point to the completion of the divine intention of salvation for humankind.

---

73. Mitchell notes that in Heb 2:10–18, the author deals primarily with the identity of the Son and mentions his priesthood in anticipation of what he begins in Heb 5:1–10. For further details, see Mitchell, *Hebrews*, 112.

74. Ibid., 114.

As in the case of Heb 2:10, the idea of completion or perfection in 5:9 has puzzled interpreters.[75] Many scholars[76] affirm the reality of a moral or ethical achievement in Jesus' personality in terms of his learning obedience, including moral virtues. For instance, P. E. Hughes argues that for Jesus, as the incarnate Son who fully shared humanity, "it was absolutely necessary for him to learn obedience, since his obedience was essential for the offsetting of our disobedience."[77] The implication here is that Jesus needed to undergo some inner growth or development into obedience. For many scholars, such emphasis on Jesus' moral development seems to contradict Hebrews' teaching in passages that speak of Christ's supreme spiritual stature (Heb 4:15 and 7:26).[78] The language of Hebrews suggests the finished state of Christ's character as the eternal Son of God. Many interpreters would agree that although the incarnation of Christ had some moral implications, the message would forbid understanding the τελείωσις of Christ in 5:9 in terms of moral development, especially when it implies a sense of progress from some imperfection to a perfect state.[79] The text shows such perfection is not an acquisition by Jesus or something he achieved; rather, he was made perfect by God the Father, as the passive verbal forms or constructions indicate (τελειωθείς in 5:9, τετελειωμένον in 7:28; cf. 2:10). The subject of the verbal action is God, not Jesus.[80]

Some scholars follow the LXX[81] rendering of the verbal form in the phrase τέλειουν τὰς χεῖρας in the Pentateuch[82] in the sense of consecration to priestly service, thus taking the notion of the τελείωσις of Christ in Heb 5:9 as signifying that Jesus was fully equipped to come before God

---

75. For an extended discussion and review of literature, see the discussion in chapter 2 of this book.

76. For examples, see Wikgren, "Patterns of Perfection in Hebrews," 159–67; and Cullmann, *Christology of the New Testament*, 93–97.

77. See Hughes, *Hebrews*, 187. Hughes further argues that "this perfection was progressively achieved as he moved on toward the cross which marked the consummation of his suffering and obedience." His perfection consisted not only of "the retention of his integrity," but also the "establishment of his integrity" (ibid.)

78. Scholer, *Proleptic Priests*, 188.

79. For further details, see Ellingworth, *Hebrews*, 294; and Kurianal, *Jesus Our High Priest*, 224.

80. The same construction is found when it comes to the perfecting of the believers. The subject of the verbal action is Christ, not the believers (cf. Heb 10:14).

81. In the LXX, the material and technical notion of consecration is apparent in the whole phrase τέλειουν τὰς χεῖρας. But in Hebrews, the verb alone (τελειοῦν) occurs in a more experiential context of sufferings and death, as described in 2:10 and 5:9 (Kurianal, *Jesus Our High Priest*, 221; see also Attridge, *Hebrews*, 85).

82. For example: Exod 29:9, 29, 33, 35; Lev 4:5; 8:33; 16:32; 21:10; Num 3:3.

The Notion of Τέλειος in Hebrews 145

in priestly or cultic action.[83] For instance, in the notion of the perfecting of Christ, DuPlessis discerns what he calls "a cultic sacral character."[84] This implies the author of Hebrews is primarily concerned with establishing Jesus' legal qualifications as priest, rather than with the surpassing nature of the character of his priesthood as compared with the character of the Levitical priesthood. The text of Hebrews indicates that Christ's priesthood is superior not only on a legal ground of valid qualifications, but especially because his priesthood is inherently superior by nature.[85] This makes sense, since it was by divine decree that Christ was exalted as the Son of God (Ps 2:7; 110:4) and appointed High Priest in the order different from Aaron's, the order of Melchizedek (cf. Heb 7:24).

The question remains as to how specifically one should view the notion of Christ "having been made perfect" in Heb 5:9. The author of Hebrews uses the aorist passive participle τελειωθείς. The aorist participle refers to Christ's suffering, death, and exaltation seen as a single event in the past, not necessarily prior to the action of the main verb (ἐγένετο)[86] but contemporaneous to the action of the main verb ἐγένετο, or "he became." In other words, the formula τελειωθεὶς ἐγένετο ("having been perfected, he became") becomes similar to the formula ἀποκριθεὶς εἶπεν ("answering, he said") in Matt 13:37.[87] If this reconstruction is correct, then one may argue that the perfecting of Christ (τελειωθείς)[88] occurs simultaneously with

83. Delling, "τέλειος," *TDNT* 8:83. For further details, see Vanhoye, *Situation du Christ*, 326; Spicq, *L'Épître aux Hébreux*, 221–24. Spicq sees the applicability of a cultic interpretation, but he is also open to other possibilities. For instance, he further affirms that the verb is susceptible to other interpretations, including eschatological understanding.

84. DuPlessis, Τέλειος: *Idea of Perfection*, 217.

85. McCruden, *Solidarity Perfected*, 17. See also Kurianal, *Jesus Our High Priest*, 224–25.

86. Some scholars logically take τελειωθείς, "having been perfected," as occurring before the action of the main aorist verb ἐγένετο, "he became" (Ellingworth, *Hebrews*, 294). While the aorist participle should be generally seen as antecedent in time to the action of the main verb, this is not without exception. Wallace posits that "when the aorist participle is related to an aorist main verb, the participle will often be contemporaneous (or simultaneous) to the action of the main verb" (Wallace, *Exegetical Syntax*, 624–25). In fact, the two actions not only occur at the same time, they are the same action. For this discussion, see also Burton, *Syntax of the Moods and Tenses*, 64–65.

87. Wallace states, "The answering does not occur before the saying—it is the speaking" (e.g., Matt 26:23; Mark 11:14; Luke 5:22; 7:22). See Wallace, *Exegetical Syntax*, 625.

88. Some scholars take the aorist participle as indicating the means of Christ's becoming the source of salvation (Kistemaker, *Hebrews*, 139; Guthrie, *Letter to the Hebrews*, 131). But it is perhaps best to take it as temporal ("When he was made

Christ's becoming the source of eternal salvation.[89] The phrase "having been perfected" does not imply a progression from imperfect to perfect or from incomplete to complete. This phrase cannot be taken as simply pointing to Christ's consecration as High Priest.[90] In addition, while it may be true that some vocational or experiential aspects are present in the work of Christ or his experience (suffering, death and exaltation),[91] these categories are inadequate in providing a better understanding of the phrase. For instance, if the vocational or experiential approach to the notion of perfection presumes the necessity for Christ's developmental process, such as having to prove Christ to be fit vocationally,[92] then the approach could be said to open itself to the same criticism leveled against the moral or ethical approach.[93] In his incarnation, God's design for redemption was completed through his suffering, death,[94] and exaltation,[95] with the result that he became the author

---

perfect. . ."). See, for instance, Lane, *Hebrews 1–8*, 110; and Hagner, *Hebrews*, 85.

89. The author's focus in the text suggests that the aorist tense could be taken as conveying an "ingressive" (or "inchoative") force (Wallace, *Exegetical Syntax*, 558), with an emphasis on the continuing result of Christ becoming the source of eternal salvation to all who obey.

90. Attridge believes that the participle τελειωθείς, "having been perfected," cannot be taken simply as synonymous with προσαγορευθείς (in verse 10), with the idea that it points to Christ's consecration as High Priest (*contra* Käsemann, *Wandering People of God*, 218). Naturally, the participle refers to the result of the process described in the preceding verses, which point to Christ's redemptive work as seen in his suffering, death, and exaltation. For further details, see Attridge, *Hebrews*, 155.

91. For further details, see ibid., 87, 153. Cf. Peterson, *Hebrews and Perfection*, 93–94.

92. Peterson, *Hebrews and Perfection*, 67.

93. The participle cannot be taken as referring to a "moral perfection" of Christ in his humanity (Moffatt, *Hebrews*, 67; Hughes, *Hebrews*, 187; and Vanhoye, *Situation*, 321). For this discussion, see Attridge, *Hebrews*, 153.

94. "To suffer death for God's sake" is sometimes taken by scholars as the same thing as "the attainment of perfection" (Bruce, *Hebrews*, 132). For example, Eusebius, reporting on the martyr of Marinus, states, "Having been led off to death, he was perfected" (τελείουται) (Eusebius, *Ecclesiastical History*, VII. 15. 5). Considering the context, it is not Marinus' death *per se* that made him perfect. Rather his good deeds were brought to completion, perfected, or sealed; his good deeds were completed in his martyrdom. While Christ's suffering and death can be seen as bound up with his "being made perfect" in the context (Bruce, *Hebrews*, 132), the essence of the terminology of τέλειος should perhaps be perceived only in terms of completion of God's redemptive work of salvation. As DeSilva indicates, the passage is fully comprehensible if one allows the phrase "having been perfected" in 5:9 to simply carry its formal sense of "having been brought to the final goal" of the work of the journey described in 5:7–8. For further details, see also DeSilva, *Perseverance in Gratitude*, 198.

95. Scholars who advocate the exaltation or glorification approach to the τέλειος notion may see Christ's glorification as a distinct step from his suffering or death, but

or source of eternal salvation to all who obey him. Kenneth S. Wuest thus argues that the main idea behind the notion of τέλειος is the bringing of the Son to the goal of redemption as fixed by God.⁹⁶ This relates to the divinely appointed discipline of suffering for the Messiah as the means of becoming the eternal High Priest and Mediator of the better promises of the new covenant. The perfecting of Christ, accordingly, should be seen not only in his exaltation to the right hand of God the Father, but also in his suffering in order to complete the eschatological fulfillment of the destiny of humankind as he brings many believers to their future glory.⁹⁷

The author of Hebrews indicates that Christ was made complete⁹⁸ as the source of eternal salvation to all who obey him. When his redemptive work on the cross was completed, Christ became the source⁹⁹ of eternal salvation—a step that could only be fulfilled by one who was truly subjected to the human condition in suffering and who fully experienced the cost of obedience.¹⁰⁰ Hugh A. Montefiore believes that the notion of a "source of salvation" was very common in the Hellenistic world,¹⁰¹ perhaps in the general sense of a source of escape or deliverance. However, the phrase αἴτιος

---

the author is not necessarily interested in creating such a dichotomy. Christ's "suffering," "death," and "exaltation" can be seen as one event that fulfills divine salvific design for mankind. In this case, the notion of τέλειος is primarily seen as expressing the "idea of fulfillment or reaching the goal," especially when viewed in contrast with the author's description of Christ's redemptive mission in 5:7–8 (Ellingworth, *Hebrews*, 294). The completion or accomplishment of Christ's redemptive mission in his suffering, death, and exaltation is an integral part of the larger eschatological design for salvation through Christ, which is to be fully realized and enjoyed by the worshipers at his second coming. See also Lane, *Hebrews 1–8*, 122.

96. For further details, see Wuest, *Hebrews in Greek New Testament*, 102.

97. For this discussion, see also Westcott, *Hebrews*, 131.

98. The perfecting of Christ is connected to his learning obedience through suffering (v. 8), a conceptual connection already laid in Heb 2:10 between perfection and suffering.

99. The Greek noun αἴτιος, "source" or "author," (see BDAG, 31) is understood by most expositors as carrying the same connotation as ἀρχηγός, "originator," "author," "champion," or "chief leader" in Heb 2:10. See Kistemaker, *Hebrews*, 139.

100. Christ's "being made perfect" (and thus his "becoming source of eternal salvation" [5:9]) is connected with his "learning obedience through suffering" (v. 8). This reinforces the conceptual connection already laid out in 2:10 between his perfecting and suffering in order to lead many sons to eternal glory.

101. Similar reasoning is found in Philo when he alludes to the notion that a "source of salvation" brings salvation just as the serpent on the pole (Num 21:8–9) brought life (Philo, *On Agriculture*, 96). Also, Josephus refers to the same notion in terms of a general who brings his troops through battle to victory and safety (Josephus, *Jewish Antiquities*, XIV. 136).

σωτηρίας αἰωνίου, or "source of eternal salvation," is unique[102] as an appropriate expression of the divine redemptive work through Christ.[103] This goes beyond the "help we may find in time of need" (χάριν εὕρωμεν εἰς εὔκαιρον βοήθειαν), in Heb 4:16, to include the future deliverance from sin and death at the second coming of Jesus Christ when he appears again to bring salvation to those who believe (Heb 1:14; 9:28). For the author of Hebrews, the future inheritance of salvation is guaranteed based on the work Christ already accomplished in his suffering, death, and exaltation to the right hand of God, the Father. For the author of Hebrews, therefore, there is no escape for anyone who neglects such a great salvation (2:3). Craig R. Koester remarks that this "entails favorable judgment from God rather than condemnation (6:10) and in its fullest sense means glory in the presence of God (2:10)."[104]

It appears the perfected Christ met all the requirements for the High Priest. The proof of completeness or fulfillment, realized through his suffering, death, and exaltation, is enriched by his appointment as the High Priest according to the order of Melchizedek (5:10), not after the order of Aaron. The eternal priesthood of Christ implies the overthrow of the Levitical priesthood (Heb 7:1–10; Gen 14:17–20; Ps 110:4) in favor of a new hope and better new covenant promises inaugurated by the new and better High Priest (7:11–19).[105] The notion of τέλειος has an eschatological significance pointing to completion of the divine salvific intention. The final order has been inaugurated, accomplishing what the former Levitical order was unable to accomplish on behalf of the worshipers.[106] Thus Lindars rightly posits, "perfection in Hebrews means the completion of God's plan of salvation."[107] Similarly, Koester posits that the notion of τέλειος

---

102. Montefiore, *Hebrews*, 100.

103. The word αἰωνίος, or "eternal," can be taken to mean "without an end" or "pertaining to the timelessness of eternity." Montefiore comments that it is used in the customary way in this Epistle to denote that which belongs to "the world to come," and more importantly, Montefiore suggests that the notion of "eternal" connotes the idea of "participation in the life that is God's own" (Montefiore, *Hebrews*, 100). The eternal salvation that is available to those who obey him (5:9–10) is "more than possession of the land and success; it is 'heavenly' (3:1; 4:14), transtemporal because also transmaterial" (Johnson, *Hebrews*, 148) as the believers participate to their fullest in Christ's glory at the second coming of Christ.

104. Koester, *Hebrews*, 290.

105. Cockerill, "Melchizedek Christology in Hebrews 7:1–28," 24–25.

106. Michel, *Der Brief an die Hebräer*, 138.

107. Lindars, *Theology of Hebrews*, 44.

("completion" or "perfection") "is a fitting way to speak about the outcome of God's purposes, since words based on the root *tel-* have to do with reaching a goal."[108]

The author has already indicated that Christ learned all that obedience entails by enduring suffering beyond what any mortal man has experienced (5:7–8; cf. Phil 2:8). The obedience of Christ is the basis for obedience of those who believe in his name. The author does not suggest that Christian obedience is a prerequisite for receiving salvation, but rather that it is a faith characteristic of those on the journey toward the goal of their eternal salvation. The eternal Son of God was made perfect through all he suffered.[109] As a result, he became the source of eternal salvation, making a way for believers to move with hope into the future that God promised them (1:14; 2:3, 10; 5:8–9; 9:28; 12:1–3). For the author of Hebrews, τέλειος implies that God's eschatological salvation has been made available as a gift to the worshipers. They will ultimately come to its full realization if they followed the path Christ has set before them.[110] This implies that Christ is not just another human hero but is indeed the Son of God. The believers do more than simply imitate his example—they obey and follow him as they approach him as Lord, the one who shares God's life and power, and the one seated at the right hand of the throne of majesty.[111] This is further amplified in the author's next usage of the τέλειος notion.

Hebrews 7:28

The author's final reference to the perfecting of Christ is found in Heb 7:28,[112] where he states, "For the Law appoints as high priests men subject to weakness, but the word of solemn affirmation that came after the Law, appoints the Son made perfect forever." In chapter 5, the author attached the

---

108. For further details, see Koester, *Hebrews*, 122.

109. The notion that "Christ learned obedience through the things he suffered" (Heb 5:8; cf. 2:10) may suggest some kind of development in the Son's personality related to his being perfected. However, the concept of τέλειος ("completion" or "perfection") should not be understood in terms of moral progress or moral development. It is true Hebrews is concerned with the conquest of sin, but the author does not use this concept to convey the notion of "moral ideal," except insofar as it is entailed in the broader theme of completion of God's design for redemption of mankind. For further details, see Lindars, *Theology of Hebrews*, 44.

110. For further details, see Koester, *Hebrews*, 291.

111. Johnson, *Hebrews*, 149.

112. This final verse of chapter 7 is the climax of the author's argument that began at Heb 5:1. For further details, see O'Brien, *Letter to the Hebrews*, 282.

title of high priest to Melchizedek, pointing to Christ's superiority over the Levitical priests. The author concluded his long argumentation for Christ's qualifications by using another citation of Ps 110:4, stating Christ became the High Priest in the order of Melchizedek based on the divine appointment (Heb 5:10). The author elaborates this theme as he continues his argument further on the nature of the Melchizedekian priesthood by divine appointment (προσαγορευθείς).[113]

In Heb 7:1–28, the author shows how Christ's priesthood in the order of Melchizedek is superior to the Levitical priesthood. For the author, Christ is superior for: (1) his priesthood is perpetual as the Son of God (7:1–10); (2) the Scripture testifies to his eternal priesthood in the order of Melchizedek (7:11–19); (3) he is superior because his priesthood is based on a divine oath to be the eternal High Priest (7:20–25); and (4) his priesthood is based on his once-for-all self-sacrifice (7:26–28). Significantly, the same thought introduced previously in Heb 5:8–10 reappears at 7:28, where the author indicates that it was by the word of divine oath that Christ was appointed as the Son made perfect forever. The statement serves as a bridge to the longer section, in which the author will elaborate more on the superiority of Christ based on his better priestly work as the Mediator of the new covenant with its better promises (cf. 8:1—10:39).

The concluding verses (7:26–28) form a crucial conclusion to the chapter, recalling and restating its major themes, but also preparing the readers for the long section that follows (8:1—10:39). Most interpreters recognize the profound difference between the two priesthoods detailed in these verses (vv. 26–28) through a series of important contrasts that summarize the argument of the entire chapter, which is then restated more forcefully in the concluding statement in Heb 7:28.[114] In the first contrast, the Law (ὁ νόμος) served as the basis for the appointment[115] of earthly high priests;[116] the word

---

113. The Greek word προσαγορευθείς is used in the sense of "being appointed" or "being designated" by another and implies the notion of "recognition" (Xenophon, *Memorabilia*, III. 2. 1; Wis 14:22; 2 Macc 1:36; Philo, *On the Life of Abraham*, 121). Thus, Christ is designated not by man, but by the Most High God, the Father, because he fulfills the qualifications for such a higher appointment. For further details, see Johnson, *Hebrews*, 195–96.

114. See Lane, *Hebrews 1–8*, 194.

115. Some scholars take the use of the present tense καθίστησιν (present active indicative of καθίστημι, "to appoint, to set, or put in charge") as suggesting that the Levitical priesthood was still functional at the time of composition of Hebrews with an implication that the temple was still standing in Jerusalem (see Hughes, "Epistle to the Hebrews," 279). However, one may argue that it implies this only indirectly, since what is set forth in Scripture is viewed as present—it exists there for all to read.

116. Their weaknesses and ineffectiveness are described in 7:11–19.

of the oath (ὁ λόγος τῆς ὁρκωμοσίας) served as the basis for the new and perpetual High Priest in the order of Melchizedek (7:1–10, 20–22). Second, whereas the old priesthood consisted of ἄνθρωποι, "men" with their weaknesses, the new high priesthood consists of the υἱός, "Son,"[117] the appointed eternal High Priest of the new covenant who continues forever. Lane indicates the argument recalls the weakness and mortality of the old (or earthly priests) in sharp contrast with the eternal or eschatological finality of the Son as the new High Priest (vv. 23–25).[118] Finally, the author's third contrast in verse 28 is related to verses 26–27, which take readers back to the beginning of the discourse in Heb 5:1–3.[119] The many earthly priests are characterized as ἔχοντας ἀσθένειαν ("having weaknesses"),[120] but Christ, as the new High Priest, is characterized as υἱὸν εἰς τὸν αἰῶνα τετελειωμένον, or "the Son who has been made perfect forever." The earthly priests of the Aaronic order are presented as "having weaknesses" in the sense that they needed to offer sacrifices not only for the people, but for themselves as well (cf. 5:3). As an antithesis, the author provides a majestic final statement (7:28)[121] as he points to the Son as the new High Priest who has been made perfect forever.[122] Most interpreters indicate the three contrasts in the passage restate the lines of argument expounded in the preceding verses (vv. 11–25).[123]

The author's description of the perfected High Priest as "the Son" reminds readers of the arguments of Heb 1:2–14 and 5:5–10. The Son is the one who has been appointed as "heir of all things and through whom God created all things" (1:2); yet the Son's entrance into his inheritance is related

117. The anarthrous use of υἱός emphasizes the character of the Son (cf. 1:2–3, 5; 3:6). Whereas the OT system, with its Law characterized by weaknesses (7:19), appoints earthly priests who have infirmities, the word of τῆς ὁρκωμοσίας, "the sworn oath" or "the oath-taking," which comes after the Law (cf. Ps 110:4) appoints the Son, who has been made perfect forever. For this discussion, see also Anderson, "Root Teleios in Hebrews," 27.

118. For this discussion, see Lane, *Hebrews 1–8*, 195.

119. O'Brien, *Hebrews*, 283.

120. The phrase ἔχοντας ἀσθένειαν, "having weaknesses," is related to ἀνθρώπους, "men," or ἀρχιερεῖς, "earthly priests," as those who have infirmities, pointing to their human or sinful condition. For further details, see Kistemaker, *Hebrews*, 208. The earthly priests or Aaronic priests are described as "having weaknesses" in that they needed to offer sacrifices not only for the people, but also for themselves as well (Heb 5:3).

121. Some scholars draw attention to the emphatic climax of τετελειωμένον, "perfected," the perfect participle placed at the end of the sentence. See, for example, Robertson, *Grammar of the Greek New Testament*, 418.

122. For further details, see also O'Brien, *Hebrews*, 283.

123. See Lane, *Hebrews 1–8*, 194; See also Peterson, *Hebrews and Perfection*, 117.

to the completion of the purification of humankind's sins through his suffering, death, and exaltation to the right hand of the Majesty on high (1:5; Ps 2:7).[124] Many scholars prefer to emphasize the quality of Christ's work; they interpret the notion of the τελείωσις of Christ in Heb 7:28 following not a moral or ethical[125] approach, but a "vocational model" instead. David Peterson posits that the perfecting of Christ as Son in 7:28 points to Jesus' vocation,[126] with his sacrifice being the basis for his high-priestly work and his exaltation. This makes it possible for him to apply continuously the benefits of the once-for-all sacrifice to the needs of the worshipers. Peterson posits, "the 'vocational' understanding of Christ's perfecting is appropriate here (7:28) as well as in 2:10 and 5:9."[127] While this reading of the perfection motif in Hebrews may be disputed,[128] Peterson is nevertheless correct that "the Son's eschatological inheritance could not be secured nor his Sonship decisively manifested for the salvation of his people until he had carried out the earthly ministry destined for him as Messiah."[129] It is best to look at the era of the fulfillment of the Messianic role of the Son not in terms of an

---

124. Peterson posits that the enunciation "You are my Son, today I have begotten you" (Ps 2:7) can be understood at Heb 1:5 and 5:5 "as applying to the inauguration of Christ's heavenly rule as Son, and to the manifestation of his Sonship which takes place through his ascension-enthronement" (Peterson, *Hebrews and Perfection*, 119). However, many expositors would suggest that the author of Hebrews is thinking of the Son as the Davidic Heir (Ps 2:7; 2 Sam 7:14), who will inherit and rule the nations.

125. See Dods, "Epistle to the Hebrews," 319: "Forever perfected is directly contrasted with the sinful yielding to infirmity exhibited by the Levitical priests, and must therefore be referred to moral perfection."

126. Peterson, *Hebrews and Perfection*, 120. Similarly, Walters sees a link between the notion of τέλειος in Hebrews with the sufferings endured by Jesus as a kind of educational or experiential test of obedience to the Father. For further details, see Walters, *Perfection in New Testament Theology*, 88.

127. Peterson, *Hebrews and Perfection*, 119. Peterson emphatically states, "The vocational understanding of the perfecting of Christ is the only interpretation that allows for all the dimensions in our writer's presentation" (ibid., 73, cf. ibid., 204). O'Brien follows Peterson's model and argues that the perfecting of Christ in 7:28 should be understood in "vocational" terms (O'Brien, *Hebrews*, 284).

128. For a critic of Peterson's approach, see McCruden, *Solidarity Perfected*, 20–24. DeSilva notes that while some vocational issues may be regarded as indeed present, they are not to be regarded as attached to the terminology of τέλειος. According to DeSilva, "God may have used sufferings to develop certain qualities in Jesus without using sufferings to 'perfect' him per se." In the case of the worshipers, he indicates, "It is even clearer that these hardships are not the means of their being perfected, which is rather effected by the sacrifice of Christ and fully manifested at the eschatological intervention of God" (DeSilva, *Perseverance in Gratitude*, 198).

129. Peterson, *Hebrews and Perfection*, 119.

educational or experiential test of obedience,[130] nor in terms of his arrival at the heavenly destination or his exaltation,[131] but as eschatological in the sense that the Christ event—his suffering, death, and exaltation—fulfilled the divine intention for the eschatological salvation of humankind. For the author of Hebrews, it is not Jesus' sufferings leading to his vocational qualifications per se, but Christ's person as the eternal Son of God, perfected as the eternal High Priest and Mediator of the new covenant with its better promises, which constitutes the focal point of the argument. Only this reading allows a better appreciation of the eschatological revelation of Christ as final and providing the ultimate, eschatological access to God for those who believe. Having said that, it is now important to focus on the meaning and significance of the τέλειος notion in Heb 7:28.

The Hebrews author indicates that it was by the word of a solemn oath that came after the OT system and the Law in particular that Christ was appointed the Son τὸν αἰῶνα τετελειωμένον, or "made perfect forever."[132] This is the final step by the author to present Christ as the exalted Son of God, who has been perfected as High Priest with the result that he forever stands to provide the final access to God in a way that the Levitical or earthly priests could not.[133] In the first two instances, the author described the "perfected" Christ as the "pioneer of salvation" (2:10) and the "source of eternal salvation for all who obey" (5:9).[134] Consequently, he is seen as the one who

130. This would make this approach very close to the moral/ethical reading of the perfection motif in Hebrews. Thus, it is difficult to substantiate "how a notion of development—moral/ethical or vocational" could agree with passages in Hebrews that emphasize Christ's sinlessness and his undefiled character (Heb 4:15; 7:26). For details, see McCruden, *Solidarity Perfected*, 20–21.

131. DeSilva, *Perseverance in Gratitude*, 199.

132. The perfect passive participle τετελειωμένον implies a completed action with continuing result (Hagner, *Hebrews*, 114–15). This is close to the argument by interpreters who believe that it implies the notion of "permanence" (Kistemaker, *Hebrews*, 210). It may be said to have an intensive (or resultative) force with "results existing in the present" (Wallace, *Exegetical Syntax*, 573).

133. As Mitchell states, Christ provides this final access to the Father, as God's representative, in a way the earthly priests could not. This is the reason the author has presented him first as the "pioneer of salvation" (2:10), "the source of salvation for all who obey Him" (5: 9), and the one who makes it possible for the worshipers to approach "the throne of grace" (4:16) (Mitchell, *Hebrews*, 113).

134. Both verbs as used previously τελειῶσαι (Heb 2:10) and τελειωθείς (5:9) are aorist verbs with ingressive action indicating the "decreed character" of Jesus' entrance into a state (DuPlessis, Τέλειος: *Idea of Perfection*, 214). Some scholars take them as constative aorists summing up what God has accomplished during the entire lifetime of Jesus on earth. For this position, see Hoekema, "Perfection," 33. Others prefer to take them as culminative aorists indicating the historical realization of the process. For this position, see Westcott, *Epistle to the Hebrews*, 198. More likely, the aorists point to a

makes it possible for the believers to approach the throne of grace in order to receive forgiveness of sins, mercy, and grace in times of need (4:16), but he is also seen as the one who forever secures their future salvation (cf. 2:3, 10). It is with this background in mind that one should seek to understand the author's final reference to the τελείωσις of Christ in 7:28, where the author elaborates on the notion of τέλειος by focusing on the abiding efficacy of the work of redemption in Christ. The author includes the phrase εἰς τὸν αἰῶνα, "forever," connected to the participle τετελειωμένον[135] in order to emphasize the permanent effectiveness of the priestly work of Christ as realized in his suffering, death, and exaltation. The author's language once again presupposes the completion of God's eternal design for the salvation of humankind through Christ, the eternal High Priest, and the Mediator of the new covenant (8:1–10:39). That the new is superior is demonstrated in the fact that the old economy proved to be unable to secure eternal salvation on behalf of the worshipers, as shown in the following section.

The theme of the τελείωσις of Christ, introduced in 2:10 and elaborated on in 5:8–9 culminates in the author's solemn statement that "the Son... has been made perfect forever" in 7:28. The author links "perfection" to the salvific, eschatological import of Christ's incarnation, including his suffering, death, and exaltation as the perfected High Priest in the order of Melchizedek.[136] The τελείωσις, or "perfecting," of Christ (Heb 7:22, 25 and 9:28) can be seen as a pledge for his ability not only to intercede on behalf of his brethren, but also to lead them to their future eschatological salvation. Thus, the perfected Christ is presented not only as the author but also the cause of eternal salvation for believers. Unlike the former earthly priests, Jesus, as the perfected High Priest, is presented as the one who has forever secured a final and abiding access to God the Father (7:28) because he is the perfect Mediator and the one who fulfills the better promises of the new covenant.

The perfected Christ as the new definitive and final agent of God's redemption is presented as the source of eschatological salvation based on the better provisions of the new covenant he mediates.[137] This fits well with his exaltation above the heavens, where he sits at the right hand of the throne

---

decreed character of Jesus' entrance into a state with continuing results. In Heb 7:28, the perfect tense τετελειωμένον is used to point to the decreed character of the act as that which has an abiding efficacy. Cf. MacLeod, "Theology of Hebrews," 352–53.

135. The passive voice is used to imply that it God who is the agent. For further details, see Kistemaker, *Hebrews*, 210. For further details on the use of the passive form of the verb τελειοῦν, see Kurianal, *Jesus Our High Priest*, 225.

136. Lehne, *New Covenant in Hebrews*, 96.

137. This is primarily the focus of the author of Hebrews in Heb 8:1–10:39.

of majesty (4:14; 7:26; 8:1; cf. Ps 110:1).[138] Readers must know that as such, he is the High Priest, who not only meets their need, but also offers them all the resources they need (7:26–28) to draw closer to God and attain eschatological glory. There is no doubt that the terminology of "perfection" could be seen as including some nuances or aspects of the "vocational," "moral," "cultic," and "exaltation" shades of meaning.[139] More likely however, the general eschatological sense of "completion" or "eschatological fulfillment" seems to better convey the message of Hebrews.[140] Specifically, the notion of the perfecting of Christ should be understood eschatologically as pointing to the fulfillment of God's design for the salvation of humankind as God's people are drawn closer to their eternal glory to be fully realized at the second coming of Jesus Christ.[141] Having examined the notion of τέλειος with regard to Christ, one is now in a position to examine how the same notion is used with reference to the limitations of the old covenant.

INABILITY OF THE OLD COVENANT TO EFFECT ΤΕΛΕΙΩΣΙΣ

This section examines how the author elaborates on the major theme of the superiority of Christ as he establishes an argument regarding the weaknesses of the old covenant ritual in contrast to the new.[142] For the author, the new order is superior because the former system, including its law and priestly regulations, was unable to lead the worshipers to the goal of τελείωσις, or "perfection" (7:11, 19; 9:9, 11; 10:1),[143] and was inadequate to secure eternal salvation for the believers.

---

138. Christ's exalted status is emphasized (O'Brien, *Hebrews*, 181) as one who also fulfills prophetic and eschatological hopes for God's people (Heb 8:8–12; Jer 31:31–34).

139. Peterson, *Hebrews and Perfection*, 166.

140. Koester, *Hebrews: A New Translation*, 122–25. Koester rightly posits that "completion [perfection] is a fitting way to speak about the outcome of God's purposes, since words based on the root *tel-* have to do with reaching a goal" (ibid., 122).

141. The believers' hope and better provisions of the new covenant can only be understood as a future reality. It is the better promises of the new covenant (Jer 31:31–34; Heb 8:7–12) that, according to the author, guarantee the believers' final or future eschatological access to God. For similar reasoning, see ibid., 187.

142. The language of "two stage process" may be applied here: the first stage is the era of the old covenant made up of laws and regulations already due to pass away (Heb 8:14), but the second stage is "the coming age or end of time in which the new covenant will come into operation" (Lindars, *Theology of Hebrews*, 44). For the author of Hebrews, a transition has already occurred.

143. Rathel, "Soteriological Terminology in Hebrews," 126.

Hebrews 7:11, 19

Hebrews 7:1-28 is an extended sermonic exposition of Gen 14 and Ps 110[144] through a series of contrasts[145] aimed at presenting Christ as the High Priest in an order that is superior to the former Levitical priestly order. In Heb 6:20, the author brought readers back to the concept of the High Priest in the order of Melchizedek[146] introduced first in 5:1-10. In chapter 7, he elaborates further on his presentation of Christ's priesthood in the order of Melchizedek as superior to the priesthood of the descendants of Aaron. The author uses two major arguments to validate his claim about the superiority of Christ's priesthood. First, Abraham paid tithes to Melchizedek and received a blessing from him; in a sense, Levi participated in the action,[147] so it follows that the priesthood of Melchizedek was superior to the priesthood of Levi (7:1-10).[148] This is amplified in the author's second argument that the priesthood that emanated from Levi and the Law upon which it was based was unable to achieve the goal of the priesthood on behalf of the worshipers: providing access to God (7:11-19).[149] Before attempting to determine the meaning and significance of the passage, particularly the use

---

144. Although the historical account about Melchizedek in Gen 14 provides more information than Ps 110, the details are nevertheless not elaborate (Kistemaker, *Hebrews*, 184-85).

145. For a survey of these contrasts, see the previous discussion.

146. The name Melchizedek means "king of righteousness" and is identified also as "king of Salem," which means king of peace. He was "priest of the Most High God" (Gen 14:16-20). The community at Qumran thought of him as a heavenly being. For this discussion, see Fizmyer, "Further Light on Melchizedek," 25-41. For further details, see also Fitzmyer, *Genesis Apocryphon of Qumran Cave 1 (1Q20)*, 245. According to Philo, Melchizedek's priesthood originated with himself, since he was a self-taught individual (Philo, *On the Preliminary Studies*, 99). There is a common interpretation of the figure of Melchizedek as "king of Salem" (with "Salem" identified with Jerusalem), as reflected in the Hellenistic world (see ibid., *Allegorical Interpretation*, III. 79, 82; cf. Josephus, *Jewish War*, VI. 438; ibid., *Jewish Antiquities*, I. 181). For further details, see Fitzmyer, *Genesis Apocryphon of Qumran*, 245-48.

147. According to the author of Hebrews, it could be said that even though Levi received tithes, he paid a tithe through Abraham because he was in his ancestor Abraham's loins when Melchizedek met him. Thus, Levi himself participated in Abraham's action of paying a tithe to Melchizedek.

148. The author of Hebrews uses the figure of Melchizedek as the type of a priesthood that is superior to the Levitical priesthood in order to establish the basis for his argument for the unique high priesthood of the perfected Christ. For this discussion, see Mitchell, *Hebrews*, 139. The paragraph (Heb 7:1-10) begins and ends with a reference to the name Melchizedek, thus forming an *inclusio*. See Vanhoye, *Structure and Message*, 125, 37.

149. Rathel, "Soteriological Terminology in Hebrews," 126.

The Notion of Τέλειος in Hebrews

of the notion of τέλειος, it is important to think through theological truths presented by the author in reference to the historical incident of Melchizedek in Heb 7 (cf. Gen 14:18-20; Ps 110:4).[150]

This incident occurs after Lot separated from Abraham in order to settle in the fertile land of Sodom. Thereafter, a coalition of the Elamites under the leadership of Chedorlaomer successfully invaded the kingdom of Sodom and Gomorrah, taking Lot's family among their captives. Significantly, Abraham had previously been with his nephew Lot when he called on the name of the Lord (Gen 13:1-5). Perhaps, Abraham believed that Lot was also a son of the promise. J. Dwight Pentecost states, "Abraham evidently believed that God would give him victory over the conquerors so that Lot could inherit God's promised blessings."[151] Following his great victory over the Elamites, Abraham returned with the spoils of battle to meet Melchizedek, king and priest like the Son of God (7:1-10). The text indicates how Melchizedek blessed Abraham and received a tithe of Abraham's battle spoils (vv. 1-3; cf. Gen 14:20). The author of Hebrews drew from this historical event some important truths that are relevant to this discussion.

Melchizedek is described first as βασιλεὺς Σαλήμ, "king of Salem,"[152] perhaps with a connotation that he ministered in Jerusalem.[153] Most scholars indicate that the association comes naturally since the noun Salem is included in Jerusalem and Abraham's place of meeting with Melchizedek is said to be at the King's Valley, which is in or around Jerusalem.[154] If this

---

150. Many expositors indicate that much of the theme of Hebrews revolves around the figure of Melchizedek, who is referred to only twice in all previous Scripture (Gen 14:18-20; Ps 110:4). The number of occurrences is insignificant, yet the author of Hebrews uses these two references to firmly demonstrate how Christ's priesthood is superior to the Levitical priesthood. For further details and historical background, see Pentecost, *Faith That Endures*, 116-24.

151. Ibid., 118.

152. "Salem" means "peace" and "Melchizedek" means "king of righteousness." Clearly, the author has in mind a king/priest whose reign will be characterized by peace and righteousness (see Koester, *Hebrews*, 138-39.). As Pentecost observes, "These are the two principle characteristics of the reign of the Messiah as described by the OT prophets (Isa 9:6-7; 48:18)" (Pentecost, *Faith That Endures*, 119).

153. As Koester indicates, "*Salēm* is the LXX's transliteration of the Hebrew placename *Shālēm*, which many identified with Jerusalem" (Koester, *Hebrews*, 341; cf. 1QapGen 22:13; Josephus, *Jewish War*, VI. 438; ibid., *Jewish Antiquities*, I. 180; Targums to Gen 14:18; cf. Jerome, *Hebrew Questions*, 14:18-19). While most of the Targums assume that Salem is the same as Jerusalem, Jerome identified it with the Salim of John 3:23 (Ellingworth, *Hebrews*, 355). For the Targums' reference, see Drazin and Wagner, *Targum Onkelos on the Torah*, 79. For further details, see Etheridge, *Targums of Onkelos and Jonathan ben Uzziel on the Pentateuch*, 199-200.

154. See Gen 14:17; 2 Sam 18:18; Ps 72:2 (MT); Josephus, *Jewish Antiquities*, VII. 243. Thus, Koester observes that "listeners would probably have associated Salem with

reconstruction is correct, then some parallels can be identified between Jerusalem as the center of David's reign and the ultimate center of the earthly reign of Christ following his second coming. The author's identification of Melchizedek as priest of the Most High God emphasizes the universality of Christ's ministry in contrast to the ineffectiveness of the Levitical priesthood, which ministered only to Israel. The figure of Melchizedek unites two offices in one person, born king and priest. Most interpreters agree the only Bible figure who exercises these two offices will be Christ at the second coming when as the King/Priest he will ultimately sit on David's throne to rule over David's kingdom.[155] This background is insightful when examined in light of the theme and purpose of Hebrews. For the Hebrews' author, not only is the king-priest Melchizedek superior to the Levitical priesthood since his priesthood is perpetual like the Son of God (Heb 7:1–10; cf. Ps 110:4), but also Christ, the new High Priest in the order of Melchizedek, is superior because of the ineffectiveness of the old *cultus* to effect τελείωσις (7:11).[156] Thus, the old has been replaced by the new, which is based on the hope that draws worshipers near to God (7:19). For the author, τελείωσις that was not available through the agency of the Levitical priesthood is now made available to the worshipers through the perfected Christ,[157] as the High Priest in the order of Melchizedek.

The question is, what does the author imply by the idea that the Levitical priesthood was unable to accomplish τελείωσις, or "perfection"? A look at the text reveals that Heb 7:11–19 constitutes a single paragraph in the Greek NT framed together by the notion of τέλειος that occurs in both verses 11 (τελείωσις) and 19 (ἐτελείωσεν).[158] In 7:11, the author states, Εἰ μὲν οὖν τελείωσις διὰ τῆς Λευιτικῆς ἱερωσύνης ἦν, or "If on the one hand therefore perfection had been possible through the Levitical priesthood. . ." The writer goes on to say, "what further need would there have been for another priest to arise, said to be in the order of Melchizedek and not in Aaron's order?" The author is emphatic that a change in priesthood has taken place in the appointment of Christ as the High Priest. He indicates that Christ is a priest (ἕτερος) not of the Aaronic order (Heb 7:11), from a

---

Jerusalem rather than with Shechem (Jer 48:5 LXX [41:5 MT]; Jdt 4:4; cf. Gen 33:18 LXX. . .) or with the Salim near Aenon (John 3:23; cf. Jerome, *Ep.* 73.7)" (Koester, *Hebrews*, 341).

155. For this discussion, see Pentecost, *Faith That Endures*, 118–24.

156. The suffix of τελείωσις (-σις) indicates that this is the *nomen actionis*, the action of making perfect; its use specifically implies that the Levitical priests were unable to provide perfection (Kurianal, *Jesus Our High Priest*, 107, 233).

157. Rathel, "Soteriological Terminology in Hebrews," 126–27.

158. Ibid.

The Notion of Τέλειος in Hebrews

different tribe (ἑτέρας) other than Aaron (7:13), and from the tribe of Judah (7:14). As most interpreters would indicate, in Christ's appointment as High Priest in the order of Melchizedek, an ἀθέτησις, "removal," of the previous precepts has occurred (7:18) which would serve as the basis for the appointment of the Levitical priests.[159] The reason for the removal of the previous precepts is suitably summarized by Kurianal when he states, that Christ "having been born in the tribe of Judah and not in the tribe of Aaron, the appointment of Jesus as priest contravenes the prescriptions of the Law and implies that a change of law has taken place (7:12–14)."[160]

Right from the start of this section, the Hebrews' author introduces the need for the new kind of priesthood in the order of Melchizedek because of the failure of the Levitical priesthood (7:11). The particle εἰ "if," introduces a second-class, contrary-to-fact conditional sentence, or an "unreal condition."[161] Often, contrary-to-fact conditional sentences would have the particle ἄν in the apodosis (cf. Heb 4:8; 8:4, 7; 11:15), but as most grammarians indicate, this is not the case here, and it is not necessary,[162] since it has been absorbed by the interrogative clause that follows.[163] The author's purpose is to firmly establish that the goal of true τελείωσις[164] could not be

---

159. For further details, see Kurianal, *Jesus Our High Priest*, 201–202.

160. Ibid.

161. See Koester, *Hebrews*, 353; Ellingworth, *Hebrews*, 370; and Hagner, *Hebrews*, 84, among others. Most interpreters construe the sentence as a past contrary-to-fact condition (see NJB, NASB, NAB, NRSV): "If perfection had occurred, which it had not," or "If perfection had been attained through the Levitical priesthood." Other scholars, however, including Attridge, consider the argument in the text as general and abstract and posit that "the ordinary syntactical pattern of a present contra-factual condition is appropriate" (Attridge, *Hebrews*, 199). It is perhaps best to take this as a past contrary-to-fact condition. As many scholars agree, the whole tenor of the argument in the text indicates the author thinks of the condition as unreal as far back as the time of the Psalmist (Ps 110:4), but also "most of the exceptions from the normal imperfect + imperfect second class conditions relate to the use of εἰμί as is the case here" (Oyediran, *Lexical and Exegetical Analysis*, 69). For further details, see Boyer, "Second Class Conditions in NT Greek," 85–86.

162. Blass and Debrunner, *Greek Grammar of the New Testament*, 360–61. For further details, see also Robertson, *Grammar*, 1015.

163. Winner, *Grammar of the Idiom of the New Testament*, 304. There are many other examples in the NT where "unreal conditions" are expressed without the particle α‡ν in the apodosis as in Gal 3:18 (cf. 2:21).

164. The author uses a noun form τελείωσις with an active ending, which may be rendered "perfecting" or "completing." As Anderson notes here, the act appears to be in view rather than the state as in τελείοτης (cf. Heb 6:1; 12:2). For further details, see Anderson, "Root *Teleios*," 25. It is the action of making perfect (τελείωσις as the *nomen actionis*) that is emphasized. This is contrary to scholars who take the noun as implying that the Levitical priests were not perfect. For example, Guthrie states, "the necessity of

reached through the Levitical priesthood: there is no perfecting that could be brought about by the Λευιτικῆς ἱερωσύνης, Levitical priesthood.[165] With a presupposition that the ultimate purpose of the priesthood is to lead the worshipers to τελείωσις, or "perfection," it is well established that the old Levitical system is unable to accomplish the goal of leading the worshipers to true "perfection," which is linked with the better hope that guarantees access to God for those who are drawing near (7:19). The author reminds his readers of the ineffectiveness of the Levitical priesthood (in contrast to the priesthood of Christ), which he vividly describes in terms of its inability to accomplish or fulfill the goal of τελείωσις, or "perfection."[166] This is the better hope for the believer who is drawing near to uninhibited access to God.

As discussed previously,[167] a similar noun form (τελείωσις) appears in Luke 1:45, where it expresses Mary's belief in the fulfillment of God's promise and prediction to her. Bock observes that God's promise coming to completion is part of Luke's fulfillment motif—the key term being τελείωσις, which carries the notion of "fulfillment or completion."[168] For Luke, the fulfillment of the promise to Mary is an assurance to the readers that the final or definitive completion of all of God's promises[169] will come to pass. The context includes future eschatological fulfillment of God's promises that are yet to be realized.[170]

In Heb 7:11, the extent of what the noun form τελείωσις entails is suggested by the context, especially other passages (7:19; 9:9; 10:1)[171] where the notion is applied to the inability of Levitical priests to secure eternal salvation for worshipers, but also the author's affirmation that the per-

---

the new priest arising according to the order of Melchizedek came about... because of the imperfection of the law ordained priesthood" (Guthrie, *Structure of Hebrews*, 84).

165. Anderson, "Root *Teleios*," 25.

166. The noun form appears here and in Luke 1:45, where it points to the "fulfillment of God's promise." For further details, see Attridge, *Hebrews*, 200.

167. See previous discussion on the notion of τέλειος in the "Synoptic Gospels, John, and Acts" section in chapter 3.

168. For further details, see Bock, *Luke 1:1–9:50*, 139.

169. In Luke's context, the promise includes Christ's seating on the throne of his ancestor David (Luke 1:32) and his rule over the House of Jacob forever (v. 33), thus establishing the everlasting Davidic kingdom forever (2 Sam 7; Jer 31:31–34) in fulfillment in God's promise to Abraham (Luke 1:55).

170. Bovon, commenting on Luke's use of τελείωσις, remarks that Luke 1:45 "speaks of the eschatological fulfillment that Mary awaited for." Further validating his observation about future eschatology in the context, he observes that for the evangelist, "Les vv. 51–55 célèbrent l'accomplissement eschatologique encore entendu dans la foi" (Bovon, *L'Évangile sélon Saint Luc*, 93).

171. For further details, see the discussion following in this chapter.

The Notion of Τέλειος in Hebrews

fected Christ has perfected the believers forever. Specifically, its meaning is elucidated by the author's descriptions of the effects of the redemptive work of the perfected Christ as the Eternal Son of God and the perfected High Priest according to the order of Melchizedek.[172] The author presents Christ as the one who has secured eternal salvation for the believers by removing the obstacle of sin (Heb 9:9, 13; 10:2-4), which laid on people's consciences and impeded access to God. This is well reasoned by A. B. Davidson when he alludes to the idea that an institution can only bring τελείωσις ("perfection") "when it effects the purpose for which it was instituted, and produces a result that corresponds to the idea of it."[173] If the true design of the priesthood was to bring people near to God (cf. Heb 7:19), then it would have been effected by the removal of the obstacle: people's sin (cf. Jer 31:31-34). The obstacle of sin preying on people's consciences would prevent their access to God.[174] Thus, for the author of Hebrews, the inadequacy of the Levitical system is equated with its inability to effect the "removal of sin."[175] By contrast, Christ—in his suffering, death on the cross, and exaltation—has truly removed the obstacle of sin (Heb 9:9, 13; 10:2-4) by cleansing believers' consciences and sanctifying them forever (9:14, 28; 10:10, 14).[176] Koester suggests that the noun form τελείωσις ("completion") "points to the establishment of the right relationship with God through the cleansing of conscience and the consummation of this relationship in everlasting glory, rest, and celebration in God's heavenly city."[177] If this reconstruction is correct, then the terminology cannot be limited to a moral/ethical, consecratory,[178] or even vocational sense; but the language looks beyond what is present in anticipation of future eschatological consummation.

---

172. Attridge, *Hebrews*, 200.

173. Davidson, *Epistle to the Hebrews*, 136.

174. Ibid.

175. Peterson, *Hebrews and Perfection*, 108-12.

176. For further details, see Attridge, *Hebrews*, 200. Yet the full enjoyment of such a removal of sin can only be perceived as a future eschatological reality when the effect of sin is completely and forever removed.

177. Koester, *Introduction to the New Testament*, 122-25, 353.

178. As Attridge writes, τελείωσις, is not just a technical term for priestly consecration (*contra* Delling, *TDNT* 8:84-86; DuPlessis, *Τέλειος: Idea of Perfection*, 229), but rather refers to that relationship with God that the covenant inaugurated and provided by Christ's sacrifice. While Attridge and many scholars see in these passages only realized eschatology (see Attridge, *Hebrews*, 200; and Hagner, *Hebrews*, 112), the position expounded in this study is that the context is full of unrealized eschatology pointing to the future, when God will ultimately fulfill all the better provisions of the new covenant on behalf of his people (Heb 8:6-12; cf. Jer 31:31-34).

In Heb 7:19, the author further elaborates on the inadequacy of the former order, which he introduced in verse 11 by again using the notion of τέλειος. He states, "For the Law made nothing perfect (ἐτελείωσεν); on the other hand, a better hope is introduced through which we draw near to God" (7:19). In Heb 7:11, the author introduces a parenthetical phrase pointing to the idea that the Law was under a priesthood that was inadequate in leading the worshipers to τελείωσις, "perfection, completion" or their final access to God. In the succeeding verse, the author also indicates that "whenever the priesthood changes, a change in the Law must come as well" (7:12). Perhaps the question here is, "If the Levitical priesthood was inadequate in bringing the people to τελείωσις, what about its law?"[179] The question is addressed in verse 19, where the author elaborates on his thoughts through another parenthetical phrase,[180] οὐδὲν γὰρ ἐτελείωσεν ὁ νόμος, or "for the law made nothing perfect" (v. 19a).

The Hebrews' author establishes his argument about the superiority of the new order by showing that Christ has become High Priest not according to legal precepts of fleshly descent (7:16),[181] but by divine appointment as evidenced in Scripture (7:17; Ps 110:4).[182] Christ was designated as High Priest with the divine word of a sworn oath (7:20–21). It was, therefore, by necessity that the former Law, including its legal precepts, was set aside because of its inability to effect the purpose for which it was instituted (7:18)—that is, to bring the worshipers to their intended goal. However, a better hope (δὲ κρείττονος ἐλπίδος) has been introduced through which the worshipers can draw near to God (7:19). Most interpreters indicate that the phrase implies a contrast between the old and new order. Kurianal observes that "the difference between the two orders is one of life and death."[183] In addition, it points to the superiority of the new order inaugurated by Christ. As Ellingworth notes, the phrase should not be understood psychologically[184] but should instead be regarded in terms of grounds for hope: it is

179. For this discussion, see also Anderson, "Root *Teleios*," 26.

180. The parenthetical phrase is explanatory with γάρ, explaining the author's comments in the preceding verse that the Law was inadequate, weak, and therefore useless as far as complete and lasting access to God is concerned. For this discussion, see Morris, "Hebrews," 69. Other scholars take the whole verse as parenthetical. See, for example, Hagner, *Hebrews*, 109.

181. Fleshly descent implies death, as the context indicates (cf. 7:23, 27), which is an implicit reference to the mortal nature of the earthly priests in contrast to Christ as the new, eternal High Priest who remains forever (cf. 7:24). For this discussion, see also Kurianal, *Jesus Our High Priest*, 202.

182. The author builds on his previous argument (Heb 5:5–6, 10; cf. Ps 2:7; 110:4).

183. Kurianal, *Jesus Our High Priest*, 202.

184. This would imply that "God has made us more hopeful" (Ellingworth, *Hebrews*,

the hope for "something better" (cf. Heb 3:6) and is related to the promise that remains to enter God's future rest (4:1–11; Ps 95:1). The "something better" is immediately defined as "a better covenant" (7:22),[185] which guarantees future eschatological access to God through Christ, who "is able to save for all times those who approach God through him" (v. 25). Montefiore contends that in both Judaism and Christianity, this hope signifies the same goal, which is the realization of God's final destiny for God's people. For the worshipers or believers under the new order, this "hope is eschatological, looking beyond the present to man's ultimate goal" of complete and lasting access to God.[186] The author does not explicitly point to this future intended goal in Heb 7:11, but it is clearly specified as the future or final access to God in verse 19.[187]

The author again cites the word of a sworn oath (Heb 7:17; Ps 110:4; cf. Heb 7:20) affirming Christ, the Son of David, as the eternal High Priest in the order of Melchizedek; then he introduces a parenthetical phrase to validate his previous assertions. He states, "For the Law made nothing perfect" (οὐδὲν γὰρ ἐτελείωσεν ὁ νόμος), as he explains the disannulling of the Law because of its inability to effect "completeness" or "a complete access to God" on behalf of the worshipers. The τέλειος notion carrying the idea of "complete and lasting access to God," should be viewed as pointing to future eschatological blessings to be fully realized on behalf of the worshipers at the second coming of Christ, when the worshipers are finally made complete.

The concept of τέλειος cannot, therefore, be uniquely perceived in terms of present cultic or consecratory fitness,[188] nor can it be comprehended simply in terms of a vocational or experiential qualification in the sense of a right relationship or participation in the experience of Christ in the present.[189] The finite verb implies that the Law is unable to accomplish

---

382).

185. The author of Hebrews develops the theme of the new covenant in Heb 8:6–13, where he elaborates on the better provisions of the new order with a guarantee for future eschatological blessings for God's people.

186. For this discussion, see Montefiore, *Hebrews*, 126–27. It is in view of this hope that the believer can do what could have never been fully achieved under the Jewish Law, that is, "he can draw near to God" (ibid.).

187. Rathel, "Soteriological Terminology," 127.

188. Ellingworth, *Hebrews*, 381. See also Delling, "τέλειος," *TDNT* 8:84–86.

189. See Lane, *Hebrews 1–8*, 185. However, Lane is correct when he argues that the finite verb ἐτελείωσεν implies that "the law did not bring the eschatological fulfillment intended by God" (v. 11). While the "drawing near to God" can be taken in terms of a right relationship with God in the present, the context points to something beyond the present—the ultimate or complete access to God, which is associated with a complete

the intended eschatological goal designed by God to draw many believers to their eschatological glory in their complete enjoyment of uninhibited access to God. The believers have already tasted some aspects or benefits of their status as those in Christ,[190] but such complete access can only be understood as expected in the yet to be fully realized future, when believers will perfectly share in Christ's glory and fullness of their eternal salvation. Further evidence is implied in the author's use of the τέλειος notion in Heb 9:9, 11 and 10:1, where he elaborates on the limited provisional character of the old tabernacle in contrast to the singular and new sacrifice of Christ.

Hebrews 9:9, 11

In Heb 9:9, 11, the author emphasizes the inability of the older sacrificial rituals of the earthly tabernacle (cf. 9:6–10) in contrast to the once-for-all greater and complete sacrifice of the heavenly sanctuary in Christ (9:11–28). Although only the high priest was allowed to enter the inner sanctuary once a year on the Day of Atonement,[191] the perfected Christ entered into the most Holy Place once-for-all, not with sacrificial blood of animals, but his own blood (9:11–14). While the Levitical priests needed to offer sacrifices for their own sins (cf. 5:3; 7:27), Christ did not because he is without sin (4:15). Thus, Christ inaugurated the new covenant (9:15–22) through his provision of a more perfect sacrifice (9:23–27) that guarantees the future eschatological salvation for the worshipers (9:28).

In verse 9, the author writes, "This was a symbol for the time then present, when gifts and sacrifices were offered that could not τελειῶσαι, 'make perfect,' the conscience of the worshipers." In 9:1–10, the author describes the provisional character of the first tabernacle as having limitations to access the most holy place and to cleanse people from sins. He describes the

---

removal of sin in the future (Heb 8:8–12; cf. Jer 31:31–34). For other scholars who see only vocational or experiential aspects in the present, see Attridge, *Hebrews*, 204; and Peterson, *Hebrews and Perfection*, 166. Cf. Riggenbach, *Hebräer*, 201.

190. This portion of the argument becomes clearer in Heb 8:1–10:39, as the following lines will indicate. Rathel argues that the tenth chapter is especially insightful, since the author develops there "the unstated portion of Heb 7:11–19" (Rathel, "Soteriological Terminology in Hebrews," 127).

191. See Philo, *On the Special Laws*, I. 72; Josephus, *Jewish War*, V. 236; Diodorus Siculus, *Library of History*, XXXIV. 1. 3; Exod 30:10; Lev 16:2, 29, 34; *m. Yoma* 5:1–7; 7:4. Koester observes that though the high priest could enter the chamber more than once (cf. *m. Yoma* 5:1–7; 7:4; Philo, *On the Embassy to Gaius*, 307), everything was accomplished on a single day. Accordingly, his entry only "once" per year "foreshadowed Christ's self-sacrifice made "once" for all times (Heb 7:27; 9:12, 26, 28; 10:10)" (Koester, *Introduction*, 396).

The Notion of Τέλειος in Hebrews

first sanctuary (9:1–5), then he gives details about the nature of the ministry of the high priest, pointing to its limitations to the Holy of Holies and the cleansing of the worshipers (vv. 6–10). In verses 8–10, the author provides two related reasons why the ministry of earthly priests was ineffective. The former priests were effective only for ritual or external matters until the new order could be revealed (9:10); therefore, they could not perfect the conscience of the worshipers (9:9). This line of thought presents some interpretative issues[192] that necessitate one's attention in order to appreciate the author's meaning of the passage. The antecedent of the Greek relative pronoun ἥτις, "which, this," and the implied τῆς πρώτης σκηνῆς, "first tabernacle" (v. 8) are debatable. Also the ambiguity presented by the phrase τὸν καιρὸν τὸν ἐνεστηκότα translated the "present time," has led to varying interpretations by different scholars. A brief evaluation of these interpretative issues follows before an attempt to elucidate the meaning of the passage.

The indefinite relative pronoun ἥτις introduces a parenthetical clause, but its antecedent is unclear. Grammatically, the most natural assumption is that it is related to τῆς πρώτης σκηνῆς, "the first tabernacle," in the preceding verse.[193] However, some interpreters take the antecedent of this pronoun to be the whole situation or state of affairs depicted in verses 6–8[194] in which case the gender of the relative pronoun is seen as related to the feminine noun παραβολή, translated as "symbol" or "illustration."[195] From the context, the relative pronoun should be seen as referring back to τῆς πρώτης σκηνῆς, "the first tabernacle," and denoting that it was of such a kind as a παραβολή, "symbol" or "parable," according to which "gifts and sacrifices were offered that could not cleanse the conscience, and thus make

---

192. For a summary evaluation of these interpretative issues, see Attridge, *Hebrews*, 240–42.

193. Moffatt, *Epistle to the Hebrews*, 118; Riggenbach, *Hebräer*, 252; Rathel, "Soteriological Terminology," 128. On the issue regarding gender, one may assume that the τῆς πρώτης σκηνῆς is the whole earthly tabernacle, in which case there would not be a problem. For this discussion, see Attridge, *Hebrews*, 241.

194. See, for example, Montefiore, *Hebrews*, 149.

195. Michel, *Der Brief an die Hebräer*, 307. See also Bruce, *Hebrews*, 195–97. The Greek feminine noun, παραβολή is translated as "symbol" (BDAG, 559; cf. NASB, NJB, NRSV). Other interpretations include "figure" (Louw and Nida, *Greek English Lexicon*, 33:15. Cf. KJV), "allegory" (ibid.), "illustration" (Lane, *Hebrews 9–13*, 223; cf. NIV). Attridge rightly posits, "the term is widely used for various sorts of figurative speeches." In fact, "In the NT, it is used outside of Hebrews (cf. also Heb 11:19) only in the Synoptics for similitudes and pointed narratives of Jesus" (Attridge, *Hebrews*, 241). Koester comments that "Hebrews uses the term for typological connections between the old and new covenants." Accordingly, the first tabernacle, which is associated with Jewish sacrificial rituals, is only a symbol for "the present time" (Koester, *Hebrews*, 398). Further details are alluded to in the discussion that follows.

the worshipers perfect."[196] Mitchell contends that the symbolic significance of "the first tabernacle" lies in the fact that the sacrificial rituals continuously performed in it were unable to grant permanent access to God in the way Christ's once-for-all sacrifice did.[197] The author contrasts the limited access available through the old earthly tabernacle to the free access made available through Christ. Accordingly, the gifts and sacrifices offered on the basis of the old *cultus* were unable to make perfect (τελείωσις) the worshiper.[198]

The other interpretative issue is the ambiguous phrase τὸν καιρὸν τὸν ἐνεστηκότα, "the present time, " which features the first tabernacle as a "parable,"[199] symbol, type, or a shadow, pointing to the reality to come. Some scholars interpret the phrase as referring to the time that was then present (KJV),[200] implying the past OT time when the earthly tabernacle existed.[201] If this is correct, the presence of the veil is seen as an "outward and visible sign" of the spiritual condition of the worshipers during that time: they could not draw near because the way to God had not yet opened up.[202] Most scholars consider this as referring symbolically to the unfulfilled old covenant that was still in effect at the time of writing of Hebrews (cf. RSV, NEB), implying that the OT sacrificial rituals were still perhaps taking place when Hebrews was written.[203] Koester observes that the "present time" is one of nonfulfillment, because the sacrificial rituals performed on behalf of the worshipers were unable to bring the conscience to "completion" (9:9b).[204] Many scholars identify "the present time" with the time of

196. Anderson, "Root *Teleios*," 29.

197. Mitchell, *Hebrews*, 177.

198. The participial phrase τὸν λατρεύοντα, "the one worshipping," is rendered as "the worshiper" (BDAG, 587; Montefiore, *Hebrews*, 149). Lane alludes to the idea that the phrase should be interpreted in the context of the LXX usage, where the notion touches on cultic worship in general (see Exod 3:12; 4:23; 7:26): "The expression describes the individual in his role as worshiper, who would 'draw near to God' (10:1)" (Lane, *Hebrews 9–13*, 224).

199. The word "parable" is not to be taken like a "narrative parable" as in the Synoptics; rather, it is "a rhetorical figure of speech involving a comparison" (Ellingworth, *Hebrews*, 440).

200. For this approach, see Westcott, *Epistle to the Hebrews*, 252–53; and Dods, "Hebrews," 331. Cf. KJV, NET.

201. Koester proposes that "the present time" is the author's own time, since that is the way the phrase τὸν καιρὸν τὸν ἐνεστηκότα would have been used (Koester, *Hebrews*, 398; see also Polybius, *Histories*, I. 60. 9; 21.3.3; Philo, *On the Sacrifices of Cain and Abel*, 47; and Josephus, *Jewish Antiquities*, XVI. 162).

202. Bruce, *Hebrews*, 209.

203. For this approach, see Montefiore, *Hebrews*, 149; Hagner, *Hebrews*, 134; and Hughes, *Epistle to the Hebrews*, 323–24.

204. Koester, *Hebrews*, 398. Koester states, "The negative connotations echo Jewish

restoration or "time of correction," which is the age of the new order or the new dispensation (9:10),[205] when "salvation and effective sacrifice are available." Speaking of the old tabernacle, Attridge states, "It is the inverse image of the present when 'the age to come' can already be experienced."[206] Yet, while it is true that the "age to come" can be experienced now, its full realization can only be perceived as a future reality. Montefiore concludes that, while the way to God has already been opened through the sacrifice of Christ, "It will not be until the full establishment of the world to come that the way to God will be absolutely opened."[207] In either case, the author of Hebrews contrasts the limited access to God which the worshipers had under the old covenant with the free and complete access to God which has been made possible on behalf of the worshipers by "the person and work"[208] of Christ. The author elaborates further as he shows how the first tabernacle only served as a shadow of what was to come. For the Hebrews' author, the earthly sacrificial rituals under the old system could not "perfect" the conscience of the worshipers.

The author of Hebrews previously referred to the weakness of the old sacrificial rituals and their inability to provide "perfection" given their association with the realm of the flesh (cf. Heb 7:16). In Heb 9:9b, he repeats

---

teachings concerning the two ages: the present age is dominated by sin and death, and the age to come brings redemption and resurrection (4 Ezra 6:7–8; 8:1; 2 Bar 17:7; *m. Pe'ah* 1.1; *m. Abot* 4:17; cf. Mark 10:30; Rom 8:18)" (ibid.).

205. The phrase καιροῦ διορθώσεως ἐπικείμενα may be rendered as "time of correction," or "time when the new order is put into effect," or "time of setting things right" (cf. NJB, NRSV). The context seems to indicate it points to the full benefits of the new covenant as the reality that will ultimately replace the shadow, or the old covenant. Many interpreters see the new covenant as already fully in effect through the sacrifice of Christ (for examples, see Peterson, *Hebrews and Perfection*, 135; Morris, "Hebrews," 84; Hagner, *Hebrews*, 130; Lenski, *Hebrews*, 288; and Bruce, *Hebrews*, 212). Koester argues, "The time of correction arrived when Christ inaugurated the new covenant by his self-sacrifice, which provides complete cleansing" (Koester, *Hebrews*, 398). It is safer to argue that though it is true that the age of the new covenant was inaugurated by Christ (Ellingworth, *Hebrews*, 444), its full realization and final restoration belong to the future eschatological age to come. See also Montefiore, *Hebrews*, 149.

206. Attridge, *Hebrews*, 242. For further details, see also Westcott, *Hebrews*, 255.

207. Montefiore, *Hebrews*, 149–50.

208. Christ's redemptive work cannot be separated from his person as the Son of God. DuPlessis observes, "His mediatorial and personal qualities are so intertwined that to regard the consummation only in respect of one or the other means violation of the unity of his personality" (DuPlessis, Τέλειος: *Idea of Perfection*, 219). Westcott also contends that one must take account of both Christ's life as the one who personally fulfilled in one true, human lifetime the destiny of humankind *and* Christ's life as the appointed Son of God, who fulfills, as Head of the race, the destiny of humanity by redemption and consummation (Westcott, *Hebrews*, 66).

this claim more precisely as he points to the concept that "gifts and sacrifices were offered that could not perfect (τελειῶσαι) the conscience of the worshipers." This passage focuses on "bringing to completion" the worshipers "with regard to conscience" (κατὰ συνείδησιν).²⁰⁹ Interpreters believe the noun συνείδησις, which is prominent in Paul's letters,²¹⁰ grew out of the classical usage of the verbal expression for "consciousness" or "awareness" (συνειδέναι ἑαυτῷ) and was used in a moral sense for "awareness of transgressions or the faculty for such awareness" as it appears in Greco-Jewish writings.²¹¹ For Paul, "the conscience was a part of the human constitution, and thus all people had accountability before God (Rom 2:15)."²¹² For Hebrews, a clear conscience is to be seen as the basis for the future hope and confidence needed to approach God and to maintain such convictions.²¹³ A conscience such as this, with its deep religious overtones, is directed toward God and embraces the whole person in relationship to God (9:9, 14; 10:2, 22; 13:18). Yet, as an awareness of human transgressions, the term seems to have a negative connotation²¹⁴ of an unceasing internal witness that human defilement extends to the heart and mind. The ceremonial ritual on the Day of Atonement provided temporary relief, but the renewal was short-lived, since its annual repetition indicated that sin and guilt had again come into remembrance (10:3-4).²¹⁵ The repetitive nature of the sacrificial offerings points to its limitations with regard complete removal of sin.

The author of Hebrews specifies that such "gifts and sacrifices" were offered under the old covenant, but they could not τελειῶσαι²¹⁶ ("make

209. The phrase κατὰ συνείδησιν is perceived as an adverbial accusative of reference. The term συνείδησις, or "conscience," is rare in the LXX, where it is restricted to wisdom literature (Job 27:6; Eccl 10:20; Wis 17:11, cf. Sir 42:18). However, it appears to have been common in the Hellenistic world (Philo, *Who Is the Heir?* 6-7; ibid., *On the Special Laws*, I. 203; Josephus, *Jewish Antiquities*, II. 52; XVI. 4. 2; cf. Maurer, "συνείδησις," TDNT 7:898-19). For further details, see Koester, *Hebrews*, 399.

210. Cf. Rom 2:15; 13:5; 1 Cor 4:4; 8:7, 10, 12; 10:25-28; 2 Cor 1:2; 4:2; 5:11; 1 Tim 1:5; 3:9; 4:2; 2 Tim 1:3; Titus 1:15; cf. 1 Clem 1:3.

211. Cf. Wis 17:10; Josephus, *Jewish Antiquities*, XVI. 4. 2. For this discussion, see Attridge, *Hebrews*, 242.

212. Koester, *Introduction*, 399.

213. A similar notion is found in Philo, *Who Is the Heir?* 6-7; and Josephus, *Jewish Antiquities*, II. 53; XVI. 4. 2.

214. Lane observes that συνείδησιν is not involved in the moral decision-making process but rather in the process of remembering ("uneasy conscience") due to the defilement of the mind and heart as an obstacle to approach God, which calls for a more decisive purgation. For this discussion, see Lane, *Hebrews 9-13*, 225.

215. Ibid.

216. The Greek verb τελειῶσαι (aorist active infinitive of τελειόω) may be translated as "to perfect" (NRSV, NET), "to make perfect" (NAB, NASB, TEV; BDAG, 996), or "to

perfect") the worshipers' consciences. The object of the verbal action is the attached participial phrase τὸν λατρεύοντα, "the one worshipping."[217] Accordingly, the sacrifices and offering under the old *cultus* could not perfect the worshiper with regard to the conscience. Such Levitical regulations were designed to convey the belief that the true way to God did not lay through them, as they could not meet the deepest human need: the removal of the obstacle for approaching God. For the author, concern with externals only would apply until the "time of correction," or the time of the new order (cf. 9:9–10) that allows a final, definitive access to God. The reference to the worshipers' τελείωσις, regarding the cleansing of the conscience from the burden of sin and guilt, coincides with the fulfillment of the new covenant prophecy of Jeremiah (31:31–34; cf. Heb 8:6–11).[218] The context indicates the new order has been inaugurated with the appearance and death of Christ, whom the author presents as the High Priest of the good things that have come (cf. 9:11). However, contrary to many interpretations, full enjoyment of its better provisions for God's people is still future.

In Heb 9:1–10, the author shows that the Aaronic sacrificial system of the old *cultus* had limitations to access the holy place and perfect the worshiper with reference to his conscience. Then in 9:11–28, he introduces a contrast to his discussion of old covenant sacrifices that the High Priest of the heavenly sanctuary has provided a "perfect" sacrifice inaugurating the new covenant. First, Christ entered the heavenly sanctuary with his own sacrificial blood (9:11–14); second, Christ's sacrificial death has inaugurated the new covenant, thus providing redemption and eternal inheritance for those who have been called (vv. 15–22); third, Christ's better sacrifice of his once-for-all own blood guarantees future salvation for the believers awaiting the second coming of Christ, when he shall appear again to bring them the fullness of their salvation (9:23–28). This context is important for a more suitable appreciation of the author's message in Heb 9:11.

In Heb 9:11, the author states, "But now Christ has come as the high priest of the good things to come. He entered the greater and more perfect tent, not made with hands, that is not of this creation" (NET). The

---

bring to perfection" (NJB). Other interpretations include: "to bring decisive purgation" (Lane, *Hebrews 9–13*, 224–25); "to bring to the goal" (Lenski, *Hebrews,* 289), and "to cleanse or make clean" (NLT). It may be understood as stressing entrance into a state of completeness or cleansing of the conscience (ingressive), or as stressing the whole act in summary of the process by which the worshipers are consecrated to the service of God (constative). For further details, see Greenlee, *Exegetical Summary of Hebrews*, 319.

217. The majority of scholars interpret the participial phrase τὸν λατρεύοντα, as "the worshiper" (see BDAG, 587, as well as most Bible versions).

218. For similar reasoning, see Attridge, *Hebrews*, 242.

passage begins with the title Χριστός in a contrastive phrase "Χριστὸς δέ . . .," translated, "But Christ. . .," which is unique in Hebrews. The nearest parallel is found in the phrase Ἰησοῦς Χριστός in Heb 13:8.[219] In both cases, the author's emphasis is on Jesus Christ, Χριστός, used here not as a title, "the Messiah," but as an already well-known name to the Christians in and around Rome, which implies "the fulfillment of type and prophecy."[220] The Greek conjunction "but" (δέ)[221] highlights the contrast between the Levitical system's "work of Aaron on the Day of Atonement, and the work of Christ,"[222] in order to demonstrate the superiority of his accomplished work of redemption. In contrast to the old Levitical order, the author emphasizes that Christ "has appeared"[223] in history as the High Priest of "the good things that have come" (τῶν γενομένων ἀγαθῶν),[224] or the blessings that Christ has proleptically secured on behalf of his people.

219. The effect of the construction is emphatic (Ellingworth, *Hebrews*, 448).

220. For further details, see Alford, *Hebrews, James and Peter*, 686.

221. The adversative particle (δέ) complements the μέν οὖν of Heb 9:1 ("Now on the one hand. . . But on the other hand") announcing a major contrast in the argument (Lane, *Hebrews 9–13*, 229).

222. Pentecost, *Faith That Endures*, 149.

223. The Greek aorist middle participle of παραγίνομαι meaning "to come to be," "to come," or "to appear" (NAB, NRSB, NET, cf. BDAG, 197) points to Christ's appearance in history, including his work. The aorist may indicate a historical realization of a process ("culminative aorist"). However, it also may be identified as an "ingressive aorist," implying entrance into a state. The incarnation event is in view, rather than just his consecration as High Priest (Ellingworth and Nida, *Translator's Handbook on Hebrews*, 190–91), or his exaltation/glorification alone, or even his entrance into heaven (Ellingworth, *Hebrews*, 449). For this position, see Alford, *Hebrews, James and Peter*, 686.

224. The external evidence for this reading (γενομένων) includes:

P46 B D* 1739 pc 1611 2005 itd, e syr[p], h, [pal]
as opposed to the alternative reading (μελλόντων), as evidenced in

א A Dc Ivid 0278 33 0150 K L P
and the majority of texts, including the Byzantine Koine and Eusebius.

Some scholars have adopted the latter on contextual grounds, arguing that it fits well with Heb 10:1 (μελλόντων ἀγαθῶν) and explains γενομένων by parablepsis from παραγενόμενος (cf. Riggenbach, Michel, Spicq, and Montefiore, among others). If one would take μελλόντων as the correct reading, this implies that Christ has appeared as High Priest, making available either the predicted eschatological blessings (as in 10:1) or the good things that are yet to come in the believers' future. For some scholars, this fits better in a context that speaks more about past works of Christ and its present and future effect. For other scholars, the more difficult reading of γενομένων fits the context better (Ellingworth, *Hebrews*, 449–50). Both readings are well attested, but γενομένων has superior attestation based on age and diversity of the text type. Besides, the presence of the phrase τῶν μελλόντων ἀγαθῶν in Heb 10:1 appears to have influenced the scribes. For further details, see Metzger, *Textual Commentary on the Greek New Testament*, 594.

The Notion of Τέλειος in Hebrews

Some scholars parallel the phrase τῶν γενομένων ἀγαθῶν with a similar phrase τῶν μελλόντων ἀγαθῶν, "the good things to come," that occurs in Heb 10:1, suggesting the phrase points to "the good things which are about to come referring to the future inheritance from the Hebrews author's point of view.[225] According to Moffatt, such "good things to come" or "blessings" consist of what already began in this world and will be completed in the future world to come.[226] For Gottlieb Lünemann, this points to the full realization of salvation in the future.[227] Similarly, Marcus Dods argues that the phrase refers to the good things to be realized under the new covenant.[228] This approach makes sense in view of the context of Hebrews as a whole. Most interpreters, however, hold to an alternative difficult reading of τῶν γενομένων ἀγαθῶν ("the good things that have come"), implying that the eternal redemption with all its benefits have already been made available through the person of Christ. While it is true the phrase points to all the blessings Christ has secured on behalf of his people,[229] the decisive removal of the obstacle of sin and full access to God or complete realization and ultimate fulfillment of the better provisions of the new covenant should be perceived as future and yet to be fully realized (cf. Heb 9:28; 10:1).[230]

The author refers to "the good things" as something accessible in the present, but just as in the previous section, the "present" intermingles with the coming or future "time to set things right" (9:10). Mitchell fittingly observes, "In the sermon's eschatology, the tension between present and future is evident."[231] Thus, in Heb 10:1, the author speaks of "the good things" as future, awaiting completion of what is presently available when Christ will appear a second time (9:28; cf. 13:14). If this reconstruction is correct, then what "the good things" in this context refer to are: the "eternal redemption" (9:12, 15), "purification of conscience" (v. 14), "a promised eternal

---

225. For this reading, see Lenski, *Hebrews*, 293. The "good things" in the context belong to the world to come and constitute the hope for God's people. In the present, the believer embraces them as one tasting the word of God and the powers of the world to come (cf. Heb 6:5).

226. Moffatt, *Hebrews*, 120–21.

227. Lünemann, *Critical and Exegetical Handbook*, 327.

228. Dods, "Epistle to the Hebrews," 332.

229. The aorist (ingressive) tense of the participle should be seen as pointing to what began with Christ's suffering on the cross and is to be fully realized in the future, in view of the better promises of the new covenant that are yet to be fully realized for God's people. For similar reasoning, see Morris, "Hebrews," 85.

230. For further details, see also Guthrie, *Hebrews*, 185; Kistemaker, *Hebrews*, 266; and Westcott, *Hebrews*, 278–80, 305.

231. Mitchell, *Hebrews*, 181.

inheritance" (v. 15), "forgiveness and putting away of sins" (v. 22), and "salvation" (v. 28),[232] which make the new covenant better.

The author validates his statement by indicating that Christ "entered the greater and more perfect tent, not made with human hands—not of this creation" (9:11b)—as he provides a further description of the nature of the heavenly sanctuary into which Christ entered to secure eternal salvation for the worshipers (cf. v. 12). The author states, "He passed through the greater and more perfect (τελειοτέρας) tent."[233] The author's purpose is to draw the readers' attention to key contrasting aspects between the work of the Aaronic priesthood on the Day of Atonement and the work of Christ in order to demonstrate the superiority of Christ's person, as evidenced in all he has accomplished. First, the superiority of Christ's work as the perfected High Priest is evidenced in the sphere of his service: it is heavenly, the very presence of God. The old tabernacle erected by Moses' human hands was merely a shadow. Second, Christ's sacrifice is unique and of greater value: while in the former order, the high priest entered with blood of goats and calves, both for himself and for the people every year,[234] the perfected Christ entered once-for-all into the most Holy Place without animal blood. Shedding his own blood, he forever secured eternal redemption on behalf of the worshipers. The third aspect of the superiority of Christ's work is evidenced in the salvation that has resulted from his sacrificial work. The author shows that Christ secured eternal salvation on behalf of the worshipers through his sacrifice, unlike the old covenant rituals, which proved unable to accomplish eternal redemption.[235]

From the previous discussion, the author of Hebrews has linked "perfection" to the "sanctifying" effectiveness of the blood of Christ's new covenant sacrifice in securing eternal salvation for the believers. The high priestly ministry of the perfected Christ revealed in the new order is presented as superior to that of the earthly priests not only because the sphere of its service is the heavenly sanctuary or true tabernacle, but also because

---

232. For this discussion, see ibid.

233. The true tabernacle is described as τελειοτέρας (Heb 9:11b). The comparative degree of the adjectival form (τέλειος) is used here to qualify the completeness of the true or heavenly tabernacle in contrast to the inability and failure of the former to secure eternal salvation on behalf of the worshipers.

234. Pentecost indicates that since the blood of goats and calves lost its effectiveness with the expiration of the year, the sacrificial ritual needed to be repeated again and again. Not so with Christ's unique and greater sacrifice (Pentecost, *Faith That Endures*, 150).

235. See ibid., 149–50. For further details about contrasting features between the old and new covenant, see Lehne, *New Covenant in Hebrews*, 96–99. See also Moffatt, *Hebrews*, 107.

he is the Mediator (μεσίτης) of a new and better covenant that guarantees better promises (8:8–12; 9:11, 15, 26–28; cf. Jer 31:31–34). In contrast to the old economy, the new covenant is described as better because it is enacted on better promises. In this context, the notion of τέλειος carries a future eschatological significance seeing that "the greater and more perfect tent" (9:11) can be best understood in terms of what it points to—the worshiper's complete union with Christ and full enjoyment of the eternal salvation (9:28) that will be realized at the second coming of Christ.

Hebrews 10:1

Hebrews 10:1 is the last instance of τέλειος with reference to the inability of the old order to effect τελείωσις. The author writes, "For the Law possesses a shadow of the good things to come but not the reality itself, and is therefore completely unable, by the same sacrifice offered continually, year after year, to perfect those who come to worship." The exposition in Heb 10:1–18 brings to a close the argument that began in Heb 7:1, where he contended for the superiority of Christ as the High Priest after the order of Melchizedek over the Levitical priests. The argument in Heb 8:1–9:28, is about the superiority of Christ's priestly ministry, which entails a superior sacrifice based on a finer covenant enacted on better promises. In Heb 10:1–18, the author reasons that Christ's better and superior sacrifice has a continual effect on making perfect the new covenant worshiper. The author shows that: (1) the Law's sacrifices were unable to remove sins but instead reminded the people of their sins (10:1–4); (2) Christ became the new sacrifice according to God's will (10:5–10); and (3) his once-for-all sacrifice, unlike animal sacrifices, has a recurrent influence for continual forgiveness of sins and therefore makes perfect those who are being sanctified (10:11–18).[236] On these grounds, the readers are urged to hold fast, to endure, and to live in faith in view of God's future judgment to come (10:19–39). It is in light of this broader context that Heb 10:1 is to be understood.

The passage (10:1) is connected to the preceding paragraph by the particle γάρ, "since" or "for," which introduces a further explanation of the finality and superiority of Christ's sacrifice over the Levitical sacrifices of the old order. In the opening phrase, the author writes, Σκιὰν γὰρ ἔχων ὁ νόμος τῶν μελλόντων ἀγαθῶν, "For the Law has only a shadow of the good things to come." Earlier in Heb 8:5, the author referred to the earthly tabernacle as

---

236. Lane believes the argument establishes a context for defining the blessings or better provisions of the new covenant already secured through Christ's death (Lane, *Hebrews 9–13*, 259).

a ὑπόδειγμα ("sketch")[237] and σκιᾷ ("shadow") of the heavenly tabernacle. In Heb 9:23, the author again referred to the earthly tabernacle as a "sketch" or "prototype" (ὑποδείγματα) and representation of the true heavenly sanctuary (cf. v. 24). In Heb 10:1, the author does not make an explicit mention of the earthly sanctuary, but rather speaks of the Law as having a σκιάν, "shadow,"[238] of the things to come. However, he implicitly has it in mind as he concludes his argument contrasting the sacrificial rituals of the old covenant with Christ's once-for-all sacrifice of the new covenant that secures the future blessings to come. If it is true that the Law (ὁ νόμος)[239] was indeed "a witness to the future eschatological salvation," then it could be described as possessing a "shadow" or a "foreshadowing quality" of the good things that were yet to come.[240] Lane correctly posits that the substantive participle τῶν μελλόντων ἀγαθῶν, "the good things which are yet to come," should be clearly regarded as expressing the contrast between the preliminary, incomplete, and limited character of the Law and the ultimate future salvation that was foreshadowed by its cultic provisions.[241] Thus, "the good things that are yet to come" point to the reality of which the Law was merely a shadow. This refers to the blessings or better provisions under the new covenant that are still in the future but are made certain in Christ.[242] The believers may have

237. Some interpreters render ὑπόδειγμα as "copy" or a "prototype." For further details, see BDAG, 1037.

238. The Greek word σκιά should not be understood as referring to the "unreal" or "deceptive" as it is always seen in Platonism. Rather, the term suggests the notion of what is "imperfect" or "incomplete." Thus, Lane argues that the term "reflects not Platonic idealism but the eschatological outlook of primitive Christianity 'the contrast implied being' temporal and eschatological in character; the Law is a past witness to a future reality" (Lane, *Hebrews 9–13*, 259). For further details, see Williamson, *Philo and Hebrews*, 174–75, 566–70; cf. Schultz, "σκιά," *TDNT* 7:398.

239. The Law (ὁ νόμος) in a strict sense refers to the Law of Moses; but in the context of Heb 10, it is accepted as standing for the whole OT, with particular reference to the Levitical system. For further details, see Morris, "Hebrews," 94. The cultic language is used to point to the limited aspects of the Levitical sacrificial system (Ellingworth, *Hebrews*, 449).

240. For further details, see Barrett, "Eschatology of Hebrews," 386.

241. For this discussion, see Lane, *Hebrews 9–13*, 260.

242. Some scholars, such as Ellingworth, take a different approach by arguing that τῶν μελλόντων ἀγαθῶν, or "the things to come," refers to things that had not been fulfilled under the old covenant but that were already realized through the past event of Christ's priestly work (Ellingworth, *Hebrews*, 492). For Westcott, "the good things to come" are spoken of "as future from the standpoint of the Law," and "have been realized by the accomplishment of Christ's work," but "still remain in part yet future in regard to man's full enjoyment of them" (Westcott, *Hebrews*, 305). Other scholars interpret the phrase as referring to Christ's sacrifice, his present ministry, and his eternal redemption, plus the uninhibited access now available to the believers to worship God (Bruce,

tasted some of the spiritual benefits of the new era already inaugurated, but under the new covenant, the worshiper will only enjoy such good things to the fullest at the second coming of the Lord Jesus Christ.

Since the Law possesses simply a shadow and not the reality of the good things that are yet to come, the author shows how, by its sacrificial rituals offered continually, it was unable (δύναται/ δύνανται)²⁴³ to completely make perfect those who come to worship (10:1). The textual problem here makes it debatable whether the proper form of δύναμαι should be singular or plural. If the correct reading is the plural δύνανται, then the reference presents the inability of the Levitical sacrifices to make perfect those who worship. However, if the correct reading is the singular δύναται, the reference conveys the inability of the Law to make perfect those who worship. Although the external evidence for the plural form δύνανται is stronger, both the syntax as well as the context argue against it. As Jean Héring observes, the plural is slightly better attested, but its usage rather than the singular form would leave ὁ νόμος "the Law" without a predicate.²⁴⁴ Similarly, Ellingworth notes that the plural form "makes ἔχων ὁ νόμος an ungrammatical 'hanging participle' phrase."²⁴⁵ It is possible that a scribe forgot that the subject was singular, or perhaps the plural is due to a scribal modification that was

---

Hebrews, 235; Wilson, Hebrews, 171–72). This is similar to the view that it refers to the blessings of salvation, the gospel, and its spiritual high priesthood, as evidenced in the church's work (cf. Kistemaker, Hebrews, 272; Lane, Hebrews 9–13, 266–71; and Guthrie, Hebrews, 201). While all these approaches are insightful, the context of τῶν μελλόντων ἀγαθῶν points to the future eschatological blessings or better provisions of the new covenant, which are to be fulfilled at the second coming of Christ (see Heb 9:10, 12, 15, 28; 13:14).

243. There is a textual problem here that impacts the interpretation of the passage. Two variant readings (either the singular δύναται or the plural δύνανται) are suggested in the context. The external evidence in support of the plural δύνανται include:

ℵ A C D1 P 0278 33 81 104 614 1241 1505 pm ar b z* vgms sy.

On the other hand, the external support for the singular δύναται include:

P46 D*.2 H K LS 0285 326 365 629 630 1739 1881 pm f r vg.

The evidence for the plural is stronger but not necessarily decisively so (cf. Ellingworth, Hebrews, 491). The plural appears to have been inserted by a scribe who was influenced by προφέρουσιν. For further details, see Metzger, Textual Commentary, 600.

244. Héring, Epistle to the Hebrews, 86.

245. Ellingworth, Hebrews, 491.

influenced by the presence in the context of the plural verb προσφέρουσιν,[246] (they/priests) "offered."[247]

The author of Hebrews states that the Law, by its continuously offered sacrifices, is unable to make perfect (τελειῶσαι) those who come to worship (10:1). The argument is similar to what the author has already presented in Heb 9:9: that gifts and sacrifices offered on the basis of the old *cultus* were unable to decisively purge the sin and guilt from the worshiper to allow a complete access or an uninhibited access to God. The aorist active τελειῶσαι appears in Heb 10:1, conveying the same meaning as in Heb 9:9. The object of the verb is "the ones approaching God to worship" or "the worshipers." In Heb 9:9, it is with regard to the cleansing of the conscience from the burden of sin and guilt (10:2) that sacrificial gifts and offerings under the old covenant are acknowledged as unable to make the worshipers perfect. Again, this is seen as how the better provisions of the new covenant prophecy of Jer 31:31–34 (cf. 8:6–12) are to be fully realized in the future. It is with this eschatological understanding that in Heb 10:1 the author speaks of the good things as a future reality, when Christ will appear a second time in order to bring salvation to God's people (cf. 9:28; 13:14). The context indicates that this future aspect awaits completion of what is presently certain and available through the incarnation of Christ.

The τέλειος notion in Heb 7:11, 19; 9:9, 11; 10:1 has an eschatological significance that points to the future realization of the new covenant promises, which though made certain in Christ, will be fulfilled at the second coming of our Lord Jesus Christ. Like in Heb 7:11, 19 and 9:9, the author makes it clear in Heb 10:1 that the Levitical system cannot bring God's people the desired completeness that allows an uninhibited access to God. Christ alone is presented as the perfected High Priest and Mediator of the better provisions that are yet to be fully realized. For the author of Hebrews, the τελείωσις, "perfecting," of Christ is, therefore, the determining factor for that of the believers.

THE ΤΕΛΕΙΩΣΙΣ OF THE BELIEVERS

Having delineated how the author uses the τέλειος notion with reference to Christ and the inability of the old *cultus* to effect the desired completeness that allows an uninhibited access to God, one is now in a position to

---

246. The present active indicative of προσφέρω ("to offer") is used here as an impersonal verb in a passive mood, the implied subject being the priests. For further details, see Lane, *Hebrews 9–13*, 255.

247. For this discussion, see Ellingworth, *Hebrews*, 492.

The Notion of Τέλειος in Hebrews

describe how he uses the same terminology in reference to believers (Heb 5:14; 6:1; 10:14; 11:40, and 12:2, 23). The purpose of this portion of the chapter is to examine the usage of the notion in these passages in order to fully appreciate its meaning and import in Hebrews for believers. This portion will show that the notion of τέλειος has an eschatological significance for believers, pointing toward their complete and final access to God. The Son was made perfect as the "leader" or "pioneer" of believers' sanctification with the goal of leading them to their future eschatological destination and complete enjoyment of their eternal inheritance.

Hebrews 5:14 and 6:1

One implication that emerges from the previous discussion is the deciding significance of the perfecting of Christ to that of the believers.[248] The author writes, "But solid food is for 'the ones perfected' whose perceptions are trained by practice to discern both good and evil. Therefore, we must progress beyond the elementary instructions about Christ and move on to 'perfection,' not laying this foundation again: repentance from dead works and faith in God" (5:14–6:1). In Heb 4:14–7:28, the author has made a case for the superiority of Christ because he is the High Priest after the order of Melchizedek. This section begins with a description of Christ's higher qualifications as High Priest in the order of Melchizedek (4:14–5:10), which leads naturally to "a transitional digression"[249] in Heb 5:11–6:20, concluding the first series of expositions and preparing the readers for his next major section, which begins at 7:1.[250] The author's reproof is evident when he writes that despite what Christ has accomplished through his once-for-all sacrifice, the readers are not growing in understanding as they should (5:11–6:3). They ought to be as teachers, but instead are as those still in elementary teachings who are slow in understanding like infants (v. 13).[251]

---

248. In the context, Heb 5:14 and 6:1 are interconnected, so they are examined together in the following discussion.

249. For the significance and use of rhetorical digression in Hebrews (Quintilian, *Institutio oratoria*, IV. 3. 1–17; Cicero, *De inventione rhetorica*, I. 51), see Koester, *Hebrews*, 306–307.

250. The rhetorical function of such digressions is to prepare the readers to give full attention to what follows. Koester notes that this digression in Hebrews "is designed to secure their attention by addressing them with reproof, warning, and encouragement" (ibid., 307).

251. Verse 13 is an elaboration on those described as νωθροὶ ταῖς ἀκοαῖς, or "slow in understanding," in verse 11 (cf. 6:12). The adjective νωθρός suggests the notion of "lethargic" or "careless" (cf. Prov 22:29; Sir 4:29; 11:2). When combined with a dative of respect such as ταῖς ἀκοαῖς ("in hearing"), it indicates a "dullness or even a

In contrast, self-training in discernment of good and evil would lead to the goal of τελείωσις, that is, "completeness" or "maturity" (5:14). The readers must pursue this goal of "completeness" or "maturity" (6:1–3). The author's reproof is followed by a warning of the devastating consequences of the danger of "apostasy" (6:4–8) prior to his words of encouragement for the readers to persevere until the end as they imitate those who had faith and waited with hope their inheritance of God's promises (6:9–20).[252]

A survey of the context shows that, just as Christ has entered the heavenly sanctuary on their behalf, the worshipers under the new covenant have hope to enter the heavenly sanctuary as they follow the example of Christ, the perfected High Priest after the order of Melchizedek. As the supreme exemplar of τελείωσις, the perfected Christ is presented as the one enabling the worshiper to walk, in faith and hope, toward the attainment of the same goal of perfection even as they share in similar trials and temptations. Such "perfection" or "maturity," while presented as attainable in the present time from the standpoint of the author, remains a goal to be pursued and to be fulfilled at the second coming of Christ (9:28; 13:14).

In Heb 5:14, the author states, τελείων[253] δέ ἐστιν ἡ στερεὰ τροφή, "But solid food is for the mature people." The author elaborates on his rebuke in verses 13 and 14 by using a common metaphorical contrast between νήπιοι ("infants") and τέλειοι ("mature") with the food appropriate to each category. The infants who are still living on milk are inexperienced in the λόγου δικαιοσύνης, "word of righteousness" (v. 13).[254] The word

---

reluctance to listen" (see Heliodorus, *Ethiopians,* V. 1. 5; and Epictetus, *Discourses,* I. 7. 30). Thus, Johnson translates the notion as "reluctant listeners," pointing to those who are described as sluggish in hearing and inexperienced in the message of righteousness (Johnson, *Hebrews,* 155).

252. Many interpreters suggest that Heb 5:11–6:20 should be taken as a unit. Some scholars divide this unit into two sections distinguished by the change of tone at 6:9 (e.g., Spicq and Michel). Other interpreters follow Vanhoye, who argues that the word νωθρός, "sluggish" or "dull," in Heb 5:11 and 6:12 frames the whole section (Vanhoye, *La structure,* 116–20; see also Koester, *Hebrews,* 307). Those who favor this approach take the major division to be between 5:11–6:3 and 6:4–6. See, for example, Attridge, *Hebrews,* 156.

253. The genitive adjective τελείων, "of mature people," is emphatic (Lünemann, *Critical and Exegetical Handbook,* 220). It refers to those for whom solid food is intended. In the Hellenistic world, the word was also used for individuals who had completed the course of education and were in a position to be teachers (Philo, *On the Special Laws,* 4.140; ibid., *On the Change of Names,* 270). The Greek form τελείων, a predicate genitive of possession, is rare in Hebrews. For further details, see Allen, *Hebrews: Exegetical and Theological Exposition,* 337.

254. The phrase λόγου δικαιοσύνης, or "word of righteousness," can also be rendered as "speech concerning righteousness" or "righteous speech" with reference to a particular form of reasoning (as evidenced in Herodotus, *Persian Wars,* I. 209; Plato,

δικαιοσύνης, "righteousness," does not carry the same meaning as it does in Pauline sense of God's righteousness. Thus, Ellingworth suitably observes that it is misleading to introduce the special Pauline significance of δικαιόω and cognates even though the association of faith and righteousness is present in Hebrews (cf. 11:7, 33).²⁵⁵ That the noun δικαιοσύνης should be taken as carrying the notion of a moral or ethical virtue enabling the worshiper to make an appropriate choice between right and wrong is debatable.²⁵⁶ The point of the metaphor is that the readers are like infants who are sluggish in learning and not fit for solid teaching. This does not indicate that all that they need to do is learn moral or ethical principles. Rather, as most commentators indicate, the phrase should be taken in a general sense as referring to advanced Christian teaching.²⁵⁷

Further reflection on the metaphor is found in verse 14, where the author draws the readers' attention to the other side of the dichotomy as he points to the analogy of solid food as the sustenance of those who are τέλειοι ("mature"). Käsemann rejects the moral-ethical approach²⁵⁸ to the notion of τέλειος, but he advocates for the glorification or exaltation view. He goes even further suggesting that there is a link between the language of Hebrews and the gnostic enlightenment through initiation into the mystery through baptism.²⁵⁹ Considering the context of Hebrews, the technical sense of "initiation into the mysteries through baptism" as the way to "maturity" is debatable. Thus, Attridge states that the initiation of baptism of the readers does not guarantee their "maturity" or "perfection" as implied in Käsemann's argument.²⁶⁰ Rather, those who are τέλειοι ("mature") are

---

Republic, 529d; Aristotle, *Eudemian Ethics*, 1149a; and Epictetus, *Discourses*, II. 2. 20), especially because "the contrasting ability among the mature involves a mental/moral activity" (Johnson, *Hebrews*, 156).

255. For further details, see Ellingworth, *Hebrews*, 306. Ellingworth also offers a detailed discussion on the major interpretative views regarding the phrase λόγου δικαιοσύνης and the force of its grammatical construction.

256. It is commonly found carrying the moral/ethical meaning in Hellenistic moral discourse. For example, see Plato, *Republic*, 433a; Aristotle, *Politics*, 1291a; cf. Heb 12:11. For further insightful details, see Johnson, *Hebrews*, 156; and Ellingworth, *Hebrews*, 306–307.

257. Attridge observes it is this general sense of "advanced Christian teaching or message" that conforms to the author's evocative use of illustrations elsewhere. See Attridge, *Hebrews*, 160. Similarly, see Spicq, *L'Épître aux Hébreux*, 144; Westcott, *Epistle to the Hebrews*, 138; Peterson, *Hebrews and Perfection*, 181; and Windisch, *der Hebräerbrief*, 46–47.

258. Peterson indicates that "the moral element appears to be secondary in the context" (Peterson, *Hebrews and Perfection*, 181).

259. Käsemann, *Wandering People of God*, 188–89.

260. Attridge, *Hebrews*, 161.

those who have been "trained" or "practiced" through habit with the goal of becoming fully able to distinguish between good and evil (v. 14b).[261]

In the second part of verse 14, the author states, τῶν διὰ τὴν ἕξιν τὰ αἰσθητήρια γεγυμνασμένα ἐχόντων πρὸς διάκρισιν καλοῦ τε καὶ κακοῦ, "whose perceptions are trained by practice to discern both good and evil" (NET). Allen recognizes the difficulty faced by interpreters seeking to capture the feel of the Greek word order and syntax in the English translation of verse 14b.[262] For instance, some translations, like the NIV, fail to make explicit the meaning of the noun αἰσθητήρια, "sense," "faculty," or "capacity to understand." While it is true that this word may seem difficult to define, it includes intellectual, moral, or spiritual capacity, perception, or sense. This capacity or "perception" can be learned through practice with the result that one is able to discern both good and evil. The ability of the one who is "mature" to decide or judge between καλός καὶ κακός, "good and evil," may be an allusion to Num 14:23 (LXX) given its significance for Heb 3–4, where the children are said to be unable to decide between "good and evil" because of lack of maturity.[263] The section deals with an issue of sanctification rather than salvation.[264]

According to Attridge, the notion of τέλειος, "maturity," involves a process of learning as an exercise and requires an effort of listening to a "lengthy and difficult discourse."[265] The process of learning becomes "experiential" as

---

261. Ibid. Accordingly, the author is said to be "operating within the framework of philosophical and educational imagery and what the trained person is supposed to have is 'ethical discernment'" (ibid.).

262. Allen, *Hebrews*, 337–38. Allen notes a particular weakness in the NIV in its rendering of the second half of verse 14. The genitive article τῶν governs the participle ἐχόντων, which stands in apposition with τελείων placed at the beginning of the verse for emphasis. Between the article and the participial noun are:

> (1) an adjectival participle γεγυμνασμένα in the predicate position, which stands in agreement with (2) αἰσθητήρια, which functions as a direct object of ἐχόντων. "This is preceded by (3) διά with its accusative object ἕξιν, which may indicate means (NIV) or reason (KJV, NASB)" (ibid.).

As one may also observe, "the final prepositional phrase following the participle ἐχόντων is introduced with πρός with its accusative object διάκρισιν which can be taken as purpose, result or content." According to Allen, a literal rendering of verse 14 would be: "but solid food is for the mature, namely, those who have the senses trained by/because of constant use for the purpose/with the result of/to distinguish(ing) both good and evil" (ibid.).

263. For this discussion, see ibid., 338.

264. Allen sees this as the clue for proper interpretation of the following passage (6:1–8). See ibid., 339.

265. Attridge, *Hebrews*, 162.

The Notion of Τέλειος in Hebrews

one progressively achieves the goal of maturity. This is similar to Peterson's vocational understanding that the "mature" are "those who have their faculties trained by practice to distinguish good from evil."[266] Accordingly, the ones who are "mature" are perfected "experientially or vocationally" and are qualified to worship God. However, the author's metaphorical language and the analogy used in a pedagogical context should not be solely seen as focusing primarily on some kind of educational experience or vocational fitness, nor should the language be understood as conveying some moral or ethical principles of discernment. Rather, this shows that the author uses familiar language in order to effectively draw attention to the theological backwardness of his readers. They ought to live as those who have already attained some skills and abilities, with the result that they can handle solid truths or distinguish between good and evil.

Having shown how self-training and discernment regarding good and evil stand as characteristics for the one pursuing after the goal of τελείωσις, "maturity" or "completeness" (Heb 5:14), the author exhorts the readers to pursue the same goal of "completeness" or "maturity" (6:1–2).[267] In Heb 6:1, the author states, "Therefore we must progress beyond the elementary instructions about Christ and move on to maturity, not laying the foundation again: repentance from dead works and faith in God." The author elaborates on his exhortation with a challenge to the readers to move on to τελειότης, "maturity," by progressing beyond the basic or elementary teaching (τὸν τῆς ἀρχῆς τοῦ Χριστοῦ λόγον)[268] about Christianity[269] already referred to in

---

266. Peterson, *Hebrews and Perfection*, 181. Similarly, Owen uses Philo's distinction of three stages in the learning process (i.e., beginner, progresser, and perfect) and argues that there are three stages involved in the educational program of Hebrews (Owen, "Stages of Ascent in Hebrews 5:11–6:3," 243–53). Accordingly, ethical perfection comes before the reception of "solid food." However, as Attridge rightly contends, Owen's argument "misapprehends the function of the complex metaphor" (Attridge, *Hebrews*, 162).

267. Hebrews 6:1–2 constitutes one sentence in the Greek text and is governed by one key verb, as will be shown in subsequent discussion. For the purpose of this study, the focus is only on the first verse (Heb 6:1), which is examined in the light of its immediate context.

268. In the genitive construction τὸν τῆς ἀρχῆς λόγον, literally "the teaching of the beginning," the noun ἀρχῆς is taken as an attributive of λόγον, "the teaching." The phrase means "the basic teachings" or "the elementary teachings" (NRSV, NASB, NJB, NIV) about Christ. See Montefiore, *Hebrews*, 104. See also Lane, *Hebrews 1–8*, 131. The alternative, taking ἀρχῆς as the object of τὸν λόγον ("teaching the rudiments," cf. REB, NLT, and Lenski, *Hebrews*, 174–75) is unlikely, given the context.

269. The Greek clause τὸν τῆς ἀρχῆς τοῦ Χριστοῦ λόγον would literally be translated as "the word of the beginning of Christ." Some scholars, including Adams, take the genitive construction (τοῦ Χριστου) as a subjective genitive: "let us leave on one side Christ's original teaching and let us advance toward maturity." According to Adams, the

his previous discussion. In Heb 5:11–14, the tone is that of a rebuke, but in 6:1–2, it is one of encouragement. There is a shift from the accusatory second-person plural (5:11–12) to the hortatory first-person plural (6:1–2).[270] The conclusion deduced from the preceding passage and introduced by the inferential Διό ("therefore" or "so then")[271] is that the readers should move on to "maturity." The controlling verb φερώμεθα[272] is in the subjunctive mood (hortatory) expressing a command with an imperatival force: "let us move on to maturity" or "we must move on to maturity." The inclusion of himself conveys to the readers the preacher's heart,[273] placing himself at the readers' level in order to provide encouragement. Simon J. Kistemaker observes that the author places himself on his readers' level even though, as a teacher, he really occupies a higher position.[274] From this discussion, the notion of τελείωσις—"perfection" or "maturity"—is the goal toward which Hebrew believers must always be advancing (Heb 6:1, 12:1; cf. Matt 5:48).

---

nature of the apostasy referred to in Heb 6:6 is the readers' acceptance of the message of Jesus, but not his person and work. Therefore, what they must leave behind is their "preoccupation with the content of Christ's own teaching" (Adams, "Exegesis of Hebrews 6:1f.," 378–85, esp. 383–84). A better alternative is proposed by scholars such as Allen, who interprets the genitive as an objective genitive expressing the content of the teaching about Christ (Allen, *Hebrews*, 339). Lane also argues for the latter (objective genitive) "descriptive of Christian instruction. Cf. TEV: 'the first lessons of the Christian message'" (Lane, *Hebrews 1–8*, 131). This is against Wuest's position that the clause "the word of the beginning of Christ" refers to the OT sacrifices and the priesthood, in contrast to the new sacrifice and the new priesthood of Christ (Wuest, *Hebrews in Greek New Testament*, 111–12).

270. Johnson, *Hebrews*, 157.

271. The inferential Διό ("therefore" or "so then") provides a deduction or conclusion to the preceding discussion (5:11–14). It may be understood as having an adverbial function of cause ("Because of this"). For this discussion, see Wallace, *Exegetical Syntax*, 673–74. (Cf. Heb 3:7, 10; 10:5; 11:12, 16; 12:12, 28; 13:12).

272. The present subjunctive verb φερώμεθα is in the passive voice, which suggests continued action as the reader yields to the influence of another person. This suggests the activity of God, as is made explicit in Heb 6:13–19. For further details, see Ellingworth, *Hebrews*, 212.

273. The Apostle Paul conveys similar truth: "I have not already been perfected, but I strive to lay hold of that for which Christ Jesus also laid hold of me" (Phil 3:12).

274. For further details, see Kistemaker, *Hebrews*, 152.

The key verb φερώμεθα[275] is placed between two participles: ἀφέντες (cf. "leaving [we must leave][276] behind the elementary") and καταβαλλόμενοι ("not laying again the foundation"). By urging the readers "to leave behind the elementary Christian teaching," the author does not dismiss its importance but rather regards the foundation as solid and already established (cf. 5:12). If that is true, then the need is to urge readers to demonstrate a fuller appreciation and application of that teaching as people who have attained some degree of maturity. For the optimistic author of Hebrews, the foundation has been laid (cf. Heb 2:3-4) and there is no need to lay it again (6:1-4). As Lane correctly states, the exhortation, which is extended to the community (6:1-12), is a reminder of that solid foundation.[277] Thus, the notion conveyed by the second participle ("not laying the foundation again") is intended to clarify, in a negative manner, the meaning of the positive injunction in the opening clause, "let us leave behind. . ." and "move on to maturity."[278]

The notion of "leaving behind" implies moving on to something else. The context does not indicate an abandonment of the basic instructions about Christ but rather the notion of building on an earlier foundation, which is not to be reestablished again.[279] The established "foundation" or "elementary teaching about Christ" is assumed in the context; thus, the readers are urged to move from one level to another, which is commensurate with those who have attained a degree of "completeness" or "maturity." According to Lane, the readers are urged to move to a level of "fuller appreciation and application of that teaching."[280] Ellingworth argues similarly that it is a level or goal "to be reached by means of more advanced teaching."[281] Thus,

---

275. The Greek aorist participle of ἀφίημι, "to leave," does not suggest the notion of "an abandonment" of the elementary teaching. Lane compares this with other usages of the verb (cf. Heb 2:8; Matt 22:22, 25; 24:2; John 11:48; 14:27) and concludes that the word may carry the notion of "leaving standing" or "let it remain" (Lane, *Hebrews 1-8*, 131). "Leaving behind" does not imply the notion of "neglecting" or "forsaking." For further details, see Attridge, *Hebrews*, 162; and Manson, *Epistle to the Hebrews*, 61.

276. The aorist participle ἀφέντες gains an imperatival force from the hortatory subjunctive φερώμεθα: "let us be carried forward" or "we must leave behind" (Lane, *Hebrews 1-8*, 139).

277. For this discussion, see Lane, *Hebrews 1-8*, 139.

278. Ibid. For further details, see also, Allen, *Hebrews*, 340; and Ellingworth, *Hebrews*, 311.

279. As Johnson observes, "'Laying a foundation again' will be an exercise in futility" (Johnson, *Hebrews*, 158).

280. Lane, *Hebrews 1-8*, 139.

281. Ellingworth, *Hebrews*, 312.

the readers are urged to move "from one stage of learning to another."[282] The doctrinal elements the author includes among the elementary teaching are merely outlined, not explained: "repentance, faith in God, ceremonial washings, laying on of hands, resurrection of the dead, and eternal judgment" (6:2). These elements may have been very familiar to readers and given much more prominence in the Christian church. As Kistemaker comments, they may have been used as a catechism new converts were required to learn before they could be fully accepted in the assembly of believers.[283]

The author of Hebrews elaborates on his exhortation as he urges the readers, saying, τὴν τελειότητα φερώμεθα, "we must move on to maturity." The Greek noun τελειότητα appears only here and in Col 3:14, where it is used of love that is the perfect bond (τὴν ἀγάπην,... τῆς τελειότητος)[284] drawing believers together in perfect unity. In Heb 6:1, this noun picks up the contrast between the infant and the "mature" in the preceding passage (5:11-14), setting before the readers the goal of τελειότης, "maturity," "completeness," or "a state of full growth,"[285] in contrast to elementary teaching about Christ. The idea of "pressing on" is presented as the means to reach the goal of "maturity." P. E. Hughes argues that the sense of community in progress is intensified in the Greek text by the fact that the Greek expression τὴν τελειότητα φερώμεθα, translated in our versions as "let us move on," means literally "let us be carried forward,"[286] suggesting that it is not a matter of the readers being carried by their instructor, but of both being moved

---

282. Johnson, *Hebrews*, 157.

283. For further details, see Kistemaker, *Hebrews*, 152-56.

284. The Greek genitive τῆς τελειότητος is taken here as an attributive genitive, "the perfect bond."

285. Some interpreters (including Ellingworth, *Hebrews*, 312; Montefiore, *Hebrews*, 104; and Hagner, *Hebrews*, 87) take τελειότης as referring to "mature teaching" or "mature doctrine" (NJB, TEV, and TNT), in which case "mature teaching" is seen as the means through which the readers come to maturity: "let us move on to discuss mature things." More likely, the author is referring to the maturity of the believers. For this reading, see Guthrie, *Hebrews*, 137; Kistemaker, *Hebrews*, 152; Bruce, *Hebrews*, 138; Hughes, *Hebrews*, 194; and Hewitt, *Hebrews*, 104; among others (NAB, NASB, NIV, NRSV): "let us move on to maturity." The notion of gradual development or personal effort is rejected, since it is an action by God to bring the worshipers to their intended goal. The worshipers' responsibility is to yield their lives into the hands of Christ so that they may be borne on together with others unto τελειότης, "perfection," or "maturity." For further details, see Hewitt, *Hebrews*, 104; and Lane, *Hebrews 1-8*, 139-40.

286. The Greek verb φερώμεθα carries a passive nuance (Lane, *Hebrews 1-8*, 140; and Ellingworth, *Hebrews*, 312), implying the agency of God as the one who moves the worshipers along to their intended goal. For this discussion, see Hughes, *Hebrews*, 194. See also Allen, *Hebrews*, 340. Alternatively, "the verb may be construed in the middle voice in the sense of 'to bring oneself forward'" (Lenski, *Hebrews*, 175), but the passive voice makes more sense.

forward together by God through the hidden inward activities of the Holy Spirit.[287] The implication is that if evidence of Christian progress toward "maturity" would be lacking in the life of a believer, it would be doubtful whether there had been a genuine experience of conversion. This explains the extremely solemn character of the author's warning in Heb 6:4–8. Yet at the same time, the author is optimistic[288] and convinced that the gospel message has fallen onto good ground and will therefore yield a harvest to the glory of God.[289] If it is true that God moves the worshipers along their intended goal of τελειότης, "maturity," or "a state of full growth," then it naturally follows that they are dependent upon God and his grace to enable them to move on to "maturity"[290] through faith and hope.

The way toward the goal of τελειότης, "maturity," or "perfection," for the worshipers becomes possible only as a result of God's enablement in Christ, who is presented in the context as the supreme and final exemplar of "perfection" (12:2; cf. 2:10; 10:14). He is the one who enables the worshiper to walk in faith and hope as one who has attained the same goal of "perfection" even as the worshiper shares in similar trials and temptations. Even though "perfection" or "completeness" is attainable in the present, it remains a future reality to be fully realized at the second coming of Christ. P. E. Hughes concludes that the worshipers will not attain the goal of τέλειος until the second return of the glorified Christ at the end of the age, when the transformed believers see the glorified Savior face to face and are fully conformed to his image (cf. 1 John 3:2).[291] The Apostle Paul conveys a similar truth when he points to the criterion of τελειότης—"maturity," "perfection,"

---

287. According to Hughes, God himself, through the Holy Spirit's hidden and inward energizing activities, becomes the true dynamic of spiritual maturity (*Hebrews*, 194). He sees some similarities with Paul in Rom 8:14: "all who are led by the Spirit of God are sons of God," but also with Peter, who uses the same verb when he asserts that the prophets of old were "moved by the Holy Spirit" (1 Pet 1:21).

288. The author's optimism lies in his hope of the better promises of God's salvation, which is secured in Christ, the eternal High Priest, and is based on God's faithfulness (Heb 6:9–20). Thus, the readers are encouraged to be faithful and persevere as they imitate those who have inherited the promises. To the author of Hebrews, the fact that Christ as the πρόδρομος, "the forerunner" (cf. ἀρχηγόν, "the pioneer" [Heb 2:10] and αἴτιος σωτηρίας αἰωνίου, "the source of eternal salvation" [Heb 5:8–9]), has entered the more perfect tabernacle on behalf of the worshipers is clear evidence that they will inherit the better promise of salvation. For the christological significance of the Greek word πρόδρομος, see Allen, *Hebrews*, 403–404; cf. Bauernfeind, "πρόδρομος," *TDNT* 8:235; BDAG, 867; and Attridge, *Hebrews*, 185.

289. Hughes, *Hebrews*, 194.

290. Allen, *Hebrews*, 340.

291. For this discussion, see Hughes, *Hebrews*, 192.

or "completeness"—as the fullness of the perfection of Christ.[292] In Phil 3:12 he states, "I have not yet reached perfection, but I press on. . ." In Eph 4:13, he states, "until we all attain the unity of the faith and of the knowledge of the Son of God—a τέλειον 'mature' person, attaining to the measure of Christ's full stature."

If the notion of τέλειος in Hebrews is closely related to Paul's notion in these passages, then the idea of "maturity" or "completeness" conveyed in the notion of τέλειος could be perceived as having an eschatological significance pointing to the future realization of God's promise, which in essence is the hope of the Hebrew worshipers. The hope for the future completeness serves as an incentive for the believers to persevere and walk by faith, looking forward to completion of the journey they have embarked on in Christ—their final access to God. The author amplifies this meaning in the remaining passages (10:14; 11:40; 12:2, 23), where he further elaborates on the perfecting of the believers.

Hebrews 10:14

The author has already referred to the inability of the old system, through its Law and repeated sacrifices, to effect the desired τελειότης, "completeness," or "perfection" on behalf of the worshipers (Heb 10:1; cf. 7:11, 19; 9:9, 11). In Heb 10:14, he elaborates on the same theme with reference to the believers, not with regard to the Law or the repeated nature of its sacrifices under the old covenant. The author writes, Μιᾷ γὰρ προσφορᾷ τετελείωκεν εἰς τὸ διηνεκὲς τοὺς ἁγιαζομένους, "For by a single offering, he [Christ] has perfected for all times those who are sanctified" (10:14).

The author's exposition in Heb 10:1–18 brings the argument that began at 7:1 to a close with respect to the superiority of Christ as the High Priest after the order of Melchizedek. In Heb 8:1–9:28, the author's concern is with the superiority of Christ's priestly ministry, which entails a superior sacrifice based on a better and superior covenant enacted on better promises. In Heb 10:1–18, the author argues that Christ's superior sacrifice has a continual effect to make the new covenant worshiper perfect. The author of Hebrews shows: (1) that the Law's sacrifices were unable to remove sins, but instead reminded the people of their sins (10:1–4); (2) that Christ became the new sacrifice according to God's will (10:5–10); and (3) that

---

292. It can be argued that "completeness" or "perfection" belongs properly to God alone. In fact, "absolute maturity," which is conveyed in the notion of τέλειος, has been achieved at the human level only by the incarnate Son, Jesus Christ (Heb 2:10; 4:15; 5:8–9).

Christ's once-for-all sacrifice, unlike animal sacrifices, has a perpetual effect for complete forgiveness of sins and to make perfect those who are being sanctified (10:11–18).²⁹³ On these grounds, the author urges his readers to hold fast, to endure, and to live in faith in view of God's future judgment (10:19–39). It is in light of this broader context that Heb 10:14 should be understood.

The author's statement in Heb 10:14 is tied to the preceding passage by the explanatory conjunction γάρ ("for") as he points to the decisive character of Christ's finished work of redemption. Whereas in Heb 10:1 the Law, with its repeated sacrifices, was proved to be inadequate to reach the goal of "completeness," in verse 14 the one προσφορά, "offering,"²⁹⁴ of Christ makes perfect for all times those who are sanctified. As Westcott indicates, it is not the one offering *per se*, but rather Christ who perfects by his single offering:²⁹⁵ "His action is personal in the application of his work,"²⁹⁶ which is a clear demonstration of his superiority over the Levitical priests. Because he is superior, he offers a better sacrifice, with the lasting result that he is able to make perfect for all times "those who are being made holy."²⁹⁷ The

---

293. As suggested in this discussion, this argument serves to sharpen the readers' appreciation of the ultimate character of Christ's once-for-all sacrifice for sins also establishes a context for defining the blessings and better provisions of the new covenant already secured through his death. For further details, see Lane, *Hebrews 9–13*, 259.

294. Westcott argues that the Greek word προσφορά carries a wider significance than the word θυσία in Heb 10:12. It refers to "Christ's perfect life as a whole, which culminated in his death by which he fulfilled the destiny of man" (Westcott, *Hebrews*, 315). This implies a distinction between the two words (cf. 10:5, 8, 10, 18). The word προσφορά, or "offering," appears only in Heb 10 and can be taken as synonymous to the word θυσία, or "sacrifice." See Attridge, *Hebrews*, 280. However, while both may be taken as referring to the death of Christ, Christ's death on the cross is not to be isolated from his person and life. DuPlessis proposes, "His [Christ's] entire life is presented as a unity with one single purpose, to serve as the all-sufficient atonement" (DuPlessis, Τέλειος: *Idea of Perfection*, 232).

295. In this context, Christ is the implied subject (cf. 10:12); he appears more prominent than the sacrifice or offering itself. For this discussion, see Ellingworth, *Hebrews*, 511.

296. Westcott, *Hebrews*, 315.

297. The participial phrase τοὺς ἁγιαζομένους in the passive voice points to the work of God in drawing his people closer to himself as they are progressively made holy. The present tense of the participle is understood differently by various interpreters:

> (1) it is taken as timeless and refers to "the sanctified ones" (Bruce, *Hebrews*, 247; Lünemann, *Critical and Exegetical Handbook*, 368; Moffatt, *Hebrews*, 141); (2) it is taken as iterative, referring to "those who from time to time receive sanctification" (Guthrie, *Hebrews*, 208); and more likely, (3) it should be taken as having a progressive or durative force, indicating the process of being made holy or the entire course of

use of the present participle ἁγιαζομένους²⁹⁸ conveys the notion that believers have already been made holy positionally, but absolute holiness remains a goal to be enjoyed in the future. Attridge contends that "it is the appropriation of the enduring effects of Christ's act that is portrayed as an ongoing reality"²⁹⁹ even though perfect holiness or sanctification can be perceived only as a future reality to be realized when God's people will be definitively transformed in the presence of their glorified Savior and King. The language anticipates the full realization and enjoyment of the better provisions of the new covenant promise of Jer 31:31–34, which the author refers to in Heb 10:16–18 (cf. 8:6–11).

For the author of Hebrews, Christ has made perfect (τετελείωκεν)³⁰⁰ those who are being sanctified for all times. He uses the notion of τέλειος with reference to the believers but relates it positively to the work of Christ,³⁰¹ which is portrayed as a completed act in the past with abiding results—not only in the present as some scholars emphasize,³⁰² but forever, as is clearly

---

sanctification as a process (Lane, *Hebrews 9–13*, 256; Wilson, *Hebrews*, 182; Kistemaker, *Hebrews*, 282).

Ellingworth correctly notes that the present tense is used here in order to create some balance with the previous words and avoid the possible implication that the believers had already attained the goal of perfection or sanctification (Ellingworth, *Hebrews*, 512).

298. One witness, P46, reads ἀνασωζομένους, "who are being saved" instead of ἁγιαζομένους, "who are being sanctified," perhaps by transcriptional error. As Attridge observes, "the variant has been defended by Hoskier (*Readings*, 27–30), but it is certainly a simple transcriptional error" (Attridge, *Hebrews*, 278).

299. Ibid., 281.

300. The perfect active indicative of τελειόω, "to perfect" or "to make complete," has in view the completed work of Christ. The completed work cannot be perceived as an end in itself; it has an abiding result into the future, when the believers will attain absolute completeness and enjoy full access to God.

301. Rathel, "Soteriological Terminology in Hebrews," 130.

302. Peterson, while recognizing that "perfection in a true sense is a future reality," as he expresses it in his own words, argues nevertheless that "10:14 clearly locates this perfecting in the past with respect to its accomplishment and in the present with respect to its enjoyment" (Peterson, *Hebrews and Perfection*, 152). Referring to the better provisions of the new covenant promise in Jer 31, Peterson also emphasizes the already-accomplished aspects of the believer's relationship with God that, according to him, were foretold in the oracle of Jeremiah cited by the author of Hebrews in the paragraph immediately after Heb 10:14. Thus, Peterson concludes: "The terminology of perfection is used by our writer here to stress the realized aspect of Christian salvation" (ibid., 153). Following this reasoning, the believers are said to be perfected (vocational approach) as worshipers who are enabled to approach God. Rathel follows this line of reasoning and argues that the primary significance of τέλειος in Hebrews is the present enjoyment of relationship with God. For further details, see Rathel, "Soteriological Terminology," 131.

The Notion of Τέλειος in Hebrews

indicated in the adverbial expression εἰς τὸ διηνεκὲς, which qualifies the participial verb ἁγιαζομένους.[303] If the attainment of the goal of "perfection" in the true sense of the word can be perceived as a future reality, then there is a reason to appreciate the anticipation that is implied in the use of the language of Hebrews. The "better things that are yet to come" become the motivating factor for readers to persevere even in the midst of trials as they look forward with great anticipation to the fullness of their salvation, when they will finally be made complete in the presence of their glorified Lord and Savior.

Some scholars take the notion of τελειόω as synonymous to ἁγιάζω,[304] which is sometimes rendered "to consecrate."[305] For instance, DuPlessis applies the cultic tradition of the OT (LXX) to Hebrews when he argues that unlike the old *cultus* that required repeated consecratory duties (cf. Heb 10:1), the all-sufficient sacrifice of Christ removed once-for-all the self-incrimination of sin and the bondage of slavery (Heb 10:14) with the result that consecrated worshipers are enabled to participate in the priestly consummation as they draw near to God.[306] Here, the life of the worshiper is conceived in sacral terms applicable to those who are priests. Such phrases as "drawing near to God" (7:25; 10:22), "being sanctified/perfected" (9:14; 10:14), "entering the holy places by the blood of Jesus" (10:19–20), are all interpreted in the light of the cultic language of the LXX and perceived as sacral actions of those who are priests.[307] Interestingly, apart from such cultic allusions, the author of Hebrews does not refer to the priestly status of worshipers in contrast with 1 Pet 2:9–10 and Rev 1:5–6; 5:9–10.[308] However, such allusions—including descriptions of Christian activity as "service," "worship," (9:14; 12:28) and the calling of the believers to continuously offer up a sacrifice of praise to God (13:15–16)—can be perceived as setting the believers in the role of priests who enjoy a better access to God now than

---

303. In Hebrews, this adverbial expression would normally follow the verb it qualifies (cf. 7:3; 10:1). For this discussion, see Lane, *Hebrews 9–13*, 256.

304. So Ellingworth, following Michel's *Der Hebräer*, writes: "Ἁγιάζω and τελειόω are used interchangeably in Hebrews" (Ellingworth, *Hebrews*, 511). For alternative views, see Peterson, *Hebrews and Perfection*, 151.

305. This is common among scholars who hold the view that the notion of τέλειος should be interpreted in terms of cultic consecration, which is sometimes referred to as the priestly ordination approach.

306. DuPlessis, Τέλειος: *Idea of Perfection*, 231–32.

307. For this discussion, see also DeSilva, *Perseverance in Gratitude*, 329.

308. Scholer observes that the high priesthood of Christ is explicitly portrayed in a unique fashion in Hebrews, but the priestly status of the readership is not even mentioned or considered explicitly, except for some cultic allusions. For further details, see Scholer, *Proleptic Priests*, 9–11.

the priests of the OT tabernacle.[309] This does not suggest that the notion of τέλειος should be perceived in terms of priestly consecration or priestly ordination.

It is doubtful whether the technical idea of "priestly consecration" or "priestly ordination" should be seen as conveying a better rendering of the notion of τέλειος in Hebrews. As discussed in previous chapters, the author is not primarily concerned with establishing the legal qualifications of Christ as High Priest or implicitly that of the worshipers, but rather the surpassing nature of Christ's priesthood as inherently superior, with its eternal benefits on behalf of worshipers based on the better provisions of the new covenant that, unlike the old Levitical order (7:11, 19; 9:9; 10:1), guarantees believers' eternal salvation (10:14; cf. 9:28). One would argue, therefore, that the cultic interpretation does not help appreciate the definitive nature of the work of Christ and the believers' sanctification, which according to Hebrews is eternal.

The same criticism is leveled against interpreters who, on the basis of the verb ἁγιάζω in Heb 10:14 (cf. 12:10, 14), suggest that the notion of τέλειος should be seen as carrying the idea of "holiness," implying "moral development."[310] David Peterson agrees that when the author emphasizes "consecration" or "holiness" as the only way to God (12:14), he does not suggest that the believers must make moral progress to prove their sanctification. However, he also observes, "A sense of moral development cannot be excluded from 12:10, 14."[311] According to Peterson, "The consummation of man in a direct and lasting relationship with God... is proclaimed as a present possibility, through the finished work of Christ." To Peterson, the notion of τέλειος (10:14; cf. 9:9; 10:1; 12:23) applied to believers carries not merely a sense of moral development, but also a "vocational" significance,[312] which calls believers to a life of consecration that should be evidenced in their worship and service to God. Accordingly, the verb τετελείωκεν of 10:14 should be understood in light of the writer's description of the readers as τοὺς ἁγιαζομένους. Peterson posits, "Such consecration to God cannot be restricted in a sense to the sphere of 'worship', but includes the life of faith,

---

309. DeSilva, *Perseverance in Gratitude*, 329.

310. Westcott, *Hebrews*, 317.

311. McCruden sees Peterson's model as closely related to the moral/ethical approach. For further details, see McCruden, "Christ's Perfection in Hebrews 2:10," 20.

312. Reading τέλειος in a "vocational sense," Peterson contends that "believers are perfected as would-be worshipers, as those who would draw near to God, through the work of Christ" (Peterson, *Hebrews and Perfection*, 166). Peterson's vocational model is similar to what Attridge describes as an "existential or experiential model of perfection" (Attridge, *Hebrews*, 87).

hope and love as the proper response to God's grace."³¹³ This implies that the perfecting of believers (Heb 10:14) was accomplished in the past and is being fully enjoyed in the present, since the focus is on the accomplishment of the relationship with God, which was foretold in Jeremiah (Jer 31:31–34; cf. Heb 10:16–17).³¹⁴ A better approach is to see the fulfillment as already begun but not yet brought to complete fulfillment.

That believers are "the ones being sanctified," at least in a positional sense, is made clear in the context. It is difficult, however, to argue that they have attained the ultimate goal of "perfection" or "completeness," which can be perceived solely in the context of a future reality. For the author of Hebrews, the better provisions that are yet to come should serve as a great incentive for the readers to hold on to their faith with conviction as they await the full realization of their eternal salvation. In fact, Heb 11 serves as an illustration of this truth.

Hebrews 11:40

In Heb 10:1–18, the author argues that Christ's better sacrifice has the perpetual effect of making new covenant worshipers perfect forever. This serves as the basis for the exhortation to enter the new sanctuary by enduring and holding fast to the confession of faith, especially in view of the judgment to come (10:19–39).³¹⁵ The exhortation in Heb 10:19–39 falls into two segments. The first segment, which is fundamentally positive (10:19–25), builds directly on the long argument concerning the superiority of Christ as the perfected High Priest over the Levitical priests. Since the perfected Christ has made the eternal access to God's presence available, the worshipers can confidently approach the holy sanctuary with the same disposition, enduring and holding fast to the confession of their faith. The second segment of the exhortation, in the form of a warning (10:26–39), encourages

---

313. Peterson, *Hebrews and Perfection*, 151.

314. Many commentators have followed Peterson's lines of argument by proposing that what was seen as a future expectation from the time of Jeremiah is now seen as a present reality not only for the readers, but also for subsequent believers of all times because of the atoning death of Christ. See Lane, *Hebrews 9–13*, 268; Attridge, *Hebrews*, 226; and, more recently, O'Brien, *Hebrews*, 358. *Contra* the above approach, one would argue that while the era of fulfillment has begun, a complete enjoyment of the better provisions of Jer 31:31–34 remains in the future for God's people, looking forward to the second advent of the glorified Christ.

315. This section includes the author's fourth warning and concludes his long stretch of exposition extending from Heb 4:14–10:39.

the worshipers to live by faith in view of their future rewards.³¹⁶ The warning precedes the author's long exposition on the nature of faith as illustrated and exemplified in lives of OT heroes of faith in Heb 11:1–40.³¹⁷

In Heb 11:39–40, the author concludes his lengthy list of faith examples with a summary statement reiterating the objective of chapter 11. The author's twofold purpose in this concluding statement is to provide a summary of chapter 11 in succinct fashion and to serve as a transition to chapter 12.³¹⁸ In verse 39, two related truths are stated: (1) all the heroes mentioned were commended by God for their faith, and yet (2) none of them received what had been promised. The remark πάντες μαρτυρηθέντες, "all were commended," recalls the initial commendation of the ancients for their faith; it forms an *inclusio* with Heb 11:2.³¹⁹ Although the people of ancient times received God's commendation³²⁰ in Scripture because of their faith, they never received what God had promised to his people. The commendation of their faith in Scripture warrants the author's presentation of the heroes of faith as examples to emulate. Yet, contrary to expectations, none of them received³²¹ in their lifetimes the fulfillment of the promise (τὴν ἐπαγγελίαν).³²² The Greek word translated "promise" is used in the

316. For a discussion of the future eschatological import of the warning passages (e.g., 10:26–39), see Toussaint, "Eschatology of the Warning Passages," 67–80.

317. Heb 11:1–40 can be subdivided into five subsections:

(1) faith produces the assurance and certainty for what we do not see (11:1–2); (2) by faith, Israel's ancestors obeyed God's command and became heirs of God's promise (11:3–22); (3) by faith, saints during the Exodus obeyed God's command, expecting restoration in the promised land (11:23–31); and (4) by faith, other saints endured sufferings, expecting a better hope (11:32–39).

318. For further details, see Allen, *Hebrews*, 566.

319. Vanhoye argues that chapter 11 begins and concludes with a reference to commendation of faith. For further details, see Vanhoye, *La structure littéraire*, 191–94. See also Attridge, *Hebrews*, 351–52.

320. The aorist participle μαρτυρηθέντες is used concessively: "although they had been commended for their faith." The passive voice implies God as the actor. See Lane, *Hebrews 9–13*, 382. Cf. NAB, NIV, NJB, NRSV, TEV.

321. The aorist tense ἐκομίσαντο is used constatively, summarizing the actions of a number of persons (Robertson, *Grammar*, 833). For other usages of the verb κομίζομαι, see Heb 10:36; 11:13, 19; 1 Pet 1:9; 5:4.

322. A few witnesses, the most prominent being A, change the singular (τὴν ἐπαγγελίαν, "the promise") to plural (τὰς ἐπαγγελίας, "the promises"), perhaps because the verb is seen here in direct contrast to Heb 11:13, 33, where the plural is referred to. For further details, see Johnson, *Hebrews*, 306. The phrase οὐκ ἐκομίσαντο τὴν ἐπαγγελίαν recalls what God promised τὴν ἐπαγγελίαν in Heb 10:36 and is not to be distinguished from τὰς ἐπαγγελίας in 11:13. In 11:13–16, the promise is seen as related to the possession of a secure homeland, a heavenly one, or a city (cf. v. 16). In verse 35,

singular, pointing to the ultimate promise of salvation in Christ.³²³ Kistemaker fittingly notes that although the OT saints were heirs of the messianic kingdom prophesied in the Scriptures,³²⁴ they never received the promised future everlasting salvation through the Messiah.³²⁵

The truth delineated in verse 39 is complemented by the contents of verse 40 to conclude the lengthy list of examples of faith in the OT. The author states, τοῦ θεοῦ περὶ ἡμῶν κρεῖττόν τι προβλεψαμένου,,³²⁶ literally, "God having provided something better for us." Peterson proposes that the stress of the verse is on "the gracious providence of God (τοῦ θεοῦ ... προβλεψαμένου), who, with us in mind (περὶ ἡμῶν), had a better plan (κρεῖττόν τι)."³²⁷ The notion that God had intended something better (κρεῖττόν τι)³²⁸ "on our behalf" does not imply that the readers are better off than the heroes of faith.³²⁹ For most interpreters, Hebrew believers in the Christian era are better off in the sense that they have become recipients of the promised salvation in Christ.³³⁰ Thus, Ellingworth posits that the "something bet-

---

it is associated with the resurrection and is later seen as fulfilled through faith together with the glorified Christ (Heb 12:1–3) within a great and wider festal communion of all the saints of all times (12:21–24). Both OT and NT believers are bound up together in God's ultimate design for the salvation of mankind. For this discussion, see also Ellingworth, *Hebrews*, 635.

323. For further details, see Allen, *Hebrews*, 567.

324. See Gen 3:15; 49:10; Num 24:17; 2 Sam 7:13; Ps 2:6–12; 16:10; 22:1; 45:6–8; 110:1.

325. For this discussion, see Kistemaker, *Hebrews*, 358.

326. The verb προβλεψαμένου is an aorist middle participle of προβλέπω, "to look ahead" or "to provide," and occurs only here in the NT. It is used once in the LXX in Psa 36:13. Although it carries the notion of "looking ahead" or "foreseeing," in secular Greek it means "provide for." See BDAG, 866; and Mitchell, *Hebrews*, 261.

327. Peterson, *Hebrews and Perfection*, 156.

328. Kistemaker observes that the comparative Greek adjective κρεῖττον, "better," appears nineteen times in the NT, thirteen of which are in Hebrews (1:4; 6:9; 7:7, 19, 22; 8:6 [twice]; 9:23; 10:34; 11:16, 35, 40; 12:24). Most commentators take this as related to "the era of fulfillment in Christ" or its benefits. The believers of the Christian era are portrayed as recipients of the promised salvation in Christ (Kistemaker, *Hebrews*, 358), to be fully enjoyed in the future.

329. Westcott argues that the believers in the Christian era have actually seen in part that towards which the OT saints strained. Accordingly, the heroes of faith "looked for a fulfillment of the promises which was not granted to them." To the believers in the Christian era, "the fulfillment has been granted" (Westcott, *Hebrews*, 384). This conveys a general truth from Hebrews' perspective, but there seems to be something deeper, as the context indicates.

330. The assumption here is that the believers in the Christian era enjoy the blessings of the new covenant mediated by Christ. Given the context, this is too strong a statement, as will be shown later in this study.

ter" involves the salvation brought to the believers or "the age of fulfillment" in Christ, at least by anticipation.[331] The general tenor seems to indicate that compared to the OT saints, who lived in anticipation of promised salvation, the believers of the NT era have tasted some of the promised benefits of salvation made available through the suffering, death, and exaltation of Christ. Yet they too anticipated the better things to come, which serve as an incentive for their walk of faith and perseverance. The author has already indicated they have "a better hope" (7:19) and have witnessed a superior ministry (8:6), but they have not yet attained the goal or completed their course (12:1). As R. McLachlan Wilson indicates, their place is assured in God's eternal purpose, but they still need to endure to the end (10:36).[332] The readers' advantage is seen in the fact that the unseen truth under the OT era is not entirely unseen in the NT era because of the manifestation of Christ (Heb 1:2–3).[333] By "something better," the author has in mind "life in the presence of God"[334] as God's elect are made perfect in the presence of the glorified Savior.

The author of Hebrews brings the OT saints and NT believers together in the great anticipation of what is yet to come. Some commentators use Pauline language[335] to explain that Heb 11:40 refers to the perfection of the body, which lies in the members' interdependence. While some similarities could apply, Paul's language is foreign to the thought of Hebrews. Others prefer a "social ecclesiology" (*contra* an "anatomical ecclesiology"), arguing that the Hebrews' author thinks of the church as a city, "heavenly city," or "household," not after the model of the human body[336] Montefiore is perhaps correct when he contends that the author in Heb 11:40 is more concerned with the inclusive nature of τελείωσις—God's eternal plan concerns all his elect, whether they belong to the old or new dispensation.[337] In this passage, both OT and NT saints are brought together as one family in great

---

331. Ellingworth, *Hebrews*, 636. Also recently, Allen, *Hebrews*, 567. More likely, the believers have tasted spiritual benefits of what was promised but are still awaiting final fulfillment and attainment of the goal of their Christian faith to be realized when they meet the Lord face to face.

332. Wilson, *Hebrews*, 218.

333. Ibid.

334. Peterson argues, "The final clause (ἵνα μὴ χωρὶς ἡμῶν τελειωθῶσιν) is epexegetical and shows that the κρεῖττόν τι should be taken absolutely: the 'better thing' is that 'the transfer of the elders to the state of perfection would not happen without us'" (Peterson, *Hebrews and Perfection*, 156–57).

335. See also Paul, in 1 Cor 12:12–26; Eph 4:16; Col 2:19.

336. For this discussion, see Montefiore, *Hebrews*, 212.

337. Ibid., 213.

The Notion of Τέλειος in Hebrews

anticipation of the perfected Christ leading them to the final stage of their perfection.[338] Thus, the author states that God had "chosen ahead of time to make provision"[339] for something better, ἵνα μὴ χωρὶς ἡμῶν τελειωθῶσιν, "in order that they should not be made perfect apart from us." The promise is not simply on behalf of Hebrew believers of the Christian era, but also the OT saints, "So that they should not be made perfect (τελειωθῶσιν) apart from us (χωρὶς ἡμῶν)."[340]

This discussion suggests "perfection" carries the formal idea of "completion" and "fulfillment" throughout Hebrews as well as an eschatological significance. While most interpreters disagree on the eschatological nature of previous occurrences of this notion in Hebrews, the majority agree that in Heb 11:40 the notion has an eschatological focus. Thus, Lane,[341] seeing in verse 40 an emphasis on the final realization of the relationship with God, argues that the notion "should be interpreted in terms of entrance into the promised inheritance."[342] Contrary to Lane's position that the present benefit of access to God motivates the readers to be more willing to endure,[343] it is the Christian hope for better things yet to come (futurist eschatology) that serves as a motivation for the readers to endure. In his early work, Ellingworth observes that τέλειος is the author's favorite word to describe "the final aim or end of salvation."[344] Accordingly, the notion expresses the idea

---

338. Montefiore argues, "A family is not complete unless all its members are present" (Montefiore, *Hebrews*, 212). The same thought is present in Heb 12:1–2, where the "great cloud of witnesses and the readers are brought together" in great anticipation of Christ leading them to perfection. For further details, see Kistemaker, *Hebrews*, 358.

339. BDAG, 866; NASB, KJV, NRSV; cf. NAB, TEV.

340. The Greek preposition χωρίς is used with the genitive object and carries the sense of "apart from" (BDAG, 1095; NASB, NRSV, NAB). Cf. "except with" (NJB); "only together with" (NIV).

341. Lane uses Kogel, "Der Begriff," 55–6. See also Riggenbach, who suggests that the "promise" (τὴν ἐπαγγελίαν) in Heb 11:39 should be seen in reference to the eschatological salvation viewed from the perspective of OT prophecy (Riggenbach, *Hebräer*, 383).

342. Lane, *Hebrews 9–13*, 393. However, a point of disagreement would be Lane's failure to distinguish between the nature of the blessings said to be presently available to the believers of the Christian era and the future blessings to come. *Contra* Lane's point that the believers now enjoy unrestricted access to God as a fulfillment of the promise of the new covenant (see also Peterson, *Hebrews and Perfection*, 150–59), one could argue that many aspects of the new covenant's better provisions are still in the future for God's people.

343. Ibid., 394.

344. Ellingworth and Nida, *Handbook*, 285. In this work, Ellingworth sees a relationship between to notion of τέλειος and "the kingdom of God" in Mark and Luke, "the kingdom of heaven" in Matthew and "eternal life" in John (ibid.).

of "being as one ought to be" or "being completely what God intended us to be."[345] If this reconstruction is correct, then "perfection," in the truest sense of the word, should be perceived as eschatological, pointing to the complete realization and enjoyment of eternal salvation at the second coming of Christ. For the author of Hebrews, that stands as the goal as the readers continue running the race that has been set before them (Heb 12:1-2).

Hebrews 12:2, 23

The final two references to the notion of τέλειος in Hebrews are found in Heb 12:2, 23. In chapter 11, the author traced the line of the ancient heroes of faith from Abel down to the NT-era readers themselves. Now, the author returns to his exhortation motif as he summons the readers to persevere in the "race"[346] that has been "set before us"[347] for the prize of God's approval and entrance into God's eternal realm (Heb 12:1-2).[348] The exhortation is embellished with athletic imageries in which the believers' Christian experience is portrayed as a "race" or "marathon."[349] The believers' performance is depicted as being witnessed not merely by a crowd of flaccid spectators or "mere onlookers," but by the assembly of those who have run the race before

---

345. Ibid.

346. The Greek word ἀγῶνος, "race" (Heb 12:1), may apply to any kind of athletic contest from wrestling to racing, but in this context, it must be seen as pointing to the imagery of "footracing" because of the verb τρέχειν, "to run" (see Euripides, *Orestes*, 847; Herodotus, *Persian Wars*, VIII. 102; IX. 60. 1; VII. 11. 3; Plato, *Phaedrus*, 247b; Lucian, *Gymnosophists*, 15; and Philo, *Allegorical Interpretation*, III. 48). The context in Heb 12:1-2 suggests "not a short sprint where speed is important, but a lengthy race where endurance is essential to passing the finish line" (Allen, *Hebrews*, 573-74). For further details, see also Johnson, *Hebrews*, 316.

347. According to DeSilva, the notion of the "race set before us" (τὸν προκείμενον ἡμῖν ἀγῶνα) is a "fixed classic expression" for a race whose course is determined by the masters of the game (DeSilva, *Perseverance in Gratitude*, 429). See also Attridge's allusions to the following documents: Euripedes, *Orestes*, 846; Plato, *Laches*, 182a; Epictetus, *Discourses*, III. 25. 3; Josephus, *Antiquities of the Jews*, XIX. 1. 13. For further details, see Attridge, *Hebrews*, 355.

348. DeSilva, *Perseverance in Gratitude*, 425.

349. For examples of such common athletic imageries or metaphors used to depict the moral/religious life, see 2 Macc 13:14; 4 Macc 17:10-14; Philo, *On Agriculture*, 112, 119; ibid., *On Rewards and Punishments*, 5; ibid., *On the Migration of Abraham*, 133; Epictetus, *Discourses*, I. 24. 1-3, III. 22. 51-52, III. 25. 1-5; Cicero, *De officiis*, III. 10. 12; 4 Ezra 7:127. So also the Apostle Paul in 1 Cor 9:24-27; Gal 2:2; Phil 1:30; 2:16. For further details, see Attridge, *Hebrews*, 354.

them³⁵⁰ and have run it well.³⁵¹ Thus, Attridge observes, the introductory segment of the author's call to endurance begins with imagery that is evocative of a stadium and a call to "run the race" (v. 1) followed by a focus on "the primary paradigm of faithful endurance, Jesus (v. 2)."³⁵²

At this point, the original readers need no further evidence to believe that faith will support them through the course of the race until they reach the goal of τελείωσις, "maturity," or "perfection" (Heb 6:1). The exhortation to the readers is that they should lay aside (ἀποθέμενοι)³⁵³ all the hindrances of sin and run (τρέχωμεν)³⁵⁴ the course with patient endurance by faith. The race must be run with perseverance.³⁵⁵ Since the goal is τελείωσις, the author elaborates on the believers' attitude of patient endurance by pointing to Jesus as the one who truly exemplified patient endurance in all he suffered (v. 2). The readers are called to follow Christ's example, not the example of the heroes of faith.³⁵⁶ F. F. Bruce contends, "The earlier witnesses supply incentive in abundance; but in Jesus we have one who is *par excellence* 'the faithful witness.'"³⁵⁷ For the author, not only is Jesus the pioneer of faith, it is also in Jesus that the faith endurance of the believer will reach its perfection or completion.

350. The "cloud of witnesses" are "the heroes of faith" of Heb 11, who themselves received God's commendation for their faith (Heb 11:2, 3, 5, 39) and are fellow pilgrims who have run the same race to which the believers are also committed in order to be made perfect together (Heb 11:40). For this discussion, see Johnson, *Hebrews*, 316.

351. Pentecost, *Faith That Endures*, 210.

352. Attridge, *Hebrews*, 354.

353. The Greek aorist middle (deponent = act) participle of ἀποτίθημι "to lay aside" may be taken as expressing the means of running: "by means of having thrown off . . . let us run." More likely, however, the participle should be taken as expressing "attendant circumstance" with a hortatory force because of the present tense and subjunctive mood of the main verb τρέχωμεν, "let us run." For this discussion, see Wallace's argument that the word is used in Rom 13:12 with the idea of "casting off" the works of darkness; in 1 Peter 2:1 as "putting away" all evil, deceit, and hypocrisy; and in Jas 1:21 as "putting away" all filthiness and wickedness (Wallace, *Exegetical Syntax*, 640–44). In the context, sin (e.g., unbelief) is like a long, heavy flowing garment that would hinder one's free movement. For further details, see Wilson, *Hebrews*, 220.

354. The present subjunctive τρέχωμεν, "let us run," implies both an effort and a continuing action. The author uses the first-person plural in order to include himself. For this discussion, see Ellingworth, *Hebrews*, 384.

355. The imagery of a race run with perseverance and endurance is also seen in Epictetus when he states, "No contest is held without turmoil" (Epictetus, *Dissertations*, IV. 4. 31). For further details, see also Mitchell, *Hebrews*, 265.

356. Pentecost argues that the ancient heroes of faith ran well but that they cannot be presented as ideal examples because they all had some failures (Pentecost, *Faith That Endures*, 213).

357. Bruce, *Hebrews*, 337.

In Heb 12:2 the author states, "let us keep our eyes fixed on Jesus, the pioneer and perfecter of our faith (ἀφορῶντες εἰς τὸν τῆς πίστεως ἀρχηγὸν καὶ τελειωτὴν Ἰησοῦν).[358] The verse begins with a participial phrase that may be literally translated, "keeping our eyes fixed on Jesus" (ἀφορῶντες εἰς τὸν Ἰησοῦν). As believers set out on the race laid before them, the author challenges them to keep their eyes fixed (ἀφορῶντες, lit. "looking away")[359] toward Jesus, the one who has run ahead of them and has already attained the goal of τελείωσις (Heb 2:10; 5:8–9; 7:28). The author uses the name "Jesus" to emphasize the shared experience with believers who are called upon to fix their eyes on him.[360] The image allows the readers to visualize the perfected Jesus as one who had run the same contest ahead of them. The language allows the readers to keep their focus toward the one on whom they must constantly rely[361] throughout their Christian experience as they endure to the end.

The author distinguishes Jesus from the ancient heroes of faith by using two qualifying epithets standing in apposition to the name Ἰησοῦν, "Jesus," giving him special recognition as τῆς πίστεως ἀρχηγὸν καὶ τελειωτήν, "the pioneer and perfecter of our faith." This description echoes the earlier

358. In his examination of the structure of Heb 12:1–2, Horning concludes that the passage shows an inverse parallelism with nine clauses, of which the centerline is "Keeping our eyes fixed on Jesus, the pioneer and perfecter of the faith" (Horning, "Chiasmus, Creedal Structure, and Christology in Hebrews 12:1–2," 37–48). If this reconstruction is correct, the main emphasis of the passage lies in the first clause, which deserves particular attention. As Kistemaker fittingly observes, the rest of the clauses in verse 2 are descriptive of Jesus with respect to his work, endurance on the cross, and position (Kistemaker, *Hebrews*, 367).

359. The present participle ἀφορῶντες emphasizes a continued action concurrent with that of the main verb τρέχωμεν, "let us run," in the preceding clause (Lane, *Hebrews 9–13*, 398). The prefixed particle ἀφ, or "from," implies looking away from all others toward one (ibid., 410; see especially, O'Brien, *Hebrews*, 453) in order to focus on the goal of the prescribed course. As Ellingworth rightly explains, this points to the constant attention the author has repeatedly recommended to the readers since Heb 2:1. For further details, see Ellingworth, *Hebrews*, 640.

360. See Heb 2:9; 3:1; 6:20; 7:22; 10:19; 12:24; 13:12.

361. So Koester suitably argues that the verb ἀφορᾶν "could mean relying on someone in authority (see Josephus, *Jewish War*, 2. 410; ibid., *Jewish Antiquities*, XII. 431; XVI. 134) or on God" (Koester, *Hebrews*, 523). There is a sense of "fixing one's eyes trustingly" on Jesus (BDAG, 158). The verb is used in a description of the Maccabean martyrs, who "avenged their nation, *looking to God,* and enduring torment to the point of death" (4 Macc 17:10; cf. Josephus, *Jewish Antiquities*, XII. 431). Michel alludes to an interesting parallel (see Michel, *Hebrews*, 265) in which Epictetus, as a teacher, exhorts his students to help him complete his purpose to bring them to maturity (cf. Heb 6:1). Furthermore, he encourages them to intently look (ἀφορᾶν) to God in things small and great (Epictetus, *Dissertations*, II. 19. 29; III. 24. 16; see also Josephus, *Jewish Antiquities*, XX. 48; *Against Apion*, II. 166).

The Notion of Τέλειος in Hebrews

statement regarding Christ and believers. In Heb 2:10, the author indicates how "it was fitting for God to make perfect the 'pioneer' (ἀρχηγὸν)[362] of their salvation in leading many sons to glory." In Heb 5:9, the author declares how "by being made perfect, Christ has become the 'source' (αἴτιος) of eternal salvation" to all who obey him. In Heb 6:20, the author depicts Christ as the "forerunner" (πρόδρομος) who has entered the better sanctuary on behalf of the many believers who are in the process of being brought to their future eschatological glory. The racing metaphor in Heb 12:2 suggests the word ἀρχηγόν should be understood in the light of the author's Christology in these previous passages[363] and in Hebrews as a whole. It is in his eternal status as the "forerunner," "pioneer," or "source" of eternal salvation that Christ has proleptically made perfect forever those who are being sanctified (Heb 10:14). Yet, in his providence, God has provided something better for the purpose that the ancient heroes of faith would not be made perfect apart from Hebrew believers of the Christian era (Heb 11:40). Though they were all well attested by faith, none of them received the "promise" (v. 39), which is an indication that there is something better that is still future[364] and points to the fullness of salvation in Christ.[365] Building from this context, the athletic metaphor of "running the race"[366] suggests that the Greek epithet ἀρχηγός functions similarly in the verses preceding Heb 12:1–2. As the "initiator," Jesus is the one on whom the Christian faith depends from start to finish. He is the source, but he is also the first person to have attained faith's ultimate goal, which is the inheritance of the promise that the ancient heroes of faith only saw from afar (Heb 11:13, 39).[367]

---

362. In Heb 2:10, the author portrays a vivid image of Christ's salvific activity as the "chief leader," "champion," or "forerunner" (cf. 6:20) of the many sons who are in the process of being brought to their future eschatological glory.

363. Attridge, *Hebrews*, 356. See also Peterson, *Hebrews and Perfection*, 171.

364. The fulfillment and realization of the new covenant, including all its benefits, are viewed and perceived as a future reality.

365. The Greek word rendered "promise" is singular. It points to the eschatological salvation in Christ (Heb 10:36; 11:13). For further details, see Allen, *Hebrews*, 567. In Heb 11:13–16, the possession of a "secure homeland," a "city," or a "heavenly one" is connected to the promise. In verse 35, it is associated with the resurrection, and in 12:1–2, it is seen as fulfilled through faith together with the glorified Christ in the context of a greater celebration of all the saints. For further details, see Ellingworth, *Hebrews*, 635.

366. Among Hellenistic moral philosophers, "such metaphors liken the moral life and progress in virtue to a struggle that calls for steadfast determination toward reaching a goal" (Mitchell, *Hebrews*, 268). See Mitchell's discussion of Heraclitus, *To Hermadorus*, qtd. in Malherbe, *Cynic Epistle*, 192; and Epictetus, *Dissertations*, I. 4. 20–23; I. 24. 1–5; IV. 12. 15–17 (ibid.).

367. For further details, see Attridge, *Hebrews*, 356.

Not only is Jesus portrayed as the "initiator," "source," or "pioneer" of the believers' faith and salvation, he is also the τελειωτής, "perfecter" or "completer," of the Christian faith.[368] For the Christian believers, running the race until the end would require keeping their eyes fixed on Jesus, the "perfecter" of their faith. DuPlessis appropriately argues that the author is not primarily concerned with the believers' acceptance of some catechetical proposition or teaching about faith, but rather with what it produces:[369] a life of endurance and persistent attachment to Christ as they run the race toward the final goal of τελείωσις (Heb 6:1). Attridge concludes the focus is not on the "faith" (πίστεως) *per se*, which Christ inaugurates and brings to perfect expression, but rather on the content of the Christian walk of faith: "the fidelity and trust that Jesus himself exhibited in a fully adequate way, and that his followers are called upon to share."[370]

The point of contention is whether the believers' faith has already reached its perfection in Christ's past work, or if the "perfecting" of the believers' faith is still to be anticipated in the future. Some commentators acknowledge that the believers are called upon to keep their eyes fixed on Jesus because, in him, the believers' faith has already reached its perfection (in the past).[371] Some scholars believe that the athletic metaphor of the race contest intends to communicate something about the moral life of the believers.[372] For instance, Johnson remarks, "This 'race' is a matter of moral and religious transformation in which the 'faithful' Jesus (3:1) and believers are intimately linked."[373] Implicitly, the believers' faith has already been per-

---

368. The Greek noun is usually translated as a relative clause: "one who perfects" (NAB); "one who brought faith to complete expression" (Lane, *Hebrews 9–13*, 397, 412); and more likely, "one who will bring [believers'] faith to fulfillment or completion" (NJB).

369. DuPlessis, Τέλειος: *Idea of Perfection*, 218–19; 22–24; and Ellingworth, *Hebrews*, 640.

370. Attridge, *Hebrews*, 356. This is similar to Westcott, who interprets the expression as referring to Jesus as the perfect example, in terms of both realization and effect, of the faith the believers are supposed to imitate as they trust in him (Westcott, *Hebrews*, 397). Similarly, Moffat argues that it points to Jesus as the perfect example of πίστις, or "faith," in Jesus' earthly life as the supreme pioneer and the perfect embodiment of the faith, as well as the one who has realized faith to the full from start to finish. See Moffatt, *Hebrews*, 196.

371. Bruce, *Hebrews*, 337; *contra* the eschatological approach, which holds that the Christian faith will ultimately reach its intended goal of "completeness" in the future. The former approach is held by most scholars within the moral, cultic, and vocational model of perfection.

372. See Epictetus, *Discourses*, I. 24. 1–3; III. 22. 51–52; III. 25. 2–5; Cicero, *De officiis*, III. 10. 12.

373. Johnson, *Hebrews*, 315, 17.

fected with the perfecting of Christ, their moral exemplar, with whom they are deeply intertwined. DuPlessis, who holds to the cultic view of τέλειος, sees a correlation between the perfecting of Christ and his function as the τελειωτής. He argues that by his achievement, Christ secured the τελείωσις for all who believe and obey.[374] Delling also notes that in Heb 12:2, Jesus is presented as the one who has brought faith to completion in the sense that he has given it a perfect basis through his work as High Priest.[375] Peterson concludes that Christ's faith is qualitatively greater than that of the ancient heroes of faith because "Jesus is the one in whom faith has reached its perfection."[376] Peter T. O'Brien clarifies the same thought when he argues that through his suffering, death, and exaltation, the perfected Christ brought faith to its ultimate goal.[377] Accordingly, the emphasis in Heb 12:2 is placed on Jesus as the "perfect example"[378] of one who fully exercised "the faith" (τῆς πίστεως).[379] If this interpretation is deemed correct, then Jesus should be perceived exclusively in terms of a virtuous person who is embodied with the moral ideal, which he demonstrates in words and deeds,[380] fostering reasons to follow his example.

374. DuPlessis, Τέλειος: *Idea of Perfection*, 224.

375. Delling, "τέλειος," *TDNT* 8:86. For further details, see Peterson, *Hebrews and Perfection*, 171–72.

376. Ibid., 171. For an emphasis on Jesus as exercising faith himself, see Dods, *Hebrews*, 365; Hughes, *Hebrews*, 522; Ellingworth, *Hebrews*, 640; Lane, *Hebrews*, 411–12; and Westcott, *Hebrews*, 395. More likely, the emphasis of the contest metaphor is not on Jesus as exercising faith but is rather on the worshipers, who are urged to run the race with their eyes fixed on Jesus as the perfecter (12:1–2; cf. Heb 2:10; 5:9) of their faith. For the latter position, see Montefiore, *Hebrews*, 214; Hewitt, *Hebrews*, 191; Lenski, *Hebrews*, 434–35; and Kistemaker, *Hebrews*, 368.

377. O'Brien, *Hebrews*, 454.

378. The use of examples was standard approach in moral exhortation among Hellenistic philosophers. Mitchell shows how it was not uncommon for philosophers to use examples of individuals who succeeded in reaching their moral purpose (Seneca, *Moral Epistles*, 71, 4; 75, 9, 51:1–9; Pseudo-Isocrates, *To Demonicus*, 9–15; Malherbe, *Moral Exhortation*, 62–64, 125–26, 135–41). See Mitchell, *Hebrews*, 268. For further treatment of philosophical background on the use and function of personal examples, see Fiore, *Function of Personal Examples*, 45–163.

379. The phrase τῆς πίστεως ("the faith") with the definite article is taken by some interpreters as "faith" in the absolute and unqualified sense. For examples, see Hughes, *Hebrews*, 522; Lane, *Hebrews*, 412; Bruce, *Hebrews*, 338; Westcott, *Hebrews*, 395; cf. NASB. More likely, it points to the faith of the author and the readers and less directly to the faith of the OT witnesses referred to in Heb 12:1 and 11:39. The rendering "our faith" (the readers and author included, cf. RSV) is acceptable, given the context. See Montefiore, *Hebrews*, 214; Guthrie, *Hebrews*, 250; NAB; KJV; NJB; NIV; NRSB; TEV; and NET.

380. Mitchell, *Hebrews*, 268–69.

There is reason to believe that the emphasis in Heb 12:1-2 is not simply on Jesus as a perfect model of faith, but also on believers, who are exhorted to focus their full attention on Jesus as the one who perfected their faith. Montefiore contends that the believers would only run with endurance of faith if they kept their eyes fixed on Christ as the object of their faith.[381] The ground for this exhortation has already been laid; Christ is the one who originates, but also the one who will bring faith to its triumphant issue.[382] The goal of "completion" or "perfection" is perceived as a future reality. The implication is that attaining the goal of τελέωσις is assured only in Christ, since he is the one who will ultimately bring it to its completion. The author's reasoning is almost identical to Paul's thought in Phil 1:9: "He who began a good work in you will bring it to completion at the day of Jesus Christ." In the meanwhile, however, the Hebrew believers must keep their eyes fixed on him.

That Jesus himself is the one who will bring the readers' faith journey to completion serves as an incentive for the readers to keep their eyes fixed on him as they continue to run the course toward the ultimate goal of their faith and the future enjoyment of their eschatological salvation.[383] Just as Jesus endured the cross and its shame, assessed his circumstances in light of the glorious future, then was glorified to the right hand of God the Father, so also the readers should endure present hardship, counting on the reality of the future eschatological promise that is assured in Christ. This future orientation appears even clearer in the author's last usage of τέλειος (Heb 12:23).

In Heb 12:22-23, the author states, "But you have come to Mount Zion, the city of the living God, the heavenly Jerusalem, and to myriads of angels, to the assembly, and congregation of the first born who are enrolled in heaven, and to God, the Judge of all, and to the spirits of the just men made perfect." Having urged the readers to run with steadfast endurance the race set before them (12:1-3), to endure discipline as the mark of God's Sonship (12:4-11), and to pursue peace and holiness (12:12-17), the author turns to present a picture of the final goal toward which the readers are to

---

381. The faith of those called to endure by faith is in view, not the faith of Jesus. For further details, see Montefiore, *Hebrews*, 214.

382. Hewitt, *Hebrews*, 191. See also Hagner, *Hebrews*, 212.

383. Their faith and hope serve as the basis for the optimism; *contra* Hellenistic moral philosophers, who held that individuals involved in moral development and progress could fail to reach their moral goal (Epictetus, *Dissertations*, I. 4. 20-23; I. 24. 1-5; IV. 12. 15-17). Consequently, the philosophers' role was likened to a coach encouraging an athlete not to lose heart when setbacks occur (ibid., IV. 9. 15-18; ibid., *Enchiridion*, XXIX. 1-2; Seneca, *Moral Epistles*, LI. 1-9).

The Notion of Τέλειος in Hebrews 203

strive. In Heb 12:18-24, he provides an antithesis[384] contrasting the quality of the Israelites' approach to God at Mount Sinai (12:18-21) with the quality of the believers' new approach to God under the new dispensation (12:22-23).[385] The author's general purpose is to build the readers' confidence by reminding them they are not connected to the terror associated with Sinai,[386] but rather to the joyful things associated with the future Zion, the heavenly Jerusalem, and the glorified Jesus, Mediator of the new covenant (v. 24).

In context, the apocalyptic overtones are seen in the author's vivid description of the realization of the eschatological hopes of the people of God announcing the objective realization of the better promises of the new covenant[387] on behalf of God's people. Because of their new identity and the prospect of the final judgment to come, the readers must not ignore God's warning (12:25-26). Instead, they should give thanks and render their worship to God as citizens of the "unshakable kingdom" that is yet to come (12:27-29). The removal of what is shakable to give way to what cannot be shaken points to the future fulfillment of salvation for God's people. Clearly, the author intends to attune believers' imaginations to the final goal of their pilgrimage. Johnson rightly asserts that the vision the author presents to the readers is proleptic as he draws an imaginative picture of what their future inheritance and reward would be.[388]

In Heb 12:22, the scene shifts from the terror of Sinai (cf. v. 18)[389] to the joy of Mount Zion. The contrast introduced is governed by the verb προσεληλύθατε, "you have come" (v. 22),[390] which recalls the same verb Οὐ

---

384. This popular rhetorical or stylistic device is also found in Aristotle, *Rhetoric*, III. 10. 5.

385. In his analysis of Heb 12:22-24, DeSilva observes that the passage points to the ultimate approach to God, which marks the believers' entrance into glory and their final perfection. For further details, see DeSilva, *Perseverance in Gratitude*, 464.

386. Heb 12:19-21, cf. Exod 19:12-13; Deut 9:19. At Mount Sinai, the Israelites of old, including Moses, were filled with terror to approach God. In contrast, the readers' approach to Mount Zion—the city of the Living God, the heavenly Jerusalem in presence of myriads of angels in joyful assembly—is assured (12:22-23) as a future reality to continue anticipating.

387. Scholars such as DeSilva and Lane take these eschatological hopes or promises as already realized. However, the context seems to indicate more than what has already been realized.

388. Johnson, *Hebrews*, 328.

389. The phrase "Mountain of Sinai" does not occur in verse 18, but the context suggests that it is implied, given the author's citation of Exod 19:12-13; 20:18-21, and Deut 9:19; cf. Heb 12:20-21.

390. The verb προσεληλύθατε, "you have come," is a perfect tense (προσέρχομαι), pointing to a continuing result from a past action. The emphasis is on the lasting result

προσεληλύθατε, "you have not come," in verse 18. The explanatory[391] sentence (about the benefits of the new covenant's approach to Mount Zion) that begins in verse 18 continues through verse 22: Οὐ γὰρ προσεληλύθατε ψηλαφωμένῳ... ἀλλὰ προσεληλύθατε Σιὼν ὄρει, "For you have not come to what can be touched. . .; on the contrary,[392] you have come to Mount Zion." The believers' experience of "coming" is construed differently by various interpreters. According to some scholars, the verb προσεληλύθατε, "you have come," points to the spiritual realities that the believers have already experienced in Christ and indicates that they have already entered a permanent place through conversion.[393] O'Brien cites Peterson in arguing that the author "uses the metaphor of journey or pilgrimage to the city of God to speak of the listeners having come to their heavenly destination, which occurred at their conversion."[394] The indicative perfect active verb προσεληλύθατε ("you have come") indicates that the believers have drawn near to God. The suggestion that the verb indicates they have already attained the goal of permanent enjoyment of their salvation is an overstatement. More likely, the verbal imagery should be taken as indicating that the believers have spiritually drawn nearer to God by faith in Christ, not in the sense of full enjoyment or realization of the benefits of their salvation, which is the anticipated goal of their Christian faith (cf. 11:39).[395] This is the reason why the author additionally indicates that because of the absence

---

of a past action (Zerwick, *Biblical Greek*, 285).

391. The use of the inferential γάρ, or "for," at the beginning of verse 18 links the whole unit (vv. 18-24) with the preceding paragraph (vv. 14-17). Lane fittingly posits that "the motif of judgment developed in vv. 14-17 informs the formulation of vv. 18-24, lending to this unit the urgent tone of pastoral concern that characterizes the prior warning" (Lane, *Hebrews 9-13*, 459).

392. Lane observes that the adversative particle ἀλλά, "but" or "on the contrary," in verse 22 is correlative to the emphatic negative particle Οὐ, "not," at the beginning of the sentence. This indicates that the latter Σιὼν ὄρει, or "Mount Zion," must be appreciated as decisively different from Sinai. For further details, see ibid., 465.

393. For examples of this approach, see: Kistemaker, *Hebrews*, 392; Allen, *Hebrews*, 590; Dods, *Hebrews*, 472; Johnson, *Hebrews*, 326; and O'Brien, *Hebrews*, 478. Most scholars in this camp follow Peterson's approach of associating the believers' present benefits with the promised blessings of the new covenant (Jer 31:31-34).

394. O'Brien, *Letter to the Hebrews*, 482. Peterson, supporting the notion of a journey or "pilgrimage motif" (*contra* "a cultic fellowship motif" in Hebrews; cf. Barrett, "Eschatology of the Epistle to the Hebrews," 376), argues that the perfect tense in Heb 12:22 (προσεληλύθατε) indicates that "the believers have already reached their heavenly destination in their conversion" (Peterson, *Hebrews and Perfection*, 160). In the context, the focus appears to be a picture of what is yet to come (future).

395. The goal of the Christian faith is perceived as a future reality that has yet to be fully experienced. For this approach, see Koester, *Hebrews*, 544; and Montefiore, *Hebrews*, 229.

The Notion of Τέλειος in Hebrews

of a "lasting city" on earth, the believers are anticipating "the city that is to come" (Heb 13:14).[396] The author's interest seems to be in presenting the readers with an imaginative picture of what the future inheritance would be for God's people (Heb 12:22, 23).

The final destination of the believers is assured[397] when the author states, "But you have come "to Mount Zion, the city of the Living God, the heavenly Jerusalem... and to the spirits of the just men made perfect" (Σιὼν ὄρει καὶ πόλει θεοῦ ζῶντος, Ἰερουσαλὴμ ἐπουρανίῳ, . . . καὶ πνεύμασι δικαίων τετελειωμένων). Most interpreters would indicate that the locatives "Mount Zion," "city of the Living God," and "heavenly Jerusalem" stand in apposition to one another referring to the same location, emphatically referred to as Σιὼν ὄρει, or "Mount Zion."[398] The description of Zion as "the city of the Living God" recalls the notion of God's dwelling place in the OT. This was traditionally known as the "city of God" and also referred to as the "city of David."[399] However, the second description of Σιὼν ὄρει, "Mount Zion, as Ἰερουσαλὴμ ἐπουρανίῳ, "the heavenly Jerusalem,"[400] implies that the author has in mind not the former earthly city of David, but a heavenly city that is yet to be revealed (cf. Heb 13:14). As Kiwoong Son suitably states, considering that the notion of πόλει θεοῦ ζῶντος, the "city of the living God," or "heavenly Jerusalem" was so common in apocalyptic tradition,[401] it is possible that the author of Hebrews may have been aware of this tradition as referring not to earthly Jerusalem but rather to the true dwelling place of God.[402]

The name "Zion" was not only used as a reference to the temple hill, but also the whole city of Jerusalem as a place where the Israelites gathered for worship and hoped to see the manifestation of God in his glory.

---

396. "The city that is to come" (Heb 13:14) is perceived in terms of the eschatological kingdom, which is yet to come. For further details, see Koester, *Hebrews*, 544; Ellingworth, *Hebrews*, 677–78; Lane, *Hebrews 9–13*, 465; and Colijn, "'Let Us Approach': Soteriology in Hebrews," 571–86.

397. Johnson indicates that the final destination of the pilgrimage is suggested by a set of deeply evocative images, including "Mount Zion," the "city of the living God," and the "heavenly Jerusalem" (Johnson, *Hebrews*, 332–33).

398. For an excellent historical survey of Zion symbolism in Hebrews, see Son, *Zion Symbolism in Hebrews*, 77–145.

399. See 1 Kgs 14:21; Ps 2:6; 48:2, 8; 74:2; 78:68; 110:2; Isa 8:18; 18:7.

400. The description Ἰερουσαλὴμ ἐπουρανίῳ, , or "heavenly Jerusalem," stands in apposition to πόλει θεοῦ ζῶντος,, or "the city of the Living God."

401. See 4 Ezra 7:26; 8:52; 10:60; Tob 13:16–18; 14:5; T. Dan 5:12; 2 En 55:2; 2 Bar 4:2–4; 32:2–4. Käsemann sees "Zion" as the goal of pilgrimage in the light of gnostic background (Käsemann, *Wandering People of God*, 22–23).

402. Son, *Zion Symbolism in Hebrews*, 89.

Significantly for Hebrews, Ps 110:1-4 speaks of Zion as the place where the Messiah, the one seated at the right hand, would display his kingly royal authority and dominion (cf. 2 Sam 7:9-11; Ps 89:22-23). There are some OT prophetic passages that allude to Zion in the context of the future restoration of the Davidic kingdom. For instance, Amos 9:11 speaks of Yahweh's restoration of David's fallen tent—a reference to the tent pitched at Zion. Isa 16:1 exhorts Israel to bring sacrifices "to the hill of the daughter Zion," with a promise in verse 5 that a righteous man from the house of David will sit on the throne to establish justice and the cause of righteousness. Furthermore, Isaiah refers to "Zion" as giving birth to sons or countrymen who are taken from all the nations (cf. Isa 66:20-21).[403] John also refers to the "heavenly Zion" and the "New Jerusalem" (Rev 14:1; 21:1) as the future dwelling place for all the saints.[404] This is the place where the Living God himself will live among his people and be their God forever (Rev 21:3).[405]

The author indicates that the citizens of the heavenly Jerusalem include not only myriads of angels in joyful assembly (v. 22), but also the "congregation of the first-born who have been enrolled in heaven" (v. 23a),[406] and

403. For this discussion, see Allen, *Hebrews*, 591.

404. The participial form ἀπογεγραμμένων, "registered-ones," is attributive to πρωτοτόκων, "firstborn-ones," and points to the citizens of the heavenly Jerusalem known as sons and daughters of Zion, whose names have been inscribed permanently in heaven. Alford indicates that they are assured of heavenly citizenship, but they are not yet in heaven (Alford, *Hebrews*, 254; cf. Hewitt, *Hebrews*, 201). These include believers both living and dead (Westcott, *Hebrews*, 416), and are counted among those who have been justified by God on account of Christ (Lenski, *Hebrews*, 466).

405. For further details, see Kistemaker, *Hebrews*, 392.

406. Some scholars take the phrase ἐκκλησίᾳ πρωτοτόκων, "congregation of the firstborn," to refer to angels who have not fallen (μυριάσιν ἀγγέλων, "myriads of angels") known widely as "elect angels" in heaven (Montefiore, *Hebrews*, 231; Käsemann, *Wondering*, 50, 231; and Spicq, *Hébreux: Introduction*, 407). *Contra* this reading, the author indicates that "they are enrolled," a notion that is associated not with "angels" but with human beings (Luke 10:20; Phil 4:3; Rev 21:27, and Acts 13:48). Others take the phrase as a reference to the OT saints who are already in heaven (Lünemann, *Critical and Exegetical Handbook*, 463). Differing from this view, it is argued from Heb 11:40 that the ancient heroes of faith have not yet been perfected. More likely, the phrase should be taken as referring to all the elect believers, both living and dead (Hughes, *Hebrews*, 555; Bruce, *Hebrews*, 359; Lenski, *Hebrews*, 466; and Guthrie, *Hebrews*, 262), who are so designated because of their heavenly inheritance. It is perhaps true that all the believers in Christ "are the 'firstborn' children of God, through their union with Him who is the Firstborn *par excellence*" (Peterson, *Hebrews and Perfection*, 162). For this discussion, see also O'Brien, *Hebrews*, 485. Regardless of their identity, the significance of the gathering is that all stand united in one assembly to enjoy the immediate presence of God in the joyful celebration that is yet to come. For further details, see Son, *Symbolism in Hebrews*, 90. For a general meaning of ἐκκλησία as the "official gathering of the citizens" or "assembly," see Josephus, *Jewish Antiquities*, XII. 164; XIX. 332;

"the spirits of the righteous made perfect" (v. 23b), joined together in joyful assembly (πανηγύρει).[407] These references point to all who will ultimately enjoy the full realization of the privileges of being the people of God (Heb 2:10; 12:5ff.), seen in this context as "the whole communion of the saints."[408] The author depicts them as united in one joyful assembly in God's presence as the "Judge of all" and are together with "Jesus the mediator of the new covenant" (v. 24). The heavenly Jerusalem is the place Jesus referred to as "my Father's house" (John 14:2)—a place where the believers will ultimately share in Christ's glory (John 14:3). Thus, Pentecost rightly observes that this is the city to which Abraham looked forward with great anticipation (Heb 11:10).[409] It is further described as "the holy city" (Rev 21:1-8) and the eternal dwelling place of all who have been redeemed. In that city, which is yet to come, God's tabernacle shall be with men, he shall dwell with them, and they shall be his people forever.[410]

Included in the city will be the πνεύμασι δικαίων τετελειωμένων, "spirits of the righteous who have been made perfect." As the author draws to the close of Hebrews, it is important to consider his final reference to the notion of τέλειος in Heb 12:23b. The reference echoes the first usage of τελείοω in Heb 2:10, where the author declared God's intention to bring many sons to glory through the perfecting of the Son as the pioneer of their salvation through suffering.[411] The first occurrence appeared in the context of eschatological hope and anticipation for the final realization of the promises on behalf of the worshipers. The final occurrence in 12:23 appears in the context of the eschatological realization of the promise—the

---

1 Macc 3:13; Sir 26:5; Acts 19:32, 40; *contra* the narrow sense of "church" as made up of a local body of believers (cf. Heb 2:12). Furthermore, the author has used the Greek word ἐπισυναγωγή in reference to a "gathering of the community on earth" (Heb 10:25). For further details, see Johnson, *Hebrews*, 332. Cf. Scmidt, "ἐκκλησία," *TDNT* 3:501–36.

407. The author conveys a picture of a joyful gathering of all God's people and the angels in the presence of God whom he described as the Judge of all (v. 23), and Jesus, the Mediator of the new covenant (v. 24). For the use of the notion in wider Greek literature, see Herodotus, *Persian Wars*, II. 59. 58; Xenophon, *Cyropaedia*, VI. 1. 10. Cf. Hos 2:11; 9:5; Amos 5:21; and Ezek 46:11.

408. So also, Peterson, *Hebrews and Perfection*, 162. The "congregation" is said to be earthly as in terms of the origin of its participants; it is clearly distinguished from the heavenly element (the angels). See also Westcott, *Hebrews*, 417.

409. Pentecost, *Faith That Endures*, 190–91. For further details, see 2 *Bar* 4:2–6 (cf. 32:2–4), where reference is made to words that came to Baruch (ca. AD 70) on the eve of the destruction of the first temple: this is not the true city of God, for the true city was revealed to Abraham when God made a covenant with him. For this discussion, see also Bruce, *Hebrews*, 356.

410. For further details, see Pentecost, *Faith That Endures*, 223.

411. Cf. also Heb 5:8–9; 7:19, 28; 9:9; 10:1, 14; 11:40.

contest has been won, the pilgrimage has been accomplished, and the goal has been reached.[412] For the author, the readers encounter not only myriads of angels as previously discussed, but also "spirits of the just men" (πνεύμασι δικαίων)[413] who "have been made perfect." The identity of the "righteous" or "just men" in question varies among commentators.

Some commentators take the phrase πνεύμασι δικαίων τετελειωμένων, "spirits of the righteous men made perfect," as referring to both Old and New Testament saints. Many commentators believe that they are "the faithful departed, including the saints of both covenants, who have already been led by the Captain of their salvation to the higher state of blessedness,"[414] in the presence of God who is the Judge over all; and far from finding condemnation, they have found fellowship. So, P. E. Hughes argues, Christ being uniquely the firstborn (Heb 1:6) is "heir of all things" (Heb 1:3) and the status of "firstborn" has been bestowed upon the total number of believers in him as the guarantee of their eternal inheritance with him (cf. Rom 8:17).[415] Delitzsch concludes that "they [both] are now πνεύματα, spiritual beings freed from assaults and defilements of the flesh."[416] Accordingly, it is all the saints together who will "have been made perfect" (τετελειωμένων) in fulfillment of the anticipated promise alluded to in Heb 11:40.[417]

More likely, the expression should be understood as referring to the OT saints[418] based on the earlier usage of δίκαιος, "just" or "righteous," in Heb 10:38 (cf. 11:40) and 11:4.[419] F. F. Bruce argues that "they are most probably believers of pre-Christian days, like those mentioned in 11:40 who could not attain perfection until Christ came in the fullness of time. . ."[420] Hagner differs when he contends that the clause refers to all the people of

---

412. For further details, see Johnson, *Hebrews*, 333.

413. For the use of this expression in Jewish apocalyptic literature, see *Jub* 23:30–31; 1 *En* 22:9; 102:4; 103:3–4; 2 *Bar* 30:2. Cf. Lane, *Hebrews 9–13*, 470. Lane suitably argues that the expression πνεύμασι δικαίων, "spirits or souls of righteous persons," was used as an idiom for those who had died after living a godly life.

414. Hewitt, *Hebrews*, 201.

415. Hughes, *Hebrews*, 555.

416. Delitzsch, *Epistle to the Hebrews*, 352. For further details, see also Lane, *Hebrews 9–13*, 470.

417. They have reached the ultimate goal of perfection, having reached the end of the journey and their stated destination (Heb 11:10, 13–16; 13:4).

418. See, for example, Bruce, *Hebrews*, 360. See also Hagner, *Hebrews*, 214.

419. In Heb 10:38, the author quotes Hab 2:4: "the righteous shall live by faith," and applies it to the ancient heroes of faith in Heb 11. For instance, in Heb 11:4, Abel is described by the author as a "righteous man." So, Hagner concludes, "The word is thus ideal to describe the heroes of faith mentioned in chap 11" (Hagner, *Hebrews*, 214).

420. Bruce, *Hebrews*, 360 (cf. Heb 10:14; 11:40).

faith in all eras, old and new;[421] accordingly, all believers from different entities, both old and new, will be present in the ultimate reunion of all God's people. This reunion will take place at the final eschatological celebration of the victory won at the second advent of the glorified Savior. If this is true, those present will include not only "an innumerable company of angels and the assembly of the firstborn or believers of the present age" (cf. 1 Thess 4:13–17), but also the OT saints, who will have waited for the realization of the promise (Heb 11:10, 13–16, 39) to be made forever perfect together with all the NT believers.

Theologically, the position held by Pentecost deserves some consideration. He argues that the phrase "the spirits of just men made perfect" should be taken as referring to all the OT saints, who will be resurrected together with the tribulation saints at the second advent of the glorified Christ (Isa 26:19–20; Dan 12:12; Rev 20:6).[422] This final eschatological event will complete the eschatological reunion so that the NT believers will be fully made complete, having been brought to glory together with the OT saints (cf. Heb 2:10; 11:40; 13:14) in order to enjoy their promised eternal inheritance (Heb 9:15, 28).

The readers are presented with a picture of the ultimate eschatological encounter of all the saints with God as the Judge of all and Jesus Christ, the Mediator of the new covenant. From the perspective of the author, the vision points to the future eschatological realization of the blessings of salvation made available in Christ. This differs from the approach held by many scholars who follow Peterson in locating the "perfection" language "in the past with respect to its accomplishment and in the present with respect to its enjoyment."[423] Given the broader context of Hebrews, the participle τετελειωμένων in Heb 12:23 should be understood eschatologically,[424] with reference to those who will have passed through divine judgment and obtained the final verdict that they are righteous and can therefore enjoy divine presence without any hindrance. For Hebrews, the worshipers will

---

421. For further details, see Hagner, *Hebrews*, 214. For a detailed discussion, see Dumbrell, "Spirits of Just Men Made Perfect," 154–59.

422. Pentecost, *Faith That Endures*, 223, 22. He distinguishes this group from the ἐκκλησίᾳ πρωτοτόκων, "congregation of the firstborn," whom he takes to be "all believers of this present age, which had its beginning on the day of Pentecost and will continue until the translation of the saints out of this world into glory (1 Thess 4:13–17)" (ibid.).

423. For further details, see Peterson, *Hebrews and Perfection*, 167. He interprets the participle as referring to those who have been consecrated to God through the sacrificial death of Jesus (Heb 10:14) and who now enjoy the blessings of the new covenant. See also Attridge, *Hebrews*, 375–76.

424. Lane sees an eschatological understanding as a possibility, but Lane leans more toward Peterson's vocational approach.

ultimately enter this final access to God's presence on the basis of the new covenant blood of Jesus that has already guaranteed forever their eternal peace and rest.

In light of this vision of future eschatological-eternal peace and rest, based on their identity (Heb 12:22–24), the readers are urged not to ignore the warning from the heavenly voice regarding the future rewards and the unshakable kingdom to come (12:25–29), but rather to continue in brotherly love (13:1–8) to imitate Jesus who is their ultimate leader (13:7–16) while they honor, submit, and pray for those who are in positions of leadership (13:17–19).

SUMMARY AND EVALUATION

The author of Hebrews has presented Christ as the supreme and final exemplar of τελείωσις, or "perfection," who enables the worshiper to walk in faith and hope as one who has attained the same "perfection" even as he shares in Christ's trials and temptations. Such "perfection" or "completeness," while presented as a possibility in the present, remains nevertheless a future reality to be realized at the second advent of the glorified Christ. From a general point of view, the notion of perfection corresponds to the larger divine intention that encompasses the future eschatological glory of humanity as fulfilled in the person of Christ, which will be fully realized at his second coming. The preceding discussion has shown that there is a consistent eschatological fulfillment motif not just as realized eschatology, but more significantly, as unrealized eschatology. In the case of Hebrews, it is intended to serve as an incentive for the Hebrew believers and believers of all ages to continue walking by faith with perseverance, looking forward to the fullness of their complete and final uninhibited access to God, which is yet to come, and the enjoyment of their eternal inheritance. For the author of Hebrews, the perfected Christ implies this final and complete access to God. The Son was perfected as the leader or pioneer of the believers' sanctification with the goal of leading them to their future destination and access to God, which is their eternal inheritance.

Chapter 6

Summary Assessment and Conclusions

THIS FINAL CHAPTER OF THE study provides a summary assessment of the major findings in the preceding chapters and draws some theological and practical conclusions based on the previous discussions.

SUMMARY ASSESSMENT

The focus for this study has been the τέλειος, or "perfection," motif in Hebrews and its contribution to the argument of the book. This study's thesis is that the notion of τέλειος has a futurist eschatological significance and is linked to the better provisions of the new covenant, which guarantee the believer's salvation and future eternal inheritance. The entire study has argued that the τελείωσις of Christ (Heb 2:10; 5:8–9; 7:28) implies that of the believer (5:14; 6:1; 10:14; 11:40; 12:2, 23) and guarantees final, complete, and uninhibited access to God as never before (7:11; 9:9, 11; 10:1). This has been found to be true, especially because the Son has been made perfect as the pioneer, the source, and the leader of the believer's sanctification with the goal of leading his many followers to their future "perfection" or "completeness."

The first chapter of this book addressed the preliminary issues related to the study. The need for, purpose, and general line of argument of the study was addressed. Chapter 1 illustrated that the author of Hebrews develops his argument around an overriding theme of τέλειος through a series of contrasts or comparisons aimed at presenting the perfected Christ as the one who originates and leads the many worshipers to their future eternal inheritance. The chapter also showed how the notion of τέλειος is central to a proper interpretation of the message of Hebrews. Chapter 1 also proposed the need for a comprehensive study aimed at ascertaining the meaning and message of τέλειος and its contribution to the argument of Hebrews. This was especially necessary because of the lack of scholarly consensus on the precise meaning of "perfection" as well as the differing positions taken by various scholars.

After outlining the argument of the entire study, plus its need, scope, and purpose, chapter 2 addressed the various interpretative approaches to the τέλειος motif in Hebrews and related literature. The five proposed interpretative views included: (1) a moral-ethical, (2) a cultic-religious, (3) a glorification-exaltation, (4) a vocational-experiential, and (5) a definitive attestation approach. Following an assessment of the strengths and weaknesses of these interpretative approaches to the notion of τέλειος, a sixth model has been proposed—namely, an eschatological model—which is defended in this study. This approach is based on the belief that Hebrews is framed within an eschatological orbit. For that reason, its eschatological dimension should be seen as setting up the motivation for the way the Hebrew believers should lead their life of persevering faith as they look forward to their future eschatological inheritance.

Thus, the third chapter moved naturally to a discussion of the usage of the concept of τέλειος in the ancient world, including its usage in classical Greek, the Jewish tradition (MT and LXX), Second Temple Judaism, and the New Testament world. While the author of Hebrews may not have borrowed directly from these ancient sources, they nevertheless provided crucial insights that illuminate the meaning of τέλειος in Hebrews. First, Plato's usage of τέλειος and its cognates reveals a sense of "perfection" with a future orientation. Platonic "perfection," perceived in terms of philosophical virtue and contemplation of the world of ideas through the eyes of the soul, is very strange to the language of Hebrews. Second, although Plato's student Aristotle provides crucial insights that link the notion of τέλειος to that of τέλος as "end" or "goal," an Aristotelian understanding of "perfection" based on subjective reasoning and contemplation of nature is contrary to the teaching of Hebrews, which assumes human sinfulness and need for the Savior. Therefore, contrary to Aristotle and later Stoicism, humankind cannot rely on subjective reasoning to attain the goal of τελείωσις, "perfection," or "completeness." Third, the MT and LXX provide a closer context to Hebrews by conveying the idea of perfection in terms of "wholehearted devotion to Yahweh" with a connotation of belonging to him, as opposed to those who practiced idolatry, sorcery, and other abominations. Yet the meaning of the concept in Hebrews is distinct from these sources.

Fourth, while the realized eschatology of Qumran is insightful, the notion of exclusion and particularization assigned to the notion of τέλειος is very strange to the language of Hebrews, where the author points to the privileges of approaching God as available to all the worshipers who are willing to draw near. Fifth, Philo's system of values sees wisdom and virtue as constituting the path to "perfection," with God being the source of both. Wisdom and virtue for Philo are seen as emanating from God, since he is the great cause of all things. Accordingly, only a person who strives to live in accordance with the Torah is "a perfect person," pure in word, deed, and in conduct. Yet Philonic interest in philosophy, his notion of progress toward philosophical virtue, and his emphasis on ethics as well as the notion of training or pedagogy limit the privilege of access to God to a philosophical minority. This differs from the language of Hebrews, where the privilege of unhindered access to God is available to all believers. Sixth, distinctive traditions forming the rest of the NT are crucial because they serve as the more immediate context of the language of Hebrews.

Chapter 4 covered background issues related to the literary nature and purpose of Hebrews. Although Hebrews is still considered by many scholars as standing apart from other NT epistles, the book nevertheless remains a profound piece of literature that builds a case for the supremacy of the Son in a uniquely cumulative argument that evolves around the notion of τέλειος. An examination of issues related to the authorship and date, historical setting, conceptual background, literary genre, and message of Hebrews concluded that for the author of Hebrews, the eschatological revelation of the perfected Christ means the final and complete access to God for believers because Christ's person and work guarantee believers' perfection and complete access to God.

The fifth chapter provided a detailed analysis of the notion of τέλειος in light of the broader parameters discussed in earlier book chapters, which form the basis for an examination of the τέλειος concept in Hebrews. This chapter formed the heart of the book, as it illustrated the import of the notion of τέλειος by examining how this concept is used throughout Hebrews.

First, the fifth chapter examined how the Hebrews author uses the concept of τέλειος in reference to Christ (Heb 2:10; 5:8–9; 7:28), linking the notion of perfection to the eschatological, salvific import of Christ's person and work as the perfected High Priest in the order of Melchizedek and Mediator of the new covenant. The author of Hebrews presents the τελείωσις of Christ as a pledge for his ability to intercede and lead many followers to their eschatological glory. As the perfected Son, Christ fulfills the eschatological design for salvation of his brethren, whom he is drawing nearer to their eternal glory, which is to be fully realized at the second coming of Christ.

Second, the chapter analyzed how the author of Hebrews elaborates on his argument about the superiority of Christ by establishing a case regarding the weaknesses of the old economy versus the new (Heb 7:11, 19; 9:9, 11; 10:1) to effect the desired τελείωσις on behalf of the believer. The concept of τέλειος has an eschatological significance that points to the future realization of the better provisions of the new covenant, which are to be fulfilled at the second coming of Christ. Such desired completeness, which allows an unhindered access to God, could not have been achieved under the old system.

Finally, the fifth chapter investigated how the author uses the same terminology of τέλειος with reference to believers (Heb 5:14; 6:1; 10:14; 11:40; 12:2, 23). Following an analysis of these passages, it was argued, first, that the perfecting of believers is guaranteed based on the perfecting of Christ, who has secured forever the final and complete access to God on their behalf. Having been made perfect as the pioneer, source, and forerunner of their faith, the perfected Christ is seen as the one leading many brethren to their final eschatological destination and full enjoyment of their eternal inheritance in glory. Second, the way toward the goal of "perfection" or "absolute maturity" (cf. Heb 5:14; 6:1) is possible only as a result of God's enablement in Christ, who is presented as the supreme and final exemplar of τελείωσις. This enables believers to press on with perseverance, likewise walking in faith and hope even as they share in similar trials and temptations. Third, an examination of the notion of τέλειος, when properly understood eschatologically, allows the readers to fully appreciate the future dimension of Hebrews' language, especially as it is seen in the abiding nature of Christ's work as the perfected eternal High Priest. This invites the readers to look beyond their present circumstances with hope for the better provisions that are yet to be fully realized. These better, future things serve as a great incentive for the believer to continue in perseverance until the end (10:1, 14). The notion of τέλειος in the true sense of the word is therefore seen as carrying an eschatological significance, pointing to the complete realization and enjoyment of the future blessings of eternal salvation (11:40). This is understood as the goal for the readers (cf. 5:14; 6:1) as they continue running the race set before them.

Finally, chapter 5 also presented a discussion regarding what has already been achieved through the incarnation and ascension of Christ. The final eschatological destination is assured for the believers (Heb 12:2, 23)— the heavenly Jerusalem, where they will be perfected in glory in order to fully enjoy the anticipated eternal privileges (cf. 11:40) reserved for God's people. Hebrews, as a "word of exhortation," reassures believers that their final access to God's presence in glory is guaranteed based on the new covenant blood of Jesus, which has secured their eternal peace and rest forever.

THEOLOGICAL AND PRACTICAL IMPLICATION

This study confirms that there is a consistent eschatological fulfillment motif—not just as realized, but also significantly as futurist eschatology—that serves as an exceptional incentive for believers of all ages to walk by faith with perseverance, looking forward to the fullness of salvation in Christ. As a result of the abiding effect of Christ's work on the cross and his ascension, God's people are being drawn to their eternal glory, which is to be fully realized at the second coming of our Lord Jesus Christ. The τέλειος motif in Hebrews, when properly understood, carries an eschatological overtone that points to the future realization of the new covenant promises (Jer 31:31–34; Heb 8:6–12). These promises are made certain in the Christ event and will be fully realized at Christ's second coming, when the believers will see him face to face. Only then will the knowledge of God be universal, covering the earth.

While believers can now approach God through faith, they are still looking forward to the ultimate eschatological fulfillment of God's promises, when all the people will experience God fully. It is only in the future that all the aspects of the better provisions of the new covenant will be fully operational. In the interim, believers can enjoy some spiritual aspects of these better provisions, while at the same time anticipating full enjoyment of the time when they meet the Lord in eternal glory.

For the believers who have experienced genuine or saving faith in Christ, the present interim becomes the time for proclamation of the gospel and a time of realization of the ethical teaching of Christ, even as they await the future enjoyment of their eternal inheritance at the eschaton. The work of Christ as the perfected High Priest is therefore foundational to the hopefulness for what is yet to be fulfilled. The believers live, therefore, in great anticipation of their unhindered access to God in eternal glory. In the meantime, their saving or genuine faith will persevere and bear fruit. Such persevering faith cannot go untested. When the genuine faith of the believer is tested through divine discipline, it responds positively, producing the peaceful fruit of righteousness (Heb 12:11). This is the kind of persevering attitude that is modeled in the perfected Christ, upon whom believers are called to fix their attention (12:2, 23) in the pursuit of the goal of "perfection" and final access to God (5:14; 6:1).

The attitude of perseverance in good works not only provides assurance, but also an evidence of salvation. The call to pursue the goal of "perfection" or "completeness" becomes a call to commitment to the gospel message, following the example of Christ as the one who endured the suffering of the cross and its despised shame in order to bring many sons to eternal glory (cf. 2:10; 5:9). The one who accepts the commitment to follow after the goal of "perfection" also accepts the call to follow Christ to the place of shame and contempt (Heb 13:13), bearing the cross with him even to death itself. On the other hand, the one who rejects the call and commitment to follow after this goal has joined the enemies of the gospel. The teaching of Hebrews thus squarely echoes the synoptic traditions and Jesus's challenges to his disciples to take up their cross and follow him (Matt 16:24–26; Mark 8:34–38; Luke 9:23–26, 57–62) to the way of life and eternal glory. Following the way Jesus prescribes for his followers leads to "perfection" or "completeness," which guarantees a final and complete access to God and the glorious eternal inheritance in Christ Jesus.

Bibliography

Adams, J. C. "Exegesis of Hebrews 6:1f." *NTS* 13 (1967) 378–85.
Aeschylus. *Oresteia: Agamemnon, Libation-Bearers, Eumenides*. Vol. 2. Translated by Herbert W. Smyth. 2 vols. Loeb Classical Library. Reprint. Cambridge: Harvard University Press, 1983.
Alford, Henry. *The Greek New Testament: Hebrews to Revelation*. Vol. 4, revised by Everett F. Harrison, 1902. Cambridge: Deighton, Bell, 1874. Reprint, Chicago: Moody, 1958.
Allen, David L. *Hebrews: An Exegetical and Theological Exposition of Holy Scripture*. Edited by E. R. Clendenen, K. A. Mathews, and D. S. Dockery. New American Commentary 35. Nashville: B. & H., 2010.
Anderson, Bernhard W. *The New Covenant and the Old: A Theological Discussion*. Edited by Bernhard W. Anderson. The Old Testament and the Christian Faith. New York: Harper & Row, 1963.
Anderson, Charles P. "The Epistle to the Hebrews and the Pauline Letter Collection." *HTR* 59 (1966) 429–38.
Anderson, Leonard C. "The Root *Teleios* in Hebrews." ThM thesis, Dallas Theological Seminary, 1952.
Aristotle. *Generation of Animals*. Translated by A. L. Peck and edited by T. E. Page, E. Capps, and W. H. D. Rouse. Loeb Classical Library. Cambridge: Harvard University Press, 1953.
———. *The Metaphysics*. Translated by Hugh Tredennick and edited by G. P. Goold. Loeb Classical Library 5. Reprint, Cambridge: Harvard University Press, 1980.
———. *The Nicomachean Ethics*. Translated by H. Rackham and edited by T. E. Page, E. Capps, and W. H. D. Rouse. Loeb Classical Library. Reprint, Cambridge: Harvard University Press, 1956.
Arminius, Jacobus. "A Letter." In vol. 2 of *The Works of Jacobus Arminius*, translated by James Nichols and William Nichols, 731–54. Grand Rapids: Baker, 1986.
Attridge, Harold W. *The Epistle to the Hebrews: A Commentary on the Epistle to the Hebrews*. Edited by Helmut Koester Hermeneia: A Critical and Historical Commentary on the Bible 72. Philadelphia: Fortress, 1989.
———. "Paraenesis in a Homily: The Possible Location of, and Socialization in, the 'Epistle to the Hebrews.'" *Semeia* 50 (1990) 211–26.
———. "Hebrews, Epistle to the." In vol. 3 of *Anchor Bible Dictionary*, edited by David Noel Freedman et al., 97–105. New York: Doubleday, 1992.

Aune, David E. *The New Testament and Its Literary Environment.* LEC. Edited by Wayne A. Meeks. Philadelphia: Westminster, 1987.
Bachmann, H., and W. A. Slaby. *Concordance to the Novum Testamentum Graece of Nestle-Aland, 26th Edition, and to the Greek New Testament, 3rd Edition.* Institute for New Testament Textual Research and Computer Center of Münster University. Berlin: Grüyter, 1987.
Bailey, Mark, and Tom Constable. *The New Testament Explorer: Discovering the Essence, Background, and Meaning of Every Book in the New Testament.* Edited by Charles R. Swindoll. Nashville: Word, 1999.
Ballarini, T. "*Archegos* (Acts 3:15; 5:31; Heb 2:10; 12:2)." *Sacra doctrina* 16 (1971) 535–55.
Barrett, C. K. "The Eschatology of the Epistle to the Hebrews." In *Background of the New Testament and Its Eschatology*, edited by W. D. Davies and David Daube, 363–93. Cambridge: Cambridge University Press, 1956.
———. *The Gospel according to St. John: An Introduction with Commentary and Notes on the Greek Text.* 2nd ed. Philadelphia: Westminster, 1978.
Bartlet, J. V. "Barnabas and His Genuine Epistle." *The Expositor* 6, no. 5 (1902) 409–27.
———. "The Epistle to the Hebrews as the Work of Barnabas." *The Expositor* 6, no. 7 (1903) 381–96.
Barton, George A. "The Date of the Epistle to the Hebrews." *JBL* 57 (1938) 195–97.
Batdorf, Irvin W. "Hebrews and Qumran: Old Methods and New Directions." In *Festchrift to Honor F. Wilbur Gingrich: Lexicographer, Scholar, Teacher and Committed Christian Layman*, edited by Eugene Howard Barth and Ronald Edwin Cocroft, 16–35. Leiden, Netherlands: Brill, 1972.
Bauder, W. "Fall Away." In vol. 1 of *The New International Dictionary of New Testament Theology*, edited by Colin Brown, 606–11. Grand Rapids: Zondervan, 1975.
Bauer, Walter. *A Greek-English Lexicon of the New Testament and Other Early Christian Literature.* 3rd ed. Translated by F. W. Danker, W. F. Arndt, and F. W. Gingrich and edited by F. W. Danker. Chicago: University of Chicago Press, 2000.
Beardslee, W. A. "James." In vol. 2 of *The Interpreter's Dictionary of the Bible: An Illustrated Encyclopedia*, edited by George A. Buttrick, 790–94. 4 vols. New York: Abingdon, 1962.
Beare, F. W. *A Commentary on the Epistle to the Philippians.* Edited by Henri Chadwick. BNTC. London: Black, 1973.
Benko, Stephen. "The Edict of Claudius of AD 49 and the Instigator Chrestus." *TZ* 25 (1969) 403–18.
Berkhof, Louis. *Systematic Theology.* Grand Rapids: Eerdmans, 1937. Reprint, Edinburgh: Banner of Truth, 2000.
Black, C. Clifton, II. "The Rhetorical Form of the Hellenistic Jewish and Early Christian Sermon: A Response to Lawrence Wills." *HTR* 81 (1988) 1–18.
Black, David Alan. "The Problem of the Literary Structure of Hebrews: An Evaluation and a Proposal." *GTJ* 7 (1986) 163–77.
Blass, F., and A. Debrunner. *A Greek Grammar of the New Testament and Other Early Christian Literature.* Translated by Robert W. Funk. Chicago: University of Chicago Press, 1961.
Bloomfield, S. T. *The Greek New Testament.* Vol. 2. 3rd ed. London: Longman & Longmans, 1839.

Bock, Darrell L. *A Biblical Theology of the New Testament*, edited by Roy B. Zuck and Darrell L. Bock, 11–17. BECNT. Chicago: Moody, 1994.

———. "Use of the Old Testament in the New." In *Foundations for Biblical Interpretation*, edited by David S. Dockery, Kenneth A. Matthews, and Robert B. Sloan, 97–114. Reprint, Nashville: Broadman & Holman, 1999.

Boisé, James R. *The First Six Books of Homer's Iliad: With Explanatory Notes*. Chicago: Griggs, 1977.

Borchert, Gerald L. *Assurance and Warning*. Nashville: Broadman, 1987.

Bovon, François. *L'évangile sélon Saint Luc (1:1–9:50)*. CNT 3a. Geneva: Labor et Fides, 1991.

Braun, Herbert. *An die Hebräer*. Edited by Hans Lietzmann, Günther Bornkamm, and Andreas Lindemann. Handbuch zum Neuen Testament 14. Tübingen, Germany: Mohr Siebeck, 1984.

Brown, Francis, et al. *The Brown-Driver-Briggs Hebrew and English Lexicon*. Reprint of 1906 ed., Peabody: Hendrickson, 1979.

Brown, Raymond E. *An Introduction to the New Testament*. Edited by David Noel Freedman. Anchor Bible Reference Library. New York: Doubleday, 1997.

———. *Christ above All: The Message of Hebrews*. Downers Grove, IL: InterVarsity, 1982.

Bruce, Alexander B. *The Epistle to the Hebrews: The First Apology for Christianity*. Edinburgh: T. & T. Clark, 1899.

Bruce, F. F. *The Canon of Scripture*. Downers Grove, IL: InterVarsity Press, 1988.

———. "Christianity under Claudius." *BJRL* 44 (1961–1962) 309–26.

———. "The Kerygma of Hebrews." *Interpretation* 23 (1969) 3–19.

———. "Recent Contributions to the Understanding of Hebrews." *ExpTim* 80 (1968–1969) 260–64.

———. "To the Hebrews or to the Essenes?" *NTS* 9 (1963) 217–32.

———, ed. *The Epistle to the Hebrews*. Rev. ed. New International Commentary on the New Testament. Grand Rapids: Eerdmans, 1990.

Buchanan, George Wesley. *To the Hebrews: Translation, Comment and Conclusions*. Edited by William Foxwell Albright and David Noel Freedman. AB 36. Garden City, NY: Doubleday, 1978.

Burns, Lanier. "Hermeneutical Issues and Principles in Hebrews as Exemplified in the Second Chapter." *JETS* 39 (1996) 587–607.

Burton, Ernest De Witt. *Syntax of the Moods and Tenses in New Testament Greek*. Chicago: University of Chicago Press, 1900.

Caird, George B. "Just Men Made Perfect." *LQHR* 191 (1966) 89–98.

Calvin, John. *Commentaries on the Epistle to the Hebrews*. Translated by John Owen. Reprint. Grand Rapids: Eerdmans, 1949.

Campbell, J. Y. "Perfection." In vol. 3 of *The Interpreter's Dictionary of the Bible: An Illustrated Encyclopedia in Four Volumes*, edited by George A. Buttrick et al., 730. Nashville: Abingdon, 1962.

Carlston, Charles. "The Vocabulary of Perfection in Philo and Hebrews." In *Unity and Diversity in New Testament Theology: Essays in Honor of George E. Ladd*, edited by Robert A. Guelich, 133–60. Grand Rapids: Eerdmans, 1978.

Carson, D. A. *Exegetical Fallacies*. 2nd ed. Grand Rapids: Baker, 1996.

———. "Reflections on Christian Assurance." *WTJ* 54 (1992) 1–29.

———. *Still Sovereign: Contemporary Perspectives on Election, Foreknowledge, and Grace*. Edited by Thomas R. Schreiner, and Bruce A. Ware. Reprint, Grand Rapids: Baker, 2000.

Carson, D. A., and Douglas J. Moo. *An Introduction to the New Testament*. 2nd ed. Grand Rapids: Zondervan, 2005.

Chamberlain, William Douglas. *An Exegetical Grammar of the Greek New Testament*. New York: Macmillian, 1941.

Charlesworth, James H., ed. *The Old Testament Pseudepigrapha*. 2 vols. Anchor Bible Reference Library. New York: Doubleday, 1985.

Clark, Kenneth W. "Worship in the Jerusalem Temple after AD 70." *NTS* 6 (1959–1960) 269–80.

Cockerill, Gareth Lee. "The Melchizedek Christology in Hebrews 7:1–28." ThD diss., Union Theological Seminary, 1976.

Colijn, Brenda B. "'Let Us Approach': Soteriology in the Epistle to the Hebrews." *JETS* 39 (1996) 571–86.

Compton, R. Bruce. "Persevering and Falling Away: A Reexamination of Heb 6:4–6." *Detroit Baptist Seminary Journal* 1 (1996) 135–67.

Coppens, J. *Les affinités Qumrâniennes de l'Épître aux Hébreux*. Louvain, Belgium: Publications Universitaires, 1962.

Cosby, Michael R. *The Rhetorical Composition and Function of Hebrews 11: In Light of Example Lists in Antiquity*. Macon, GA: Mercer University Press, 1988.

Croy, Noah Clayton. "Endurance in Suffering: A Study of Hebrews 12:1–13 in its Rhetorical, Religious, and Philosophical Context." PhD diss., Emory University, 1995.

Cullmann, Oscar. *The Christology of the New Testament*. Translated by Shirley C. Guthrie and Charles A. M. Hall. Philadelphia: Westminster, 1963.

Dahms, John V. "The First Readers of Hebrews." *JETS* 20 (1977) 365–75.

Daly, C. B. "Novatian and Tertullian: A Chapter in the History of Puritanism." *Irish Theological Quarterly* 19 (1952) 33–43.

Daly, Robert J. "The New Testament Concept of Christian Sacrificial Activity." *Biblical Theology Bulletin* 8 (1978) 99–107.

Davidson, A. B. *The Epistle to the Hebrews*. Edinburgh: T. & T. Clark, 1882.

De Vogel, Cornelia J. *Greek Philosophy: A Collection of Texts with Notes and Explanations*. Vol. 3. 2nd ed. Leiden, Netherlands: Brill, 1964.

Deasley, A. R. G. "The Idea of Perfection in the Qumran Texts." PhD thesis, University of Manchester, 1972.

Deissmann, Adolf. *Bible Studies*. Translated by Alexander Grieve. Reprint, Grand Rapids: Baker, 1979.

Deissmann, Adolf. *The New Testament in the Light of Modern Research: The Haskell Lectures*. Garden City, NY: Doubleday, 1929.

Delitzsch, Franz. *Commentary on the Epistle to the Hebrews*. Translated by Thomas L. Kingsbury. 2 vols. Reprint, Minneapolis: Klock & Klock, 1978.

Delling, Gerhard. "τέλειος." In vol. 8 of *Theological Dictionary of the New Testament*, edited by Gerhard Friedrich and translated by Geoffrey W. Bromiley, 67–87. Grand Rapids: Eerdmans, 1972.

DeSilva, David A. "Despising Shame: A Cultural-Anthropological Investigation of the Epistle to the Hebrews." *JBL* 113 (1994) 439–61.

———. *Despising Shame: Honor Discourse and Community Maintenance in the Epistle to the Hebrews*. Edited by Pheme Perkins. SBLDS 152. Atlanta: Scholars, 1995.

———. "The Epistle to the Hebrews in Social-Scientific Perspective." *Restoration Quarterly* 36 (1984) 1–21.

———. "Exchanging Favor for Wrath: Apostasy in Hebrews and Patron-Client Relationships." *JBL* 115 (1996) 91–116.

———. "Hebrews 6:4–8: A Socio-Rhetorical Investigation (Part 1)." *TynBul* 50 (1999) 33–57.

———. "Review of the Structure of Hebrews: A Text-Linguistic Analysis, by George H. Guthrie." *Catholic Biblical Quarterly* 57 (1995) 395–97.

———. *Perseverance in Gratitude: A Socio-Rhetorical Commentary on the Epistle to the Hebrews*. Grand Rapids: Eerdmans, 2000.

DeVaux, Roland. *Ancient Israel: Its Life and Institution*. Translated by John McHugh. Biblical Resource Series. Grand Rapids: Eerdmans, 1961.

Dey, Lala Kalyan Kumar. *The Intermediary World and Patterns of Perfection in Philo and Hebrews*. Edited by Howard C. Kee and Douglas A. Knight. SBLDS 25. Missoula, MT: Scholars, 1975.

Dibelius, Martin. "Der himmlische Kultus nach dem Hebraerbrief." In vol. 2. of *Botschaft und Geschichte: Gesammelte Studien*, edited by G. Bornkamm and H. Kraft, 160–76. Tübingen, Germany: Mohr Siebeck, 1959.

Dickie, J. "The Literary Riddle of the Epistle to the Hebrews." *Expositor* 8th Series, 5 (1913) 371–78.

Dillow, Joseph C. *The Reign of the Servant Kings: A Study of Eternal Security and the Final Significance of Man*. Miami Springs, FL: Schoettle, 1992.

Diogenes Laertius. *Lives of Eminent Philosophers*. Vol. 2. Translated by R. D. Hicks. 2 vols. Loeb Classical Library 185. Cambridge: Harvard University Press, 1952.

Dods, Marcus. "The Epistle to the Hebrews." In vol. 4 of *The Expositor's Greek Testament*, edited by W. Robertson Nicoll, 219–381. Grand Rapids: Eerdmans, 1980.

Doty, William G. *Letters in Primitive Christianity*. Philadelphia: Fortress, 1973.

Drake, Henri L. *Plato's Complete Works Abridged*. Paterson, NJ: Littlefield Adams & Co., 1959.

Drazin, Israel, and Stanley M. Wagner. *Targum Onkelos on the Torah: Genesis, Including Original English Translation, Commentary, and Appendix*. Jerusalem: Gefen, 2006.

Dumbrell, W. J. "'The Spirits of Just Men Made Perfect.'" *EvQ* 48 (1976) 154–59.

Dunn, J. D. G. *Unity and Diversity in the New Testament: An Inquiry into the Character of Earliest Christianity*. London: SCM, 1977.

Dunnill, John. *Covenant and Sacrifice in the Letter to the Hebrews*. Edited by Margaret E. Thrall. SNTSMS 75. Cambridge: Cambridge University Press, 1992.

DuPlessis, Paul Johannes. Τέλειος: *The Idea of Perfection in the New Testament*. Theologische Academie Uitgande van de Johannes Calvijn Stichting te Kampen. Kampen: Uitgave J. H. Kok, 1959.

Eaton, Michael. *No Condemnation: A New Theology of Assurance*. Downers Grove, IL: InterVarsity, 1995.

Edman, Irwin, ed. *The Works of Plato*. New York: Modern Library, 1928.

Ehrhardt, Arnold. *The Framework of the New Testament Stories*. Cambridge: Harvard University Press, 1964.

Eisenbaum, Pamela Michelle. *The Jewish Heroes of Christian History: Hebrews 11 in Literary Context*. Edited by Michael V. Fox, and Pheme Perkins. SBLDS 156. Atlanta: Scholars, 1997.

Ellingworth, Paul. *The Epistle to the Hebrews: A Commentary on the Greek Text*. Edited by I. Howard Marshall and W. Ward Gasque. NIGTC. Grand Rapids: Eerdmans, 1993.

———. "Hebrews and 1 Clement: Literary Dependence or Common Tradition." *BZ* 23 (1972) 262–69.

Ellingworth, Paul, and Eugene A. Nida. *A Translator's Handbook on the Letter to the Hebrews*. New York: United Bible Societies, 1983.

Ellis, E. Earle. *The Gospel of Luke*. Rev. ed. New Century Bible Commentary. London: Marshall, Morgan, & Scott, 1966.

Etheridge, J. W. *The Targums of Onkelos and Jonathan ben Uzziel on the Pentateuch: Genesis and Exodus: with the Fragments of the Jerusalem Targum from the Chaldee*. New York: Ktav, 1968.

Eusebius. *The Ecclesiastical History*. Vol. 2. Translated by J. E. L. Oulton and edited by E. Capps, T. E. Page, and W. H. D. Rouse. 2 vols. Loeb Classical Library. London: Heinemann, 1982.

Fanning, Buist M. "A Theology of Hebrews." In *A Biblical Theology of the New Testament*, edited by Roy B. Zuck and Darrell L. Bock, 369–415. Chicago: Moody, 1994.

———. *Verbal Aspect in New Testament Greek*. Edited by J. Barton et al. Oxford Theological Monographs. Oxford: Clarendon, 1990.

Fensham, F. C. "Hebrews and Qumran." *Neotestamentica* 5 (1971) 9–21.

Ferguson, E. "Religion, Greco-Roman." In *Dictionary of the Later New Testament and Its Development: A Compendium of Contemporary Biblical Scholarship*, edited by Ralph P. Martin and Peter H. Davids, 1006–11. Downers Grove, IL: InterVarsity, 1997.

Filson, Floyd V. "The Epistle to the Hebrews." *JBR* 22 (1954) 22–23.

———. *A New Testament History: The Story of the Emerging Church*. Philadelphia: Westminster, 1964.

———. *'Yesterday:' A Study of Hebrews in Light of Chapter 13*. Edited by C. F. D. Moule et al. Studies in Biblical Theology 4. London: SCM, 1967.

Fiore, Benjamin. *The Function of Personal Examples in the Socratic and Pastoral Epistles*. AnBib 105. Rome: Pontifical Biblical Institute, 1986.

Fitzmyer, Joseph A. "Further Light on Melchizedek from Qumran Cave II." *JBL* 86 (1967) 25–41.

———. *The Genesis Apocryphon of Qumran Cave 1 (1Q20) A Commentary*. Biblica et orientalia 18b. Rome: Pontificio Instituto Biblico, 2004.

———. *The Gospel According to Luke (X–XXIV) Introduction, Translation and Notes*. AB 2. Garden City, NY: Doubleday, 1985.

Flew, Robert N. *The Idea of Perfection in Christian Theology: An Historical Study of the Christian Ideal for Present Life*. Oxford: Oxford University Press, 1934.

Gambiza, Farai K. Moyo. "*Teleiosis* and *Paideia* as Interpretation of Suffering: The Perfecting of Jesus and the Disciplining of Christians in the Letter to the Hebrews." ThD diss., Christ Seminary, 1981.

García Martínez, Florentino, ed. *The Dead Sea Scrolls Translated: The Qumran Texts in English*. 2nd ed. Translated by Wilfred G. E. Watson. Grand Rapids: Eerdmans, 1996.

Gelardini, Gabriella. "Hebrews, an Ancient Synagogue Homily for Tisha Be-Av: Its Formation, Its Basis, Its Theological Interpretation." In *Hebrews: Contemporary Methods-New Insights*, edited by R. A. Culpepper and Ellen van Wolde, 107–27. Biblical Interpretation Series 75. Leiden, Netherlands: Brill, 2005.

Gleason, Randall C. "The Old Testament Background of the Warning in Hebrews 6:4-8." *BSac* 155 (1998) 62–91.

Goold, G. P., ed. *Clement, II Clement, Ignatius, Polycarp, Didache*. Vol. 1 of *The Apostolic Fathers*, translated by Kirsopp Lake. 2 vols. Loeb Classical Library. Cambridge: Harvard University Press, 1977.

Goppelt, Leonhard. *Theology of the New Testament: The Variety and Unity of the Apostolic Witness to Christ*. Vol. 2. Translated by John E. Alsup and edited by Jürgen Roloff. Grand Rapids: Eerdmans, 1982.

Gouge, William. *Commentary on Hebrews*. Edinburgh: Nichol, 1886. Reprint, Grand Rapids: Kregel, 1980.

Grässer, Erich. *An die Hebräer*. Edited by Norbert Brox, Rudolph Schnackenburg, et al. Evangelisch-katholischer Kommentar zum Neuen Testament 1. Zurich: Benziger Verlag, 1990.

———. *Der Glaube im Hebräerbrief*. Marburger theologische Studien. Marburg, Germany: n.p., 1965.

———. "Der Hebraerbrief 1938–1963." *TRu* 30 (1964) 128–36

Greenlee, Harold J. *An Exegetical Summary of Hebrews*. Dallas: Summer Institute of Linguistics, 1998.

Greer, Rowan A. *The Captain of Our Salvation: A Study in the Patristic Exegesis of Hebrews*. Edited by Oscar Cullmann, Nils A. Dahl, et al. Beiträge zur Geschichte der biblischen Exegese 5. Tübingen, Germany: Mohr Siebeck, 1973.

Grenfell, Bernard P., and Arthur S. Hunt, eds. "P.Oxy I.63." In *Oxyrhynchus Papyri*, translated by Bernard P. Grenfell and Arthur S. Hunt. London: Egypt Exploration Fund, 1898.

———. "P.Oxy III.483." In *Oxyrhynchus Papyri*, translated by Bernard P. Grenfell and Arthur S. Hunt. London: Egypt Exploration Fund, 1903.

Grenfell, Bernard P., et al, eds. "Ptebt 2.316." In *Tebtunis Papyri: Part 2*, translated by Bernard P. Grenfell, Arthur S. Hunt, and J. Gilbert Smyly, 116–20. London: Frowde, 1902.

Grudem, Wayne. "Perseverance of the Saints: A Case Study from the Warning Passages in Hebrews." In *Still Sovereign: Contemporary Perspectives on Election, Foreknowledge, and Grace*, edited by Thomas R. Schreiner and Bruce A. Ware, 133–82. Grand Rapids: Baker, 2000.

Gundry, Robert H. "Grace, Works, and Staying Saved in Paul." *Biblica* 66 (1985) 1–38.

———. *Matthew: A Commentary on His Handbook for a Mixed Church under Persecution*. 2nd ed. Grand Rapids: Eerdmans, 1994.

Guthrie, Donald. *The Letter to the Hebrews: An Introduction and Commentary*. Edited by Leon Morris. TNTC. Grand Rapids: Eerdmans, 1983.

———. *New Testament Introduction*. Rev. ed. Leicester, UK: Inter-Varsity, 1990.

Guthrie, George H. *Hebrews*. Edited by Terry Muck et al. NIV Application Commentary. Grand Rapids: Zondervan, 1998.

———. *The Structure of Hebrews: A Text-Linguistic Analysis*. BSL. Grand Rapids: Baker, 1998.

Hagen, Kenneth. *Hebrews Commenting from Erasmus to Beze 1516-1598*. Edited by Oscar Cullmann, Nils Dahl, et al. Beiträge zur Geschichte der biblischen Exegese 23. Tübingen, Germany: Mohr Siebeck, 1981.

———. *A Theology of Testament in the Young Luther: The Lectures on Hebrews*. Edited by Heiko A. Oberman et al. Studies in Medieval and Reformation Thought 12. Leiden, Netherlands: Brill, 1974.

Hagner, Donald A. *Encountering the Book of Hebrews: An Exposition*. Edited by Walter E. Elwell, and Eugene H. Merrill. Encountering Biblical Studies. Grand Rapids: Baker, 2002.

———. *Hebrews*. Edited by W. Ward Gasque. GNC. Cambridge, MA: Harper & Row, 1983.

———. *Hebrews*. Edited by W. Ward Gasque. NIBC 14. Peabody: Hendrickson, 1990.

———. "Interpreting the Epistle to the Hebrews." In *The Literature and Meaning of Scripture*, edited by Morris A. Inch and C. Hassell Bullock, 217-23. Grand Rapids: Baker, 1981.

———. *The Use of the Old and New Testaments in Clement of Rome*. Edited by W. C. van Unnik et al. Supplements to *NovT* 34. Leiden, Netherlands: Brill, 1973.

Hamm, Dennis. "Faith in the Epistle to the Hebrews: The Jesus Factor." *Catholic Biblical Quarterly* 52 (1990) 270-91.

Häring, Theodor. "Über einige Grundgedanken des Hebräerbriefs." *MP* 17 (1920-1921) 260-76.

Harnack, A. von. "Probabilia über die Adresse und den Verfasser des Hebräerbriefes." *Zeitschrift für die neutestamentliche Wissenschaft* 1 (1900) 16-41.

Harrison, Everett F. *Introduction to the New Testament*. Grand Rapids: Eerdmans, 1971.

Hartin, Patrick J. *A Spirituality of Perfection: Faith in Action in the Letter of James*. Collegeville, MN: Liturgical, 1999.

Hatch, William H. P. "The Position of Hebrews in the Canon of the New Testament." *HTR* 29 (1936) 131-51.

Hawthorne, Gerald F. *Philippians*. Edited by Ralph P. Martin. WBC 43. Waco, TX: Word Books, 1983.

Hengel, Martin. *The Son of God: The Origin of Christology and the History of Jewish-Hellenistic Religion*. Philadelphia: Fortress, 1976.

Héring, Jean. *The Epistle to the Hebrews*. 1st English ed. Translated by A. W. Heathcote and P. J. Allcock. London: Epworth, 1970.

Herodotus. *The Persian Wars*. Vol. 3. Translated by A. D. Godley and edited by T. E. Page, E. Capps, and W. H. Rouse. 4 vols. Loeb Classical Library. Cambridge: Harvard University Press, 1963.

Hewitt, Thomas. *The Epistle to the Hebrews: An Introduction and Commentary*. Edited by R. V. G. Tasker. TNTC. Grand Rapids: Eerdmans, 1975.

Hiebert, D. E. *An Introduction to the New Testament*. 3 vols. Chicago: Moody, 1977.

Hodges, Zane C. *Absolutely Free! A Biblical Reply to Lordship Salvation*. Grand Rapids: Zondervan, 1989.

———. *The Gospel under Siege: Faith and Works in Tension*. 2nd rev. ed. Dallas: Redencion Viva, 1992.

———. *Grace in Eclipse: A Study on Eternal Rewards*. 2nd ed. Dallas: Redencion Viva, 1985.

———. "Hebrews." In *BKC*, edited by John F. Walvoord and Roy P. Zuck, 777-813. New Testament ed. Wheaton, IL: SP Publications, 1983.

Hoekema, Anthony A. "Perfection of Christ in Hebrews." *CTJ* 9 (1974) 31–37.
Holmes, Michael W., ed. *The Apostolic Fathers: Greek Texts and English Translations*. Grand Rapids: Baker, 1999.
Homer. *The Iliad*. Translated by A. T. Murray. Loeb Classical Library. New York: Putnam's, 1928.
Horning, E. B. "Chiasmus, Creedal Structure, and Christology in Hebrews 12:1–2." *BR* 23 (1978) 37–48.
Horton, Michael. "Preface." In *Christ the Lord: The Reformation and Lordship Salvation*, edited by Michael Horton, 11–13. Grand Rapids: Baker, 1992.
Hughes, Graham. *Hebrews and Hermeneutics: The Epistle to the Hebrews as a New Testament Example of Biblical Interpretation*. Edited by R. McL. Wilson and M. E. Thrall. SNTSMS 36. Cambridge: Cambridge University Press, 1979.
Hughes, Philip Edgcumbe. *A Commentary on the Epistle to the Hebrews*. Grand Rapids: Eerdmans, 1977.
———. "The Epistle to the Hebrews." In *The New Testament and Its Modern Interpreters*, edited by Eldon J. Epp, and George W. Macrae, 351–70. Society of Biblical Literature: The Bible and Its Modern Interpreters 3. Philadelphia: Fortress, 1989.
———. "Hebrews 6:4–6 and the Peril of Apostasy." *WTJ* 35 (1973) 137–55.
Hurst, Lincoln D. *The Epistle to the Hebrews: Its Background of Thought*. Edited by G. N. Stanton. SNTSMS 65. Cambridge: Cambridge University Press, 1990.
———. *Eschatology and Platonism in the Epistle to the Hebrews*. Edited by Kent H. Richard. Society of Biblical Literature: 1984 Seminar Papers. Chico, CA: Scholars, 1984.
Husselman, Elinor M., ed. "P.Mich 9.568–69." In *Papyri from Karanis, Third Series*, 116–18. Vol. 9 of *Michigan Papyri*. American Philological Association Monograph 29. Cleveland, OH: Case Western Reserve University, 1971.
Isaacs, Marie E. *Reading Hebrews and James: A Literary and Theological Commentary*. Macon, GA: Smyth & Helwys, 2002.
———. *Sacred Space: An Approach to the Theology of the Epistle to the Hebrews*. Edited by Stanley E. Porter. JSNTSup 73. Sheffield, UK: Sheffield Academic, 1992.
Isaak, Jon M. *Situating the Letter to the Hebrews in Early Christian History*. Studies in the Bible and Early Christianity 53. Lewiston, NY: Edwin Mellen, 2002.
Jeffers, James S. *The Greco-Roman World of the New Testament Era: Exploring the Background of Early Christianity*. Downers Grove: InterVarsity, 1999.
Jewett, Robert. "Conflicting Movements in the Early Church as Reflected in Philippians." *NovT* 12 (1970) 362–90.
———. *Letter to Pilgrims: A Commentary on the Epistle to the Hebrews*. New York: Pilgrim, 1981.
Johnson, Luke Timothy. *Hebrews: A Commentary*. Edited by C. Clifton Black and John T. Carroll. NTL. Louisville: John Knox, 2006.
Johnson, Richard W. *Going Outside the Camp: The Sociological Function of the Levitical Critique in the Epistle to the Hebrews*. Edited by Stanley E. Porter. JSNTSup 209. Sheffield, UK: Sheffield Academic, 2001.
Johnsson, William G. "The Cultus of Hebrews in Twentieth-Century Scholarship." *ExpTim* 89 (1977–1978) 104–108.
———. "Issues in the Interpretation of Hebrews." *Andrews University Seminary Studies* 15 (1977) 169–87.
———. "The Pilgrimage Motif in the Book of Hebrews." *JBL* 97 (1978) 239–51.

Josephus. *Jewish Antiquities*. Translated by Ralph Marcus and edited by G. P. Goold. 9 vols. Loeb Classical Library. Cambridge: Harvard University Press, 1929.

Käsemann, Ernst. *The Wandering People of God: An Investigation of the Letter to the Hebrews*. Translated by Roy A. Harrisville and Irving L. Sandberg. Minneapolis: Augsburg, 1984.

Katz, Peter. "The Quotations from Deuteronomy in Hebrews." *Zeitschrift für die neutestamentliche Wissenschaft* 49 (1958) 213–23.

Kendall, R. T. *Once Saved, Always Saved*. Chicago: Moody, 1983.

Kent, Homer A. *The Epistle to the Hebrews: A Commentary*. Grand Rapids: Baker, 1972.

Kistemaker, Simon J. *Exposition of the Epistle to the Hebrews*. NTC. Grand Rapids: Baker, 1984.

Klijn, A. F. J. "Paul's Opponents in Philippians 3." *NovT* 7 (1964) 278–84.

Koehler, Ludwig, and Walter Baumgartner. *The Hebrew and Aramaic Lexicon of the Old Testament*. 2 vols. Study ed. Translated by M. E. J. Richardson. Leiden, Netherlands: Brill, 2001.

Koester, Craig R. *Hebrews: A New Translation with Introduction and Commentary*. Edited by William Foxwell Albright, and David Noel Freedman. AB 36. New York: Doubleday, 2001.

Koester, Helmut. *Introduction to the New Testament: History and Literature of Early Christianity*. Vol. 2. 2nd ed. Berlin: Grüyter, 2000.

———. "The Purpose of the Polemic of a Pauline Fragment." *NTS* 8 (1961) 317–32.

Kögel, J. "Der Begriff τελειοῦν im Hebräerbrief im Zusammenhang mit dem neutestamentlichen Sprachgebrauch." In *TSMK*, 35–68. Leipzig, Germany: Deichert (Böhme), 1905.

Konkel, August. "The Sacrifice of Obedience." *Didaskalia* 2 (1991) 2–11.

Kümmel, Werner Georg. *Introduction to the New Testament*. Rev. ed. Translated from the 17th German edition by Howard Clark Kee. Nashville: Abingdon, 1975.

Kurianal, James. *Jesus Our High Priest: Psalm 110:4 as the Substructure of Hebrews 5:1–7*. European University Studies 23:693. Frankfurt: Peter Lang, 2000.

Ladd, George Eldon. *A Theology of the New Testament*. Rev. ed. Grand Rapids: Eerdmans, 1974.

Lane, William L. "Hebrews." In *Dictionary of the Later New Testament and Its Developments: A Compendium of Contemporary Biblical Scholarship*, edited by Ralph P. Martin and Peter H. Davids, 443–58. Downers Grove, IL: InterVarsity, 1997.

———. *Hebrews: A Call to Commitment*. Peabody: Hendrickson, 1985.

———. "Hebrews: A Sermon in Search of a Setting." *SJT* 28 (1985) 13–18.

———. *Hebrews 1–8*. Edited by David A. Hubbard and Glenn W. Barker. WBC 47A. Dallas: Word Books, 1991.

———. *Hebrews 9–13*. Edited by David A. Hubbard, Glenn W. Barker, John D. Watts, and Ralph P. Martin. WBC 47B. Dallas: Word Books, 1991.

———. "Social Perspectives on Roman Christianity during the Formative Years from Nero to Nerva: Romans, Hebrews, 1 Clement." In *Judaism and Christianity in First-Century Rome*, edited by Karl P. Donfried and Peter Richardson, 196–244. Grand Rapids: Eerdmans, 1998.

LaRondelle, H. K. *Perfection and Perfectionism: A Dogmatic Ethical Study of Biblical Perfection and Phenomenal Perfectionism*. 2nd ed. Andrews University

Monographs Studies in Religion 3. Berrien Springs, MI: Andrews University Press, 1975.

LaSor, William. *The Dead Sea Scrolls and the New Testament*. Grand Rapids: Eerdmans, 1972.

Legg, John D. "Our Brother Timothy: A Suggested Solution to the Problem of Authorship of the Epistle to the Hebrews." *EvQ* 40 (1968) 220–23

Lehne, Susanne. *The New Covenant in Hebrews*. Edited by David Hill and David E. Orton. JSNTSup 44. Sheffield, UK: Sheffield Academic, 1990.

Lenski, R. C. H. *The Interpretation of the Epistle to the Hebrews and of the Epistle of James*. Columbus, OH: Lutheran Book Concern, 1938.

Leon, Harry J. *The Jews of Ancient Rome*. Peabody: Hendrickson, 1960.

Leonard, William. *The Author of the Epistle to the Hebrews: Critical Problem and Use of the Old Testament*. Rome: Vatican Polyglot, 1939.

Liddell, Henry George, and Robert Scott. *A Greek-English Lexicon: With a Revised Supplement*. Revised and augmented by Henry Stuart Jones and Roderick McKenzie. Oxford: Clarendon, 1996.

Lightfoot, Neil R. *Jesus Christ Today: A Commentary on the Book of Hebrews*. Grand Rapids: Baker, 1976.

Lincoln, A. T. "Sabbath, Rest, and Eschatology in the New Testament." In *From Sabbath to Lord's Day: A Biblical, Historical, and Theological Investigation*, edited by D. A. Carson, 197–220. Grand Rapids: Zondervan, 1982. Reprint, Eugene, OR: Wipf & Stock, 1999.

Lindars, Barnabas. "The Rhetorical Structure of Hebrews." *NTS* 35 (1989) 382–06.

———. *The Theology of the Letter to the Hebrews*. Edited by J. D. G. Dunn. New Testament Theology. Cambridge: Cambridge University Press, 1991.

Linss, Wilhelm C. "Logical Terminology in the Epistle to the Hebrews." *Concordia Theological Monthly* 37 (1966) 365–69.

Lobel, E., and C. H. Roberts, eds. "P.Oxy 22.2349." In *Oxyrhynchus Papyri*, translated by E. Lobel and C. H. Roberts, 142–46. London: Egypt Exploration Society, 1954.

———. "P.Oxy 27.2349." In *Oxyrhynchus Papyri*, translated by E. Lobel and C. H. Roberts. London: Egypt Exploration Society, 1954.

Logan, Stephen Philip. "The Background of *Paideia* in Hebrews." PhD diss., Southern Baptist Theological Seminary, 1986.

Lohse, Eduard. *The New Testament Environment*. Rev. ed. Translated by John E. Steely. NTL. London: SCM, 1974.

Long, Thomas G. *Hebrews*. Interpretation: A Bible Commentary for Teaching and Preaching. Louisville: John Knox, 1997.

Longacre, Robert E. *The Grammar of Discourse*. 2nd ed. New York: Plenum, 1996.

Louw, Johannes P., and Eugene A. Nida, eds. *Greek-English Lexicon of the New Testament Based on Semantic Domains: Introduction and Domains*. 2 vols. New York: United Bible Societies, 1988.

Lünemann, Gottlieb. *A Critical and Exegetical Handbook to the Epistle to the Hebrews*. Translated by Maurice J. Evans and Edited by H. Meyer. MCNT 18. Edinburgh: T. & T. Clark, 1890.

Mackie, Scott D. *Eschatology and Exhortation in the Epistle to the Hebrews*. Edited by Jörg Frey. Wissenschaftliche Untersuchungen zum Neuen Testament 223. Tübingen, Germany: Mohr Siebeck, 2007.

MacLeod, David John. "The Literary Structure of the Book of Hebrews." *BSac* 146 (1989) 185–97.

———. "The Theology of the Epistle to the Hebrews: Introduction, Prolegomena and Doctrinal Center." ThD diss., Dallas Theological Seminary, 1987.

Maier, Paul L. *The New Complete Works of Josephus*. Rev. ed. Translated by William Whiston. Grand Rapids: Kregel, 1999.

Manson, William T. *The Epistle to the Hebrews: An Historical and Theological Reconsideration*. London: Hodder & Stoughton, 1951.

———. "The Problem of the Epistle to the Hebrews." *Bulletin of the John Rylands Library* 32 (1962) 1–17.

Manuel, Donald Gordon. "The Religious Identity of the Recipients of the Epistle to the Hebrews." ThD diss., New Orleans Baptist Theological Seminary, 1965.

Marshall, I. Howard. *A Critical and Exegetical Commentary on the Pastoral Epistles*. Edited by J. A. Emerton, C. E. B. Cranfield, and G. N. Stanton. ICC. Edinburgh: T. & T. Clark, 1999.

———. *Kept by the Power of God: A Study of Perseverance and Falling Away*. 3rd rev. ed. Minneapolis: Bethany, 1969.

Martin, John A. "Dispensational Approaches to the Sermon on the Mount." In *Essays in Honor of J. Dwight Pentecost*, edited by Stanley D. Toussaint and Charles H. Dyer, 34–48. Chicago: Moody, 1986.

Mason, Elliot James. "The Position of Hebrews in the Pauline Corpus in Light of Chester Beatty Papyrus II." PhD diss., University of Southern California, 1968.

Mason, John. "The Exhortation in Hebrews: Its Basis in Exposition." PhD diss., Vanderbilt University, 2001.

Matera, F. J. "Moral Exhortation: The Relation between Moral Exhortation and Doctrinal Exposition in the Letter to the Hebrews." *Toronto Journal of Theology* 10 (1994) 69–82.

Mayer, Günther. *Index Philoneus*. Berlin: Grüyter, 1972.

McCown, Wayne Gordon. "Ὁ λόγος τῆς παρακλήσεως: The Nature and Function of the Hortatory Sections in the Epistle to the Hebrews." ThD diss., Union Theological Seminary, 1970.

McCruden, Kevin B. "Christ's Perfection in Hebrews: Divine Beneficence as an Exegetical Key to Hebrews 2:10." *BR* 47 (2002) 40–62.

———. *Solidarity Perfected: Beneficent Christology in the Epistle to the Hebrews*. Edited by James D. G. Dunn, Carl R. Holladay, et al. BZNW 159. Berlin: Grüyter, 2008.

McKay, K. L. "Time and Aspect in New Testament Greek." *NovT* 34 (1992) 209–28.

McKnight, Scot. "The Warning Passages of Hebrews: A Formal Analysis and Theological Conclusions." *TJ* 13 (1992) 21–59.

McNeil, John T., ed. *Calvin: Institutes of the Christian Religion, Book I*. Translated and indexed by Ford Lewis Battles and edited by John Baillie et al. Library of Christian Classics 20. Louisville: Westminster John Knox, 2002.

Metzger, Bruce M. *The Canon of the New Testament: Its Origin, Development, and Significance*. Oxford: Clarendon, 1987.

———. *A Textual Commentary on the Greek New Testament*. 2nd ed. Stüttgart, Germany: Deutsche Bibelgesellschaft, 1994.

Michel, Otto. *Der Brief an die Hebräer*. 12th ed. Edited by Heinrich August et al. Kritisch-exegetischer Kommentar über das Neue Testament 13. Göttingen, Germany: Vandenhoeck & Ruprecht, 1984.

———. "Die Lehre von der Christlichen Volkommenheit nach der Anschauung des Hebräerbriefes." *TSK* 106 (1935) 333–35.

Miller, Neva F. *The Epistle to the Hebrews: An Analytical and Exegetical Handbook*. Dallas: Summer Institute of Linguistics, 1988.

Milligan, Robert. *Epistle to the Hebrews*. NTC 9. Cincinnati, OH: Chase & Hall, 1876.

Mitchell, Alan C. *Hebrews*. Edited by Daniel J. Harrington. Sacra pagina 13. Collegeville, MN: Liturgical, 2007.

Moffatt, James. *A Critical and Exegetical Commentary on the Epistle to the Hebrews*. Edited by Alfred Plummer. ICC. Edinburgh: T. & T. Clark, 1924.

Montefiore, Hugh. *A Commentary on the Epistle to the Hebrews*. Edited by Henry Chadwick. BNTC. London: Black, 1964.

Morris, Leon. "Hebrews." In *Hebrews–Revelation*, edited by Frank E. Gaebelein, 1–158. EBC 12. Grand Rapids: Zondervan, 1981.

Morrison, Michael D. *Who Needs a New Covenant? Rhetorical Function of the Covenant Motif in the Argument of Hebrews*. Edited by K. C. Hanson, C. M. Collier, and D. C. Spinks. Princeton Theological Monograph 85. Eugene, OR: Pickwick, 2008.

Moule, C. F. D. "Commentaries on the Epistle to the Hebrews." *Theology* 61 (1958) 228–32.

———. *An Idiom Book of New Testament Greek*. 2nd ed. Cambridge: Cambridge University Press, 1971.

Moulton, James H., and George Milligan. *The Vocabulary of the Greek Testament: Illustrated from the Papyri and Other Non-Literary Sources*. Reprint, Grand Rapids: Eerdmans, 1972.

Moulton, W. F., and A. S. Geden, eds. *A Concordance to the Greek New Testament according to the Texts of Westcott and Hort, Tischendorf, and the English Revisers*. Rev. ed. Edinburgh: T. & T. Clark, 1978.

Mugridge, Alan. "Warnings in the Epistle to the Hebrews." *Reformed Theological Review* 46 (1987) 74–82.

Muller, P. G. Χριστός Αρχηγός: *Der Religionsgeschichtliche und Theologische Hintergrund einer neutestamentlichen Christuspradikation*. Frankfürt: Peter Lang, 1973.

Nairne, Alexander. *The Epistle of Priesthood*. Edinburgh: T. & T. Clark, 1913.

———. *The Epistle to the Hebrews*. Cambridge: Cambridge University Press, 1917.

Nardoni, Enrique. "Partakers in Christ (Hebrews 3.14)." *NTS* 37 (1991) 456–72.

Nauck, Wolfgang. "Zum Aufbau des Hebräerbriefes." In *Judentum Urchristentum Kirche: Festschrift für Joachim Jeremias*, edited by Walther Eltester, 199-206. Berlin: Töpelmann, 1960.

Neighbour, R. E. *If They Shall Fall Away: The Epistle to the Hebrews Unveiled*. Miami Springs, FL: Conley & Schoettle, 1984.

Nestle, E., and K. Aland, eds. *Novum Testamentum Graece*. 27th ed. Stüttgart, Germany: Deutsche Bibelgesellschaft, 1998.

Neufeld, Vernon. *The Earliest Christian Confessions*. Edited by Bruce M. Metzger. New Testament Tools and Studies 5. Grand Rapids: Eerdmans, 1963.

Ngoupa, Hans Ejengele. "La perfection dans l'Épître aux Hébreux." ThD thesis, Institut Protestant de Théologie, 1982.

Nunn, H. P. V. *A Short Syntax of New Testament Greek*. Cambridge: Cambridge University Press, 1951.

O'Brien, Peter T. *The Letter to the Hebrews*. Edited by D. A. Carson. Pillar NTC. Grand Rapids: Eerdmans, 2010.

Oberholtzer, Thomas K. "The Eschatological Salvation of Hebrews 1:5–2:5 (Part 1 [of 5 Parts] of the Warning Passages in Hebrews)." *BSac* 145 (1988) 97.

Osborne, Grant R. "Soteriology in the Epistle to the Hebrews." In *Grace Unlimited*, edited by Clark Pinnock, 144–66. Minneapolis: Bethany Fellowship, 1975.

Osborne, Grant R. *The Hermeneutical Spiral: A Comprehensive Introduction to Biblical Interpretation*. Rev. ed. Downers Grove, IL: InterVarsity, 2006.

Owen, H. P. "The Stages of Ascent in Hebrews 5:11–6:3." *NTS* 3 (1956–1957) 243–53.

Owen, John. *An Exposition of the Epistle to the Hebrews with Preliminary Exercitations*. Edited by W. H. Goold. The Works of John Owen 21–22. Edinburgh: Johnstone & Hunter, 1854–1855. Reprint, Edinburgh: Banner of Truth, 1991.

Oyediran, Richardson Ademitoye. "A Lexical and Exegetical Analysis of the Soteriology of the Epistle to the Hebrews." PhD diss., Dallas Theological Seminary, 2009.

Padva, Paul. *Les citations de l'Ancien Testament dans l'Épître aux Hébreux*. Thèse présentée à l'Université de Paris, Faculté de Théologie Protestante, vol. 380. Paris: N. L. Danzig, 1904.

Peake, A. S. *Hebrews*. Century Bible. Edinburgh: T. C. & E. C. Jock, n.d.

Pentecost, J. Dwight. *A Faith that Endures: The Book of Hebrews Applied to the Real Issues of Life*. Grand Rapids: Discovery, 1992.

Peterson, David. "The Prophecy of the New Covenant in the Argument of Hebrews." *Reformed Theological Review* 38 (1979) 74–81.

Peterson, David. *Hebrews and Perfection: An Examination of the Concept of Perfection in the Epistle to the Hebrews*. Edited by R. McL. Wilson and M. E. Thrall. SNTSMS 47. Cambridge: Cambridge University Press, 1982.

Peterson, Robert A., and Michael D. Williams. *Why I Am Not an Arminian*. Downers Grove, IL: InterVarsity, 2004.

Philo. *Philo*. Translated by F. H. Colson and G. H. Whitaker and edited by E. H. Warmington. 10 vols. Loeb Classical Library. Cambridge: Harvard University Press, 1968.

Plato. *Phaedo*. Vol. 1. Translated by Harold N. Fowler. 12 vols. Loeb Classical Library. Cambridge: Harvard University Press, 1977.

———. *Phaedrus*. Translated by Harold N. Fowler. 3 vols. Loeb Classical Library. Cambridge: Harvard University Press, 1977.

———. *The Republic*. Translated by Paul Shorey. 12 vols. Loeb Classical Library. Cambridge: Harvard University Press, 1980.

Porter, Stanley E. *Verbal Aspect in the Greek of the New Testament, with Reference to Tense and Mood*. Edited by D. A. Carson. Studies in Biblical Greek 1. New York: Lang, 1989.

Preisker, Hebert. "ἔθος." In vol. 2 of *Theological Dictionary of the New Testament*, edited by Gerhard Kittel and translated by Geoffrey W. Bromiley, 372–73. Grand Rapids: Eerdmans, 1964.

———. "μισθός." In vol. 4. of *Theological Dictionary of the New Testament*, edited by Gerhard Kittle and Gerhard Friedrich and translated by Geoffrey W. Bromiley, 695–706. Grand Rapids: Eerdmans, 1967.

———. *Das Ethos des Urchristentums*. Gütersloh, Germany: Bertelsmann, 1949.

Purdy, Alexander C., and Harry Cotton. "The Epistle to the Hebrews." In *Philippians to Hebrews*, edited by G. A. Buttrick and N. B. Harmon, 575–63. IB 11. Nashville: Abingdon, 1955.

Ramsey, William M. *Luke the Physician and Other Studies in the History of Religion.* London: Hodder & Stoughton, 1909.

Rathel, Mark A. "An Examination of the Soteriological Terminology in the Epistle to the Hebrews." PhD diss., New Orleans Baptist Theological Seminary, 1988.

Rigaux, Beda. "Révélation des mystères et Perfection à Qumran et dans le Nouveau Testament." *NTS* 4 (1957) 237–62.

Riggenbach, Eduard. "Der Begriff der telei,wsij im Hebraerbrief. Ein Beitrag zur Frage nach der Einwirkung der Mysterienreligion auf Sprache und Gedankenwelt des Neuen Testaments." *Neue kirchliche Zeitschrift* 34 (1923) 185–86.

———. *Der Brief an die Hebräer.* 3rd ed. Kommentar zum Neuen Testament 14. Leipzig, Germany: Deichert, 1922.

Robert, A., and Andre Feuillet. *Introduction to the New Testament.* Translated by P. W. Skehan et al. New York: Desclée, 1965.

Robertson, Archibald Thomas. *A Grammar of the Greek New Testament in the Light of Historical Research.* 4th ed. New York: Hodder & Stoughton, 1923.

———. *The Fourth Gospel and the Epistle to the Hebrews.* Word Pictures in the New Testament 5. New York: Harper & Brothers, 1932.

Robinson, John A. T. *Redating the New Testament.* Philadelphia: Westminster, 1976.

Robinson, Theodore H. *The Epistle to the Hebrews.* Edited by James Moffatt. NTC. New York: Harper, 1933.

Robinson, William. "The Eschatology of the Epistle to the Hebrews: A Study in the Christian Doctrine of Hope." *Encounter* 22 (1961) 37–51.

Rogers, Cleon L., Jr., and Cleon L. Rogers III. *The New Linguistic and Exegetical Key to the Greek New Testament.* Grand Rapids: Zondervan, 1998.

Rutenber, Culbert G. *The Doctrine of the Imitation of God in Plato.* Morningside Heights, NY: King's Crown, 1946.

Ryrie, Charles C. *Biblical Theology of the New Testament.* Chicago: Moody, 1959.

Sabourin, L. "Liturgie du Sanctuaire et de la tente véritable (Héb 8:2)." *NTS* 18 (1971–2) 87–90.

Salevao, Lutisone. *Legitimation in the Letter to the Hebrews.* Edited by Stanley E. Porter et al. JSNTSup 219. Sheffield, UK: Sheffield Academic, 2002.

Sanford, Carlisle J. "The Addressees of Hebrews." ThD diss., Dallas Theological Seminary, 1962.

Saucy, Mark. "Exaltation Christology in Hebrews: What Kind of Reign." *TJ* 14 (1993) 43–58.

Schierse, F. J. *The Epistle to the Hebrews.* Translated by Benen Fahy. Edited by John L. McKenzie. New Testament for Spiritual Reading. New York: Herder & Herder, 1969.

Schippers, Reinier. "*Telos. . . Teleo, Teleioo.*" In vol. 2 of *the New International Dictionary of New Testament Theology: Translated, with Additions and Revisions, from the German Theologisches Begriffslexikon zum Neuen Testament*, edited by Colin Brown and translated by Lothar Coenen et al., 59–65. Grand Rapids: Zondervan, 1971.

Schmithals, W. "The False Teachers of the Epistle to the Philippians." In *Paul and the Gnostics*, 65–122. Nashville: Abingdon, 1972.

Schnackenburg, Rudolf. "Christian Perfection According to Matthew." In vol. 1 of *Christian Existence in the New Testament*, translated by Fred D. Wieck, 158–89. 2

vols. Munich: Kösel, 1967. Reprint, Notre Dame: University of Notre Dame Press, 1968.

Scholer, John M. *Proleptic Priests: Priesthood in the Epistle to the Hebrews*. JSNTSup 49. Sheffield, UK: JSOT, 1991.

Schreiner, J. "Fuhrung-Thema der heilsgeschichte im Alten Testament." *BZ* 5 (1961) 2–8.

Schreiner, Thomas R., and Ardel B. Caneday. *The Race Set before Us: A Biblical Theology of Perseverance and Assurance*. Downers Grove, IL: InterVarsity, 2001.

Schurer, Emil. *The History of Jewish People in the Age of Jesus Christ (175 BC–AD 135) A New English Version*. Rev. ed. Edited by Geza Vermes, Fergus Millar, and Martin Goodman. 3 vols. Edinburgh: T. & T. Clark, 1986.

Scott, E. F. *The Epistle to the Hebrews: Its Doctrine and Significance*. Edinburgh: T. & T. Clark, 1923.

———. *The Literature of the New Testament*. New York: Columbia University Press, 1932.

Shank, Robert. *Life in the Son: A Study of the Doctrine of Perseverance*. 2nd ed. Springfield, MO: Westcott, 1962.

Shelton, R. Larry. "Perfection, Perfectionism." In *Evangelical Dictionary of Theology*, edited by Walter A. Elwell, 902–906. Grand Rapids: Baker, 2001.

Silva, Moisés. "Perfection and Eschatology in Hebrews." *WTJ* 39 (1976) 60–71.

Simpson, E. K. "The Vocabulary of the Epistle to the Hebrews." *EvQ* 18 (1946) 35–45.

Son, Kiwoong. *Zion Symbolism in Hebrews: Hebrews 12:18–24 as a Hermeneutical Key to the Epistle*. Paternoster Biblical Monographs. Waynesboro, GA: Paternoster, 2005.

Sophocles. *Ajax, Electra, Trachiniae, Philoctetes*. Vol. 2. Translated by F. Storr and edited by T. E. Page. 2 vols. Loeb Classical Library. Cambridge: Harvard University Press, 1961.

Spicq, Ceslas. "L'authenticité du chapitre XIII de l'Épître aux Hébreux." *Conjectanea neotestamentica* 11 (1947) 226–36.

———. "L'Épître aux Hébreux: Apollos, Jean-Baptiste, le Helleniste et Qumran." *RevQ* 1 (1958) 365–90.

———. *L'Épître aux Hébreux: Commentaire*. EBib 2. Paris: Librairie Lécoffre (Gabalda), 1953.

———. *L'Épître aux Hébreux: Introduction*. EBib 1. Paris: Librairie Lécoffre (Gabalda), 1952.

Stadelmann, Andreas. "Zur Christologie des Hebräerbriefes in der neueren Diskussion." *TB* 2 (1973).

Stanley, Steve. "The Structure of Hebrews from Three Perspectives." *TynBul* 45 (1994) 245–71.

Stein, Robert H. *Interpreting Puzzling Texts in the New Testament*. Grand Rapids: Baker, 1996.

Strachan, R. H. *The Historic Jesus in the New Testament*. London: SCM Press, 1931.

Suetonius. *The Deified Claudius*. Translated by J. C. Rolfe. 2 vols. Loeb Classical Library. Reprint, Cambridge: Harvard University Press, 1992.

Swetnam, J. "The Greater and More Perfect Tent: A Contribution to the Discussion of Hebrews 9:11." *Biblica* 47 (1966) 91–106.

Synge, F. C. *Hebrews and the Scripture*. London: S.P.C.K., 1959.

Tacitus. *Annals*. Translated by John Jackson and edited by T. E. Page, E. Capps, and W. H. Rouse. 4 vols. Loeb Classical Library. Cambridge: Harvard University Press, 1957.

Tasker, R. V. G. "The Integrity of the Epistle to the Hebrews." *ExpTim* 47 (1935–1936) 136–38.

Telfer, William. *The Forgiveness of Sins: An Essay in the History of Christian Doctrine and Practice*. Philadelphia: Muhlenberg, 1960.

Tenney, Merril C. *New Testament Survey*. Grand Rapids: Eerdmans, 1961.

Tertullian. *La Pudicité: Book I*. Translated by Charles Munier. SC 394. Paris: Les Éditions du Cerf, 1993.

Thayer, Joseph Henry. *A Greek-English Lexicon of the New Testament*. New York: American Book, 1889.

Thien, F. "Analyse de l'Épître aux Hébreux." *Révue biblique* 11 (1902) 74–86.

Thomas, C. Adrian. "A Case for a Mixed-Audience with Reference to the Warning Passages in the Book of Hebrews." PhD diss., Dallas Theological Seminary, 2006.

Thompson, James W. *The Beginnings of Christian Philosophy: The Epistle to the Hebrews*. Edited by Bruce Vawter et al. Catholic Biblical Quarterly Monographs 13. Washington, DC: Catholic Biblical Association, 1982.

Thucydides. *History of the Peloponnesian War*. Vol 3. Translated by Charles F. Smith, edited by T. E. Page, E. Capps, and W. H. D. Rouse. 4 vols. Loeb Classical Library. Cambridge: Harvard University Press, 1952.

Thyen, Hartwig. *Der Stil Des Judisch-Hellenistischen Homilie*. FRLANT 47. Göttingen, Germany: Vandenhoeck & Ruprecht, 1955.

Tönges, Elke. "The Epistle to the Hebrews as a Jesus Midrash." In *Hebrews: Contemporary Methods-New Insights*, edited by Gabriella Gelardini, 89–105. Biblical Interpretation Series 75. Leiden, Netherlands: Brill, 2005.

Toussaint, Stanley D. "The Eschatology of the Warning Passages in the Book of Hebrews." *GTJ* 3 (1982) 67–80.

Trotter, Andrew H., Jr. *Interpreting the Epistle to the Hebrews*. Edited by Scott McKnight. Guides to New Testament Exegesis. Grand Rapids: Baker, 1997.

Turner, E. G., et al., eds. "P.Oxy 27.2471." In *Oxyrhynchus Papyri*, translated by E. G. Turner, J. Rea, and L. Koenen. London: Egypt Exploration Society, 1962.

Turner, Nigel. *Syntax*. Vol. 3 of *Grammar of New Testament Greek*, edited by James Hope Moulton. Edinburgh: T. & T. Clark, 1976.

Vanhoye, Albert. *Homilie für Haltbedurftige Christen: Struktur und Botschaft des Hebräerbriefes*. Regensburg, Germany: Pustet, 1981.

———. *Le message de l'Épître aux Hébreux*. Cahiers Evangile 19. Paris: Éditions du Cerf, 1977.

———. *Prêtres anciens, prêtres nouveaux selon le Nouveau Testament*. Parole de Dieu 20. Paris: Éditions du Cerf, 1980.

———. *Situation du Christ: Épître aux Hébreux 1 et 2*. Lectio divina 58. Paris: Éditions du Cerf, 1969.

———. *Structure and Message of the Epistle to the Hebrews*. Translated by James Swetnam. *SubBi* 12. Rome: Pontifical Biblical Institute, 1989.

———. *La structure littéraire de l'Epître aux Hébreux*. 2nd ed. StudNeot 1. Paris: Desclée de Brouwer, 1976.

———. *A Structured Translation of the Epistle to the Hebrews*. Translated by James Swetnam. Rome: Pontifical Biblical Institute, 1964.

———. "La *Teleiosis* du Christ: point capital de la christologie sacerdotale d'Hébreux." *NTS* 42 (1996) 321–38.
Verbrugge, V. D. "Towards a New Interpretation of Hebrews 6:4–6." *CTJ* 15 (1980) 61–73.
Volf, Judith M. Gundry. *Paul and Perseverance: Staying in and Falling Away*. Louisville: Westminster John Knox, 1990.
Vos, Geerhardus. *The Teaching of the Epistle to the Hebrews*. Grand Rapids: Eerdmans, 1956.
Waanders, F. M. *The History of Telos and Teleo in Ancient Greek*. Amsterdam: Grüner, 1983.
Wallace, Daniel B. *Greek Grammar beyond the Basics: An Exegetical Syntax of the New Testament*. Grand Rapids: Zondervan, 1996.
Walters, John R. *Perfection in New Testament Theology: Ethics and Eschatology in Relational Dynamic*. Mellen Biblical Press Series 25. New York: Mellen Biblical, 1995.
Weiss, Bernhard. *Handbuch über den Brief an die Hebräer*. 6th ed. Göttingen, Germany: Vandenhoeck & Ruprecht, 1897.
Weiss, Hans-Friedrich. *Der Brief an die Hebräer*. Edited by Heinrich August, Wilhelm Meyer, and Ferdinand Hahn. KEK. Göttingen, Germany: Vandenhoeck & Ruprecht, 1991.
Welch, Charles H., and Stuart Allen. *Perfection or Perdition: An Exposition of the Epistle to the Hebrews*. London: Berean, 1973.
Wesley, John. "Christian Perfection: A Sermon Preached by John Wesley." In vol. 2 of *The Works of John Wesley: Sermon 2*, edited by Albert C. Outler, 96–124. Nashville: Abingdon, 1985.
———. *A Plain Account of Christian Perfection: As Believed and Taught by John Wesley, A. M., from the Year 1725 to the Year 1777*. Edited by T. O. Summers. Reprint, London: Epworth, 1952.
Westcott, Brooke Foss. *The Epistle to the Hebrews: The Greek Text with Notes and Essays*. London: Macmillan, 1889. Reprint, Eugene, OR: Wipf & Stock, 2001.
Westfall, Cythia Long. *A Discourse Analysis of the Letter to the Hebrews: The Relationship between Form and Meaning*. Edited by Mark Goodacre. Library of New Testament Studies 297. Edinburgh: T. & T. Clark, 2005.
Wikgren, Allen. "Patterns of Perfection in the Epistle to the Hebrews." *NTS* 6 (1960) 159–67.
Wilkin, Robert N. "Striving for the Prize of Eternal Salvation: A Review of Schreiner and Caneday's *The Race Set before Us*." *Journal of the Grace Evangelical Society* (2002) 3–24.
Williamson, Ronald. "The Background of the Epistle to the Hebrews." *ExpTim* 57 (1975–1976) 232–37.
———. *Philo and the Epistle to the Hebrews*. Edited by K. H. Rengstorf, J. Danielou, and G. Delling. Arbeiten zur Literatur und Geschichte des hellenistischen Judentums 4. Leiden, Netherlands: Brill, 1970.
Wills, Lawrence. "The Form of the Sermon in Hellenistic Judaism and Early Christianity." *HTR* 77 (1984) 277–99.
Wilson, R. Mclachlan. *Hebrews*. Edited by Matthew Black. NCBC. Grand Rapids: Eerdmans, 1987.

Bibliography

Windisch, Hans. *Der Hebräerbrief.* 2nd rev. ed. Handbuch zum Neuen Testament 14. Tübingen, Germany: Mohr Siebeck, 1931.

Winer, Georg Benedikt. *A Grammar of the Idiom of the New Testament.* 7th ed. Andover, MA: Drapper, 1877.

Witherington, Ben, III. *Letters and Homilies for Jewish Christians: A Socio-Rhetorical Commentary on Hebrews, James, and Jude.* Leicester, UK: Inter-Varsity, 2007.

Wuest, Kenneth S. *Hebrews in the Greek New Testament for the English Reader.* Vol. 9. Grand Rapids: Eerdmans, 1947.

Yadin, Yigael. "The Dead Sea Scrolls and the Epistle to the Hebrews." In *Aspects of the Dead Sea Scrolls*, edited by Chaim Rabin and Yigael Yadin, 36–55. 2nd ed. Scripta hierosolymitana 4. Jerusalem: Hebrew University Press, 1965.

Zahn, Theodor. *Introduction to the New Testament.* vol. 2. Translated by M. W. Jacobus. 3 vols. Edinburgh: T. & T. Clark, 1909. Reprint, Minneapolis: Klock & Klock, 1977.

Zerwick, Max, and Mary Grosvenor. *A Grammatical Analysis of the Greek New Testament.* 4th rev. ed. Rome: Pontificio Instituto Biblico, 1993.

Zimmerli, Walther. *Promise and Fulfillment.* Edited by Claus Westermann. Essays on Old Testament Hermeneutics. Richmond, VA: John Knox, 1963.

Author Index

Adams, J.C., 181–82n269
Alford, Henry, 112, 136n34
Allen, David L., 81n4, 180
Apollos, 81, 86n35
Aristion, 86
Aristotle, 14–15, 48, 212
Attridge, Harold W., 26–27, 90, 109n169, 112, 121, 123, 124, 139n55, 146, 159n161, 161n178, 179, 180, 181n266, 188, 197, 200
Augustine, 88
Aune, David E., 121

Barnabas, 81, 85
Barrett, C.K., 116
Bauer, Walter, 22n58, 50–51
Beare, F.W., 76
Black, C. Clifton, 121
Black, David Alan, 120, 124
Bloomfield, S.T., 136n37
Bock, Darrell L., 10, 160
Bovon, François, 160n170
Bruce, F.F., 32, 96, 103, 124, 129, 133, 136n36, 197, 208
Buchanan, George Wesley, 110

Caird, George B., 31, 138
Clark, K.W., 90
Clement of Alexandria, 82, 83
    Hebrews' influence on, 85
Clement of Rome, 81, 89
Cody, Aelred, 115
Cullmann, Oscar, 18, 33

Davidson, A.B., 161
de Vaux, Roland, 59
Delitzsch, Franz, 208
Delling, Gerhard, 23, 51, 58, 137, 201
DeSilva, David A., 106n156, 146, 196n347, 203n385, 203n387
Dey, Lala Kalyan Kumar, 18, 58n91
Dibelius, Martin, 27n82, 60
Dickie, J., 112
Diessman, Adolf, 113
Diogenes, 48
Dods, Marcus, 171
DuPlessis, Paul J., 6, 13, 24, 25, 26, 32, 51, 56, 63–64, 73, 75, 133, 135, 136n37, 145, 167n208, 187n294, 189, 200, 201
    on James' use of τέλειος, 78
    on Philo, 67

Ehrhardt, Arnold, 94
Ellingworth, Paul, 3n11, 24, 25, 39, 114, 136n36, 162, 174n242, 175, 179, 183, 188, 193
Eusebius, 49n30, 82, 84–85, 96, 104, 105, 146
    Ecclesiastical History, 82–83

Fanning, Buist M., 107n161
Ferguson, Everett, 101
Filson, Floyd V., 103
Fitzmyer, Joseph A., 73

Gaius, 84–85
Guthrie, Donald, 90

Author Index

Guthrie, George H., 124–25, 125, 136n36, 159–60n164

Hagner, Donald A., 208
Häring, Theodor, 2, 23–24
Hartin, Patrick J., 67, 74
Héring, Jean, 175
Holtzmann, Oskar, 88
Homer, 47
Horning, E.B., 198n358
Hughes, Philip Edgecumbe, 18, 93, 137, 144, 184, 185, 208
Hurst, Lincoln D., 115
Hyppolytus, 85

Irenaeus, 85

Jerome, 88, 157n152
Jewett, Robert, 76
John, 206
Johnson, Luke Timothy, 141–42n66, 142n69, 205n397
Josephus, 104n146, 105n149, 147n101
  use of present tense, 89n54
Jude, 86

Käsemann, Ernst, 28–29, 138, 142n72, 179
Kistemaker, Simon J., 182, 184, 193
Klijn, A.F.J., 76
Koester, Craig R., 30, 85, 107n160, 148, 155n140, 161, 164n191, 166
Koester, Helmut, 112
Kögel, Julius, 2, 14, 28
Kümmel, Werner Georg, 123
Kurianal, James, 25, 159, 162

Lane, William L., 29–30, 32, 98, 103, 106n156, 117n230, 122, 151, 163n189, 168n214, 174, 183, 203n387, 204n392
LaRondelle, H.K., 56
Leonard, William, 81n3
Lindars, Barnabas, 122
Long, Thomas G., 32
Luke, translation of Hebrews by, 83
Lünemann, Gottlieb, 171
Luther, Martin, 81, 86n33

Manson, William T., 95n87, 141n64
McCruden, Kevin B., 3, 8, 20, 21, 26, 34, 37
McNeile, A.H., 115
Michel, Otto, 4, 129
Mitchell, Alan C., 109n170, 143, 153n133, 166
Moffat, James, 28, 29, 99–100, 171, 200n370
Montefiore, Hugh A., 147, 148n103, 163, 167, 194, 202
Morris, Leon, 124
Moule, C.F.D., 101n124

Nairne, Alexander, 112
Nauck, Wolfgang, 123

O'Brien, Peter T., 201, 204
Origen, 83–84
Osborne, Grant R., 10
Owen, H.P., 181n266
Oxyrhyncus, 35

Padva, Paul, 132n17
Pantaenus, 82, 83
Paul, 73, 74–77, 102, 168, 185–86
  factors arguing against authorship, 87–88
  as possible Hebrews author, 81
Pentecost, J. Dwight, 157, 197n356, 209
Peter, 86, 88, 105, 185n287
Peterson, David, 3, 6–7, 26, 31, 33–34, 48, 58, 59–61, 76, 152, 172n234, 181, 188n302, 190, 209
  on Christ's faith, 201
Philip, 86
Philip the Evangelist, 94
Philo of Alexandria, 65–68, 213
  conceptual approach to Hebrews, 115
  On the Special Laws, 66
Plato, 48
  Hebrews and, 115
  and perfection, 212
  Phaedo, 49
  τέλειος usage, 49–51
Pliny, 102

Author Index

Priscilla and Aquila, 81

Ramsey, William M., 94
Rathel, Mark A., 58, 164n190, 188n302
Robinson, John A. T., 89n54, 90
Rutenber, Culbert G., 50

Salevao, 105
Scholer, John M., 21, 23n60, 26
Seneca, 53
Shepherd of Hermas, 89
Silas, 81–82, 86
Silva, Moisés, 29, 60, 140
Silvanus, 86
Socrates, 50
Son, Kiwoong, 205
Sophocles, 48
Spicq, Ceslas, 24–25, 65n131, 81n6, 86n35, 88, 92, 95n87, 113, 115
Suetonius, 102–3

Tacitus, 105
Tertullian, 85, 86n33, 99
Thayer, Joseph Henry Thayer, 45
Thomas, C. Adrian, 103

Thucydides, 47
Thyen, Hartwig, 111
Timothy, 87, 87n39, 92
  imprisonment, 93
Tönges, Elke, 110
Toussaint, Stanley D., 106n157

Vanhoye, Albert, 32–33, 119, 133n18, 140n63, 178n252
  literary analysis by, 122–23
Vespasian, 104, 104n147
von Harnack, Adolph, 88

Walters, John R., 31, 78
Westcott, Brooke Foss, 17, 19–20, 33, 88, 99, 167n208, 174n242, 187, 193n329
Westfall, Cynthia Long, 121
Wikgren, Allen, 18
Williamson, Ronald, 116
Wills, Lawrence, 111
Wilson, R. McLachlan, 194
Witherington, Ben III, 112
Wuest, Kenneth S., 147

Zahn, Theodor B., 99

Subject Index

שָׁלֵם, 45, 55, 56, 57, 62
תָּמִים, 45, 55, 57, 62, 64
   and James, 78

Aaron
   Christ's superiority to, 141, 143
   sacrifical system limitations, 169
Abraham, 207
   faith made complete, 78
   tithes to Melchizedek, 156, 157
achievement, 44–45
acultic sacral character, 6
ἁγιαζομένους, 188, 189
ἁγιάζω (to consecrate), 189, 190
"agnostic approach," to Hebrews structure, 124
αἴτιος (source), 199
αἴτιος σωτηρίας αἰωνίου, 147–48
αἰσθητήρια (sense; faculty), 180
αἰωνίος (eternal), 148n103
מלא, 58
Alexandria, 102
   as destination for Hebrews, 96–97
   Eastern Church at, 82
ἀλλά (but), 204n392
allegiance
   renunciation of, 71
   to Yahweh, 56
αμῶμος, 61n110
ἄμωμος, 55n78
ανάμνησις (remembrance of soul's pre-existent divinity), 51
Ananias, high priest, 105
ἀνασωζομένους, 188

ancient Israel, priests in, 59
angels, 206n406
   Christ as superior, 125, 126, 131, 143
animal sacrifice, 55, 172
antitheses, uses of, 49
aorist tense, 136n36
apostasy, 106n157, 118
   danger of, 178
   suffering and, 107
Aramaic, vs. Hebrew language, 95
Aristotle, and Stoicism, 54
Asa, 57
authorship of Hebrews, 65, 80–93
   anonymity, 9
   historical or external evidence, 82–86
   internal evidence, 86–88
ἀφ (from), 198n359
ἀφέντες, 183
ἀφορῶντες εἰς τὸν τῆς πίστεως ἀρχηγὸν καὶ τελειωτὴν ᾽Ιησοῦν, 198
ἀφορῶντες, 198n359
ἀγαγόντα (leading), 136n36, 136n37
ἀναλογίσασθε, 42n156
ἄνθρωποι, and high priesthood, 151
ἀπό, 97n102
ἀπογεγραμμένων (registered-ones), 206n404
ἀποθέμενοι, 197
ἀθέτησις (removal), 159
ἀρχῆς (teaching), 181n268
ἀρχηγὸν (pioneer), 199

ἀρχηγός, 133
  in Acts, 132n18
  Christ as, 132
  Christ perfected as, 28

βασιλεὺς Σαλήμ (king of Salem), Melchizedek as, 157
βεβαιόω (to confirm), 37
believers
  access to the Father, 25
  call for perseverance, 20
  final destination, 205
  hardship of, 32
  of NT era vs. OT saints, 194–95
  perfecting of faith, or perfecting in future, 200
  perfection of, 21–22, 176–201
  τέλειος and, 214
biblical theology, 10
⸺, 56
blamelessness, 57

Caesarea, 95n87
χάριν εὕρωμεν εἰς εὔκαιρον βοήθειαν, 148
character, fixed vs. changeable, 21
children (παιδία), 75
Chrestus, 102–3
Christ. *See* Jesus Christ
church of Hebrews, Jerusalem church as, 94
city of the Living God, 205
classical world, τέλειος (perfection) in, 46–62
  general usage, 46–48
Claudius, 101
  edict expelling Jews and Jewish Christians from Rome, 98, 102
Clement of Alexandria, 99
Clement of Rome, 91, 98
close of the age, messianic mission of Jesus at, 38
cloud of witnesses, 197n350
Colossae, 95n87
commitment, call to, 216
communion of saints, 207
communion with Christ, 25
completeness, Jesus' calls to, 70

completion, 45, 144
conceptual approach to Hebrews, 120
confidence, erosion, 117
conscience, 168
consecration, 2, 58–59, 137
  reintegration into covenant community through, 25
  of worshipers, 189
consilia evangelica, 70n166
consummation, 45n5, 48
contract, 35
conversion, 185
Corpus Paulinum, 85
covenant. *See also* new covenant; old covenant
covenant community, reintegration through consecration, 25
Χρηστιανός, 103
Χριστός, 170
cultic or religious approach to τέλειος, 3n11, 22–27
cultic sacral character, 145
cultic tradition of Old Testament, 189
cultus
  in Pentateuch, 117
  practice of, 23

ὁ ἀγῶνος (race), 196n346
ὁ ἀπόστολος, 83n18
ἡ δόξα, 136n34
date of Hebrews, 80–93
Davidic Heir, 152n124
Day of Atonement, 164, 168, 172
δὲ κρείττονος ἐλπίδος, 162
definitive attestation approach to τέλειος, 34–38
devotion, to God, 57
διὰ παθημάτων τελειῶσαι (made perfect through suffering), 134, 137, 139
διὰ τὸ πάθημα τοῦ θανάτου (through the suffering of death), 139
Dialog of Gaius, 85
diaspora, 96
δικαιοσύνης (righteousness), 179
δίκαιός (just; righteous), 208
Dionysius of Corinth, 98
discouragement, signs of, 107–8

Discourse Analysis, 124–25
Δι' ὃν τὰ πάντα καὶ δι' οὗ τὰ πάντα (he for whom and by whom all things exist), 135
divine beneficence (*philanthropia*), 3, 8, 34
divine hero, Hellenistic notion of, 133n18
divine purpose, 140
Domitian, Christian persecution under, 91
δόξαν, 134
δύναται δύνανται, 175

ε ἔμαθεν ἀφ' ων ἔπαθεν, 142n69
ε καιροῦ διορθώσεως ἐπικείμενα (time of correction), 167n205
ε πρός εβραίους (to the Hebrews), 98–100
ε τοὺς ἁγιαζομένους, 187–88n297
early church authorities, 82
earthly, vs. heavenly, 49
Eastern Church
  at Alexandria, 82
  vs. Western Church, views on authorship, 85
Ecclesiastical History (Eusebius), 82–83
ἔχοντας ἀσθένειαν (having weaknesses), 151
ἔγγυος (guarantee), 130
εἰ θέλεις τέλειος εἶναι, 70
εἰς ἄνδρα τέλειον (perfect person), 75
εἰς τὸ διηνεκὲς, 189
εἰς τὸν αἰῶνα (forever), 154
Eleazar, 58
"end of the ages," 42n156
endurance, 126, 194, 197
Enoch, 57
Ephesus, 95n87
epilogue, 120
ἔπρεπεν, 135
eschatological fulfillment, 72
eschatological peace, vision of future, 210
eschatological understanding, 209
eschatology, 116, 215
  definition, 39
  in Hebrews, ix, 11, 40–43
  of Qumran community, 213
  as scholars' focus, 30
ἔσεσθε οὖν ὑμεῖς τέλειοι, 69
ἐτελείωσεν, 158
ethical philosophy, τέλειος viewed in terms of, 52
ἐκκλησίᾳ πρωτοτόκων (congregation of the firstborn), 206n406
ἐπισυναγωγῃ, 94, 207n406
ἐπ' ἐσχάτου τῶν ἡμερῶν (at the end of these days), 116
exaltation approach to τέλειος, 27–30
exaltation of Christ, 138
exclusion, Qumran community and, 63
exegesis, 10
experiential approach to τέλειος, 31–34

faith
  commendation of, 192
  crisis of, 117
  perfection acquired through, 25
φερώμεθα, 182, 183
"filling of the hand," 59
firstborn, 206n406
  status of, 208
φοβηθῶμεν, 42n156
forgiveness, 154, 187
foundation, 183
Φρόνησις (insight; wisdom), 49
fulfillment, 45

Galilee, invasion of, 104n147
γάρ (since; for), 134, 173, 187, 204n391
γενομένων, 170n224
Gentile audience, Hebrews for, 99
geographic location for Hebrews, 93–100
  Alexandria, 96–97
  Palestine, 93–96
  Rome, 97–98
Gessius Florus, 104
Gestius Gallus, 104
γεύσηται θανάτου (he might taste death), 139

glorification, 138
  of Christ, 2
glorification or exaltation approach to τέλειος, 27, 179
glory, 134, 139
gnostic Christian missionaries, as Paul's opponents, 76
gnostic myth, 28
  on savior, 133n18
God. *See also* Yahweh
  access to, 18
  alone as perfect, 66
  danger of turning away from, 118
  devotion to, 57
  Israelites' approach to, 203
  as Judge of all, 209
  knowledge from, 64
  person in relationship, 168
  salvation plan, 43
  as source of perfection, 67
God the Father, 21
  Christ made perfect by, 22
gods, 47
God's κατάπαυσίς (resting-place), 41
God's King-Son, perfecting, 125
God's people, Hebrew believers as, 41
grace, 67

ἡ τελεία ἀγάπη (perfect love), 14
heavenly city, 42
heavenly Jerusalem, 205, 207, 214
heavenly, vs. earthly, 49
Hebrew scripture, 54–62
  use of, 116
Helenistic Jewish Christians, 100
Hellenistic devices, in Hebrews, 121
Herodotus, 47–48
heroes of faith, 192, 193n329
  vs. Christ's example, 197
  vs. Jesus, 198
עָשָׂה, 45
עָשָׂה, 46
ἡγουμένοι (leaders of community), 98
High Priest
  installation, 23
  Jesus Christ as, 26, 30, 37, 119, 132, 145, 154–55
  in order of Melchizedek, 129, 141, 143, 150–51, 213
  qualifications, 7
  surpassing nature of, 27
  Jesus' qualification to become, 7, 19, 148
  in order of Melchizedek, 143, 156
history, division of present and age to come, 116
כָּלָה, 45
holiness movements, 17
holy city, 207
Holy Land, Roman invasion, and Jewish persecution, 104–5
Holy of Holies, 165
Holy Spirit, 64
  and spiritual maturity, 185n287
"homiletical midrash," 110
homily, Hebrews as, 110–12
"hook word," 123
hope, recurrent language of, 41–42
ἥτις (which, this), 165
humanity
  Jesus' participation in, 18, 32, 137
  Philo on perfection, 67
  of Son, testing, 142

ideal sage, image of, 48
Ignatius of Antioch, 98
ignorance, 50
ιησοῦς Χριστός, 170
ἵνα ὦσιν τετελειωμένοι εἰς ἕν, 74
incarnation of Christ, 3, 8, 38, 136
infants, vs. mature, 184

James the Great (brother of John), 104n145
James the Just
  execution, 105n149
  martyrdom of, 104
James the Less, 104n145
Jerusalem
  destruction of, 104n147
  view on Hebrews as written after, 91–93
  as Jesus' goal, 73
  Jewish Christian community in, 93–94

Subject Index

Jesus Christ, 103
  call to renunciation of wealth, 71
  complete access to God through, 79
  death and life, 187n294
  death and resurrection, 72
  as enabler for worshiper to walk in faith, 178
  endurance of suffering, 31
  endurance of temptation, 32
  and eternal salvation, 118
  as forerunner, 185n288
  as High Priest, 26, 30, 37, 119, 126, 145
    in order of Melchizedek, 129, 141, 143, 150–51, 213
    qualifications, 7
    surpassing nature of, 27
  incarnation of, 3, 8, 38
  Jerusalem as goal, 73
  as leader, 136–37
  as leader for believers, 133n18
  on limited love to God, 70
  made perfect by God the Father, 22
  as Mediator, 173, 209
  messianic mission at close of the age, 38
  once-for-all sacrifice, 173
  participation in humanity, 137
  perfection of, 17–18, 125
    moral, 18
  priesthood, 190
    not of Aaronic order, 158–59
    perfected as Mediator, 5
    permanent effectiveness, 154
  προσφορά (offering) of, 187
  Sermon on the Mount, 69–70
  as Son, 141n65
  as source of perfection, 130
  suffering of, 135
  superiority, 141, 172
    to Aaron, 141, 143
    to angels, 143
    to Moses, 143
  supreme stature, 20
  τέλειος applied to, 20–21
  testing and proving of, 31
  and worshipers access to God, 167
"Jesus midrash," 110

Jewish community
  controversy within, 103
  temptation to return to ritual system, 108
  traditions, 116
Jewish War (AD 66–70), 101, 103
Jews and Christians, Roman authorities and, 103
Judaism, in Hebrews, 100
Judaizers, as Paul's opponents, 76
judgment seat of God, 43

καίπερ ὢν υἱός, 141
καθίστησιν, 150n115
κατὰ συνείδησιν (with regard to conscience), 168
καταβαλλόμενοι (not laying again the foundation), 183
κατανοήσατε, 42n156
κατέχωμεν, 42n156
knowledge, from God, 64
κρεῖττόν τι, 193

Latin (Western) Church, on Hebrews authorship, 84
Law, 174n239
  and earthly high priests, 150
  inadequacy, 187
  limitations, 176
  superiority of new order over, 87
leaving behind, 183
letter or epistle, literary genre of Hebrews as, 112–14
λευιτικῆς ἱερωσύνης (Levitical priesthood), 160
Levitical priesthood, 37–38, 118
  Christ as superior, 125
  inability to perfect worshipers, 129
  law, 162
  Melchizedek superiority to, 150, 158–59
  overthrow of, 148
  sacrifices, limitations, 175
literary genre of Hebrews, 108–14
  as letter or epistle, 112–14
  as Midrash, 109–10
  as written homily or sermon, 110–12

ְ֒יִ, 45
loan, agreement of cancellation, 35
λόγου δικαιοσύνης (word of righteousness), 178–80
λόγος τῆς παρακλήσεως, 114
Lot, 157
love, 74
LXX. *See* Septuagint (LXX)
Lycus Valley, 95n87

Maccabean martyrs, 198n361
μακροθυμία, 42n156
Marcion canon, Hebrews absence, 85
μαρτυρηθέντες, 192n320
martyrdom, and church in Jerusalem, 95
Mary, belief in fulfillment of God's prediction, 72
Masoretic Text (MT), 6, 212
  DuPlessis on, 61n110
mature (τέλειοι), 75
maturity, 53
  move to, 181
  training to distinguish good and evil, 181
Mediator
  Christ as, 173
  priestly ministry of perfected Christ as, 5
Melchizedek, 115
  as βασιλεὺς Σαλήμ (king of Salem), 157
  Christ as High Priest in order of, 129, 141, 148, 150–51, 156, 213
  historical incident of, 157
  superiority to Levitical priesthood, 158–59
memorandum, legal execution of, 35–36
Methodism, 17
Μιᾷ γὰρ προσφορᾷ τετελείωκεν εἰς τὸ διηνεκὲς τοὺς ἁγιαζομένους, 186
Midrash, Hebrews as, 109–10
moral-ethical approach to τέλειος, 20, 179
  critics of, 20–22

moral perfection, of historical Jesus, 18
moral virtue, 52
Mosaic system of worship, new covenant and, 119
Moses, Christ as superior, 125, 126, 143
Mount Sinai, 203
Mount Zion, 205
Muratorian Canon, 96
  Hebrews absence, 85
Mysteries, 22n58
mystery religions, 76n198
  initiation, 50–51

Narcissus, bank of, 35
Nathan, oracle on Davidic dynasty, 117n229
Nero, 101, 105
new covenant, x, 10, 30, 64, 92, 119, 129, 163n185, 176
  Christ's inauguration of, 164, 169
  eschatological significance, 211
  fulfillment of, 19, 199n364
  good things under, 171
  participation in blessings of, 24
  perfecting worshiper, 186–87
  realization of promises, 215
new covenant people, 29
New International version of Bible, weakness in, 180n262
New Jerusalem, 206
new order, superiority of, 162
νήπιοι (infants), 178–80
notarization, 35
νωθρός (sluggish; dull), 178n252

ὁ λόγος τῆς ὁρκωμοσίας, 151
ὁ λόγος τῆς παρακλήσεως (word of exhortation), 108, 118
ὁ τὴν βασιλείαν τῶν οὐρανῶν (kingdom of heaven), 71n170
obedience, 64, 137, 140, 141, 142, 144
  of Christ, 19, 149
  learning, 17
οἱ ἐκ περιτομῆς, 99
old covenant, 7
  and limited access to God, 167

ὁμοίωσις Θεοῦ (being made like God), 50
ον οἱ ἀπὸ τῆς Ἰταλίας (those from Italy), 97–98
On the Special Laws (Philo), 66
ου προσεληλύθατε (you have not come), 203–4n390
οὐ γὰρ προσεληλύθατε ψηλαφωμένῳ`` ἀλλὰ προσεληλύθατε Σιὼν ὄρει, 204
˚όω, verbal forms ending with, 15

παιδία ,children), 75
Palestine, as Hebrews location, 93–96
πάντες μαρτυρηθέντες (all were commended), 192
παραβολη (symbol; illustration), 165
παραγενόμενος, 170n224
παραγίνομαι (to come to be), 170n223
patchwork approach, to Hebrews structure, 124
Paul
　gnostic Christian missionaries as opponents, 76
　Judaizers as opponents, 76
　sense of God's righteousness, 179
Pentateuch, cultus in, 117
perfect love, 14
perfection. *See also* τέλειος (perfection)
　of believers, 21–22
　of the body, 194
　of Christ, 9
　　cultic installation, 24
　as future reality, 202
　in sacrificial animal, 57
　technical understanding, ix–x
　vocational model of, 3, 7
perfection models, cultic, 3n11
περὶ ἡμῶν, 193
persecution, 117
　likelihood, 92
perseverance, 20, 43, 107, 215
　in good works, 216
　in race, 197
　walking by faith with, 210
personal effort, rejection of, 184n285

philanthropia (divine beneficence), 3, 8, 34
Philo of Alexandria, 65–68
　On the Special Laws, 66
philosophical knowledge, Plato on, 50
pietist circles, 17
πίστις, 42n156
πνεύμασι δικαίων (spirits of just men), 208
πνεύμασι δικαίων τετελειωμένων (spirits of the righteous men made perfect), 207, 208
polytheism, 101
poverty, 95
present tense usages, in Hebrews, 89n54, 90
present time (τὸν καιρὸν τὸν ἐνεστηκότα), 166
priesthood, 126. *See also* High Priest
　in ancient Israel, 59
　consecration, 24, 58–59
　ordination, 137, 190
　of perfected Christ, as Mediator, 5
Priscilla and Aquila, 103
πρόδρομος (forerunner), 185n288, 199
prologue, 120, 125
προσαγορευθείς, 150
προσεληλύθατε (you have come), 203, 203–4n390, 204
προσφέρουσιν, 176
προσφορά (offering), of Christ, 187
πρὸς, 180n262
πρός Ἀλεξανδρίνους, 96
πρός εβραίους, 96
πρωτοτόκων (firstborn-ones), 206n404
purification, 29

Qumran community, 63
　eschatology of, 213
θυσία (sacrifice), 187n294

race set before us, 196
reality, Hebrews' concept of, 61
redemption, Son and, 147
religious approach to τέλειος, 22–27
rich young man, Jesus with, 70

Subject Index

right hand of God the Father, exaltation of Christ to, 27
Roman Catholic church, 70n166
Rome
　authorities' views of Christians, 101–2
　church in, 94
　as destination for Hebrews, 97–98
　fire in, 105
running the race, 200

sacrifices, 90
　of Christ, 143
　of Levitical priesthood, 118
　　limitations, 175
　　repetitive nature of, 168
sacrificial animal, 47
　perfection in, 57
saints, 208
salvation, 7, 41, 79
　of believers, 190
　Christ and, 118, 214
　Christ as pioneer, 153
　Christ as source, 130, 147
　God's plan of, 5
　secured by Christ, 161
Samaria, 95n87
sanctification, 26, 29, 161, 180
　of believers, 126
savior, gnostic redeemer myth on, 133n18
second coming of Christ, x, 7, 77, 92, 140, 148, 185, 209
　worshipers complete at, 163
Second Temple Judaism, τέλειος in, 62–68
Septuagint (LXX), 6, 54–62, 86, 95, 144, 212
sermon, Hebrews as, 110–12
Shepherd of Hermas, 89
sinlessness, progressive moral development toward, 17
sins, forgiveness of, 187
Σιὼν ὄρει (Mount Zion), 205
σκιᾷ (shadow), 174
σκια (unreal; deceptive), 174n238
σκιάν, Law as shadow of things to come, 174

Sodom and Gomorrah, 157
σοφία (wisdom), 67
Son of God, Christ's person as, 153
soul, perfection in, 50
spiritual maturity, Holy Spirit and, 185n287
Stoicism, 54
suffering, 126, 137, 142, 147
　and apostasy, 107
　of Christ, 31, 135
　in Greco-Roman world, 101
　by recipients of Hebrews, 102n133
　reward to come, 33
συναγωγή, 94
συνειδέναι ἑαυτῷ (consciousness), 168
superiority of Christ, 131, 214
　to Aaron, 141
　Hebrews 2:10, 132–40
　Hebrews 5:8–9, 140–49
　Hebrews 5:14, 177–86
　Hebrews 6:1, 177–86
　Hebrews 7:11, 19, 156–64
　Hebrews 7:28, 149–55
　Hebrews 9:9, 11, 164–73
　Hebrews 10:1, 173–76
　Hebrews 10:14, 186–91
　Hebrews 11:40, 191–96
　Hebrews 12:2, 23, 196–210
Sychar, 95n87
syncretism, 101
synoptic gospels, perfection in, 69–78

tabernacle, 119n235, 165, 172, 174
　limitations of sacrificial rites, 164
　symbolic significance of first, 166
Tacitus, 101–2
tamim, 61n110, 63
τὰς ἐπαγγελίας (the promises), 192n322
teachings, doctrinal elements for, 184
τέλειοι (mature), 75, 178–80
τέλειοι ,"the perfect ones"), 29
τέλειος τὰς χεῖρας (to perfect the hand), 137–38
τελειοτέρας, tabernacle as, 172n233
τελειότητα, 184

Subject Index

τελειότης (completeness), inability of old system to achieve, 186
τελειότης (maturity), God movement of worshipers toward, 185
τελειοῦμαι, 72
τελειοῦν τὰς χεῖρας ("to perfect or complete the hands"), 22–23, 23n60, 25–26, 60, 61
τελειοῦν (verbal form)
   in Gospels, 72
   in LXX, 26
τελειοῦσθαι, 66
τέλειουν τὰς χεῖρας, 144
τελειόω (executed; to be made perfect), 14–15, 35, 45, 137
   in Philo, 65–66
τέλειος (perfection), ix, 127, 161, 162
   basics, 1–12
   of believers, 176–201
   central function of concept, 37
   in classical world, 46–62
      Aristotle and Stoicism, 52–54
      general usage, 46–48
      Hebrew scripture and Septuagint (LXX), 54–62
      Platonic usage, 49–51
   conceptual meaning, 61
   in cultic or religious sense, 137
   eschatological approach, 5, 38–43
   final reference in Hebrews, 207
   formal meaning, 13–16
   in Gnosticism, 15n21
   goal of, 130
   interpretation of, 2
   and legal execution, 35–36
   lexical meaning, 44–46
   in New Testament world, 69–78
      synoptic gospels, John, and Acts, 69–74
   in Second Temple Judaism, 62–68
      Philo of Alexandria, 65–68
      Qumran community, 62–65
   significance of notion, 129–30
   summary assessment, 211–15
   technical meaning, 16–38, 212
      cultic or religious approach, 22–27
      definitive attestation approach, 34–38
      glorification or exaltation approach, 27–30, 179
      moral or ethical approach, 17–22, 179
      vocational or experiential approach, 31–34, 138, 146, 152, 190
τελειῶσαι, 139n56, 153n134
τελειῶσαι τὰς χεῖρας, 58
τελειῶσιξ (perfection), and goal for Hebrew believers, 182
τελείων, 178n253
τελείων δέ ἐστιν ἡ στερεὰ τροφη, 178
τελειωθείς, 57, 145, 153n134
τελειωθεὶς ἐγένετο, 145–46
τελειωθέσεται, 66
τελειωθῆναι, 28
τελειωσάντων τὰς ἡμέρας, 72n171
τελείωσιξ, 72, 118, 158, 159
   inclusive nature of, 194
   for worshipers, 118
τελειώσω αὐτοῦ τὸ ἔργον (to complete or accomplish his work), 73
τελειωτής (perfecter), 200
τελέωσις, goal of, 202
telos, 73
τέλος (goal), 15
temple
   destruction, and dating Hebrews, 88–93
   language of Hebrews on, 89–90
temptation, Christ's endurance of, 32
terminus ad quem, 88, 91, 92
terminus ad quo, 88–89
terminus technicus, 23
Tertullian, 86n33, 99
testing and proving of Christ, 31
τετελείωμαι (I have attained perfection), 76
τετελειωμένον, 153n132, 209
text-linguistic approach, to Hebrews structure, 124–25
τῆς ὁρκωμοσίας (sworn oath), 151n117

τῆς πίστεως ἀρχηγὸν καὶ τελειωτὴν (pioneer and perfecter of our faith), 198–99
τῆς πίστεως (the faith), 201n379
τῆς πρώτης σκηνῆς (first tabernacle), 165
   symbolic significance, 166
τῆς σωτηρίας αὐτῶν, 134
τῆς τελειοτέρας, 119n235
Thayer, Joseph Henry Thayer, 45
τὴν ἐπαγγελίαν (the promise), 192, 192n322
τὴν τελειότητα φερώμεθα (we must move on to maturity), 184
Timothy, 86, 114
tithes to Melchizedek, from Abraham, 156, 157
τὸν αἰῶνα τετελειωμένον (made perfect forever), 153
τὸν καιρὸν τὸν ἐνεστηκότα (the present time), 165, 166
τὸν λατρεύοντα (the one worshipping), 169
τὸν τῆς ἀρχῆς λόγον (teaching of the beginning), 181n268
τὸν τῆς ἀρχῆς τοῦ Χριστοῦ λόγον, 181n269
totality, 45
τοῦ λόγου τῆς παρακλήσεως (word of exhortation), 110–11, 112, 130
τοῦ θεοῦ περὶ ἡμῶν κρεῖττόν τι προβλεψαμένου, 193
τοὺς ἁγιαζομένους, 190
traditional approach to Hebrews, 121
τρέχωμεν, 197
Tripartite approach, 123
τῶν γενομένων ἀγαθῶν (good things that have come), 170, 171
τῶν μελλόντων ἀγαθῶν (things to come), 171, 174, 174n242

υἱὸν εἰς τὸν αἰῶνα τετελειωμένον, 151
υἱός (Son), 141n65, 151
"unshakable kingdom," 42, 203
ὑπόδειγμα (sketch), 174
ὑποδείγματα (prototype), earthly tabernacle as, 174
ὑπομονή, 42n156
Urmensch, gathering parts of, 28

Vespasian, 104, 104n147
Ἰερουσαλὴμ ἐπουρανίῳ (heavenly Jerusalem), 205
virtue, 46, 50, 53
vocational model of perfection, 3, 7, 152, 190
רֹאשׁ, 133n18

ὧν ἔπαθεν, 142
wealth, renunciation of, 70n166
Western (Latin) Church, on Hebrews authorship, 84
wisdom (σοφία), 67
ὡς τελειῶσαι τὸν δρόμον μου καὶ τὴν διακονίαν, 73
word of exhortation, Hebrews as, 4
worshipers
   consecrated, 189
   Levitical priesthood inability to perfect, 129
   at second coming of Christ, 163

Yahweh
   allegiance to, 56
   man's relationship to, 57

Zeno, 53
Zeus, 47
   τέλειος as attribute, 51
Zion, 205–6

Scripture Index

OLD TESTAMENT

Hebrews and, 87
inability to effect τελείωσις, 155–76
influence on Hebrews, 116
Jewish audience familiarity with, 100
Philo use of, 68

Genesis

6:9	56, 61n110
13:1–5	157
14	125
14:16–20	156n146
14:17–20	148
14:18–20	157

Exodus

3:8	134n23
3:17	134n23
6:6–7	134n23
6:14	133n18
7:4–5	134n23
12:5	57
19:12–13	203n386
29	59
29:6	58
29:9	23n59, 137
29:33	137
29:35	137

Leviticus

1:3	55n76
1:10	55n76
3:1	55n76
3:6	55n76
4:3	55n76
4:5	137
8:33	137
8:61	59
16:32	137
21:10	23, 26, 58, 60

Numbers

1:4	133n18
3:3	137
14:23	180
21:8–9	147n101

Deuteronomy

6:5	71
9:19	203n386
18:13	55, 61n110
32:43	132n16

Judges

17:10	59
18:4	59
20:26	56
21:4	56

2 Samuel

7	160n169
7:4	132n16

2 Samuel (continued)

7:9–11	206
7:14	117n229, 140n60, 140n63, 152n124
22:26	61n111

1 Kings

8:61	56n83, 57
11:4	56n83
15:3	56n83
15:14	56n83, 57

2 Kings

20:3	56
22:26	61n110

1 Chronicles

8:16	45
17:13	117n229, 132n16, 140n60
28:9	56, 57

Job

27:6	168n209

Psalms

2	56
2	117
2:7	130, 132n16, 140n60, 141, 143, 145, 152, 152n124
2:8	143
2:10	140n63
8	139
8:4–6	132, 134
8:6	134
37	63
45	117
45:6–7	132n16
89:22–23	206
95	116
95:1	163
97:7	132n16
102:25–27	132n16
102:26–28	140n60, 140n63
104:4	132n16
110	110, 117, 125, 140n60, 140n63, 141, 143
110:1	132n16, 155
110:1–4	206
110:4	129, 130, 143, 145, 148, 150, 157, 158, 162, 163

Ecclesiastes

10:20	168n209

Wisdom

4:13	57
17:11	168n209

Isaiah

	63
9:6–7	157n152
16:1	206
26:19–20	209
48:18	157n152

Jeremiah

13:19	56n83
31	188n302
31:31–34	43, 117, 160n169, 161, 169, 173, 176, 188, 191, 215

2 Baruch

17:7	167n204
30:1	139n55
32:4	139n55

Ezekiel

27:11	45

Daniel

12:3	139n55
12:12	209

Amos

9:11	206

Micah

63

Nahum

	63
6:10–11	98
10:33–34	98

Habakkuk

63

4 Maccabees

7:15	58, 58n91

Sirach

42:18	168n209

1 Enoch

39:4–6	139n55
45:3	139n55

2 Enoch

22:8–18	139n55

4 Ezra

6-7-8	167n204
7:91	139n55
7:98	139n55
8:1	167n204

NEW TESTAMENT

69–78
Synoptic Gospels, 92
perfection, in synoptic gospels, John, and Acts, 69–78

Matthew,

	79
5:20	71
5:43–47	70
5:48	1n1, 69
7:21	71n170
13:37	145
16:24	71
16:24–26	216
18:3	71n170
18:8–9	71n170
19:14	71
19:16–39	69
19:17	71n170
19:21	70
19:22	71
19:23	71n170
22:37–40	71
23:14	71n170
24:15	93
27:56	104n144

perfection in, 69

Mark

	88
8:34–38	216
10:30	167n204
12:30	71
13:14	93
13:14–15	90
16:1	104n144

Luke

	81
1:32	160n169
1:45	72, 160
1:55	160n169
2:43	72
9:23–26	216
9:57–62	216
10:20	206n406
10:27	71
12:50	73
13:32	17, 72, 73
13:33	73
21:5	93
22:37	73
24:10	104n144

John

	74
4:34	73, 73–74

John (continued)

5:36	73
14:2	207
14:3	207
17:4	73
17:23	74
19:28	73
19:30	73
perfection in, 69–78	

Acts

2:34	140n63
3:15	132n18
5:31	132n18
6:9	97
10:45	99
11:2	99
11:26	103
13:14–41	111
13:15	108n166, 111
13:33	87n41
13:48	206n406
20:24	72, 73
21:27	97
24:18	97
26:28	103
perfection in, 69–78	

Romans

2:15	168, 168n210
6:14	129n4
8:14	185n287
8:18	167n204
8:29	87n41
11:36	135n31
12:2	74
13:5	168n210

1 Corinthians

2:6	14, 74, 75, 77
4:4	168n210
8:7	168n210
8:10	168n210
8:12	168n210
9:6–12	85
10:11	42
10:25–28	168n210
12 — 14	42
12:4	87n41
12:11	87n41
13:10	74, 75, 75n191, 77
14:20	14, 74, 75, 77
15:25	140n63
15:54–55	75

2 Corinthians

1:2	168n210
4:2	168n210
4:4	87n41
5:11	168n210

Galatians

1:1	81n6, 87n41
1:2	86n35
1:12	81n6, 86n35
2:12	99
3:19	87n41

Ephesians

1:21	87n41
3:9	87n41
4:12–13	75
4:13	74, 77, 186

Philippians

1:1	87
1:9	202
2:6	87n41
2:8	142, 149
2:19	87
2:22	87
3:4–7	87
3:8	76
3:12	74, 75, 76, 77, 186
3:15	74, 77
3:21	77
4:3	206n406

Colossians

1:1	87
1:15	87n41
1:17	87n41

1:28	74, 75, 77	2:1–4	106, 117, 126, 131, 132, 141
3:14	74, 77, 184	2:2	87n41
4:11	99	2:3	37, 41, 86, 86n35, 87n41, 92, 94, 148, 149
4:12	74, 77		
		2:5–9	132, 134

1 Thessalonians

		2:5–18	131
4:13–17	209	2:8	132
4:13–18	42	2:9	27, 135, 139
		2:9–10	132

1 Timothy

		2:10	1n3, 2, 7, 9, 18, 21, 26, 30, 118, 126, 129, 131, 132–40, 153, 153n134, 185, 185n288, 198, 199, 207, 209, 211, 213
1:5	168n210		
3:9	168n210		
4:2	168n210		

2 Timothy

		2:10–18	132, 141
1:3	168n210	2:11	18
		2:14–15	132
		2:17–18	30, 85n29, 132

Titus

		2:43	87n41
1:10	99	3–4	116
1:15	168n210	3:1	42n156, 83n18, 106, 148n103

Hebrews

		3:1–4:13	126
1:1–2	37	3:1–4:14	122n257
1:1–4	85n29, 120, 122n257, 124n265, 125, 131	3:1–5:10	124n265
		3:1–6	141, 143
1:2	40, 87n41, 94, 116, 141n66	3:6	1n3, 41, 117, 141n66, 163
1:2–3	194	3:7	92
1:2–14	151	3:7–4:13	108, 117, 141
1:3	87n41, 141n66, 208	3:11	41
1:3–4	82n9	3:12	92, 108, 118
1:4	87n41	3:13	94, 107
1:5	87n41, 132n16, 152, 152n124	3:14	1n3, 37, 41, 92, 106, 117
		3:18	92
1:5–2:18	122n257, 124n265	4:1	42, 42n156
1:5–4:16	125	4:1–11	163
1:5–7	132	4:1–13	141
1:5–10:18	120	4:2–3	42n156
1:5–13	132	4:9	x
1:5–14	131, 140, 143	4:9–10	30, 43
1:6	87n41, 208	4:10	108
1:8	141n66	4:11	92
1:10–12	140n60	4:12	85n29
1:13	140n60, 143	4:13	42
1:14	40, 131, 148, 149	4:14	141n66, 148n103, 155
2:1	108	4:14–5:10	141

Hebrews (continued)

4:14–7:28	177
4:14–15	108
4:15	18, 20, 34, 138, 144, 164
4:15–5:10	122n257
4:16	148, 154
5:1–3	151
5:1–4	89n54
5:1–10:18	125
5:3	164
5:5	141n66
5:5–7	143
5:5–10	151
5:6	143
5:7–8	143, 147n95, 149
5:8	141
5:8–9	21, 126, 140–49, 149, 198, 211, 213
5:8–10	150
5:9	1n3, 2, 7, 9, 17, 18, 25, 26, 41, 129, 143, 144, 153, 153n134, 199
5:9–10	30, 148n103
5:10	125, 148
5:11 — 6:1	2, 9, 117, 130, 141
5:11–6:20	122n257, 177
5:11–10:39	124n265
5:11–14	107, 182, 184
5:12	95
5:14	1n3, 29, 178, 180, 181, 211, 214, 215
5:14–6:1	177
6:1	1n3, 18, 85n29, 107, 184, 211, 214, 215
6:1–2	107, 181, 181n267, 182
6:1–3	178
6:4–6	108
6:4–8	178, 185
6:5	x, 42, 43, 116
6:8	1n3
6:9	41, 106
6:9–20	185n288
6:10	95
6:10–12	107
6:11	1n3, 41, 106
6:12	41, 42n156, 117
6:16	37
6:18	41
6:18–20	117
6:19	18, 37
6:20	125, 133n18, 156, 199
7:1–10	148, 150, 156, 157, 158
7:1–10:31	108
7:1–28	122n257, 125, 150, 156
7:3	1n3, 49
7:11	1n3, 2, 7, 9, 29, 118, 126, 129, 155, 156–64, 158, 158–59, 160, 162, 176, 186, 211
7:11–19	148, 150, 156, 158
7:11–25	151
7:12–14	159
7:13	159
7:14	159
7:16	167
7:17	162, 163
7:18	159, 162
7:19	1n3, 7, 9, 18, 23, 29, 41, 58, 126, 129, 155, 156–64, 158, 160, 161, 162, 176, 186, 194
7:20	163
7:20–25	150
7:21	89n54
7:22	118, 129, 130n6, 154, 163
7:23	89n54
7:24	49
7:25	118, 129, 154, 189
7:26	20, 30, 34, 144, 155
7:26–28	150
7:27	89n54, 164
7:28	1n3, 2, 7, 9, 17, 21, 89n54, 118, 129, 139, 144, 149–55, 154, 198, 211, 213
8:1	155
8:1–13	49
8:1 — 9:28	122n257, 173, 186
8:1 — 10:39	150, 154, 164n190
8:3–4	89n54
8:5	1n3
8:6	194
8:6–11	169
8:6–12	215
8:6–13	163n185

Scripture Index

8:8	1n3	10:12	27
8:8–12	173	10:13	126
8:13	89n54	10:14	1n3, 2, 7, 9, 18, 19, 21,
9:1–5	165		25, 29, 119, 130, 185,
9:1–10	169		186–91, 189, 190, 191,
9:6	1n3, 89n54		211, 214
9:6–10	164, 165	10:14–24	18
9:8–9	18	10:16–18	188
9:9	1n3, 2, 7, 9, 29, 89n54,	10:19–21	42
	108, 126, 129, 155, 160,	10:19–39	122n257, 173, 187, 191
	161, 164–73, 168, 176,	10:19 — 13:19	120, 125
	186, 211	10:22	42, 168, 189
9:10	167, 171	10:23	41, 42, 42n156, 106
9:11	1n3, 41, 129, 130, 155,	10:23–25	117
	164–73, 169, 172, 173,	10:24–25	42
	186, 211	10:25	94, 107, 117
9:11–14	164, 169	10:26–31	118
9:11–28	164, 169	10:27	92
9:12	171	10:32	42n156
9:13	89n54, 161	10:32–34	32, 106
9:14	20, 108, 168, 171, 189	10:32–39	33
9:15	171, 172, 173, 209	10:34	49, 95
9:15–22	164, 169	10:35	117
9:17	37	10:35–37	126
9:22	126, 172	10:36	41, 42n156, 194
9:23	174	10:37	92
9:23–24	49	10:38	208
9:23–27	164	10:39	92, 106
9:23–28	169	11:1	41, 117
9:25	89n54	11:1–40	122n257, 126
9:26	1n3, 42, 42n156	subsections	192n317
9:26–28	173	11:1 — 12:13	124n265
9:28	7, 42, 118, 126, 129,	11:1 — 13:19	126
	148, 149, 154, 164, 171,	11:3	81n6
	172, 178, 209	11:6	25
10:1	1n3, 2, 7, 9, 23, 29, 58,	11:7	82n9
	89n54, 126, 129, 130,	11:10	43, 207, 209
	155, 160, 170n224, 171,	11:13	130
	173–76, 176, 186, 211	11:13–16	209
10:1–18	122n257, 173, 186	11:14	41
10:2	108, 168	11:16	41
10:2–3	90	11:26	41, 106
10:2–4	161	11:39	41, 126, 130, 209
10:3	89n54	11:39–40	30, 191
10:3–4	168	11:40	1n3, 2, 7, 9, 18, 19,
10:8	89n54		25, 29, 41, 126, 130,
10:11	89n54		191–96, 199, 209, 211,
10:11–18	187		214

Hebrews (continued)

12:1	29
12:1–2	85n29, 196, 202
12:1–3	149, 193n322
12:1–4	107
12:1–13	122n257
12:1–17	202
12:1–29	126
12:2	1n3, 2, 9, 18, 19, 25, 29, 30, 107, 130, 185, 196–210, 198, 201, 211, 214, 215
12:3	42n156, 117
12:3–14	117
12:4	92, 95, 117
12:5	207
12:5–8	107
12:10–11	33
12:11	215
12:12–13	117
12:12–15	107
12:14–13:18	122n257, 124n265
12:18–21	203
12:18–24	203
12:18–29	126
12:19–21	203n386
12:21–24	193n322
12:22	30
12:22–23	202, 203, 205
12:22–24	210
12:23	1n3, 2, 7, 9, 18, 19, 25, 29, 130, 196–210, 207, 209, 211, 214, 215
12:25	92, 108, 117
12:25–26	203
12:25–29	210
12:27	49, 94
12:27–29	203
12:28	x, 42, 43, 189
13	113, 114
13:1	117
13:1–5	107n163
13:1–8	210
13:2	95
13:5	95
13:7	92, 98, 114
13:7–9	117
13:7–16	210
13:8	43, 170
13:9	37
13:10	89n54
13:11	89n54
13:13	43, 90, 106, 130, 216
13:13–14	117
13:14	x, 42, 43, 49, 171, 178, 205, 209
13:15–16	189
13:16	95
13:17	98, 114
13:17–18	117
13:18	168
13:18–19	114
13:19	86
13:20–21	114, 122n257, 124n265
13:20–25	120, 125, 126
13:21	93
13:22	1, 1n2, 86, 111, 112
13:22–25	114
13:23	86, 87, 88, 92, 114
13:24	97, 98
19:32–34	98
20:10	17

conceptual background, 114–17
date of composition, 88–93
 as before AD 70, 89–90
 as after fall of Jerusalem, 91–93
divisions, 125–27
eschatology of, 11, 40–43
historical setting, 93–108
 geographic location, 93–100
 socio-political setting, 101–6
 spiritual and religious, 106–8
literary structure, 119–25
neglect in scholarly studies, 4
occasion and purpose, 117–19
original recipients, 98–100
salutation absence, 86
socio-political setting, 101–6
survey of literature on, 6–8
theological and practical implication, 215–16
as word of exhortation, 4

James

	78, 113
1:4	78

1:17	78	19:2	85n29
1:21	197n353	21:2	85n29
1:25	78	36:1	85n29
		36:1–2	82n9
		36:1–6	98
		36:2–5	85n29

1 Peter

1:3–9	42
1:19–21	42
2:1	197n353
2:9–10	189
4:16	103
1 John	113
2:5	74
3:2	185
4:12	74
4:16	74
4:17	74
4:18	14, 74

DEAD SEA SCROLLS

1QS

1:12	64
2:2	64
3:3	62
3:13–4:26	63
4:23	139n55
8:20	62
8:21	62
i. 15	63
perfection use in, 62	

Revelation

1:5–6	189
5:9–10	189
14:1	206
20:6	209
21:1	206
21:1–8	207
21:27	206n406

Didache

1:4	71
6:2	71

1 Clement

9:4	82n9
12:1	82n9

Odes of Solomon

36:2	28
P.Oxy III.483	35
P.Oxy XI. 1462	36
P.Oxy XXVII.2471	35

www.ingramcontent.com/pod-product-compliance
Lightning Source LLC
Chambersburg PA
CBHW050343230426
43663CB00010B/1972